Restructuring Territoriality

Europe and the United States Compared

The bundling of political authority into mutually exclusive territorial boundaries – territoriality – is a fundamental principle of modern political organization. Indeed, it provides the foundation for other cherished institutions – national sovereignty, citizenship, the modern welfare state, and democracy. Are globalization, internationalization, and Europeanization consipiring to unbundle territoriality? If so, are sovereignty, citizenship, the welfare state, and democracy unraveling as well? Is a new postnational, nonterritorial form of political organization, heralded by the European Union, being born? With a focus on Europe, this book explores these issues from various substantive and theoretical perspectives. The authors find evidence of the diffusion of authority both within and beyond the state, producing novel institutional arrangements and new modes of governance. But the United States may provide more useful insights into the new dispensation than the idea of a postnational, nonterritorial politics. Interest in contemporary challenges to democracy run throughout this book.

Christopher K. Ansell teaches organization theory, public administration, and democratic theory at the University of California, Berkeley. He is the author of numerous articles on labor politics, political parties, and European regional development strategy. He is the author of *Schism and Solidarity in Social Movements: The Politics of Labor in the French Third Republic* (Cambridge University Press, 2001) and is currently at work on a project on European food safety regulation.

Giuseppe Di Palma is Professor of Political Science at the University of California, Berkeley. Since the return to democracy in Spain, Portugal, and Greece, he has worked and published on democratic transitions (*To Craft Democracies*, 1991). More recently, his attention has moved to democratic theory, with special attention to democratic practices and institutions in contexts other than the modern nation-state.

Restructuring Territoriality

Europe and the United States Compared

Edited by

CHRISTOPHER K. ANSELL
University of California, Berkeley

GIUSEPPE DI PALMA
University of California, Berkeley

CAMBRIDGE
UNIVERSITY PRESS

PUBLISHED BY THE PRESS SYNDICATE OF THE UNIVERSITY OF CAMBRIDGE
The Pitt Building, Trumpington Street, Cambridge, United Kingdom

CAMBRIDGE UNIVERSITY PRESS
The Edinburgh Building, Cambridge, CB2 2RU, UK
40 West 20th Street, New York, NY 10011-4211, USA
477 Williamstown Road, Port Melbourne, VIC 3207, Australia
Ruiz de Alarcón 13, 28014 Madrid, Spain
Dock House, The Waterfront, Cape Town 8001, South Africa

http://www.cambridge.org

First published 2004

Printed in the United States of America

Typeface Sabon 10/12 pt.   *System* LATEX 2$_\varepsilon$ [TB]

A catalog record for this book is available from the British Library.

Library of Congress Cataloging in Publication Data

Restructuring territoriality : Europe and the United States compared / edited Christopher K.
Ansell, Giuseppe Di Palma.
   p.   cm.
Includes bibliographical references and index.
ISBN 0-521-82555-5 – ISBN 0-521-53262-0 (pb.)
   1. Political geography.   2. Sovereignty.   3. State, The.   4. Globalization – Political aspects.
5. Europe – Politics and government – 1989–   6. United States – Politics and government –
2001–   I. Ansell, Christopher K., 1957–   II. Di Palma, Giuseppe.
JC319.R43   2004
320.1–dc22   2004043579

ISBN 0 521 82555 5 hardback
ISBN 0 521 53262 0 paperback

In Memory of
Ernst Haas
Loyal Friend and Inspiring Colleague

Contents

Contributors   *page* ix

Acknowledgments   xiii

I. THEORETICAL FRAMEWORKS

1 Restructuring Authority and Territoriality   3
   Christopher K. Ansell

2 Old and New Peripheries in the Processes of European
   Territorial Integration   19
   Stefano Bartolini

3 Center–Periphery Alignments and Political Contention in
   Late-Modern Europe   45
   Sidney Tarrow

II. THE TRANSFORMATION OF GOVERNANCE

4 Sovereignty and Territoriality in the European Union:
   Transforming the UK Institutional Order   67
   James A. Caporaso and Joseph Jupille

5 Social Citizenship in the European Union: Toward a Spatial
   Reconfiguration?   90
   Maurizio Ferrera

6 Islands of Transnational Governance   122
   Alec Stone Sweet

7 Regional Integration and Left Parties in
   Europe and North America   145
   Gary Marks and Ian Down

III. EUROPE–U.S. COMPARISONS

8 The European Union in American Perspective: The
   Transformation of Territorial Sovereignty in Europe and
   the United States   163
   Sergio Fabbrini

9 Is the Democratic Deficit a Deficiency? The Case of
   Immigration Policy in the United States and the European
   Union   188
   Bruce E. Cain

10 Territory, Representation, and Policy Outcome: The
    United States and the European Union Compared   205
    Alberta M. Sbragia

IV. CONCLUDING THOUGHTS

11 Territoriality, Authority, and Democracy   225
    Christopher K. Ansell

12 Postscript: What Inefficient History and Malleable Practices
    Say about Nation-States and Supranational Democracy
    When Territoriality Is No Longer Exclusive   246
    Giuseppe Di Palma

Reference List   271
Index   297

Contributors

Christopher K. Ansell is Associate Professor of Political Science at the University of California, Berkeley. He is the author of *Schism and Solidarity in Social Movements: The Politics of Labor in the French Third Republic* (2001).

Stefano Bartolini is Professor at the European University Institute. He is the editor of the *Rivista Italiana di Scienza Politica* and a member of the scientific editorial board of *West European Politics* and *Electoral Studies*. In 1990 he was awarded the UNESCO Stein Rokkan Prize for the Social Sciences. He is author, most recently, of *The Class Cleavage: The Political Mobilization of the European Left, 1860–1980* (2000).

Bruce E. Cain is Robson Professor of Political Science at the University of California, Berkeley, and Director of the Institute of Governmental Studies. His books include *The Reapportionment Puzzle* (1984); *The Personal Vote* (1987), written with John Forejohn and Morris Fiorina; and *Congressional Redistricting* (1991), with David Butler. He received the Zale Award for Outstanding Achievement in Policy Research and Public Service in March 2000 and was elected to the American Academy of Arts and Sciences in April 2000.

James A. Caporaso is Professor of Political Science at the University of Washington. He is the editor of the journal *Comparative Political Studies* and the author of *The Changing International Division of Labor* (1987); *The Elusive State* (1989); *Theories of Political Economy*, with David Levine (1992); and *The European Union: Dilemmas of Regional Integration* (2000).

Giuseppe Di Palma is Professor of Political Science at the University of California, Berkeley, and the author of *Apathy and Participation: Mass Politics in Western Societies* (1970), *Surviving Without Governing: The Italian Parties in Parliament* (1977), and *To Craft Democracies: An Essay on Democratic Transitions* (1991).

Ian Down is currently a postdoctoral Fellow at the University of California, Davis, and the author of a forthcoming article on central bank independence in *Comparative Political Studies*.

Sergio Fabbrini is Professor of Political Science at the University of Trento. He is a member of the Steering Group on the European Union of the European Consortium for Political Research (ECPR). He has authored seven academic books, coauthored one book, edited and coedited five other books, and published several articles in journals in the fields of comparative, American, European Union, and Italian politics and political theory.

Maurizio Ferrera is Professor at the Università degli Studi di Pavia and the Università Commerciale Bocconi. He is the author of several books on the European and Italian welfare state, including *Salvati dall' Europa* (1999) with E. Gualmini, *Le Trappole del Welfare* (1998), *Modelli di Solidarietà. Politica e Riforme Sociali nelle Democrazie* (1993), and *Il Welfare State in Italia* (1984).

Joseph Jupille is Assistant Professor at Florida International University, where he is currently Associate Director of the Miami European Union Center. His first book, *Procedural Politics: Influence and Institutional Choice in the European Union*, is forthcoming (2004) from Cambridge University Press. He is also coeditor (with James A. Caporaso and Jeffrey Checkel) and contributor to a special issue of *Comparative Political Studies* entitled "Integrating Institutions: Rationalism, Constructivism, and the Study of the European Union" (February–March 2003).

Gary Marks is Professor of Political Science and founding Director of the Center for European Studies at the University of North Carolina, Chapel Hill. He has published *Unions in Politics: Britain, Germany, and the United States in the Nineteenth and Early Twentieth Centuries* (1989); *It Didn't Happen Here: Why Socialism Failed in the United States* (2000), with S. M. Lipset; and *Multi-Level Governance in the European Union* (2000), with Liesbet Hooghe. Marks is the coeditor of *Governance in the European Union* (1996) with Fritz Scharpf, Phillipe Schmitter, and Wolfgang Steeck and of *Continuity and Change in Contemporary Capitalist Societies* (1998) with Herbert Kitschelt, Peter Lange, and John Stephens.

Alberta M. Sbragia is Professor of Political Science at the University of Pittsburgh and Director of Center for Western European Studies and Director of the European Union Center. She is the author of *Debt Wish: Entrepreneurial Cities, U.S. Federalism, and Economic Development* (1996), and editor of *Euro-Politics: Politics and Policymaking in the "New" European Community* (1992).

Alec Stone Sweet is Senior Official Fellow at Nuffield College and currently Visiting Professor at Yale Law School. He is the author of *The Judicial Construction of Europe* (forthcoming); *On Law, Politics, and Judicialization* (2002), with Martin Shapiro; and *Governing with Judges: Constitutional*

Politics in Europe (2000). He is also the coeditor, with Wayne Sandholtz and Neil Fligstein, of *The Institutionalization of Europe* (2001) and, with Wayne Sandholtz, of *European Integration and Supranational Governance* (1998).

Sidney Tarrow is the Maxwell Upson Professor of Government and Sociology at Cornell University. Professor Tarrow's 1990 monograph, *Democracy and Disorder*, received the Best Book in Collective Action and Social Movements award from the American Sociological Association. More recently, he is the author of *Power in Movement* (1998). In the past five years, Professor Tarrow has also coauthored or edited four other books and monographs: *The Social Movement Society* (1998), edited with David S. Meyer; *Contentious Europeans* (1998), edited with Doug Imig; *Dynamics of Contention* (2001), written with Doug McAdam and Charles Tilly; and *Silence and Voice in the Study of Contentious Politics* (2001), with Ronald R. Amizade et al.

Acknowledgments

This book could not have come to fruition without the financial, administrative, and moral support of the University of California's Institute of European Studies (IES) and the Institute of Governmental Studies (IGS). The original idea for the project grew in part out of a proseminar sponsored by IES in the fall of 1997. Offered by Bruce Cain and Beppe Di Palma of Berkeley and Sergio Fabbrini of Trento University, the proseminar compared democracy in Europe and the United States. That same semester, a Comparative Federalism Roundtable, organized by Chris Ansell and cosponsored by IES and IGS, brought a number of scholars from outside Berkeley (including Alberta Sbragia and Alec Stone Sweet) to compare federalism in Canada, Germany, Europe, and the United States. Building on ideas explored in both the comparative democracy proseminar and the federalism roundtable, we organized a larger research project examining the changing character of center–periphery relations in Europe. With the encouragement of Fabbrini and Cain, the project was conceived from the outset with the comparative reference of the United States in mind. IES graciously funded the first set of meetings, which were held in Berkeley. The IGS sponsored the final Berkeley meeting. At IES, we especially thank Gerald Feldman, Beverly Crawford, and Gia White-Forbes for their enlightened support over several years. On the IGS side, we thank Cain and Marc Levin for their generous assistance with this project. We were also very fortunate to have additional support at a critical stage from the Robert Schuman Centre at the European University Institute (EUI). Through the good offices of Stefano Bartolini, the EUI sponsored an additional meeting in Florence in May 2000.

We also thank the participants in the project, whose good humor helped us get over some of the inevitable kinks in a transatlantic project of this kind. The advice and support of Bartolini, Jim Caporaso, and Sid Tarrow were especially appreciated at several critical junctures in the project. In addition, we would like to thank the three anonymous reviewers who charitably read through the somewhat disjointed original manuscript and offer special thanks to the reviewer who read both the original and revised manuscripts. Finally, we would like to pay special tribute to the memory of Ernie Haas. Although never a formal member of the project, Ernie gave us an encouraging kick in the pants at a number of points during the course of the project. The great thing about Ernie, which so many of us will now sorely miss, is that without coddling you, he let you know that fundamental intellectual inquiry is worth the effort. We dedicate this book to the lasting influence of Ernie's life and work.

Chris Ansell and Beppe Di Palma

Restructuring Territoriality

Europe and the United States Compared

PART I

THEORETICAL FRAMEWORKS

Restructuring Authority and Territoriality

Christopher K. Ansell

This book represents the fruits of a collective inquiry begun in 1997 with the support of the Institute for European Studies and the Institute for Governmental Studies at the University of California, Berkeley, and the European University Institute in Florence. Our inquiry was initially prompted by John Gerard Ruggie's provocative analysis about the "unbundling of territoriality" (Ruggie 1993).[1] Beginning with an analysis of authority relations in medieval Europe, Ruggie argues that the "medieval system of rule was structured by a non-exclusive form of territoriality, in which authority was both personalized and parcelized within and across territorial formations." In contrast, the distinctive feature of the modern system of rule is that it "differentiated its subject collectivity into territorially defined, fixed, and mutually exclusive enclaves of legitimate domination." Ruggie argues that, as exemplified by the project of European integration, contemporary trends represent an "unbundling of territoriality." As the foundational principle of modern politics, territoriality is receding in favor of a nonterritorial, functional organization of political authority. While some have seen this development as a return to the medieval pattern of "overlapping authorities," Ruggie interprets these developments as a postmodern turn.

In many respects, Ruggie's argument is simply one of the more subtle and provocative examples of an emerging genre arguing that the modern state and the modern state system are being challenged, and perhaps eroded, by a variety of forces ranging from domestic privatization to economic and cultural globalization. The conventional argument runs roughly as follows. After steady expansion of the size and scope of states in the postwar era, a variety of social forces have sought to curtail and reverse this expansion. Waves of privatization of public services, deregulation of utilities and markets, and deconcentration or decentralization of service and authority to

---

[1] For other discussions of unbundling, see Elkins (1995), Kratochwil (1986), and Murphy (1996).

lower levels of government appear to have reversed the trend toward expansion of the state's role in the economy and the provision of social welfare. This "retreat of the state" has coincided with a trend toward the internationalization of markets and the development of new information technologies that appear to "shrink" space by allowing denser communication across national borders. As a result, control over territorial borders has decreased as the crossborder mobility of people, goods, information, capital, and social bads like crime, drugs, and pollution have increased. This "globalization" occurs at a time when the collapse of the Soviet Union (not to mention the earlier collapse of European colonialism) has left in its wake a series of weak "quasistates" or "semisovereign" states whose territorial borders only weakly coincide with societal interests and identities. When combined, these various factors have encouraged an internationalization of governance – an expansion in the scope and role of international organizations and the creation of new "transnational" societal interests and identities. In short, just as the internal and external authority of the state seems to be entering a phase of decline, the demands of interests and identities transcending the territorial state appear to be on the rise.

As a group, we neither endorse nor reject this description of the world. Instead, we see it more as a description of the current terms of debate about the nature of political change. At the center of this debate is often the claim that what is being challenged is state sovereignty (e.g., Boon-Thong and Shamsul Bahrin 1998; Camilleri and Falk 1992; Cusimano 2000; Elkins 1995; and Ohmae 1991). The critical issue, however, is not fundamentally about the various infringements to sovereignty perpetrated or suffered by this or that country. As Stephen Krasner points out, infringements to sovereignty are nothing particularly new – they have been a continuous and ever-present dynamic in modern states and the modern state system (Krasner 1999). Rather, sovereignty is interesting precisely to the extent that it acts as the constitutive principle in organizing the territoriality referred to by Ruggie – the "fixed and mutually exclusive enclaves of legitimate domination." Sovereignty is a powerful concept because it connects the organization of "domestic" authority to claims about the autonomy and authority of one territorial state vis-à-vis others. Conceptually, and in practice, it connects the organization of modern democracy with the organization of the international system.[2]

What is important and novel about the chapters in this book is that they are all concerned with challenges or changes to this basic constitutive

---

[2] Gianfranco Poggi argues that sovereignty is the claim that the state, within a delimited territory, makes its own rules autonomously; it is the "highest level *locus* of power." In the cases in which we are primarily interested, this power is legitimated democratically by the claim that this "highest level *locus* of power" ultimately resides with the "people" – the citizens of the territory. At the same time, "the state's sovereignty and its territoriality, jointly produce a most significant consequence: the political environment in which each state exists is by necessity one which it shares with a plurality of states similar in nature to itself" (Poggi 1990: 21-4).

feature of modern political order – and ultimately, to this nexus between the organization of domestic politics and international politics. Taking the "unbundling of territoriality" or "challenges to sovereignty" as our start-ing point, we asked ourselves what this portends for the basic organization of modern political order. As with most such projects, however, we found it necessary to spend much of our time grappling with the theoretical and empirical meaning of our basic analytical framework. Quite soon, we be-came uncomfortable with the "unbundling of territoriality" as a statement of what was happening in the world. The European Union (EU), for instance, might be better described as a "rebundling" of territorialities than an "un-bundling." While neofunctionalist scholars have long interpreted the EU as a space of "functional" organization, it also appears in much recent work as a space of multiple functional and territorial jurisdictions cast on a larger scale. Our group has also noted a trend toward the increasing prominence of subnational regions in national, European, and international affairs – a ter-ritorial rebundling that arguably results from the very factors seen as making territoriality increasingly irrelevant. Gradually, we have come to believe that asking how the relationship between territory and governance is changing is more useful that asking how it is coming unglued.

From the beginning, the concept of sovereignty also posed problems for our collective inquiry. Sovereignty has been called an "essentially contested concept" – a place where scholars fear to tread. In recent years, a num-ber of scholars have sought to "deconstruct" the concept or to demonstrate the way in which it operates as a "social construction" (Bartelson 1993; Biersteker and Weber 1996; Shinoda 2000; Weber 1995). While provocative and important, these discussions have tended to make the analytical value of the concept more obscure to us. Perhaps of all the current discussions of sovereignty, we found Krasner's distinction between four different types of sovereignty (international legal, Westphalian, domestic, and interdepen-dence) as offering the most analytical clarity. He argues persuasively that it is useful to treat each of these types as independent on the grounds that they have different logics and may even contradict one another. Ultimately, however, we have adopted a somewhat different strategy. We have found it useful to focus on two common denominators in Krasner's definitions (as well as in nearly all definitions of sovereignty of which we are aware). First, all four types of sovereignty commonly presume "territoriality" – that the state is a "discrete" (and for the most part, spatially contiguous) territorial unit demarcated by boundaries, and that the world is carved up politically into discrete, territorially demarcated political units. Second, all four types of sovereignty described by Krasner concern claims about public authority over territory.[3] As Cynthia Weber puts it, "Generally, sovereignty is taken to

---

[3] Following Janice Thompson, Krasner distinguishes between authority and control. Inter-national legal sovereignty concerns authority (mutual legal recognition), but not control; Westphalian sovereignty concerns both authority (the right to nonintervention in the exercise

mean the absolute authority a state holds over a territory and people as well as independence internationally and recognition by other sovereign states as a sovereign state" (Weber 1995: 1). As Christopher McMahon's recent analysis of authority suggests, the state itself can be defined "simply as an entity that claims to have supreme authority in a given territory" (McMahon 1994: 40). As will be further explicated in this introduction, territoriality and authority are more fundamental terms than sovereignty and hence more useful in examining the basic constitutive features of modern political order.

At the core of the modern conception of state sovereignty is the ontology that a region of physical space – usually though not always contiguous – can be conceived of as a corporate personality (which includes the weak sense of an association).[4] As constructivist analyses of sovereignty have shown, this ontology was something that had to be conceived and constructed (Wendt 1992). It was not simply a fact of nature, though in many cases it has come to be conceived as such. As a corporate personality, the sovereign state was also a legal personality that could be assigned rights and duties, and more generally, authority. The legal character of this territorial corporation could vary greatly, as could the organization of offices that every corporate body must organize to execute these rights and duties. So too could the precise content and character of the rights and duties attributed to these offices.[5] The *unity* of this public authority, however, has generally been regarded as a hallmark of the so-called Westphalian states. As James A. Caporaso and Joseph Jupille succinctly put it in their contribution to this book, the creation of the Westphalian state required a movement "from parcellization to consolidation [of authority], from personalization to institutionalization [of authority], and from a nonspatial ontology to a territorial one."[6]

of domestic authority) and control (effective autonomy from external intervention); domestic sovereignty refers to the institutional location and organization of authority within the state (popular sovereignty, parliamentary sovereignty, and so on); and interdependence sovereignty refers to control (capacity to control the flow of goods, services, people, capital, information, and so on across borders). While he claims that the last, interdependence sovereignty, does not concern authority, certainly the capacity to control is in part a capacity to exercise authority.

[4] Ontology is a claim about the existence of an entity that behaves like a subject. (No claim is being made here about the debate between methodological individualism and methodological holism. No methodological individualist denies, for instance, that people believe that there exist groups that can be conceived of as persons.)

[5] It was the consolidation and institutionalization of authority that allowed the state to become distinguished as being the center of public authority – as opposed to the private authority that has always been present in families, firms, churches, and many other forms of non-state organization. This boundary between public and private has always been contested, but there is now the sense that bundles of public authority are being broken off from the state and privatized.

[6] On the Westphalian state, see Caporaso (1996). The so-called Philadelphian system (of which the antebellum United States is the predominant example) respects the second and third of these criteria, but authority remained divided between state governments and a federal government (Deudney 1996).

One important reason for focusing on authority rather than sovereignty is that sovereignty is almost inextricably linked to territoriality.[7] It is therefore difficult to examine their covariation. Arguably, it is a better formulation of Ruggie's original problem to say that what has become "unbundled" is authority rather than territoriality. In some cases, authority is being unbundled within the territorial state – as when public authority is being privatized or deconcentrated – or new forms of authority are being created beyond the state. These new forms of authority may ultimately derive their authority from the territorial state or may be constituted along nonterritorial lines.[8] In still other cases, it is useful to think of authority as being "rebundled" – when discrete bundles of functional or territorial authority are joined together in new combinations (themselves territorial or functional). To examine whether and how authority is becoming unbundled and rebundled, we must first expand our analysis of authority.

While sovereignty may be claimed to be the ultimate, supreme, or final binding authority within a territory, it is necessary to recall that this never has meant complete, comprehensive, or unlimited authority over activities and behaviors taking place within a territory. Other authorities have always existed within and beyond the territorial state. It is true that these authorities may have been subject to the state's claim of being the highest authority, yet modern democratic states have never held unlimited authority over these "private" authorities. Nor do these private authorities necessarily derive their authority from the sovereign state.[9] The American Medical Association, the

---

[7] Sovereignty is both the de jure claim and the de facto exercise of authority over this territorial political association. Often, sovereignty is regarded as a form of authority that subordinates other authorities: It is a claim about "supreme authority" (McMahon 1994: 40) or "highest degree" of authority (Lasswell and Kaplan 1950) or the location of "final binding decision" (from Hans Morgenthau as quoted by Shinoda 2000, 104). The discussion of authority is valuable because, again, it points to a common denominator between domestic and international politics – domestic authority being contingent upon international authority, and vice versa.

[8] On the expansion of private legal authority, see Cutler, Haufler, and Porter (1999).

[9] If power is "the ability to get what one wants," then the ability to get people to do things by telling them to do these things is "directive power." Authority is the "right" to exercise directive power and differs from coercion in that subordinates comply with authority because they believe it appropriate to do so rather than because of fear of the consequences if they do not. "A right, then, is a claim that certain people ought to accept" (McMahon 1994: 43). Authority is "the right to tell others, within certain limits that will vary from cases to case, what to do" (McMahon 1994: 28). Or, as James Coleman puts it: "One actor has authority over another in some domain of action when the first holds the right to direct the action of the second in that domain" (Coleman 1990: 66). McMahon distinguishes between de facto and de jure (or legitimate) authority. De facto authority is acceptance, in practice, of the authority's right to direct, regardless of whether that right is regarded as morally just. A "legitimate" authority is obeyed because it is regarded as morally right or just. With de facto authority, the "right" to direct is regarded as a prerogative; with de jure authority, it is regarded as justified.

German Lutheran Church, British firms, and Italian parents have always been bearers of "private" (and sometimes quasipublic) authority.[10] While this authority has certainly come in conflict with the "public" authority of the state (and the boundaries between public and private authority have been continuously negotiated), these authority claims have for the most part either reinforced the territorial basis of public authority or else posed no challenge to it.

This last point ultimately helps to clarify what is distinctive about current changes in the state system. The principle of territoriality, as described by Ruggie, has meant that public authority has been demarcated by discrete boundaries of national territory. But so too has the articulation of societal interests and identities that both buttress and make demands upon this authority. Nationalism is the most important and salient example of the coincidence of societal identities and territorial authority (Berezin, in press). Yet this coincidence has always been imperfect. There have always been group identities and interests that fit uncomfortably within the boundaries of the territorial state (particularly religious and ethnic identities). The Catholic Church or the international labor movement are good examples. Yet to a large degree, the evolution of forms of interest intermediation in the last century has largely conformed with national territorial boundaries. For example, while labor movements have always had a strong inclination toward internationalism, they have been *predominantly* organized around and oriented toward national authority. It is true, of course, that interests and identities *within* national boundaries have been predominantly, though not exclusively, organized along functional rather than territorial lines. They have sought to represent certain statuses or classes of actors within the territorial state. But as Stefano Bartolini argues in his contribution to this book, this is precisely because the state itself has largely monopolized territorial forms of representation.

Thus, the consolidation of territoriality, the organization of public and private authority, and the articulation of societal interests and identities have for the most part been coincident over the last century. In a sense, they have "coevolved" together in a mutually reinforcing way that makes it difficult to consider the existence of one without the other. The individual contributions to this book, which we can now introduce, all explore the political

---

[10] To see how "interests and identities" can themselves be conceived in terms of bearers of authority of various sorts, we can follow McMahon's distinction between three different subspecies of authority. E-authority is a form of nonsubordinating authority that preempts your beliefs about what is in your interest. (An example is the "epistemic community" frequently discussed in the international relations [IR] literature.) C-authority is a form of subordinating authority voluntarily accepted because it allows individuals to better realize their own interests through the achievement of cooperation. (International regimes may be a good example of this type of authority.) And P-authority is a form of subordination established by a promise, which in turn establishes an obligation (for example, treaties).

implications of a world in which the mutually reinforcing relations among territory, authority, and societal interests and identities can no longer be taken for granted.

In bringing these individual contributions together, this book suggests different theoretical logics for understanding the changing relationship between territory, authority, and societal interests and identities. While all the chapters of this book explore this new terrain, Chapters 2 and 3, by Bartolini and Sidney Tarrow respectively, explicitly seek to formulate broad theoretical models for understanding this evolving relationship. Though they share certain observations about the nature of political change, these authors' theoretical differences lead them to different conclusions about the scope and extent of this change. For these reasons, a comparison of their contributions is a very useful place to begin our discussion.

Drawing on Stein Rokkan's pioneering work on the territorial structuring of modern European states, Bartolini's chapter attempts to establish a baseline for understanding the contemporary changes wrought by economic internationalization and European integration. From this Rokkanian perspective, the territorial structuring of states was a difficult and uneven historical process in which the consolidation of the external borders of the state vis-à-vis other states was interdependent with the ability of a territorial "center" to hierarchically subordinate or subdue the territorial "periphery." The development of centralized administrative organization (the "modern bureaucratic state") allowed the center both to defend its territorial claims externally and control the periphery internally. The consequences for the subsequent evolution of political authority, interests, and identities were manifold. Drawing on Albert Hirschman's well-known "exit-voice" framework, Bartolini argues that successful state-building sharply reduced the options for "exit" and consequently created a demand for the internal structuring of "voice." The organization of interests and identities along functional and national lines was one critical consequence of the internal demands to exercise voice; democratic institutions and national citizenship were others.

In Bartolini's view, it is precisely the "coincidence of cultural, economic, and politico-administrative boundaries" achieved by this territorial structuring that economic internationalization and European integration now challenge. By increasing the "exit" options for cultural, economic, and political interests and identities, internationalization and European integration pose two fundamental challenges to the territorial dispensation achieved by modern state building. First, exit options challenge the state's domestic authority and its capacity to order domestic affairs authoritatively; second, and simultaneously, expanding exit options reduce the incentives to exercise voice in lieu of exit.

Bartolini suggests a number of important consequences that may follow from this state of affairs. One of the most important is the reemergence of the old "center–periphery" territorial cleavages and the increasing assertiveness of subnational identities and interests. The second – driven by the mobility of capital – is the appearance of a new form of "subnational" territorial competition to attract capital and to develop resources endogenously. Third, by fragmenting the sites of power and decision making, European integration challenges the functional organization of interests and identities premised on the territorial organization of nation-states. Thus, while subnational regionalization disorganizes functional interests and identities from below, European integration disorganizes them from above. The conclusion reached by Bartolini departs significantly from the expectations of neofunctionalist theory: We should expect the European political landscape to be increasingly dominated by a form of "stratarchic territorial representation" rather than national or continental functional representation.

Whereas Bartolini draws on Rokkan and Hirshman to conceptualize the current change in the relationship of territoriality, authority, and interests and identities, Tarrow approaches the issue from a quite different analytical perspective. To Bartolini's marriage of Rokkan's structural perspective with the individualist perspective of Hirschman, Tarrow proposes a different connubial arrangement: the combination of a dynamic "political exchange" model inspired by Alessandro Pizzorno with a relational approach to political contention in the tradition of Charles Tilly. In earlier work examining claims about the emerging transnational nature of contentious politics, Tarrow found examples of both transnational and supranational political mobilization (Imig and Tarrow 2001). However, he also found that evidence for this form of protest was limited and that national mobilization remained by far the dominant form of political contention. From Bartolini's perspective, this limited "Europeanization" of protest makes sense because European integration and economic internationalization have accentuated a transition from functional to "stratarchal territorial representation." But Tarrow suggests that a relational political exchange model offers a particular interpretation of the new forms of European subnational territorial mobilization pointed to by Bartolini. Subnational territories, he argues, are really behaving fundamentally like functional interests ("lobbies") because the logic of political exchange in the EU converts territorial interests into sectoral interests.

The differences between Bartolini and Tarrow are subtle, but ultimately point to different ways of conceptualizing political change. For Bartolini, territorial boundaries are the critical structural feature of modern states; political change depends on the relative ease of exit from these territorial boundaries. For Tarrow, the boundary per se is less important than examining strategies of political exchange, and ease of exit is less important than focusing on the relationships of actors within and across territorial boundaries. Ultimately, these conceptual differences lead to different judgments about whether the political change we are now witnessing is foundational or not. For Bartolini, current events may be seen as a "critical juncture" (to draw on Rokkanian language) in which one mode of interest intermediation is being disorganized and replaced with another. But for Tarrow, national and functional modes of interest intermediation are not being disorganized; rather, the process is one of layering new modes of authority and new opportunities for political coalition on top of existing ones. He sees increasing complexity as authority and coalition building become "composite" in nature, but no fundamental break with the status quo.

Several of the chapters in this book can be interpreted from the perspective of the conceptual frameworks developed by Bartolini and Tarrow. Maurizio Ferrera, for example, draws explicitly on the Rokkan/Hirschman framework to analyze the changing structure of welfare provision in Europe. He argues that the territorial bounding of the nation-state was a fundamental precondition for the making of modern welfare states. Territorial bounding and the institution of national citizenship were necessary ingredients for creating the "compulsory" social insurance programs that became the centerpiece of European welfare states. The free movement of European workers across national borders (exit) has deeply challenged the compulsory nature of these programs. Europeanization has certainly added a layer of administrative complexity to national programs and raised the legal conundrum of harmonizing different national welfare regimes. But most importantly, the expansion of legal authority at the European level has led to the erosion of national legal control over social insurance beneficiaries, creating "semisovereign" national welfare systems. While the precise mode of adaptation of national welfare systems to this external intrusion of European authority remains an open question, Ferrera suggests that one significant outcome may be a push toward the subnational regionalization of national welfare regimes.

Sergio Fabbrini's contribution to the book critically examines the Rokkanian framework from the perspective of the American experience of state building. The main thrust of his argument is to show that the pattern of development of the American state is at variance with the pattern described by Rokkan for continental European states. In Fabbrini's survey of American state building, the crucial difference is that the nation precedes the state in the United States, and democratization and nation building are synchronic in America (and diachronic in Europe). Consequently, the "center" never subordinated the "periphery," and a modern bureaucratic state emerged only much later. By constitutional design, domestic authority in the United States has remained both vertically and horizontally fragmented. Thus, from a Rokkanian perspective on European state building, the United States represents an interesting deviant case, though one with many parallels with the contemporary EU. I will return to this comparison between the EU and the United States later in this chapter.

Although published elsewhere, Jack Citrin and John Sides' (2003) contribution to our group project can be read as offering support for both Bartolini and Tarrow. They find that national loyalties remain the dominant political identities in Europe, though compatible with a European identity for a significant fraction of citizens. Their major conclusion, drawn from their assessment of Euro-barometer studies, is that "strong feelings of national identity persist" even as a "large segment of the public in all countries view themselves as simultaneously members of two communities: the nation-state and Europe." Their finding can be read as reinforcing Tarrow's argument about political contention: As with interest groups, national identities will continue to reinforce the importance of national territorial borders, even as the space for an alternative (European) identity offers a secondary venue for mobilization. But the way in which the construction of the EU evokes "strong feelings of national identity," as well as the way in which national identities are nested within a broader European identity, also imply that the "stratarchal territorial representation" that Bartolini suggests will supplant functional representation.

While other contributions to this book might be introduced in terms of how they relate to the perspectives advanced by Bartolini and Tarrow, we might then miss a broader theme that emerges in a number of the chapters. As developed in the first part of this introduction, one way to explore contemporary political change is to investigate the changing organization of authority. As some contributions to this book demonstrate, it is useful in some cases to analyze political change in terms of the "unbundling" of existing authority. "Unbundling" here means that modes of authority once packaged and organized together are becoming separated and organized as distinct bundles. However, our contributors also find cases where once-distinctive modes of authority are being brought together and joined in new ways – a process of "rebundling." And finally, some chapters describe the creation of new "bundles" of authority where they simply did not exist previously.

Chapter 4, by James Caporaso and Joseph Jupille, can be understood as a study of the changing organization and exercise of domestic political authority in the face of the development of new forms of extranational authority. Specifically, the authors examine changes in the meaning and exercise of British parliamentary sovereignty in the face of the expanding legal authority of the EU. They observe that "as the EU becomes progressively constitutionalized, it has injected its substance and procedures into the UK's constitutional order." In a country without a formal Bill of Rights, EU law creates "entrenched rights" that "the UK parliament cannot deny British citizens." The final or supreme authority of parliament on such matters is, therefore, trumped by the higher authority of the European Court of Justice (ECJ). As Caporaso and Jupille note, however, the consequences go beyond a shift in the locus of final authority from the British parliament to the ECJ. The creation of formal European rights also leads to a reorganization of domestic authority relations, because interpretation of these rights creates a demand for domestic judicial review of parliamentary law. Their chapter reveals an interesting dynamic whereby the creation of new bundles of external authority leads to an internal unbundling of authority. Their findings are similar to those described by Ferrera for European welfare states: The emerging legal authority of the EU leads to both a diminution of national authority ("semisovereign welfare state," "semisovereign parliament") and potentially a domestic unbundling of authority (the creation of regional welfare regimes, the emergence of judicial review).

One of the main consequences of the unbundling and rebundling of authority is the problem of establishing rules of priority and jurisdiction between different bundles. Although not published in this book, Martin Shapiro's contribution to our group project dealt with one of the major difficulties of creating European authority that can potentially trump national authority: the problem of delineating, legally and institutionally, the respective authority jurisdictions between the EU and its member states. Shapiro examined one very notable attempt to tidy up overlapping authority created by earlier rounds of European integration: the principle of subsidiarity. Subsidiarity, as Shapiro wrote in his paper, is a "way to make legal sense of two sovereigns sharing the same citizens and territory" (Shapiro 2000). Subsidiarity is a standard for deciding whether member states or the EU have prerogatives over particular issues. Introduced by the Maastricht Treaty, the principle of subsidarity states that the EU shall have jurisdiction "only if and insofar as the objectives of the proposed action cannot be sufficiently achieved by the Member States." Drawing a comparison with American disputes over the boundaries between federal and state authority, however, Shapiro argues that the problem is nearly impossible to settle clearly, particularly in the context of a modern economy. Subsidiarity, he argues, will ultimately be no more successful than American claims of "dual sovereignty." One of the further implications he draws from this comparison is that the precise boundaries between national and European authority can be established only through continuous political negotiation and not through conceptual fiat.

This theme of complex, overlapping authority appears in a number of the contributions. As already pointed out, Tarrow argues that Europe should be seen as a "composite polity." The essence of his argument is that "ordinary people" confront "multiple and overlapping structures of opportunity." His model argues that a variety of coalitions – both horizontal and vertical – will be possible for ordinary people in the context of this new political opportunity structure. Some of these alliances may reinforce traditional "state-centric" structures. However, the possibility will exist for translocal coalitions and transnational contention.

In a comparison of immigration policy in the United States and the EU, Bruce Cain argues that the EU creates something that bears a family resemblance to James Madison's "compound republic." The layering on of European institutions creates countervailing forms of authority that, as Madison prescribed for the United States, mediate majoritarian tendencies. In the United States, this mediating role has been played by federalism and by the courts. In Europe, Cain argues, the functional equivalent is currently the system of intergovernmental negotiation, though in time EU courts may play this role more directly. One consequence of this new compound republic, Cain argues, may be the phenomenon of "venue shopping," in which European interest groups may seek out the political arena most responsive to their needs and interests. Interestingly, this idea of venue shopping straddles Tarrow's political exchange perspective and Bartolini's exit perspective. Venue shopping suggests the sort of composite "political opportunity structures" described by Tarrow. But it also suggests the increasing prominence of exit over voice strategies highlighted by Bartolini's perspective (that is, the ability to move from venue to venue).

How does the policy process work in compound or composite polities? In a comparison of air pollution policymaking in the United States and the EU, Alberta Sbragia develops a method for explaining divergent policy outcomes consistent with this perspective on venue shopping or composite or compound "political opportunity structures." She argues that policy differences can be explained in terms of the number of institutional veto points, the majoritarian or supermajoritarian character of the institution, and the way the structures of legislative institutions shape possibilities for agreement and disagreement. She also argues that the policy outcomes mediated by these institutional structures depend on the organization of interests, which she conceives of as depending on the precise intersection between territorial and functional modes of interest representation. What is distinctive about the United States, Sbragia argues, is that functional interests are often mobilized and represented territorially, while territorial and functional representation is more disjunct in Europe. I will return to this important point later in this chapter.

My own contribution to the project (published elsewhere) can be understood as the administrative parallel of policy-making dynamics in a compound or composite polity (Ansell 2000). What types of administrative organization are possible when overlapping political authority is organized at several administrative levels? Examining regional economic development strategies in Europe, I describe the development of a "networked polity" – a functional organization of multiple public and private authorities that cuts across and links up different subnational regions and different levels of territory (subnational, national, European). As developed in Chapter 11, these functional networks reflect the domestic unbundling of authority (decentralization), the creation of new layers of authority beyond the state (EU structural policy), and the contingent rebundling of multiple sources of authority for specific development projects. While venue shopping and veto points can be easily observed in this domain, it is worth pointing out how the logic here differs from that developed by Cain and Sbragia: The distinctive feature of these functional networks is that they link together multiple venues in a common organizational framework. In this sense, these functional networks reflect the relational rather than the exit perspective.

To discuss the relative salience of relational versus exit mechanisms more generally, we can draw inspiration from Shapiro's argument about the difficulty of tidying up overlapping authority (discussed previously). To the extent that the unbundling or layering of authority creates complex patterns of shared authority, we must expect relational mechanisms to exist – in the form of political alliances or functional networks – that attempt to create an emergent form of joint authority. But to the extent that unbundling or layering creates distinct arenas that see their respective authority claims in competitive, conflictual, or exclusive terms, exit mechanisms might be more likely to operate.

The contribution of Alec Stone Sweet to this book demonstrates yet another aspect of the reorganization of authority. So far, the chapters have talked about the unbundling of authority within the context of existing states or the creation of new forms of authority at a higher territorial scale. They have not challenged the principle of territoriality per se, although the scale of territoriality has in some cases been significantly altered (shifted to subnational units in the cases of Bartolini and Ferrera; shifted to the EU in the cases of Tarrow, Caporaso and Jupille, Cain, and Sbragia).[11] Stone Sweet's contribution demonstrates the possibility of a more complete separation of authority from territory. He describes the globalization of freedom of contract and arbitration, which is designed to replace national contract law and courts as the means of regulating international commerce between private firms. His analysis describes a new private law of commercial commerce, which he compares to the *Lex Mercatoria* that regulated transactions between traders and merchants in the absence of state regulation in medieval Europe. These new "islands of transnational governance" are important in

---

[11] The "constitutionalization" of the EU described by the Caporaso and Jupille chapter implies the creation of public authority on a larger territorial scale. Bundles of authority may have migrated from the nation-state to the EU, but the new organization of authority reinforces the principle of territoriality. To the extent that the EU is simply a set of discrete functional authorities, it does represent the unbundling of territoriality identified by neofunctionalists and Ruggie. But to the extent that the EU is constitutionalized, develops a body of authoritative and integrative law, and has "offices" that speak for the EU as a whole, it operates much more like a new territorial ontology – a corporate personality – on a higher scale.

our analysis because they reflect one extreme in the development of authority relations. They clearly break with a territorial ontology. Although national law may be drawn upon to construct model rules for contracting, the whole purpose of these systems is to enable firms embedded in different legal regimes to transcend the constraints of any one legal tradition. These islands also represent a vivid example of authority established outside existing state boundaries. This authority is clearly private, at least in the sense that it does not derive its authority to regulate from state authority. This new form of governance represents a rather dramatic shift from public to private authority and from a territorial to nonterritorial organization – that is, specific bundles of activity once regulated in the public legal systems of territorial states are now regulated by a private law organized by nonterritorial actors. This new *Lex Mercatoria* has taken shape against the backdrop of state authority, while the medieval *Lex Mercatoria* emerged from the vacuum of state authority.

Closely related to changing modes of authority, changes in the nature of societal interests and identities are also explored in several of the chapters. Indeed, following the theme of alternative conceptual frameworks (structuralist/individualist versus political exchange/relational) and the theme of unbundling and rebundling of authority, this is the third major theme of this book. As with authority, it is possible to see that old interests and identities are in some cases being unbundled or rebundled, while new interests and identities are being created. Contributions by Bartolini, Tarrow, Ferrera, Sbragia, and Stone Sweet each consider, from various angles, the modes of organization and mobilization of societal interests and identities. Bartolini provides a discussion of the organization of societal interests and identities linked directly to his Rokkanian and Hirschmanian perspective: Because the territorial bounding of states reduced the options for exit, while increasing the incentive to exercise voice, societal interests and identities have been coincident with state boundaries; because the center has sought to subordinate the periphery, identities and interests have become organized along functional rather than territorial lines. The increasing options for exit, however, have tended to disorganize (unbundle) functional representation at the national level, while the lack of a real center at the European or international level discourages the creation of functional organization at a higher level. New forms of territorial mobilization are thus expected, particularly at the subnational level. My own work (Ansell 2000) and Ferrera's contribution to this book support this view that subnational mobilization is becoming increasingly important.

As already pointed out, Tarrow reaches a different conclusion about political change than does Bartolini. First, Tarrow does not predict a disorganization of functional interests at the national level; second, from his political exchange perspective, he regards functional (that is, sectoral) interests as coming to dominate European-level politics. In his focus on the increasing need for legal mediation for international joint ventures, Stone Sweet's contribution tends to reinforce the view that the representation of sectoral producer interests will increasingly be separated from territorial forms of representation. Sbragia's contribution adds an interesting nuance to Stone Sweet's emphasis on the separation of territorial and functional interests. She argues that the precise mode of organization (territorial versus functional) will depend on the extent to which functional interests are territorially concentrated. Producer (functional) interests are more territorially concentrated in the United States than in Europe, she argues, and thus more inclined toward territorial representation.

Gary Marks and Ian Down's contribution to this book draws together the themes of changing authority structures and changing societal interests. In a comparison of the respective levels of left support for the EU and North American Free Trade Agreement (NAFTA), their contribution poses the question of whether interests or identities will adapt or "coevolve" with changing authority structures. In their comparison of left support for international regimes in Europe and North America, they ask why the European left has come to embrace and support EU institutions, while labor unions and left parties in North America have been much more antagonistic toward NAFTA. Comparing the two regional institutions, Marks and Down argue that the left in Europe came to embrace the EU precisely as its "authoritative competences" became more weighty. As these competences became real, the left came to understand that the EU offers concrete leverage for organizing markets. Thus, we should expect a complex interplay between the consolidation of extranational authority and the extent that interests and identities are organized at the national level.

In many ways, this model of the coevolving relationship between authority structures and the strategies of interests and identities might be developed into a third general model that could be compared to the Bartolini and Tarrow frameworks. In a number of respects, Marks and Down's model is similar to Tarrow's in that it sees regional institutions like the EU or NAFTA as political opportunity structures that may alter the incentives and opportunities for mobilization. Especially if broadened to consider the reciprocal adaptation of authority structures and the strategies of parties and interest groups, their analysis suggests that there may be "thresholds" that if crossed will lead to a further deepening of the integration process. More broadly, Marks and Down raise a general issue about the coherence and efficiency of political change – topics that Giuseppe Di Palma devotes himself to in his postscript to this book.

This introduction can now be concluded by contemplating the comparison that many of the chapters draw between the European Union and the United States. Why does the United States pose such an appealing point of contrast to the EU? In fact, several of the chapters in this book suggest an answer. From a baseline assumption that European nation-states represent the Westphalian archetype of unified internal authority structures, European integration has encouraged a form of divided and overlapping authority much more characteristic of the "separation of powers" known in the United States. The chapters by Cain and Sbragia (while pointing out differences as well) bring these similarities to light and suggest some of the potential consequences for European integration. It is Fabbrini's contribution to this book, however, that most directly and extensively confronts the historical analogy of the United States with the United States.

Like Bartolini, Fabbrini adopts a Rokkanian perspective on political development. While Bartolini's contribution attempts to show that contemporary developments in Europe are diverging from the assumptions of the "center–periphery model" convincingly used by Rokkan to describe the political development of Europe, Fabbrini argues that the political development of territorial sovereignty in the United States never fit the European model. From the Westphalian perspective of Europe, the United States never developed a clear "state" at all – it had legal integration and nationalism, but only limited governing capacity at the center. The European Union, however, shares the highly pluralistic character of the United States: In both cases, he argues, territorial sovereignty is institutionally fragmented.[12] He concludes by suggesting that the American experience may be instructive for the political development of Europe. In his conclusion to this book, Di Palma picks up on the theme of EU/U.S. comparison, arguing that the comparison is essential because the United States represents – with all its warts and strengths – one possible image of what "democracy beyond the [Westphalian] State" may look like.

Thus, in our collective inquiry investigating the changing relationship between authority and territory, four broad themes have emerged: first, the theoretical contrast between a structural/individualist perspective and a political exchange/relational perspective; second, the emergence of compound or composite forms of authority as new forms of external authority are created or domestic authority is unbundled or rebundled; third, the increasingly compound and composite nature of societal interests and identities; and finally, the striking similarity between the pluralism and fragmented authority now seen in Europe with the institutional separation of powers so familiar in the United States.

---

[12] The fragmented authority of American institutions led Samuel Huntington (1968) to describe the United States as a "Tudor polity," a description suggestive of the "neomedievalist" analysis of the EU.

2

Old and New Peripheries in the Processes of European Territorial Integration

Stefano Bartolini

The internal political structuring of the European nation-states took place through the formation of cleavage structures, the articulation of corporate interests, and the development of center–periphery relations. This chapter deals with the third of these aspects and more precisely with the implications of the process of European integration for the established national system of terr¡torial relationships. Once the old forms of pre-modern territorial representation were superseded by functional and crosslocal systems of sociopolitical cleavages and of interest articulation, the relations between the political center of the state and the subnational territories were set up via institutional arrangements moving from a maximum of federalist decentralization to a maximum of unitary centralization, and by political arrangements involving a specific mix of partisan, bureaucratic, and "local notables" linkages. Yet, the older territorial distinctiveness of a cultural, economic, and political nature on which the boundaries of the older and newer nation-states superimposed did not disappear altogether in the process of modernization triggered by the British industrial revolution and by the French political revolution.

The following chapter considers the possibly changing nature of centers and peripheries in this new context as compared with the historical peripheries in Europe. The core theoretical question can be summarized in the following terms:

- Historical peripheries of a cultural, economic, or politico-administrative nature were the result of the process of territorial, cultural, and economic retrenchment associated with the formation of the nation-state and national economy. The closure of boundaries for various types of transactions (goods, messages, peoples, capital) that the formation of the European system of states produced actually determined the formation and strengthening of new centers and the peripheralization of other territories.[1]

- If this is the case, then the question is what happens to historical peripheries in phases of territorial, cultural, and economic expansion and opening as a result of European integration. Is this associated with a redefinition of centers and peripheries? Will other different peripheries be created? On the basis of which resource imbalances can new peripheralization occur in a loosely bounded territoriality such as that defined by the European Union (EU)? What opportunities and which costs are produced for different types of territories by the multiplication and differentiation of centers at the EU level?

HISTORICAL FORMATION OF PERIPHERY WITHIN NATION-STATES

The process of building new economic, cultural, and administrative boundaries associated with the consolidation of the European system of nation-states determined the formation of the various kinds of peripheries according to their geopolitical, geocultural, and geoeconomic position with respect to the new state geography. The European nation-state building was not exclusively – as it is often thought – a process of integration and of unification of disparate and different territories, economies, and societies. It also implied the disintegration or simply the division of *previously existing* and integrated territories, economies, and societies. When cultural identities were strong, this determined the creation of minorities on both sides of the new boundary. Border groups, economies, and societies therefore had to face a reorientation toward national centers created around the new cores of decision, production, and exchange. Their linkages with the older economies and societies were necessarily and progressively cut, and their claims redirected accordingly.

Obviously, the interaction between various types of boundaries also made for various types of peripheries.[2] Military-administrative centers, with their chancelleries, ministries, courts, legislative bodies, and so on, did not necessarily coincide with economic centers, with the headquarters of major trading firms, industrial companies, stock exchanges, banking insurance, companies, and such, or with cultural centers, with their religious and/or linguistic distinctiveness, universities, theaters, publishing houses, and so on. Territories that were culturally peripheral with respect to the dominant state center need not be economic peripheries, as much as economic peripheral territories

---

[1] In an earlier version of this work (Bartolini 1998b), I deal more extensively with the historical formation of various types of European peripheries.

[2] O. Hintze (1962) first emphasized the distinction between the core around the Frankish Empire and the peripheral areas of the British islands, Scandinavia, Castile, Naples-Sicily, and the German territories to the east.

need not be culturally distinctive with respect to the dominant cultural center. Actually, cultural peripheralization was almost exclusively the result of the reinforcement of military-administrative boundaries that cut across preexisting areas of cultural homogeneity as defined mainly in ethnolinguistic and religious terms. On the contrary, economic peripheralization was the result of the switch in the dominant trade routes. The east-west southern axis through the Mediterranean Sea civilizations was dominant until the downfall of the Roman Empire and the conquests of Islam. The dominant trade route was progressively switched northwards along the Rhine Valley and the Alps from central Italy to the Hanseatic League in the North Sea and the Baltic, and lasted as the dominant route until the seventeenth century. Later, the transoceanic trade route, along Western Europe and across world oceans, produced the relative decline of the transalpine route.

The interaction between these various processes of center building and peripheralization resulted in territorial structures that were more or less monocephalic or policephalic. The most policephalic structure remained concentrated in the Central European city belt of the former Holy Roman Empire. By contrast, during the sixteenth and eighteenth centuries, there was a continuous strengthening of dominant monocephalic administrative centers within territories to the west and east of the medieval trade-route belt: London, Paris, and Madrid on the Atlantic side; Vienna, Munich, Berlin, Stockholm, and Copenhagen on the landward side. Such centers controlled vast peripheries and accumulated large military and administrative, as well as cultural and economic, resources.

The complexity of the interaction among military-administrative, cultural, and economic boundary building does not allow a clear-cut definition of which process was the dominant one in defining the internal differentiation of territories. Immanuel Wallerstein (1974/1980) has developed a model of center–periphery relationships that assigns primacy to development in the economy sphere and, therefore, in economic centers, positing a hierarchy of economic centers and defining peripheries as territories depending on these rich urban centers. The administrative and cultural hierarchies and the processes of the rise of the bureaucratic nation-state, the Reformation, and so on, can, in this model's view, be analyzed as reactions to decisive changes brought about by the world economy with the opening up of the ocean trade routes in the sixteenth century.

Wallerstein makes a distinction among four zones generated by the emergence of the early European world economy: the *dominant core* (moving northward from Spain to the Netherlands and later England; regions with highest concentration of secondary-tertiary activities whose population welfare depend primarily on trading products brought in from distant peripheries); *long-distance peripheries* depending on the core (Latin America, Eastern Europe, and so on); *semiperipheries* (dominated by cities in decline in Italy, the French Midi, and increasingly Spain); and *external areas* (beyond the reach of the network of long-distance trade (notably Japan and China until well into the nineteenth century).

Against this interpretative paradigm, other scholars such as Perry Anderson (1974) and S. E. Finer (1997) have asserted the primacy of the state and its military-administrative apparatus. They have argued that long-distance trade was only of limited importance in this period, and what really mattered was the consolidation of the control system in the conquered immediate hinterland of each center. All this points out the importance of different centers for theories of center–periphery relations.

Rokkan underlines the importance of the interaction between horizontal (territorial) and vertical (membership) peripheralization in the three domains of cultural, economic, and politico-administrative systems for the resulting monocephalic or policephalic territorial structures. How the interaction among military-administrative, cultural, and economic centers actually operated is well illustrated by the example of how border controls and administrative boundaries determined the peripheralization of areas across the borders and reoriented them to the centers. For centuries, an important gap in the system of heavy-freight canals connecting Europe was the absence of a canal connection between the Rhone and the Rhine, and between both and the Seine. Such a Rhone-Rhine canal would have constituted an important and attractive alternative – also during the railways period – to the routes over the Alps. Yet, notwithstanding obvious economic advantages for the region and overall European trade, the administrative authorities in Paris were always reluctant to invest in a transportation system that would have made eastern France closer to the Rhineland axis, and allow also the north-south traffic to bypass Paris. To a large extent, geopolitical issues concerned military and administrative authorities in Paris (Rokkan, Urwin, Aerebrot, Malaba, and Sande 1987: 40).

In conclusion, although large-scale changes in the main trade routes might have determined the *systemic* peripheralization of certain areas within the world economy, internal economic, cultural, and politico-administrative peripheries were mainly the result of the structuring of the modern nation-state and of its capacity to limit the exit options of territories as well as of individuals and resources. These conflicts over the demarcation of boundaries and their stiffness or looseness clearly reflected oppositions and differences of interest among social groups controlling different resources within each territory in different domains: in the economy, the commercial, industrial, financial bourgeoisie controlling capital, commodities, and services; in culture, the educated elite in the churches, universities and schools, media, and telecommunication networks controlling message codes; and in the politico-administrative domain, the political and military-administrative elite controlling rule making and personnel.

The democratization process of the nineteenth century and the development of internal political oppositions were processes of internal differentiation of externally consolidated territorial units. The internal structuring of voice options was mainly a function of such external territorial consolidation and boundary stability. Voice institutionalization was a consequence of the declining opportunity for exit determined by the consolidation of the modern bureaucratic nation-state. The latter claimed control over the economic, cultural, and politico-administrative borders. The centralization of its political administrative, economic, and cultural processes meant that conflict could be voiced and solved only following the same logic – that is, by centralization of claims and political divisions. However, in the democratization process, territorial and peripheral claims were (and still are) less legitimate and less acceptable than functional interest representation and sociopolitical cleavages, due to their inherent challenge to the boundary control of the political elite and center resource controllers. This is why, with few exceptions, nineteenth- and twentieth-century politics was largely about individual rights and collective crosslocal social movements, and tended to regard as threatening the peripheral mobilization of resources.

The transformation of states from warfare to welfare entities since the middle of the twentieth century has progressively made it more evident that borders are not only military-territorial lines, but also systemic boundaries between regulatory systems. This aspect of borders' significance was obscured by their military and "high politics" nature in more stormy political periods up to recent decades. If borders come to be perceived increasingly as regulatory systemic borders, nothing implies that they should remain the same across different functional regimes. Only cultural identifications and loyalties remain to justify and legitimize the coincidence of different spheres' regulatory borders. A prevailing view of borders as regulatory systems' boundaries may raise claims to redefine such borders within or across national lines.

Both international and European integration processes progressively affect the coincidence of cultural, economic, and politico-administrative boundaries, which was the fundamental innovation, distinctive trait, and source of legitimacy of the nation-state. In the last few decades, exit options from the once-integrated cultural-economic-administrative coinciding boundaries of the state have increased rapidly. This is more obvious in the economic sphere, where such options make it more difficult for political authorities to transfer the cost of the political regulation of the market within a territory to the consumers of that same territory. Individual citizens, firms, and possibly territories can increasingly enter a different jurisdiction without moving or seceding, can enter crossborder functional regimes or appeal against national law to supranational regulative authorities. The progressive (within-state) territorial differentiation of regulatory orders does not witness the deprivation of the state along classic territorial sovereignty lines, but its deprivation through functional sovereignty transfers.[3] At the cultural

---

[3] John Ruggie's (1993) thesis that territoriality is receding in favor of a nonterritorial functional organization of political authority needs to be qualified. Although the transfers of

level, exit options are less evident. Cultural bonds – that is, the sentiment of loyalty one feels toward the group to which he/she belongs – are normally regarded as an element increasing the costs of exit options. Yet, cultural solidarities are often stronger at the subnational level than at the national one, and they may exist or have existed across national boundaries. Under the aforementioned conditions of declining exit costs in the economic and administrative spheres, such traditions of subnational or crossborder cultural identifications may be revived, reinforced, and remobilized.

What consequences may derive from the current trend toward territorial enlargement and politico-administrative integration at a level higher than the state? If the peripheralization of territories within bounded states was historically linked to the states reducing exit options, what happens to peripheries when exit opportunities – even in the "weak" or "partial" form of access to external regulative, jurisdictional, and material resources and of avoidance of internal social obligations and costs – spread from individuals and firms to territories?[4] If the historical definition of centers and peripheries resulted from boundary building in the economic, cultural, and administrative field at the state level, one may expect that boundary reshaping will have a strong influence on old and new peripheries.

New boundaries, new types of boundaries, and competition among different boundaries modify the opportunities for weak and partial exit[5] of substate territories. As a result, they also affect the conditions for and the modalities of voice of the latter. In particular, the differential distribution of economic, administrative, and cultural exit opportunities among territories (groups, individuals, and organizations) is likely to become a major source of redefining interests and changing political alignments. It is also likely that the loosening grip of state territorial boundaries leads to the reemergence of territorial oppositions as result of within-state progressive territorial cultural, institutional, and economic differentiation. The impact of European policy on subnational territories may foster a territorial definition and redefinition of interests and even of cultural loyalties. Policies directed toward territories within the boundaries of the nation-state or policies directed toward territories across such boundaries may increase claims to politico-administrative decentralization and strengthen local forms of external representation.

---

authority may be by functional areas and duties, this does not necessarily mean that the new authority center is not "territorial." Moreover, functional transfer of authority from lower to more inclusive centers is a common and frequent historical trend in federalized systems (like that or the United States). This is not regarded as necessarily entailing the receding of territoriality as such.

[4] The terms of "exit" and "voice" are inspired by the work of Albert O. Hirschman (1970, 1981).

[5] For a reelaboration of Hirschman's concept of exit to apply it to territories, see Bartolini (1998a).

The next sections of this chapter discuss the implications of this new opportunity structure. The focus will be on the substate territorial relationships; reference to the other two main dimensions of nation-state political structuring – cleavage systems and corporate interest intermediation – will be made only when directly linked to and affected by the new significance of territory. Needless to say, these latter forms of functional and crosslocal alignments continue to be relevant and interact with old and new forms of territorial representation. Sidney Tarrow's chapter in this book rightly emphasizes that different types of alignments and forms of representation will coexist in the European Union enlarged polity. Tarrow actually discusses the opportunities for new forms of crosslocal (meaning in this case cross-national) political action and political alignments in the political structuring of a united Europe. As I focus on the prospects of renewed substate territorial politics, I may tend to underscore other competing alignments.[6] In this chapter, I will argue that the current mode of market-centered European integration is likely to destructure nation-state functional alignments, while making it very difficult to restructure such alignments at the European Union level.

WITHIN-STATE TERRITORIAL DIFFERENTIATION: CHANGES AFFECTING
THE ROLE OF SUBNATIONAL TERRITORIAL UNITS

With respect to the historical distribution of resources over the national territory and among subnational territories, a number of changes should be considered that affect the within-state territorial differentiation process. I will list them as "points-questions-hypotheses."

Changing Operational Scale of Infrastructural Power?

Once the state develops and expands its ability to provide centrally – and territorially – organized services (the welfare state, the educational system, credential control, an so on), its basis of legitimacy changes and becomes increasingly dependent on this capacity (a "performance legitimacy" as opposed to "procedural legitimacy"). In this way, the state and its bureaucracy develop some element of autonomy from the dominant social elite and it is no longer a pure or simple expression of their "despotic" power. This autonomy and legitimacy depend, however, on the capacity to continue to deliver those goods that cannot be provided in other ways. Infrastructural power, as opposed to "despotic power," can therefore be defined as the capacity to provide and deliver public goods efficiently as services and

---

[6] Bartolini (1999) elaborates more thoroughly the competing relationships among politico-electoral, corporate, and territorial representation in Europe.

rules that other organizations cannot provide (or cannot provide with equal efficiency).[7]

At this stage, however, the state is subject to the challenge and competition of other organizations that prove or are thought to be most able to deliver the same goods (services, protection, and rules). In other words, the changing basis of legitimacy of the state from pure domination to performance of functional duties has eventually exposed the state itself to functional decline with respect to other forms of creation of these goods by other types of organizations. This challenge has proved more intense precisely in the realm of the specific functional regimes defining the administrative-political boundary of the state (defense of property rights connected to an increasingly mobile property, environmental protection, and so on). The application of infrastructural power can be more efficiently allocated to substate or regional communities as well as new above-state communities or international organizations.

To a certain extent, this possibility is enhanced by the devaluation of space as a result of technological development in the communication and transport system. The traditional location scheme according to which investments will tend to be located as close as possible to one of the three sources of capital, market, or raw material no longer applies. In this sense, the process of reproduction of economic peripherality is broken as greater opportunities emerge to locate resources without the constraints of preexisting resource concentration.

Moreover, technological change and international division of production labor in advanced industrial countries bring about a declining importance of asset specificity (that is, that the value of an asset is strongly connected to a specific use). A "specific" asset has no easy substitute. Its exchange requires high transaction cost and high economies of scale. Nonspecific assets (financial products, for example) are the opposite. A political hierarchy guaranteeing the complex conditions of price efficiency and market availability is required more by a predominant "specific asset economy" than by a "nonspecific asset economy."

Therefore, in this purely instrumental perspective, one can imagine that specific political structures (like the state) are more or less efficient in regulating, fostering, and controlling certain economic activities. Economic processes, depending on technological features, have different efficient or ideal political scales. With technological change and goods differentiation, the scale of the political structure becomes suboptimal (because the existing political arrangements for the regulation of production, exchange, and consumption are inadequate for the asset type and the public goods required). Then pressure may emerge for a new political scale that reflects the altered requirement for political production.

---

[7] M. Mann (1984) develops the distinction between "despotic" and "infrastructural" power.

In a growing number of areas, nation-states experience problems in providing the traditional regulatory, distributive, and redistributive public goods (Lowi 1964). For important areas of the regulatory framework of the market and economic activities, only international or crossnational regulations are effective (establishment and protection of property, currency, abolition of internal barriers of production and exchange, standardization, legal enforcement, and adjudication). Distributive activities (through state-controlled and state-sponsored production and distribution, nationalized industries, public services, public finance, and subsidies) and redistributive policies (health and welfare services, employment policies, and environmental policy) are affected by the increasingly difficult definition of which sectors are strategic, by international and regional agreements, and by international competitiveness and a favorable climate for international capital (Cerny 1995).

This increasing divergence between the scale of infrastructural power for the market activities and the scale of action of the state generates interests, ideas, and debates about the ideal and efficient political scale. Does this concern entail only the shift of functions and duties to the transnational and above-state level, or does it also imply the empowerment in certain areas of substate-level territorial organizations?

Territorial Competition?

When the concept of the "demise of the nation-state" is used, what is normally meant is the "demise of the nation-state Keynesian policy capacity." When economic boundaries are lowered or removed, mobile production factors can easily move from one jurisdiction to others according to the social costs and regulatory burdens imposed on them. The absence of European-wide market regulations forces governments to structure their economic and social policies following the requirements of European and international competitiveness (that is, attracting mobile factors). National competitiveness becomes the dominant political imperative and program as national regimes are exposed to competition that can no longer be contained either at the national level or at the EU level. The pressures for competitive de- and reregulation that result already have visible consequences: 1) shift of taxation from mobile to immobile factors; 2) shift of the financing of the welfare state from employers' contributions to general tax revenues; 3) ruling out of state aids and subsidies to domestic industries for employment protection; 4) pushes toward privatization of previously nationalized industries that protected sectors of the labor force; 5) constraints on public borrowing and the overall public deficit; and 6) rising autonomy of central banks no longer allowed to extend credit to governments.

The process of opening markets at the European and global level makes governments less able and willing to put resources into backward regions for programs of territorial redistribution and has made governments more ready and inclined to give more attention to the most dynamic and active sectors and territories in order to foster national competitiveness. In other words, there has been a certain change of priority in territorial politics, from redressing within-state territorial imbalances, to foster territorial endogenous resources and to promote national competitiveness; from territorial to sector intervention (Keating 1997: 27). In the new context, there will be a tendency to divert resources from other programs to those activities that tend to promote growth. This will tend to change the terms of the political debate, putting development and system competitiveness at the core of the political argument.

However, even if the competitive pursuit of economic development and growth will increasingly dominate territorial politics, this does not entail the reduction of the territory to a pure set of exchange relationships based on instrumental calculations. Territorial collective identities, institutional strength, cooperation traditions, and so on can all provide the basis for forms of cooperation in the production of public goods and investments in the future. They can help not only to overcome external diseconomies of competition, but also to create local conditions that, relying on historical traditions and endogenous resources of a cultural, institutional, or social nature, may favor the adaptation and the response of specific local territories. Local territorial identities may also get a new push thanks to this development in the internationalization of forces as a reaction of local defensiveness.

More precisely, territorial competition depends on the following:

- The mobility of factors (goods, firms, individuals, taxpayers, and so on) that create a potential demand. If there are no mobile factors, then there is no competition, in the sense that there are no customers to compete for. The essential element of territorial competition is therefore territorial mobility. However, also non- (or less) mobile factors do play a role, to the extent that they bear the costs of mobile factors' choices. Note that here lies a fundamental difference between economic competition and territorial public good competition. While a loyal customer may continue to buy the same good, eventually enjoying its improved quality determined by the exit options of other more volatile buyers (and even if the factory that produces the good that the buyer likes were to fail and disappear, the buyer could always have a substitute), in public goods territorial competition, the loyal customer (that customer who does not want or who cannot be "territorially mobile") is considerably affected by the deterioration of the territorial performance.
- The territorial differentiation of the public goods bidding that creates a supply. If territorial bidding is not differentiated, there is no incentive to change territorial location. Territorial competition is mainly competition through bids to offer different kinds, levels, or quality of public goods (transports, loans, and so on). There might be big differences in the

capacities of different subnational territories to differentiate the bidding according to the institutional structure, policy competence, and means of the local government. The stronger the external hierarchical control of the bidding (from the center), the less possible a territorial substate differentiation. The higher the local resources and the lower the central control, the higher the possibility for such differentiation.

To a certain extent, the standardizing element in EU policies would tend to reduce the differentiation of territorial bidding (for instance, imposing common standards on products). Everything in the direction of "positive integration" (Scharpf 2000a) sets boundaries to the differentiation of the bidding, compelling firms, territories, and so on to make a standardized European bid. On the other side, everything in the direction of "negative integration," reducing territorial (national, but also regional) barriers to competition, seems to foster that territorial mobility of factors that is a necessary condition for competition. Historically, the European obsession with exit options actually leads to measures to limit within-state territorial competition as potentially explosive for both internal cohesion and international equilibrium. Due to the EU's active engagement in removing internal boundaries and openness to new members, territorial competition is likely to be less bounded than it was within nation-states. It may resemble more the experience of the United States with the continuous addition of new states, historical legacies, technological change, the tax system, and the fragmentation of the subnational governmental structure (Sbragia 1996a: 218).

It can be argued that eliminating explicit obstacles to trade, harmonizing regulations that would otherwise segment the market, and increasing the mobility of labor, services, and capital may lead to divergence in both economic structure, and growth rates of different regions, rather than to convergence in factor prices, economic structure, and growth rates. Paul Krugman (1993) has concluded that with integration EU states and regions will become more specialized (like in the United States) and that they will therefore become more vulnerable to regional-specific shock. At the same time, they will be unable to respond with countercyclical monetary or exchange rate policy and will also tend to have an immobile fiscal policy (in the environment of high factors' mobility, the shocks tend to have permanent effects on output and therefore immobilize fiscal policy). According to Krugman, in the United States the heavily federalized fiscal system offers a partial solution to regional stabilization. In the EU, unless there is a considerable institutional change, the absence of this leverage may exacerbate problems of regional economic unbalance.

However, territorial competition is not only a process of opening. It is at the same time a process of boundary building. If territories want to compete, they have to control certain factors; otherwise they are not different bidding units. Creating regions does not only mean to create a "space of action," but also to set boundaries with other territories of an economic, administrative, cultural nature. In other words, the space of action follows from the boundary-building process. An internal territorial space of action (which I call "political structuring") cannot be successfully built unless some form of boundary consolidation has taken place. Functional, cultural, and administrative territories are characterized by different boundary-building processes.

Territorial differentiation can be based on such traditional resources of the territory as economic resources, cultural distinctiveness (ethnic, linguistic, cultural, religious distinctiveness), or institutional resources (local government tradition and capabilities). However, the most interesting and innovative processes of territorial differentiation are likely to affect the politico-administrative boundaries taking the form of regulative differentiation of previously nationalized functional regimes. We can hypothesize the tendency to create new forms of social protection, of labor market regulation, and of educational system territorially differentiated at the subnational level. This tendency may retrench social solidarity toward more restricted territorial entities, and the weakening of national integration may also reduce the possibilities of nationwide solidarity and redistribution. The underlying logic of this aspect of territorial differentiation is that the higher the systemic interdependence (the boundaries of the social division of labor), the higher the need for localized forms of social integration (the community solidarity bonds). Maurizio Ferrera has mentioned three factors that push toward subnational particularism in the specific field of the welfare state (Ferrera 1993b: 297–303), but his reasoning can be extended to other functional spheres such as labor market regulation, educational requirements, and so on.

The first factor that favors territorial differentiation is the new logic of competition of the internal market. This competition tends to create a new aggregation of territorial and sectoral interests and help the reemergence of old cleavages between centers and peripheries of production and trade (for example, such economic axes as the Renan, Catalonia, the French Midi, Padania, or Carintia axes). The various social groups that operate within these types of territorial areas tend to see the convergence of their interests and policy needs. Looking for more efficient forms of competition with respect to other territorial areas, these groups develop common interests toward institutional arrangements (welfare, fiscal, labor market, education, and so on) that do not penalize them in the competitive game. In these domains, social groups could manifest a growing interest for localized functional regimes that are efficient, flexible, and territorially circumscribed to them – that is, deprived of extensive redistributive dispersions.

The new logic of competition of the internal market sketched before might have a further implication. It will help the surfacing of old and new peripheries, regions, and territories traditionally backward or incapable of keeping up with economic modernization. The unbalances in national budgets and the growing fiscal opposition of strong social groups endowed with a high capacity for exit might challenge the traditional national redistributive circuits and mechanisms, contributing to a new dynamic of infra-European differentiation between development and underdevelopment. This may contribute to new territorial tensions along the axis of national standardization of functional regimes versus their territorial differentiation.

The second factor that may contribute to territorial differentiation is the regional policy at the EU level and more generally the process of the Union's regionalization. One of the indirect effects of the socioeconomic cohesion policies is to strengthen subnational identities and to set incentives for the formation, even at the cultural level, of territorially narrower risk-community and solidarity areas.

The third factor contributing to territorial differentiation is the changing logic of national political competition. The dealignment of traditional cleavages and forms of political control and the disappearance of antisystem oppositions in Europe can determine an opening of the politico-electoral markets that offer new spaces to political competition impinging upon the defense of interests of local type and nature, either through the mobilization of new single-issue groups or through the reactivation of the old territorial and also social-economic cleavages (urban–rural, for instance). We should add to this the potential interest and convenience for political entrepreneurs to exploit the theme of particularistic solidarity (Belgium, Italy, Catalonia, and so on).

In conclusion:

- Processes of integration and interdependence have made state boundaries more permeable.
- States have to a large extent changed their nature from territorial entities to regulatory systems.
- There is disengagement between state and territory leading to more emphasis on the nonterritorial aspects of statehood.
- Therefore, divisions within the state are highlighted and the possibility for internal differentiation has increased.

Politico-Institutional Differentiation?

At the EU level since the 1980s, the increasing level of crossborder cooperation, the extension of EU interregional policy, and the beginning of extensive territorial planning (Borras-Alomar 1995; Borras-Alomar, Christiansen, and Rodriguez-Pose 1994) have started to define new boundaries that regroup regions in different countries. At the same time, they have helped redefine boundaries within state borders. There are, in fact, internal territories of the state that are "in" or "out of" the regional policy programs or the crossborder cooperation, and to them this makes a great deal of difference:

The combination of large amounts of community funding and novel forms of territorial governance to administer them is challenging traditional state-centred politics.
But this is exactly not the withering away of either states or borders. What are withering away are the one to one matches between states and borders: borders equal
states and states equal territorial borders is a thing of the past (Christiansen and
Jorgensen 1995: 18).

Challenging the traditional role and boundary of the state may also mean
repoliticizing within-state territory differences, and the politics of the EU has
introduced new stimulus for the circuit of territorial bargaining: cooperation
but also competition. The EU has contributed to the development of a set
of new legal and financial tools for regions. The EU structural funds have
prompted even the most centralized states – such as the United Kingdom,
Greece, Portugal, and Ireland – to create entities at the regional level for
the implementation of the EU regional policy funds. The EU structure and
incentives continue to provide the legal framework and resources for regions
to compete and to form alliances that will be competitive in the economic
sphere. The EU policies have affected the decentralization trend in most EU
countries going back to the 1970s, but they have increased regional capacities in terms of economic and organizational resources to deal with territorial problems and to manage policies of local economic development. In
short, the EU has played an institution-building role for subnational regional
strengthening.

Both the national (Wright 1997) and more recently the European centers
actually aimed at increasing the endogenous capacities to achieve regional
development, trying to add to the classic redistributive measures the fostering of endogenous-oriented measures. As a result, the mobilization of the
endogenous economic and social potential was actually fostered by supra-
regional centers.

The uncertainties produced at the regional level by EU integration in the
economic field prompted relevant social forces and interests to express their
concerns about the possible impact of EU measures on regional and local
economic structures. These uncertainties generally generated demands from
local socioeconomic actors for regional action to identify areas affected by
these changes and to respond with appropriate regional structural adjustments. At the same time, regional governments have become more active
in gathering together private and public forces with a view to competing in
the wider international context of economic allocation, trying to make themselves attractive locations for investments and signing agreements with other
state and interstate governments to promote cooperation, trade, and so on.
Regions that are culturally distinctive have recently tried to develop at the
ideological and practical level a model of regionalism in which their cultural
distinctiveness might give them a competitive advantage within EU integration and within new economic internationalization trends. The reference

TABLE 2.1. *Types of Crossborder Regimes*

Regime Type	Basis for Cooperation	Geopolitical Situation	Approach
Crossborder	Common frontier	Peripherality from national centers	Problem-solving endogenous development
Big Geographic Areas	Big areas with some common characteristic	Peripherality from European centers	Endogenous development
Noncontiguity	Functional: relative affinity of economic growth/structure	Centers at national and even European level	Endogenous development

point has changed from the central state to the international (EU and world) arenas.

The growing awareness of the importance of regions in economic development has coincided with the idea that, with the creation of worldwide markets and the internationalization of certain factors of production, a number of "economic regions" are emerging as the best frame for economic activity promotion and regulation. However, some of these economic regions have boundaries that cut across national administrative regions and sometimes also national boundaries.

New regional cooperation has evolved from a problem-solving framework (determining how to provide coordinated public services – infrastructure, crossborder commuting, civilian protection, disaster control, environmental issues – on both sides of a national boundary) toward a more comprehensive approach that comprises the general economic development of these frontier regions, often at the periphery of the national economic structure. Moreover, the bases for these experiences of regional cooperation have evolved from physical continuity or some geographical principle to functional and structural characteristics. On the basis of these considerations, S. Borras Alomar provides the interesting typology depicted in Table 2.1 (Borras Alomar 1995: 135).

These structural changes, however significant, should not be regarded as increasing the role or power of *all* regions. The changes apply to each region, but obviously the structural definition of regional territorial interests may allow these fora to express very different interests and opinions; they may not necessarily and in fact may be very unlikely to express a "regional" view or a regional power increase. While regional alliances continue to develop along common economic or infrastructural interests, and regions try to establish their institutional position vis-à-vis the EU and national governments, the prospects of a harmonious "regional Europe" are nonexistent given the potential conflicts of interests among regions and areas and given the enormous differences in resources among the regions. Moreover, the relevance of territory and territoriality in Europe does not necessarily have anything to do with a regionalized Europe, and new forms of territorial politics do not need to be regionalized politics.[8]

Europeanization challenges the unity of the territorial framework within which the functional policy choices were exercised. Not only does the EU have a territorial policy that adds to that which existed at the national level, but also, in general, territorial alternatives have become more important in the political debate over functional choices. Alternatively, functional choices can be neither framed nor legitimated without a strong territorial consideration and component. The multiplication of governmental levels and sites increases the number of systemic interactions and modifies their hierarchical nature: Local government can appeal to different authorities and get access to different sources of resources. All this makes the relevance of the territorial dimension of the policy choice more salient.

CONSEQUENCES FOR POLITICAL REPRESENTATION: THE TERRITORIAL AXIS

If the hypotheses discussed in the previous section are correct, one should expect that this new constellation will redistribute territorial resources in a new way and will tend to reverberate on the forms of territorial politics and representation. However, while there is a general perception that economic regionalization prompts forms of representation of the local interests that must be relatively unitary, it is difficult to specify how the capacity to represent externally the interests of a local society is formed in the new conditions.

Functional and Territorial Representation

Political representation has traditionally taken both functional and territorial forms. In the first case, the internal social differentiation of a territorial unit becomes the basis of political representation and competition. Cross-local alliances of political entrepreneurs develop political organizations around which central political competition is organized. However, in the forms of territorial representation, existing territorial entities are the natural focus for representation, and their internal divisions tend to be either suppressed or politically diffused. Territorial politics in the consolidation of the nation-state in early-modern Europe had a distinctive stratarchic structure: It was dominated by a triadic relationship that is reappearing in the process of territorial expansion associated with the development of the EU. In different ways, J. Barrington Moore, Jr. (1966), Stein Rokkan (1999), and Wayne te Brake (1997) have elaborated this triadic view of oppositions and alignments based on the relationship between 1) ordinary people; 2) their

---

[8] For a critique of the myth of the "Europe of Regions," see Christiansen (1995: 241–5).

local rulers; and 3) the national claimants to power or nation-state builders. This early stratarchic vertical division was later complicated by the internal differentiation of interests within each strata due to the capitalist penetration of the countryside and to the industrial revolution; this is Moore's main line of reasoning. It was made more complex by the politicization of cultural and religious differences in the process of democratization since the French Revolution – which is Rokkan's main line of reasoning.

In early-modern Europe, in a situation of loose and shifting boundaries, ordinary people could take advantage of the conflicts between local rulers and national claimants. They could align themselves either with their local rulers against nation builders or with the latter against the former. In my opinion, however, real crossterritorial social movements could develop around the most broad-ranging claims only in the context of an alliance of territorial consolidation between national claimants and ordinary people. Until politics remained controlled or dominated by the local rulers, representation and conflicts tended to be of an external nature (Tarrow 1998).

This early stratarchic organization was progressively undermined and complicated by the horizontal divisions cutting across ordinary people, local rulers, and national claimants. On these new bases (primary versus secondary sector, class, religion, and so on) crossterritorial alliances could develop, eventually forming national social movements sometimes taking advantage of inter-elite competition and pluralism. This was possible only because the nation-state was becoming a relatively closed territorial unit that controlled cultural, economic, and administrative boundaries.[9] Over time, conflicts over policies tended to be shaped primarily by functional alternatives. Distributive and regulatory policies tended to concern sectors, such as industry or agriculture, education or defense policy, welfare or economic incentives, even if territorial adjustments were not absent for disadvantaged regions. That is, they tended to be national standardizing measures concerning groups or economic sectors that were not, or which were only partially, territorially characterized.

Traditional functional cleavages, therefore, are forms of "voice" within a given territory. This voice was characterized by a central decision making toward which new potential political organizations were directing their claims. These organizations are expressions of functional or cultural differentiation within a national territory and power structure. The territorial national system – and the inability to exit it – bound new political groups' opportunities for support and alliances. They are therefore confined and restricted by the set of alliances between social groups and political organizations already established within such system. Accessing mobilization resources and alliances *outside* the territory is impossible or, when this was attempted (by

---

[9] The reasons for this internal politicization of "closure rules" are developed in Bartolini (1998a).

international political movements or by secessionist interface peripheries), all other national elites saw it as a deadly challenge. This restricted the scope for new cleavage development.

Within closed territories, the possibility of functional crosslocal alliances among different section groups was essential to overcome territorial representation. The external form of territorial representation was insufficient to satisfy the complex internal differentiation of interests, and localistic ties were seen as dysfunctional to the effective structuring of functional groups' voices that required crosslocal organizations and linkages.

In the new constellation of circumstances discussed in the previous section, these possibilities for crossboundary resource mobilization and alliance building are more likely to be accessible for the structuring of new cleavage lines and political opposition. Moreover, these attempts are less likely to face coherent and cohesive repression and isolation responses from the established national elite. Forms of external representation of a cohesive local community and a new stratarchic dimension of political interaction are likely to reemerge in certain policy areas. The multicentered and multilevel polity associated with the EU offers to social movements, interest groups, and territories both new loci and sites for influence, decision making, information gathering, and so on, that are different from the national and domestic ones.

As argued so far, the historical experience of the nation-states suggests that the attempt by supralocal rulers to create higher-level states normally met with two responses: the formation of anti-establishment crossterritorial sociopolitical movements and/or the territorial resistance and persisting local control of key regulative, jurisdictional, and material resources. These two responses were not mutually exclusive. However, one of the two responses tended to prevail and weaken or subordinate the other. When the persistence and defense of local distinctiveness prevail, forms of "federalized" or "composite" polities develop in which sociopolitical cleavage systems and corporate intermediation structures remain weak, less integrated, and less centralized. When national sociopolitical alignments prevail, more unitary polities develop in which territorial representation is weakened and often only latently represented within broad partisan and corporate peak organizations.

For the new European polity, it is not surprising that both dimensions of political structuring attract the attention of scholars. Some of them (including Sidney Tarrow in Chapter 3 or this book) – with specific reference to the potential for Euro-parties, Euro-interest groups, and Euro-social movements – argue that in the long run the European Union will reproduce the formation of crossborder alliances among sociopolitical actors based on functional similarity of interests and values at the Union's expanded territorial level. I have so far argued the competing hypothesis that the predominant mode of representation will be territorial, based on the interaction among a substate territorial coalition of social groups and their territorial rulers, the national rulers, and the center builders and central claimants at the EU level.

In this sense – using the te Brake terminology – pure intergovernmentalism represents a form of "elite-consolidation" based on an accommodation between central claimants (the new Brussels center) and local rulers (state executives and central institutions). Pure supranationalism, however, would represent a form of "central-consolidation" based on an alliance between ordinary people and central claimants at the expense of local national rulers. A "local-consolidation," based on an alliance of ordinary people and local national rulers, could only result from and lead to a profound redefinition of the institutional design of the integration process, granting to the nation-state stronger constitutional protection of its prerogatives and competencies than the treaties actually specify.

To conclude, I consider the formation of a new stratarchic territorial representation as more likely than the new formation of Europeanwide, crossterritorial alliances, for the following reasons:

- The number and fragmentation of the new sites of power and decision making tend to lower the organizational cohesion of groups and movements. The plurality of loci allows different groups within the encompassing national organization to perceive that their resources might be better used in one locus rather than the other. Within organizations, conflicts may arise about the vertical decisional center toward which to act. That is, there will be differentiation among groups, movements, and interests according to their capacity to access different layers and different sites of the EU, national, and local decisional structures.
- Internal interest differentiation within and among groups may derive also from their different capacity to escape the impositions and social duties established at any of these levels and sites. In other words, previously united and centralized corporate and political organizations may internally divide on the basis of different perceptions of the costs and gains of the new exit option constellation.
- The organizational domain of interest groups will cover narrower territorial capacities than the market. The reach of the organizational resources of groups, parties, and even states will be shorter than the reach of the market:

By undermining associational monopoly and inter-associational hierarchy, the fragmentation of interests and the pluralist proliferation of political opportunities that is entailed by the "regionalization of Europe" adds to the decomposition of national-level corporatism as well as to the obstacles to its supranational resurrection (Streek and Schmitter 1991: 156).

- The emphasis on territorial competition will tend to foster regional "developmental coalitions" defined as broad and "place-based inter-class coalitions of political, economic and social actors devoted to the economic development in specific location." Such coalitions "may include locally and non-locally based business interests, regional and local bureaucracies, as well as locally based national bureaucrats, and neighbourhood and social movements" (Keating 1997b: 32–4).

• The processes of territorial negotiations among actors at the subnational level (when such negotiations become all too frequent) imply recognition of the similarity of interests (and identities). This reciprocal recognition requires relationships in which each actor is autonomous in its capacity to modify its goal through the negotiation. In turn, these relationships require the actors' to reduce their dependency on or their linkage with crosslocal encompassing national organizations. In other words, the growing recognition of common local interests (such as increasing the attractiveness of the territory for investments, increasing local infrastructures, and exploiting local assets, etc.) generates negotiation climates that inevitably tend to weaken the vertical and crosslocal relationships between local and national actors. It tends to balkanize interest representation at the local level, increase requests and needs of local autonomy, and redefine the hierarchical relationships within the national organization.

Variation in Territorial Resources

The extent to which latent territorial tensions – which are indeed very likely to develop – transform into open requests of institutionalized territorial representation will depend on the cultural, economic, and institutional resources and options of different substate territories and regional alliances within and across territories. The larger the number of different political options available to the periphery in its relations to the political center, the greater the resources that can be converted into political pressures brought to bear upon the political center.

It is likely that, in a context of loosening boundaries, interface peripheries have an advantage over external peripheries as a result of the existence of alternative and supportive cultural centers. Following the same logic, territorial spaces subject to one national politico-administrative center but fully integrated in a broader-than-national space of market transactions have greater resources to convert into political pressures brought to bear upon the politico-administrative center. They may also have another possibility rather than bearing upon the center: to find alternative resources other than those offered from the center in terms of transfers and access to international capital markets (that is, exit options based on supportive external economic centers). Territorial spaces with strong institutional autonomy and where alternative administrative borders compete in different functional

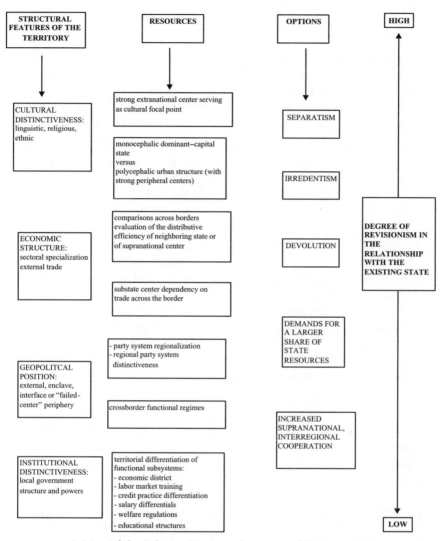

FIGURE 2.1. A Map of the Substate Territory Structure of Opportunity

areas – crossborder cooperation, functional regimes within the EU, and so on – can access external regulative and jurisdiction resources (that is, exit options based on the supportive external administrative centers of the EU). The framework of territorial resources needs to include the cultural distinctiveness resource of the peripheral territory, economic access to external resources, and institutional distinctiveness and autonomy of the territory. In Figure 2.1, I have attempted to systematize the structural feature of the territory, its resources, and its political options.

A map of the variables affecting the variation in substate territorial resources should therefore include the following:

- *Economic resources* concentrated in the territory.
- *Financial resources*, including autonomous fiscal imposition, access to nonstate financial markets, and freedom in allocation.
- *Cultural distinctiveness and resources.* A rich ethnohistory can be a significant source of cultural power and a focus of cultural politicization:

> Communities able to boast such histories have a competitive advantage over others where that history is scanty or doubtful. In the latter case the intellectuals have a double task: they must recover a sufficiently large quantity of communal history to convince their own members that they have an illustrious past, and they must authenticate it sufficiently to convince sceptical outsiders of its merits (Smith 1991: 164).

- *Institutional resources*: density of regional political and administrative but also social and economic institutions; capacity to formulate policy (the extent to which regions are political systems with a decisional capacity and the possibility to define politically a "regional interest"); competencies (autonomous versus shared with the state) (Keating 1997a: 33–5).
- *Political resources*: the level of autonomy of the local political class from the national one; political distinctiveness of the local political elite; regionalization of the party system and denationalization of the party system; territorial mobilization of support and political action.

The study of these processes of territorial differentiation requires some systematic and objective solid fact-finding and data accumulation on the within-state territorial differentiation of interests, institutions, policies, and economic and cultural resources. We need data not only on the sociodemographic and economic structure, but also on crossterritory linkages and fluxes (for example, external regional trade figures and statistics on regional foreign trade dependency), and political administrative data and synopsis about local government authority and power, fiscal powers, resort to court of justice, resort to national courts against national governments, institutional territorialization (the welfare state), chances of crossborder cooperation, and so on. Finally we need to accumulate political data about the party system's regional distinctiveness, electoral regional specificity, European versus national election differences, regional parties, and center–peripheral relationships within the structure of nationally based parties.

CONCLUSION

In this chapter, I have discussed a number of structural conditions that foster the rebirth of territorial forms of political representation within the emerging structure of loosely bounded European territories and multiple centers in the

TABLE 2.2. *Winning and Losing Territories and Groups*

		Territories within States	
		Losers	Winners
Groups within Territories	Losers	Loser group within losing territories	Loser group within winning territories
	Winners	Winner group within losing territories	Winner group within winning territories

areas of politico-administrative, cultural, and economic transactions. Can we also identify the dimensions of territorial conflict and opposition that might emerge from this structure? Which territories will be peripheralized within the new large-scale territorial differentiation process?

I hypothesized that loosely bounded territories are subject to the mobility options of crucial factors such as capital, taxpayers, consumers, skilled professions, and so on, and that a potential conflict line will run along the institutional territorial competition for the acquisition of such factors. The emphasis shifts from intraterritorial functional conflict to intraterritorial competition. This will tend to foster a new emphasis on external territorial representation, with a corresponding decline of intraterritorial functional differences to the advantage of external representation cohesion and efficacy. Actually strong intraterritorial functional conflicts may weaken territorial capacity to compete or to retain mobile resources. This dimension of conflict along the axis of the differential distribution exit options among territories may represent a new line of territorial alignment within and across nation-states.

The processes of boundary removal, boundary redefinition, and new boundary creation that are linked to the European integration process will redistribute resources directly and indirectly, and this redistribution will result in "winners" and "losers," both in terms of social groups and territories (see Table 2.2).

What produces a winning or losing territory and social group? The provisional answer that was given was the structural conditions determining the capacity for exit in the sense used in this chapter. For groups, this means their "market" capacity combined with the possibility of mobility that enhances their capacity for negotiation with national and/or European authorities, or, alternatively, that ensures that their interests will be taken in account by default, as part of the systemic resources that need to be defended within and by the territory. For territories – my main focus in this chapter – this means their capacity to exit the nation-state and their negotiation and "blackmailing" potential with respect to the nation-state. In this case, the main dividing line is between the possibility to exit national frameworks accessing extranational resources (and therefore being able to extort better terms even from the nation-state) and the lack of this possibility (and therefore continuing to be dependent on national center resource distribution and interest defense). Perceptions of the potential impact of the new opportunity structure will affect losers' and winners' reactions to the speed, scope, and institutional design of the integration process. The latent conflicts may become mobilized and politicized, with some territories aiming to confine the exit options and the new opportunities available for other territories. The underlining hypothesis is that non-exiters may see the exit options of the others as bearing costs for them, as they tend to subtract and/or withhold resources for intrastate distributive and redistributive policies. In this sense, this line of conflict may generate "voice against exit."

For both membership and territorial groups, a new latent dividing line may therefore set "nomadic" against "standing." The opposition between nomadic and standing does not impinge exclusively on their physical capacity to move. One should speak of the possibility of using competing functional and regulative boundaries to their advantage.

When there is one national center (coinciding boundaries), peripheries differ in their distinctive features (cultural, economic, and politico-administrative), in their geopolitical nature (external, buffer, interface, or failed center), or in the degree of their dependency. In a system of multilevel, multicenter governance – a multicephalic structure plus a newly added center (EU) – the picture becomes complicated, and the core and periphery at the national level interact with the core and periphery at the new supranational center. There are peripheries of core territories versus peripheries of the peripheral territory. The process of integration and territorial expansion may redefine old peripheries of the nation-state as new centers. Political demands may accordingly be redefined as indicated in the options column of Figure 2.1.

The new cleavages in the globalization era develop within loosely bounded territories and may emanate exactly from the new configuration of opportunities that this new "openness" offers to individuals and groups. At the territorial level, the national revolution was about limiting still-available exit options. Actually, where such options prevailed, no state consolidation took place (as in the transalpine city belt region). The industrial revolution produced functional conflicts among groups linked to the division of labor within a consolidated territory. The rural/urban cleavage had strong territorial implications, but it was mainly expressed in functional conflicts among social groups in the production and distribution domains. What we may call the "integration" revolution rejects allegiance to the old nation-state in favor of the internationalization of chances and opportunities. This revolution has both a territorial and a functional dimension and expresses itself through *material* and *ideational* bases. It has consequences that manifest mainly in the loosening of the territorial state and the national political community and produces tensions and conflicts among groups and territories based on the

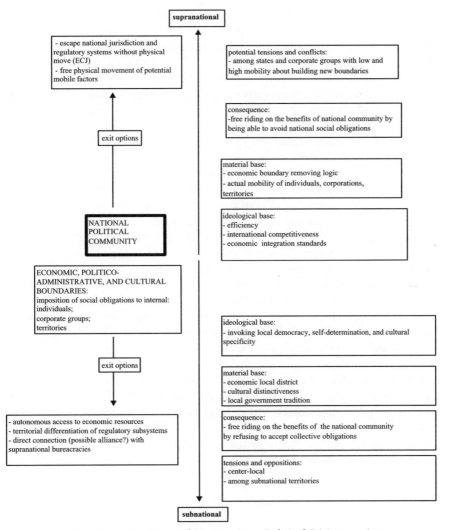

FIGURE 2.2. Exit Opportunities and Nation-State Political Disintegration

differential distribution of the capacities of exit. I have tried to summarize this interpretative framework in Figure 2.2.

At both the territorial and the individual level, the material base of nomadic/standing interest orientation rests on differences in "potential mobility": the capacities to profit from the loosening of state boundaries in the economic, cultural, and administrative spheres; the capacities to profit from territorial competition for mobile skills and resources; the capacities to avoid the costs of collective social obligation (toward other territories or social groups) within the nation-state. The ideational base of nomadic/standing ideological orientations rests on the opposition between the themes of "roots" and those of "options" and "choices": the insistence on local democracy versus international governance; the nearness of government to the citizens, new regionalism, ethnic purity and traditions, the rediscovery of old cultural traditions, decentralization, federalism, subsidiarity, fiscal transparency, and so on, versus all forms of cultural "globalization"; the criticism and dislike of all sorts of boundaries versus the quest to erect new boundaries against the "nomadism" of culture, trade, and administrative practices; multiculturalist rhetoric versus the continued lack of confidence and interest in the "foreign" and "foreigners," and the security ideology insisting on proximity and local community and "identity"; the refusal of the standardizing effects of enhanced communication and competition versus the ideology of instantaneous networks of communications and information (electronic, hertzian, as well as traditionally physical) covering the world.

I have argued in this chapter that these new potential interest orientations and ideational underpinnings may take the form of territorial alignments as much as they can become additional elements of modified crosslocal functional alignments throughout Europe. It is difficult to predict the extent to which territorial and functional conflicts in a polity are both politically active or to which one is muted to the advantage of the other. This ultimately depends on the level of closure of the systemic boundaries of the polity. The more closed and reinforcing the various types of boundaries, the more likely that territorial issues will be in the long run incorporated within broader, functional crosslocal alliances (Bartolini 1998a). The more open the polity boundaries and the more loosely bounded the polity's territories, the more likely territorial alternatives will differentiate and become the focus of political conflict. In the current mode and phase of European integration, this second situation seems predominant and likely to persist.

3

Center–Periphery Alignments and Political Contention in Late-Modern Europe

Sidney Tarrow

On February 27, 1997, the president of the ailing French firm Renault announced the imminent closure of the company's plant in Vilvorde, Belgium. Closing Vilvorde was but a prelude to politically more risky cuts, because the French state is Renault's largest shareholder, and an election was coming up in France. But the mainly Flemish and heavily unionized Vilvorde workforce would not go quietly. Workers occupied the plant and began a series of public protests that would make Vilvorde synonymous with a new term in the European political lexicon: the "Eurostrike." Vilvorde brought together Belgian, French, and Spanish workers; officials of France, Belgium, and the European Union; and the courts of both countries in a structure of multiple alignment and contention that was dramatized by the actions of the EU as well as the French and the Belgian Press and culminated in a mass demonstration before the EU's headquarters.

Many aspects of the strike were interesting, but for our purposes it will serve to illustrate this chapter's three central messages: first, that Europeanization is not occurring only at the summit – on which most of the research has been centered – but also at the grassroots of European society; second, that social actors at that level are learning to utilize Europe's variable political geometry and – though they lack the resources of the rich and powerful lobbies in Brussels – are developing a repertoire of contention to put forward their claims; third, and most central to our discussion, both contention and alignment are crossing Europe's center–periphery axes in a variety of ways. My thesis is that if polity building is occurring in Europe today, it must be seen at the intersection of elite and mass, local, national, and supranational actors and institutions.

Four axes of conflict and alignment can be seen in the Vilvorde affair:

First, in the run-up to the labor conflict, we see the effects of *elite consolidation*, as European governments, led by the European Commission and cheered on by the German government, worked out a plan for European Works Councils (EWC) (Martin and Ross 2001: 68–9; Turner 1996). These institutions, roughly based on German co-determination practices, required multinational firms to organize and consult with transnational works councils of their workers. These institutions were still in their infancy when Renault decided to close Vilvorde, and undoubtedly the firm thought it could ignore them with impunity. But it was the company's indifference to the requirement that it must inform and consult its workers that fed the workers' campaign and led the media and European officials to enter the fray.[1]

Second, we see in the conflict a *supranational/local alignment* that aligned the workers – however briefly – with European officials. In the Vilvorde case, European Commission members expressed outrage at the plant closure, at its unexpected announcement, and at the failure of the firm to consult its workers.[2] Not only the Commission, but also the European Parliament – peppered with e-mail petitions from constituents and unions – expressed shock and outrage at this "Anglo-Saxon" restructuring. Echoing the concerns of unionists from Belgium, France, and Spain, the assembly urged the EU to penalize Renault for its failure to consult and inform its workers, as EU regulations require, accusing the auto maker – and indirectly the French government – of "arrogance and disdain for the most fundamental rules of social consultation" (*Reuters*, March 12, 1997; *Le Monde*, March 13, 1997: 14).

Third, we also see a *local-national alignment*, as the Vilvorde workers benefited from their government's support and even from the king, who, in measured terms, expressed his concern. Prime Minister Jean-Luc Dehaene, as luck would have it, represented Vilvorde in the Belgian parliament and could not fail to express his constituents' outrage. More surprising was the ability of the workers to gain support from both the French and Belgian national courts, which ruled that Renault had ignored its obligations under the EWC regulations to inform and consult its workers of the plant closing. Local-national alignments were not sufficient to reverse the decision but they helped to legitimate and politicize the workers' cause.

Fourth, the Vilvorde workers became part of a *transnational alignment*, as French, Spanish, and even British workers demonstrated alongside them against the plant closure. Coordinated by the European Federation of Metalworkers – which has its headquarters in Brussels – the Belgian unions organized "guerrilla actions" in France, and brought French workers to

---

[1] On media support, see Lagneau and Lefébure (2001: 189–206).

[2] This outrage was heightened when it emerged that the French government knew of the plan months in advance and that Renault was hoping to use EU structural funds to expand its plant in Valladolid, Spain, just as it was closing Vilvorde. Competition Commissioner Karel Van Miert quickly announced that he would soon propose ways to stop companies from "aid shopping" from the EU (*Reuters*, March 7, 1997). Nearly $8 million would have come from the European Regional Development Fund, in effect helping Renault to move jobs from one member state to another, according to a spokesperson for Regional Policy Commissioner Monika Wulf-Mathies.

Belgium for a mass demonstration. When the firm refused to compromise, the Vilvorde workers responded with a surprise "commando action" across the border at the Renault plant in Douai. As they marched through the factory, about six hundred French workers joined them, and production ground to a halt (*Le Monde*, March 15, 1997: 19).

Not only French workers but also French politicians supported the Belgian workers. On television, French Union Secretary Nicole Notat chided the company for failing to consult the workers. In parliament, deputies of both the majority and the opposition were up in arms about Renault's decision (*Le Monde*, March 9–10, 1997: 5), and created an information committee to keep track of Renault and its workers (*Le Monde*, March 13, 1997: 14). Given the politically charged pre-electoral atmosphere, French Prime Minister, Alain Juppé appeared on television to announce that eight hundred thousand francs per worker would be disbursed for "reconversion and accompaniment" (*Le Monde*, March 26, 1997: 18).

The Renault crisis ended as it had to: with the plant's closure and the distribution of generous severance packages to the workers. But before the crisis ended, it angered officials of the EU, forced European Commission and parliamentary figures to take positions that were critical of a member state, united unionists of three nations against "American-style" capitalism, and involved the courts in both countries. However measured and temporary, conflicts and alignments were occurring below the summit of the European system.

MULTILEVEL CONFLICT AND POLITICAL ALIGNMENTS

What does this have to do with Europeanization? To be sure, Vilvorde was not typical; for one thing, the fact that it occurred in a suburb of the capital of Europe won it an unusual amount of EU attention and press coverage. But if the closure of one plant belonging to one firm operating in another country could produce so tangled a skein of conflicts and alignments, then we will need to look below the summit of the European project to understand the dynamics of Europeanization. To do so, we will need to study not only broad structural trends and interstate relations, but the relational mechanisms developing around European issues among ordinary Europeans, their national governments, supranational elites, and their counterparts in other countries. That will be the main goal of this chapter.

I have called for a "relational" approach, but I need to clarify what I mean by it with respect to European contention.[3] By a relational approach, I mean attention to the mechanisms that regularly bring actors into interaction with

---

[3] The approach put forward here derives from joint work with Doug McAdam and Charles Tilly in our *Dynamics of Contention* (McAdam, Tarrow, and Tilly 2001).

one another and cause change. Later in this chapter I will examine such mechanisms as:

- *Brokerage*: the linkage of two or more social sites by a unit that mediates their relations with each other and/or with yet another site (McAdam, Tarrow, and Tilly 2001: 142).

    We saw brokerage at work in the Vilvorde case in the role of the European Metalworker's Federation, which brought French and Belgian workers together; we will see it again in European structural policy.
- *Object Shift*: alteration in relations between claimants and objects of claims (ibid., p. 144).

    We saw object shift at work as the press constructed the Vilvorde strike from one of industrial relations to one of European contention (Lagneau and Lefebure 2001).
- *Scale Shift*: a change in the number and level of coordinating contentious actions leading to broader contention involving a wider range of actors and bridging their claims and identities (McAdam, Tarrow, and Tilly 2001: ch. 10).

    We saw scale shift in the Vilvorde conflict as French and Belgian opposition politicians shifted the conflict to the national and European level.

Until recently, scholars of European integration polarized around two main approaches, both of them heavily structural and institutional, and neither one paying particular attention to the mechanisms that link social actors to the European project: neofunctionalism and intergovernmentalism:

- *Neo-functionalism*, deriving from Ernst Haas' celebrated work in the 1950s, focuses on the structural trend toward supranationalism rippling outward from market opening to elite actors (Haas 1958). Haas' approach was implicitly interactive, but it did not specify the kinds of relations that would develop among social and state actors, nor did it adequately predict how states and non-elites would react to these activities outside the nation-state. His followers focus on institutional dynamics but see states responding to dysfunctionality rather than as alignment-shaping actors (Fligstein and Stone Sweet 2002).
- *Intergovernmentalism*, which insists on the centrality of the major treaty-making activities of European states, provides no more specified a guide to the relational mechanisms developing around the European project (Moravcsik 1998). Consider the conflicts we saw in Vilvorde: They brought private and public actors into relations of conflict and alignment, crossed national borders, and leapfrogged over the national states that are at the center of the intergovernmental model. States were involved, but scarcely as the only key actors in the conflict.

Two newer approaches provide a better account of some of these interactions than either of the two classical models.

Exit without Separation

Drawing on Stein Rokkan's theory of territorial cleavages and Albert O. Hirschman's trilogy of exit, voice, and loyalty, our colleague, Stefano Bartolini, has produced a model of territorial exit that might help us to find an answer (see Chapter 2 in this book; also see Bartolini 1999). Here I will summarize his argument schematically. Previously, European territorial actors could find recourse for their claims only by permanent exit (for example, peripheral nationalism) or by horizontal integration of the actors with others in mass political parties that centered on the national state. Polity building was, in large part, a process through which center–periphery cleavages were absorbed and transformed into functional ones through political parties that took the national state as their targets.

In contrast with the historical development of national territorial/functional systems, continues Bartolini, the uniqueness of the European project is, first, that national states are losing their capacity to respond to subnational claims and, second, that subnational actors who fail to find satisfaction at the national level have recourse to forms of exit less dramatic than separation. Without permanently exiting, they can extend their activities to other parts of the Union. Simultaneously, this serves as a safety valve for subnational tensions and as a weakening of the powers of the national states and party systems (see Chapter 1).

The marriage of Rokkan's structuralism with Hirschman's individualism is a unique contribution to our understanding of the dynamic of European center–periphery relations. But we may usefully interrogate Bartolini's model in three respects:

- First, do European states really lack the resources to brake or oppose the exit of constituent subnational actors?
- Second, what are the political mechanisms through which such exit occurs, and how is it mediated by state and suprastate actors?
- Third, what can we learn about territorial relations from areas of European policy making that bring local, national, and supranational actors together in relations of conflict and alignment?

Multilevel Governance

In a series of wide-ranging books and articles, Liesbet Hooghe, Gary Marks, and their collaborators join a number of American and European scholars who see late-modern Europe in terms of the problem of who is governing whom across a range of policy sectors.[4] Their valuable work leaves off the search for general covering laws in favor of a down-to-earth focus on what happens in the day-to-day negotiation among public and private actors

---

[4] Among their many contributions, the following stand out: Hooghe (1996); Marks, Hooghe, and Blank (1996); Hooghe and Marks (2001a).

in the European Union. But their accounts have several major lacunae:

- First, they do not propose a theory of intra-European alignments, offering instead a finer-grained description of day-to-day European policy making than do either intergovernmentalists or the supranationalists (Roederer 2000: 25).
- Second, they build their findings largely on one area of policy – cohesion – a policy area that was deliberately created to empower non-state actors (Fairbrass and Jordan 2000: 2), though recently they have applied their model to other areas of policy (Hooghe and Marks 2001a).
- Third, they "tend to iron social and political conflicts out of European policy-making" (Roederer 2000: 26), making it difficult to explain the kind of multilevel conflict and attempts at cooperation we have seen in the Vilvorde crisis.

Let me be clear: I have no quarrel with either Bartolini's observation that the EU offers opportunities for exit without separation, or with Hooghe and Marks' observation that multiple channels and elite interactions characterize contemporary Europe. But both approaches stop short of pointing to the kinds of mechanisms and processes through which these interactions operate. Since many of these interactions revolve around the traditional territorial institutions of government, states need to be centrally involved in any such equation; since non-state actors more than occasionally take part in such interactions, they cannot be excluded either; and since both states and private actors interact in various ways with supranational authorities, we need to develop models of multilevel interaction that specify recurring processes among constellations of private and public actors in the everyday conflicts of European integration.

The rest of this chapter will constitute an effort to identify such processes through attention to the axes of alignment and conflict we find in a number of cases of EU policy. I begin with a historical analogy, which I use to specify some processes of alignment and conflict that can be observed in many multilevel interactions in the European Union today. Then, I trace in more detail one set of mechanisms that we can observe in the area of European center–periphery relations. I close with a reflection on the so-called democratic deficit.

COMPOSITE STATES IN EARLY-MODERN EUROPE

"At the beginning of the early modern period," writes historian Wayne te Brake, "most Europeans lived within composite states that had been variously cobbled together repertoire of techniques" (1997: 14). In some states, like England or Wales or the mosaic of *pays d'élection* and *pays d'état* in France, people lived in states with continuous territories; in others, like the checkerboard of territorial units in the Hapsburg Empire, they were physically dispersed and boasted strong local rulers making competing claims on loyalties and resources – like Catalonia and Portugal (1997: 14–15). Still others lived in city-states or cathedral cities. For centuries, most people lived under the sway of local elites, bishops, merchant aristocrats, dukes, and rival princes. Te Brake writes:

Since the dynastic "prince" promised to respect the political customs and guaranteed the chartered privileges of these constituent political units, ordinary political subjects within composite states acted in the context of overlapping, intersecting, and changing political spaces defined by often competitive claimants to sovereign authority over them (1997: 14).

European state building was not simply a process of insistent nationalizing pressure from above and futile resistance from local rulers and ordinary people from below. Both territorial alignments and conflicts shifted constantly. Out of the triangular structure of relations among nationalizing princes, local rulers, and ordinary people, a variety of alignment and conflict structures developed among actors whose strategies and successes varied with the context and the strength of the pressure from their opponents:

- *Nationalizing princes* could either try to coopt local rulers or form coalitions with merchants, bankers, or the ordinary people living under their direct rule to subvert their local power.
- Facing pressure from nationalizing princes, these *local rulers* could attempt to fight them off or join them. If they chose to fight, one strategy was to oppose the creation of large, national states through coalitions with the merchants, religious groups, and even ordinary people living in their territories.
- As opportunistic as their betters, *ordinary people* sometimes made common cause with local rulers against intrusive nationalizers and sometimes reached out to the latter against the former. On occasion, but more rarely, they made common cause with people like themselves from other territorial jurisdictions in crossterritorial social movements. "It was often in the interstices and on the margins of these composite early modern state formations that ordinary people enjoyed their greatest political opportunities," concludes te Brake (1997: 15).

These alternative alignments growing out of different patterns of opposition suggest three forms of center–periphery alignment to te Brake:

- *Local consolidation:* alliance structures between local rulers and ordinary people, which produced either sovereign city-states, as in Italy, or confederated provinces, as in the low countries and Switzerland, or leagues of cities, as in the Hansa.
- *Elite consolidation:* alliances between nationalizing claimants and local rulers, creating layered sovereignties, as in Catalonia or the Habsburg Empire.

- *Territorial consolidation:* the erosion of the power of local rulers leading to unitary states, as in Britain or France.

Possibly because the period he studied offered less evidence of it than the centuries before or since, te Brake ignores a fourth form of alignment:

- *Crossterritorial political alliances:* secular alignments or religious denominations that united horizontally against either nationalizing princes or local rulers.

For a longer period than is often realized, politics in Europe were fought not only between or within territories but also among a triad of players with unequal resources whose playing field was both intra- and extraterritorial. In Figure 3.1, I present an expanded version of te Brake's three forms of historical alignments and conflicts with the addition of a fourth pattern of crossterritorial political alliances.

I do not rehearse te Brake's argument here because I think twenty-first-century Europe is subsiding into a pre-Wesphalian jumble of territorial jurisdictions; nor do I think that Europe is segmented into four watertight patterns of alignment and conflict. But as we saw in the Vilvorde case, te Brake's model has strong analogies with what is happening in Europe today, in processes in which citizen groups and their representatives both conflict and align with "local" rulers (that is, national governments), with

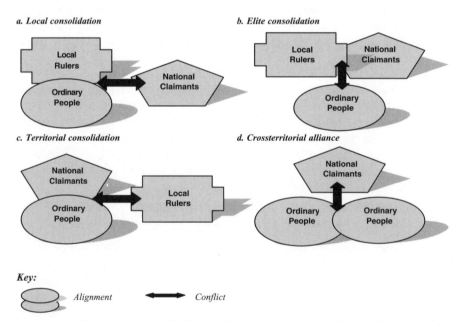

FIGURE 3.1. Four Patterns of Political Contention in Early-Modern Europe (after te Brake 1997)

(supra)nationalizing claimants (that is, European authorities), and with one another. As we saw in the Vilvorde case, all four patterns of political alignment and conflict coexist in the current phase of European integration. In the rest of this chapter, I illustrate this argument, and specify some of the mechanisms that produce these interactions.

BEYOND EXIT AND GOVERNANCE: ALIGNMENT AND CONFLICT
IN LATE-MODERN EUROPE

Early-modern Europe possessed an overlapping checkerboard of political jurisdictions that is analogous to the variable geometry of today's Europe. This produces what te Brake calls "multiple and overlapping structures of opportunity" (1998: 14). These intricacies exist below, and to some extent subvert the more linear changes predicted by intergovernmentalist and neofunctionalists. They also elude Bartolini's concept of exit and are more political than Hooghe and Marks' focus on governance.

"Ordinary people" are better organized today than they were in early-modern Europe and even than they were a few short decades ago. With modern means of communication, a loosening and hybridization of the organizational forms of private associations, public interest groups, and social actors have access to a broader range of channels of influence than at any time in the past. With the aid of transnational instruments of communication and organization, farmers, workers, women's groups, immigrants, and consumer and environmental advocates can combine in transnational collective action (Imig and Tarrow 2001). And finally, these Europeans are learning to profit from "dual networks" with both national governments and supranational authorities (Ansell, Parsons, and Darden 1997).

How do these aggregate trends play out in Europe's emerging polity? Rather than evolving toward territorial exit or neofunctional restructuring, the map of Europe today offers the potential for coalition building, political exchange, and the construction of mechanisms of alignment and conflict among social actors across states, sectors, and levels of decision making. These can take horizontal as well as vertical form. Regional governments, political parties, and even social movements are reaching across and above their territories to exercise leverage against other actors, national states, and supranational authorities. Figure 3.2 proposes a typology of political contention in contemporary Europe that parallels the patterns of alignment and conflict in te Brake's work. The next sections elaborate and illustrate each of them.

Elite Consolidation and Its Victims

In early-modern Europe, local rulers frequently aligned themselves with nationalizing princes to suppress efforts of their restive subjects for autonomy.

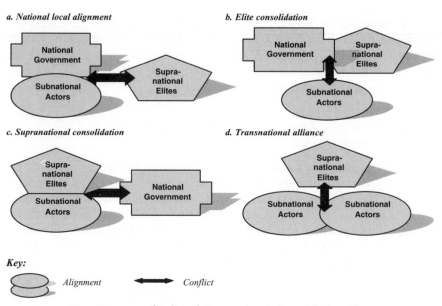

a. National local alignment

b. Elite consolidation

c. Supranational consolidation

d. Transnational alliance

Key:

Alignment   Conflict

FIGURE 3.2. Four Patterns of Political Contention in Late-Modern Europe

Where this succeeded, local liberties were suppressed. Subnational actors in today's Europe worry less about such elite alliances suppressing their liberties, but in the late 1990s the implementation of the Maastricht Treaty caused ripples of protest on the part of social actors against their own governments. These aligned with European institutions to slash social entitlements.

From the signature of the Maastricht Treaty onward, it was clear that the historic beneficiaries of the European welfare systems were in for a shock. Farmers, pensioners, workers in state-run or state-subsidized industries – all those who benefited from what are loosely termed "transfers" – would have their payments from the state shaved in order to meet the stabilization requirements for their countries' entry into the European Monetary System. Some states rejected the social costs that would be involved in such massive budget cutting; others could not meet the criteria in time; but for most, the Maastricht criteria provided a spur – and for some, an opportunity – to put their national accounts in order. Italy was an archetypical case.

Resistance, Italian Style. By the 1990s, Italy was clearly in greater need of budgetary discipline. Since the early-1970s expansion of its welfare system, it had accumulated a massive public debt, which it met only through increasingly expensive public borrowing, leading to cycles of inflation and devaluation. Even in the midst of the political turmoil around the "tangentopoli" scandals, Carlo Azeglio Ciampi and Giuliano Amato – both, it should be noted, representing the center-left – were able to use the Maastricht stabilization criteria to introduce cuts in the nation's current spending. By the

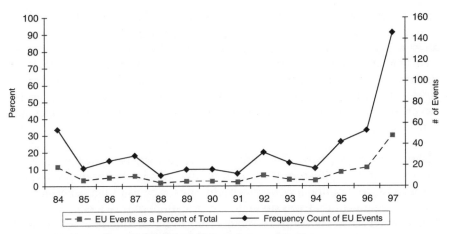

FIGURE 3.3. Euro-Centered Political Contention, 1984–97

late 1990s, current spending was being covered by revenues, and only the accumulated debt from previous decades left the budget in the red.

The Italian budget-cutting exercise was fought out politically on domestic ground. In a pattern reminiscent of te Brake's pattern of elite consolidation – but at a higher level – an objective alliance between Europe's supranational institutions and Italy's national government was struck at the cost of subnational "ordinary people." Plenty of these protested – especially the pensioners who stood to lose the most. But workers in nationalized industries, farmers and milk producers, and even shopkeepers supporting Silvio Berlusconi's right-wing effort to turn Italy toward a liberal market economy were up in arms. But in the end, a center-left government, with support from internationally oriented business and neutrality from the reluctant trade unions, used the growth and stabilization pact as a lever to pry budget cuts from many domestic actors.

Italy was not alone. Reuters European news data that I collected with Doug Imig in my study of European contention show a sharp upturn in protests by various social actors as the deadline for meeting the Maastricht criteria approached (Imig and Tarrow 2001: ch. 2). Farmers, manufacturing workers, miners, pensioners, and public welfare clients marched, demonstrated, blocked the entrances to offices and banks, and lobbied their governments to soften the blow. Figure 3.3 summarizes the trend line of protests in twelve nations of the EU as Europe implemented the Maastricht criteria. Subnational actors were protesting against an alignment of their national governments and European elites against their economic interests.

National–Local Alignments

In early-modern Europe, local rulers often aligned with their subjects against the designs of nationalizing princes. Europe today also shows a variety of crosscutting alignments and cleavages. Many of these bring the equivalents of te Brake's "local" (that is, national) rulers together with their constituents against others or the European Commission. We saw this in the support that Belgian national politicians offered the Vilvorde workers. Such alignments do not lead to exit against nationalizing princes, as in te Brake's model, but to concerted lobbying efforts and coordination of policy between subnational groups and national elites against European rules and officials.

Fishing for State Support. The conflict over fishing rights in the Bay of Biscay in 1995 is a good illustration of an objective alliance between subnational actors and their national government. In 1995, Spanish tuna fishermen, using old equipment that was no match for the modern trawlers used by their British and French competitors, sequestered a French tuna boat for allegedly using nets that exceeded the statutory EU limit of 2 kilometers. For good measure, they blocked a French ferry in the port of Hendaye. The French navy replied in kind as militants of Greenpeace entered the fray on the high seas to protest the threat to both tuna and dolphins posed by the big trawlers' industrial fishing practices. Britain, accused of snaring dolphins with its fishermen's 2 kilometer nets, insisted that its nets were equipped with holes to let the intelligent dolphins escape, while the apparently more stupid tuna allowed themselves to be caught (Tarrow 1998).

Were it not for the outcome negotiated in Brussels, this story would be no more than a folkloric intrusion on the ordinary political-economic business of three historical neighbors. Embarrassed by the daring of its fishermen and pilloried in the national press, the Spanish government was forced to demand better regulation of tuna catches from Brussels. The government succeeded in having EU inspectors placed on the bigger French and British trawlers to ensure that they were not taking more than their fair share of the catch. What began as a conflict between social actors from different European member states ended up as a national–subnational alignment vis-à-vis supranational elites.

Supranational–Local Alignments

Te Brake's category of territorial consolidation was meant to show how nationalizing claimants, trying to defeat local rulers, sometimes aligned with commoners to create centralized administrative structures and, eventually, integrated national states. Advocates of the "Europe of the Regions" advocated just such a project at a higher level, in which subnational actors – aided and abetted by Brussels – would affirm their own territorial rights vis-à-vis national states within a supranational polity. At the extreme, they called for separatism of regional governments with what they hoped would be the tacit or active support of the European Union.

European officials would not go nearly so far. European cohesion policy, as amended in 1988, was designed to establish permanent patterns of cooperation between subnational governments, interest groups, and the European Commission (Hooghe 1996), but it did not flirt with regional exit. Yet structural policy is one of the few areas where the EU, under a unique system of "partnerships," intervenes directly in the implementation of European Community funding and has developed privileged relations with subnational actors (Ansell, Parsons, and Darden 1997). This gives EU administrators leverage against national governments by encouraging some kinds of regional projects over others, stimulating the organization of the *forces vives* in the regions in which they work and occasionally overcoming national resistance.

The capacity of regional authorities to evade the control of their national governments and align themselves with supranational officials is broadly illustrated in the literature on the EU's regional policies. As Christopher Ansell, Craig Parsons, and Keith Darden summarize it:

> Politically, Commission officials do little to disguise their attempts to cultivate potential allies in subnational government.... Regional actors, in turn, may be willing to lend this political support for several reasons. From the Commission they too obtain useful information.... regions may profit from the support the Commission lends to regional priorities which diverge from national priorities in regional development (1997: 59).

The following section provides a stunning example of what Ansell and his collaborators suggest.

New Laender in an Old Economy. The inclusion of the new East German Laender – poor enough to warrant major EU structural support – into Germany's federal government brought Bonn a dilemma. Germany's federal system and the country's European vocation afford its Laender governments direct access to European institutions, but Bonn wished to set the parameters for East German development itself. Soon after the reunification of Germany, the Commission set up direct ties with the needy and inexperienced eastern regions, responding to their campaign for "Objective One" status and for a substantial injection of EU funding. "In effect," concludes Jeffrey Anderson, "unification created a new territorial constituency in Germany, one that had the opportunity, the desire, and the means to avail itself of Commission resources" (1996: 164).

West German leaders were anxious to get all the help they could to transform East Germany's crumbling infrastructure, but were uneasy about the potential interference of EU administrators in this politically delicate task. In the end, the government acceded to the new Laender's wishes for direct access to the Commission, and EU funds were employed for projects that Bonn might not have supported with its own funds. A supranational–regional alliance leapfrogged over the national state.

Transnational Alliance Building

Our fourth model of alignment and conflict examines transnational alliance building, along the lines of my addition to te Brake's threefold typology of early-modern European contention. I see few signs of exit in these alliances either, but, rather, lateral cooperation among actors with similar claims against their own governments and Europe's institutions. Although such cooperation has developed slowly in most sectors (Imig and Tarrow 2001: ch. 2), in policy sectors with strong international links – such as air and water pollution, food safety issues, and immigration – we are beginning to see evidence of transnational collective action similar in many ways to the Vilvorde case.

Seeding Europe with Conflict. My example comes from the work of Vera Kettnaker, who studied the formation of a European coalition against the importation of genetically modified (GM) seeds from the United States (Kettnaker 2001). Anti–genetic food protests lend themselves easily to transnational cooperation. The market for genetically modified organisms (GMOs) is international; member states have a stake in protecting or promoting domestic producers, farmers, and consumers; and at least four directorates of the European Commission – External Affairs, Agriculture, the Environment, and Scientific Research – have an obvious interest or competence. As American GM seeds began to enter Europe in the mid-1990s, this provided a setting that encouraged both transnational and national consumers' and environmental groups to come together in a powerful international coalition that attacked both national and supranational targets.

Before the first half of 1996, anti–genetic food protests were mostly confined to sporadic local campaigns against experimental fields of genetically modified crops. Yet in November 1996, when the first crop of genetically modified corn and soybeans was to arrive in Europe, many Europeans protested in fear of another food safety scandal like the "Mad Cow" crisis in Britain. Kettnaker writes:

Activists fervently pressured the European Union to avoid this seemingly unnecessary danger or at least to uphold the freedom of choice for consumers by imposing labeling requirements. Concurrently, consumer campaigns were launched to pressure food producers and retailers into making promises not to produce or sell products that contained genetically-modified material (2001: 207).

Although European legislators were moving closer to the position of the consumer and environmental nongovernment organizations (NGOs) by the late 1990s, the European legislative process moved slowly and both Brussels and member states were torn between the goals of calming environmental and consumer groups, supporting Europe's budding GMO industry, and keeping relations with the United States on an even keel. As policy shifted back and forth from Brussels to national governments, the campaign moved

TABLE 3.1. *Frequency of Events Targeting Different Levels of Government in the Campaign against Genetic Modification*

Target	Percentage	Frequency
Direct targets	102.4	N = 129
Subnational government	3.1	4
National government	48.1	62
U.S. government	2.3	3
EU	47.3	61
International	1.6	2
Indirect targets	105.6	N = 18
National government, indirectly EU	77.8	14
National, indirectly international	16.7	3
EU, indirectly International	11.1	2

Note: Figures add up to over 100 percent because of multiple targets for some events.
Source: Kettnaker 2001: 218.

TABLE 3.2. *Level of Government Targeted by National and Transnational Actors in the Campaign against Genetic Modification*

	National target	National (indirect supranational) target	Supranational target	U.S.	Total
National actors	81.8%	10.9%	14.5%	0%	
	(45)	(6)	(8)	(0)	(55)
Transnational actors	23.9%	12.5%	64.8%	3.4%	
	(21)	(11)	(57)	(3)	(88)

Source: Kettnaker 2001: 217.

back and forth between transnational anti-EU and national protests. This situation provided Kettnaker with the unusual opportunity to compare protest behavior against governments at both the national and European levels within the same campaign and time period.

Table 3.1, taken from Kettnaker's study, shows the percentage distribution of anti-GMO protests targeting the subnational, the national, the European, or the international level (for example, protests at international conferences or United Nations meetings).

Are national environmental and consumer groups exiting their national territories when they target the European Union? This would lend support to Bartolini's theory of territorial exit. What we find from Kettnaker's evidence is a much more differentiated picture, with national groups protesting against their own governments, while transnational social movement organizations focus mainly on European institutions. Table 3.2, also from Kettnaker's study, demonstrates this division of protest labor.

MECHANISMS OF CONFLICT AND ALIGNMENT

We can summarize as follows: A variety of deep and structural conflicts of interest divide Europeans, and the lowered borders between their states facilitate forms of territorial exit that challenge both the political parties that organize around national politics and the national states that used to monopolize authority. But while the migration of regulatory authority to Brussels has put national governments' authority at risk, territorial exit is only one of the processes in play; others – like the four that we have sketched in the preceding sections – bring states, supranational authorities, and citizen groups into recurring patterns of alignment and conflict.

Some of these patterns – such as supranational/local alignments – leapfrog over the national state. Others – such as transnational alliances – bring social actors together across Europe's increasingly permeable borders. Still others – like national–supranational alignments and national–local ones – place national governments at the center of networks of actors and institutions, providing them with leverage that they can use both to pressure European decision makers and to produce resources for restive constituents. Rather than wringing our hands over – or applauding – the supposed decline of national sovereignty in Europe, we would do better to focus on the structure of conflicts and alignments and on the mechanisms and processes that link states, social actors, and institutions to one another in the everyday processes of polity construction and management. Many of these processes preserve traditional patterns of center–periphery relations. The following section offers an illustration.

Sectoralization of Territorial Claims

In the area of European Union structural policy, a process that I call *sectorialization* (Balme and Bonnet 1995) results from a combination of mechanisms: Mobilization and claim formation start the process, brokerage brings it into the European arena, and object shift and claim shift turn what might have been efforts for territorial exit into routine claims for sectoral benefits.

- *Mobilization and claim formation:* These mechanisms occur in European politics no differently than they do when the focus is national government (Imig and Tarrow 2001: ch. 2). Regional elites mobilize support on behalf of constituents around claims that involve local interests and identities. Regional nationalism is not natural: Claims may be framed in territorial terms or in terms of satisfying the interests of specific local actors – the famous *forces vives* of French regional policy, from which EU structural policy was largely derived (Balme and Bonnet 1996).
- *Rotating brokerage:* We saw in the "tuna war" how national states can act as brokers between supranational authorities and their own domestic groups. But the brokerage role in the European Union is not limited

to national states. For many issues, conflict is regulated through an interlarded system of policy networks in which brokerage shifts from one player to another.

For example, looking at structural policy, Ansell and his collaborators pinpoint a number of exchange networks among subnational, national, and supranational officials. At first, the authors observe, national governments were the sole linchpin between subnational governments and Brussels. Now, however, "supranational and sub-national actors also have dual access to aspects of their policy-making environment" (Ansell et al. 1997: 353). During some stages of structural policy allocation, national governments align with their subnational authorities to extract the maximum of resources from the Commission; during other phases, however, the axes of brokerage shifts and subnational actors find interlocutors among Commission officials against their national officials.

- *Object and claim shift:* As Europe's history of nationalism shows, the territorialization of conflict depends on the cumulation of sectoral policy differences into indivisible and mutually exclusive territorial clusters and on the mobilization of ideologies of difference among nationalizing elites. When we turn to EU structural policy – through which the Commission allocates resources to subnational territories – the Commission frames regions as policy sectors, not as a set of territories with distinct identities and needs. Once levels of need are statistically established, structural funds are allocated for sectoral purposes and in partnership with sectoral groups who will use the funds (Balme and Bonnet 1996).

The shift of regional mobilization and potentially territorial claims to sectoral objects and claims through the brokerage of EU officials and national governments buffers the regional cleavages that might produce territorial exit and renders territorial claims divisible into budget items that can be negotiated over, compromised, and traded off for gains or losses in other areas of policy. What might have developed as a transgressive process fomenting territorial exit develops instead as a process of bargaining, alignment, and contained contention.

Sectorialization is beneficial for all the actors involved: "Through functional arguments for the need for transnational co-ordination of regional policies," the Commission has steadily expanded its own discretion. At the same time – and through similar functional "arguments" – the Commission has successfully pushed for a subnational role in European regional policy" (Ansell et al. 1997: 51–2). National states have had to give ground in this relationship, but on the other hand, they gain resources from the Commission for less-developed regions and political credit for doing so. Sectorialization of territorial policy transfers resources from the supranational to the subnational level without encouraging the territorial exit that nationalists fear and that advocates of the Europe of the Regions cheer.

CONTENTION AND THE DEMOCRATIC DEFICIT

The preceding reflections suggest that no single trend is emerging toward the construction of a European polity. Bartolini worries that the growth of supranational authority and the territorial exit that it encourages leave the classical instrument of representative politics – the national mass party – with a much reduced role. I share that concern and do not believe that existing European party groupings are an adequate substitute for national mass parties. But if our sketch of European alignment and conflict patterns has shown us anything, it is that there is more than one mechanism for ordinary people to participate in European politics and gain representation for their claims. For some issues, they unite with their national governments to face their counterparts in other countries and the European Union; for others, they find support from the Union against their own states; for still others, they combine across borders; while for others they protest domestically against EU policies (Imig and Tarrow 2001: ch. 2). Elite consolidation at the cost of Europe's "ordinary people" is one part of the equation; but another is the emerging capacity of Europe's social and political actors to align vertically and horizontally in Europe's composite polity.

What of representation? As ordinary people and the organizations that represent them increasingly target Europe with their claims, the question of democratic representation shifts from a purely national arena to a supranational and transnational one as well. Will Europe's representative institutions begin to close the representative gap that some believe has given rise to a more contentious European politics? Or will they diversify the informal channels that we have seen to provide more incentives to act collectively? A broader look at Europeans' forms of representation and participation as they cross boundaries and levels of authority may now be in order.

Ordinary people seeking representation for their interests at the European level have both informal and formal, direct and indirect pathways open to them (see Figure 3.4):

- *Indirect formal representation* through member states meeting in intergovernmental forums in which state interests, European collective goals, and interstate coalitions constrain the capacity of domestic social actors to gain direct representation for their claims – as predicted by the intergovernmental model
- *Indirect informal representation* through Euro-lobbies in which the big and the powerful possess natural advantages over the small and dispersed claims of ordinary people, as neofunctionalists would expect

	Formal	*Informal*
Direct	European Parliament	Euro- protest
Indirect	Member states	Euro- lobbies

FIGURE 3.4. Forms of Europeanized Participation and Representation

- *Direct formal representation* through elections to the (still extremely weak) European Parliament, as Bartolini and other students of party systems would hope (Bartolini 1998)
- *Direct informal participation* through protest against national governments and European institutions, as Imig and Tarrow (2001) found

The indirect nature and the biases of the first two forms of access and the weaknesses and imperfections of the latter two have led to two kinds of proposals to fill the democratic deficit: the desire to broaden the web of Euro-lobbies to so-called civil society groups, and the call for a stronger European Parliament. If these occur, are they likely to affect the magnitude and direction of contentious politics? Will European civil society lobbies and greater power for a directly elected Parliament still the voices of protest that we have seen and overcome the tendency to territorial exit that concerns Bartolini?

With respect to European-level civil society groups, recent research suggests that such groups are often little more than coopted agencies of the Commission that have great difficulty creating and maintaining representative links with their claimed constituencies in the member states (see the contributions in Imig and Tarrow 2001). Without such ties, it would be surprising if such groups gained much political clout either in Brussels or with respect to national governments. They prosper largely because it is in the interest of the Commission that they do so, for they provide EU officials with both information for policy making and legitimacy for the European project.

This takes us to the argument that increasing the power of the European Parliament will lower the incentives for ordinary people to employ contentious politics against European policy makers. The argument has a certain superficial logic: Why would people go to the trouble of protesting against European policies if Members of the European Parliament (MEPs) in a more robust European Parliament can carry their claims to Strasbourg? But there is a flaw in this logic. Historically, the strengthening of parliamentary government did *not* lead to a decline of contentious politics; on the contrary, as

Charles Tilly has shown in Britain's contentious history, parliamentarization led to a greater focus of contention on higher-level institutions (1995). If history is a guide, instead of a substitute for protest, a strengthened European Parliament will provide more channels for protest and greater incentives for taking protests to a higher (in this case *supra*national) level. The genetic modification conflict already showed hints of coordinated action between protesters and MEPs in the European Parliament.

Democracy, if it evolves at the European level, will not result from the predominance of any single channel of representation but from the capacity of social movements, public interest groups, and other non-state actors to forge workable alignments with national governmental actors, supranational institutions, and each other in Europe's increasingly composite polity (see Marks and Steenbergen, in press). We have seen illustrations of four such patterns of alignment and conflict. Research like the contributions to this book will show how durable and how useful such patterns are to Europe's ordinary people.

PART II

THE TRANSFORMATION OF GOVERNANCE

4

Sovereignty and Territory in the European Union

Transforming the UK Institutional Order

James A. Caporaso and Joseph Jupille

The thematic core of this book involves changes in the territorial basis of politics resulting from broader social, political, and economic changes in the domestic and global political economies. We focus in particular on changes in the territorial organization of authority in the modern state. One of the documents we read at the beginning of this project was titled "Beyond Center and Periphery or the Unbundling of Territoriality" (Ansell and DiPalma 1998). In an effort to galvanize our energies into a collective project, this paper enjoined us to examine ways in which contemporary territorial structures of authority could be "unbundled" or "unpacked" so as better to understand changing configurations of power and authority in the modern state.

In part, this guidance was motivated by an emerging literature on the "new medievalism" (Anderson 1996) as well as by persistent critiques that contemporary research in comparative and international politics was state-centric and caught in a "territorial trap" (Agnew 1994). Just as the transition to the Westphalian order involved a consolidation of rule and territory, so the neomedieval turn implies a loosening of the ties among authority, sovereignty, and territory.

The medieval model of rule was marked by three integrated properties of governance. Governance was parcellized and personalized in use and function and aspatial in its underlying conception and physical organization. Parcellization implies no overarching system of rule for all subject matters. Separate authorities existed within the same physical space, without clearly demarcated jurisdictions. The distinction between public and private realms was vague and that between domestic and foreign largely nonexistent. In the German Empire during the first part of the seventeenth century, C. V. Wedgewood (1981) tells us, 21 million people depended on more than two thousand authorities for their government. Personalization implies that rights and duties were based on ties among individuals rather than institutions. During the Battle of Agincourt (1415), Henry the Fifth's order to kill prisoners recently taken was disobeyed by his men at arms, arguably because the prisoners were seen as property of the vassals who had accepted their surrender (Keegan 1976: 109). The aspatial ontology of this world implies that rule was not organized over a definite territory by an exclusive political authority. To be sure, rule took place somewhere; it had its specific sites. But the idea of rule was not necessarily limited by a conception of permanent borders within which authority applied and outside of which it did not. During the medieval period, territoriality did not have the habitual, seemingly essential, taken-for-granted status that it does today (Ruggie 1993).

The move from the medieval form of rule to the modern world, punctuated most sharply by the "Westphalian moment," involved a broad and deep countering of these three aspects of rule. Of course, the development of the Westphalian state did not occur abruptly in 1648. It is a process that is still going on and it preceded 1648 by centuries (Bueno de Mesquita 2000). Yet movement on all three dimensions cannot be denied: from parcellization to consolidation, from personalization to institutionalization, and from an aspatial ontology to a territorial one. This transformation thoroughly conditioned many of our modern touchstones of society and politics, including, among others, citizenship, nationalism, participation, and modernization.

Our attempt to understand changes in the modern system of rule – the Westphalian system – raises difficult conceptual and theoretical, not to mention research design, issues. In this chapter, we attempt to probe some of the relationships previously alluded to by focusing on the United Kingdom's participation in the European Union (EU). Of particular interest to us is parliamentary sovereignty, since it is through the sovereignty of parliament that the United Kingdom has institutionally expressed its final right to decide. Participation in the EU raises troubling questions about the sovereignty of parliament when its acts conflict with provisions of European law. If capacity to exclude external authority structures is a hallmark of the sovereign (territorial) state (Krasner 1999), the intrusion of European law into the domestic order of member states provides, at a minimum, a challenge.

Two problems with our macrohistorical focus stand out, one of them related to research design and the other to the basic conceptual materials from which we work. The design problem relates to a temporal mismatch between the relatively short contemporary time period during which territorial changes are examined compared to the long geological era over which the territorial state developed and took shape. The relative thinness and limited duration of our hypothesized determinants of territorial transformation – the growth and institutionalization of the rule of law and specific conceptions of rights at the EU level – stand in stark contrast to the institutional durability and longevity of our dependent variables (sovereignty, citizenship, territorial authority). At most, we can identify incipient changes, point to emerging trends, and speculate on their significance. Without a more complete time series, it is difficult to distinguish among short-term anomalies, cyclical fluctuations, and durable secular trends. The second complication has to do with the complex nature of territorial authority per se. The first complication requires us to set out our baseline expectations. The second directs our attention toward clarification of the basic concepts used here.

In what follows, we focus on a crucial aspect of territoriality, the right to establish and preserve a basic domestic institutional structure and to remain immune from authoritative external transformation of that structure. We emphasize the authoritative aspect of this relationship, as opposed to the material or even ideational capacity to resist. The linkage between the physical territory of the state and the sources and scope of public authority is central to this chapter, as to the project as a whole. We are particularly interested in the way the capacity to resist authoritative intrusion (or loss of such capacity) plays a role in preserving (eroding) the domestic political order. Our empirical application focuses on the United Kingdom and European law and the ways in which external legal pressure has been brought to bear to constrain progressively the traditional functioning of and relationship between the parliament, the executive, and the courts. As with "foreign" capital in dependency theory, the forces in question do not present themselves merely as external, but instead surface partly through domestic agents and structures.

The story of domestic institutional change in the face of a transnational authority structure is not a simple one, nor can it be easily told with off-the-shelf vocabularies provided by international relations and comparative politics subfields. The institutional variation in question involves changes in the territorial structure of authority in the UK, a loosening of the links between the scope of authority and the boundaries of the state, and a territorial reconstitution of authority so as to commingle domestic and external sources of authority. Two levels of authority (national authority in the British parliament, supranational authority in EU law and the European Court of Justice [ECJ]) sit uneasily next to one another. Thus the process of institutional competition has begun, with the judiciary and parliament often in opposition to one another, even if reluctantly. This is a competition not only between domestic and foreign, inside and outside (Walker 1993), but also among different domestic institutions. Indeed, as we shall argue, one of the most striking effects of the territorial changes examined is a reconfiguration of functions among domestic institutions in the United Kingdom, with "domestic" courts acting as witting or unwitting agents of territorial transformation.

Exploring changes in the territorial organization of authority implies examining the links between borders and the reach of public authority. This is a more difficult exercise than examining the constraints of globalization on national policy making. It is generally accepted that the globalization of trade, capital flows, and technology restrict national policy making. France and Sweden, to take just two obvious examples, cannot set interest rates or employment and inflation goals exactly where they want, as if capital controls were still in place. However much is "left for the left" (Garrett and Lange 1991), it is hard to argue that all policy options remain on the table. However, we are not examining policy options in this chapter. Instead, we focus on the much more difficult issue of transformations in the domestic constitution of authority and territoriality.

Authority, sovereignty, and territoriality are broad terms, quite abstract, and difficult to link to specific research questions. It is important for us to proceed in a deliberate way, first to explore the meaning of these key concepts and to move from them to our more concrete research. In this spirit, we organize this chapter in the following way. In the second section we attempt to clarify the notions of authority, sovereignty, and territoriality, and ask what transformations of this syndrome of characteristics might look like. The third section proceeds more operationally, specifying how each of these abstract concepts takes concrete form in one EU member state, the United Kingdom, and identifying some of their observable implications. The fourth section develops two case studies intended to illuminate the ways in which, the extent to which, and the effects with which EU law can transform Westphalian sovereignty, British style. The fifth section summarizes the arguments and findings, draws out the implications of European law for the UK constitutional polity, and considers issues of broader concern to the project as a whole.

AUTHORITY, SOVEREIGNTY, AND TERRITORIALITY IN MODERN POLITICS

Authority

The significant aspect of authority from our perspective is "right to rule" or "recognized right to rule." Since politics is about systems of rule, claims about the right to rule are distinctive claims about both legitimacy and capacity to govern. However, while authority claims rest partly on acceptance and legitimacy, modern understandings of legitimacy, informed by theories of public opinion, seriously overstate the importance of political support. Max Weber's famous definition of authority as "power wielded legitimately" was not intended to imply that authority exists only when a democratic citizenry actively supports the policies and governance structures of the state. Instead, authority is best conceived as a relation of command and obedience, as a set of claims "to the exclusive right to make rules" (Thomson 1995: 223). The success or failure of these claims can rest on a variety of bases, including active political support, a generalized acceptance of the rules of the game, deference to experts, fear of retaliation, and/or sheer indifference to the process and outcomes. In short, the effectiveness of authority can best be seen by the extent to which individuals will obey even when their interests diverge from the command in question.

In sum, the presumptive right to rule, which is a structural relation joining both rulers and ruled, represents the distinctive characteristic of authority. The foregoing suggests that "private authority" (Cutler et al. 1999) is not a contradiction in terms nor is the phrase "sovereign authority" redundant. These two concepts are separable in principle and in practice.

Sovereignty

The international relations literature advances four broad uses of sovereignty: as control over borders, as external recognition, as the ultimate legal right to decide, and as the capacity to exclude external authority structures (Krasner 1999). In the context of our chapter, we find the last two conceptions of sovereignty the most relevant.[1] Within every political system, according to the "right to decide" definition, there must be some locus of final rules, some "place" where decisions can be taken and not be overruled by some other body (Hinsley 1986: 25–6). This view of sovereignty implies that a hierarchy of norms must exist among laws and regulations within a society. When clashes among norms occur, the question arises of how to adjudicate the differences. Some institution must be vested with the power to decide (authoritatively) which rule is controlling.

The final conception views sovereignty as capacity to exclude external authority structures (Krasner 1999: 3–4). We follow Janice E. Thomson's definition of authority, which emphasizes rules establishing "which issues, activities, and practices fall within [the state's] authority realm – the political – and which lie in the province of non-state authority" (1995: 225). Redrawing the boundary between the market and the state, for example, or conferring on individuals social rights that are intended to blunt the force of the market would represent authoritative decision making in this sense. Perhaps the most crucial aspect of a state's authority has to do with its capacity to establish and reproduce its basic institutional structure. The analytical key to the conception of sovereignty as capacity to exclude external authority structures involves a distinction between external *influence* attempts and attempts by some external agent to impose its *authority*. In the former, target states decide whether or not to comply with the wishes of an external actor as a function of the relative costs and benefits of the alternative courses of action. To the extent that the external actor can alter those costs and benefits, we find ourselves in the realm of power. In the case of external authority, by contrast, actors will or will not comply out of a sense of right, obligation, or deference (or lack thereof) to the would-be external authority (May 1995).

---

[1] While we find the "ultimate right to decide" to be a useful point of departure, we also raise difficulties with this notion, such as the old and largely unanswerable question of who really has power or authority when external constraints are so strong. We elaborate this problem in the context of this chapter.

Whereas compliance with influence attempts follows a logic of consequences gauged in cost/benefit terms, compliance with authority attempts follows a logic of appropriateness gauged in normative terms (March and Olsen 1989: 160–2). Of course, power and right are categories, and ideal typical ones at that. In the empirical world, we do not observe them in pure form. A mixture of power (a purely utilitarian calculation) and right (based on standards of appropriateness and legitimacy) inevitably arises in practice.

Territoriality

Territoriality involves the physical organization of political space, in particular the principles underlying the way political space is organized. Political organization is territorial when the legal reach of public authority is coterminous with certain spatial boundaries, for example, those of the national state, or of federal jurisdictions within a state. Other principles of political organization exist: rule by and over tribe (which might be dispersed in different territories), rule over believers (such as over Catholics worldwide), and rule in terms of administrative task (for example, independent regulatory agencies that are not limited to state borders) (Ruggie 1993).

The emergence of the territorial principle, of rule over territory by a single ruler or political institution, subverts multiple claimants of authority. Absent territoriality, we could imagine separate authority structures coexisting. Indeed, the medieval principle of organization in which multiple authorities exist within the same territory, each authority making claims based on use, customary rights, and personal relations, provides a case in point. However, the persistence of competing claims depends in part on nonterritorial forms of organization. When the territorial principle emerges, it immediately raises the issue of rule over space, regardless of substantive domain. When conflict occurs, it is more difficult to resolve by more finely honed specialization of function or by exit.

The territorial state is of course a state with physical boundaries, and a well-developed sense of inside-outside and us-them (Walker 1993). As Bartolini (1998; Chapter 3 of this book) has persuasively argued, the modern state erects boundaries and thus alters the relative incentives in favor of voice as against exit. The rise of political parties, the expansion of the electorate, the growing importance of formal representation and parliaments, and the development of interest group lobbying may be seen as indicators of this selective but powerful tightening of the borders of states. With the movement of people and capital more restricted, and with claims to rule by the state more pervasive, "domestic" mobilization became inevitable.

In short, territorial organization implies rule over a distinct space, the subjects inhabiting it, and the economy within it. It also implies drawing together (consolidating) scattered islands of authority into one hierarchy or separating authority into territorial spheres, as in federal systems. The territorial principle implies neither total control nor absolutism. The authority of the territorial state can be quite limited and carefully circumscribed. Constitutions, formal and informal, may spell out the precise range of authorities of the state and may divide the powers of the state among several institutions. But whatever the boundaries of the state with respect to society, when conflicts among authorities occur, the sovereign state can claim final right to rule.

Summary

To summarize this conceptual introduction, we rely on a state's capacity to exclude external authority as the key element of the Westphalian syndrome. This conception offers greater analytical leverage than the more commonly used "ultimate right to decide," which, while helpful for legal reasoning (hierarchy of norms, conflict of jurisdictions), has produced little but intellectual dead ends when used to assess changes in sovereignty. We are especially interested in the ways in which the erosion of the capacity to exclude compromises constitutive elements of the domestic political architecture and, in our subsequent case study, parliamentary sovereignty.

What, then, might a *European* transformation of sovereignty and territoriality look like? As a political system based on the rule of law, the EU is potentially subversive of Westphalian sovereignty. Attempts to redraw the lines of authority by the European Union, and more specifically by the ECJ, lend themselves to studying these aspects of sovereignty because the analytical separation between influence (power) and authority is less difficult to maintain with regard to the ECJ than with institutions that work more by power (such as, the North Atlantic Treaty Organization) or inducement (the market). EU law and ECJ rulings enjoy little in the way of "teeth" beyond the mere fact that they are perceived as authoritative by others in the EU system.[2] Thus, we claim that where member states comply with EU legal incursions such that they alter their course of action, we are observing the intrusion of an external authority into the territorial realm of the state, which represents a weakening of Westphalian sovereignty in the sense intended by Stephen Krasner.[3] The purest expression of authority – and we recognize that this may be controversial – is obedience to command apart from economic inducement or some form of coercion. We now turn to the case of the United Kingdom to put some more operational flesh on the conceptual bones that we have sketched.

---

[2] Of course, the fact that national courts are frequently willing partners to the ECJ nuances this position somewhat, a point to which we return later in this chapter.

[3] Krasner, of course, recognizes such transgressions of Westphalian sovereignty as an empirical regularity and considers them essential to any complete understanding of sovereignty in the international system. See also Krasner (1995/96).

The enormity of the concepts involved has hamstrung efforts at gaining systematic empirical leverage on the putative transformation of sovereignty. The key research question is where to cut into the complex mix of phenomena to gain the greatest marginal leverage in observing what are, from a long-term perspective, relatively small changes in sovereignty bargains (Litfin 2000). Focusing on the United Kingdom within the context of the European Union provides some distinctive methodological advantages. To the extent that the United Kingdom has had a clear and strong conception of domestic sovereignty, it provides a stable background against which to treat deviations. It is also worth pointing out that the United Kingdom meets some of the requirements of a "hard case." That is, the United Kingdom represents a convincing case of a country with a durable tradition of parliamentary sovereignty and resistance to judicial review. Thus, even small changes in the relationship between parliament and the courts in the United Kingdom could be significant and might provide clues to changes occurring elsewhere.

Parliamentary Sovereignty

In many systems, detecting the "locus" of sovereignty may be difficult. Does it reside with the people (and if so, which people)? The executive? God? However, identifying the locus of sovereignty in the United Kingdom poses fewer difficulties. Sovereignty resides in the parliament, which has power to legislate on any matter it wishes, in any way that it wishes, with one exception: Parliament cannot bind future parliaments. Parliamentary sovereignty means that acts of parliament are the supreme laws of the land. As A. V. Dicey put it, the British parliament has "the right to make or unmake any law whatever, and no person or body is recognized by the law of England as having the right to override or set aside the legislation of Parliament" (Dicey 1959, quoted in Levitsky 1994: 349). No other institution, neither the Crown nor the courts, can overrule parliament.

Three observable implications of parliamentary sovereignty stand out. First, parliamentary sovereignty is hostile to judicial review of primary legislation. If laws of parliament represent the supreme law of the land, no other body may interrogate or overturn them. If the courts could review laws and find them wanting, then the parliament could not be supreme:

In the nirvana of pure legal theory an Act of Parliament which has been approved by both Houses of Parliament and which has received the Royal Assent is unassailable before the Courts, however perverse, unjust, or ill-considered its contents may be (Mackenzie-Stuart 1995: 783).

Second, parliamentary sovereignty produces a particular judicial style, one that tends to oppose "purposive" or teleological interpretations of the law. The function of judges in parliamentary systems is to "find" the plain meaning of laws as drafted by legislators, "avoiding constructions that are not true to the statutory text" (Levitsky 1994: 350). Judges must not interpret the law, supply missing or ignore existing words, or point out what the legislation must mean if it is to fulfill some abstract standard or goal. This last point, of course, raises complex issues regarding the relation between the UK and (higher) EU law, and the extent to which the former should be interpreted in light of the goals and purposes of the latter (Lasok and Bridge 1991: 429–30).

Third, parliamentary sovereignty abhors "entrenched" rights, that is, rights placed on foundations that are insulated from parliamentary changes (Wade 1980: 22–40). The entrenchment of rights – the guarantee of their provision in the face of popular or other pressures to the contrary, hence their insulation from the changing fortunes of public opinion and politics – has long been considered an important aspect of democracy. It is ironic that the United Kingdom, perhaps the earliest and longest-lasting democracy, does not have an entrenched system of rights. But such a system is precisely disallowed by the British constitutional tradition of parliamentary sovereignty, because it would entail a limitation on the right of parliament to legislate.

Background Changes

Our argument that (external) European law authoritatively intrudes into the putatively sovereign domain of the British parliament and transforms the UK institutional order departs from an understanding of European law as constitutional. The "constitutionalization" of the treaty, involving its transformation from a horizontal compact among sovereign states to an integrated and vertical legal order in which European law is both supreme and applies directly to citizens, is a necessary precursor to the developments that we examine. Fortunately, others have already told, and told well, the constitutionalization story (Alter 2001; Mancini and Keeling 1994; Stone 1994; Stone Sweet and Caporaso 1998; Stone Sweet 2000). We simply note that the revolutionary doctrines of supremacy and direct effect, enunciated by the ECJ and eventually accepted by national courts, appear fundamentally subversive of parliamentary sovereignty as we have just sketched it.

Most importantly, it seems in retrospect that the doctrines of direct effect and supremacy – more generally, the process of constitutionalization – led naturally to judicial review of both legislative and executive action in the domestic sphere. If individuals were to have rights that could be exercised under European law, and these rights were to hold up even under conflicting domestic provisions, a judiciary had to exist to adjudicate claims. Judicial review involves the assessment (review) of the laws of one level of government in light of laws (including the constitution) of another level. Hierarchy is implied in the very idea of judicial review. Clearly, this gives the European Court of Justice and domestic courts, collectively charged with interpreting the highest (European) law of the land, potentially tremendous authority. Less obviously, this also opens the possibility that the external authority of European law could intrude into the domestic constitutional order and alter the interinstitutional balance between the legislature, executive, and judiciary.

How, and to what extent, might the authority claims inherent in EU law produce domestic institutional transformations eroding the practice of Westphalian sovereignty in the United Kingdom? As we have noted, the relative thinness and short duration of our independent variables contrast sharply with the thickly institutionalized, long-established, and deeply entrenched nature of our dependent variables. To echo a phrase used by James Rosenau in assessing Ernst Haas' work on the transformation of state sovereignty through the declarations and working of the International Labor Organization (ILO), we are necessarily dealing with "small increments along a vast periphery" (Rosenau 1966).

Accordingly, we seek to multiply the observable implications of a change in sovereignty and territoriality in the United Kingdom and bring a wide array of evidence to bear on the problem. We do so by focusing on the three discriminating issues identified previously. We propose that external authority intrudes into the domestic order and transforms territoriality and sovereignty as any of the following occurs: 1) judicial review of domestic laws in light of the expansion of external (European) legal norms; 2) British courts employ "purposive interpretation," reviewing laws with reference to underpinning purposes rather than the words that comprise them; or 3) domestic courts invoke superior external legal norms to create rights that are resistant to parliamentary override.

Our empirical examination consists of two case studies involving initially domestic litigation with significant European elements. We do not construe the case studies as empirical tests of the proposition that European law can alter the domestic institutional balance – indeed, we understand the cases to be instances of this phenomenon. We do find methodological defenses of this biased sample, however. First, review by domestic courts of acts of the British parliament proves exceptionally rare, a universe of a single handful of cases from among tens of thousands of judgments. Because of this, anything approaching random sampling would prove terrifically inefficient and almost perfectly uninformative (King and Zeng 2001a, b). Second, our goal here is not to test hypotheses (for example, about the conditions under which territoriality is transformed), but rather to trace and assess processes and substantive and institutional impacts. Third, it makes sense to think that in "noisy" environments, and in environments in which hypothesized causes (for example, European legal activity) are expected to produce relatively small effects (for example, in the territorial organization of legal and political authority), we should select cases not for representativeness, but for maximal signal-to-noise ratios. Finally, if the EU represents the thin end of the wedge of territorial transformation, it makes sense to focus on familiar cases involving the EU and to interrogate them for clues to broader processes.

TRANSFORMING THE UK INSTITUTIONAL ORDER: CASE STUDIES
OF PROCESS AND IMPACT

The *Factortame* Case

The *Factortame* case (actually, series of cases) raises a range of issues that are central to our examination of territoriality and the UK institutional order. The case involved several fishing companies that were incorporated under British law – that is, they registered their vessels under the Merchant Shipping Act of 1894 and flew the British flag – but the majority of directors and stockholders of which were Spanish nationals. Incorporated in the United Kingdom, these vessels enjoyed access to lucrative North Sea fishing waters, and their catches were counted against the UK's catch limits as established in a 1983 European Community (EC) regulation.[4] To British eyes, the vessels represented nothing more than "quota hoppers," stealing fish and revenues from depressed British fishing communities and repatriating profits to Spain.

In response to these concerns, in 1988 the British parliament passed a new fishing law (the Merchant Shipping Act of 1988), part II of which was explicitly intended to debar Spanish fishermen from fishing against UK quotas.[5] The act did this in a number of ways, most important of which were requiring that fishing vessels flying the UK flag have a "real economic link" with the United Kingdom and that the individuals owning, managing, and controlling the vessels be British citizens, resident and domiciled in the United Kingdom. Some (opposition) Labour members of parliament warned the UK government that these provisions contravened free establishment and nondiscrimination provisions in European law, but the measure nonetheless sailed through the House of Commons.

The provisions clearly harmed the Spanish fishermen, who accordingly sought legal redress in British courts, but invoked matters of European law. For our purposes, three legal issues stand out from the rest. The first concerned the invocation of Community law rights as against provisions of domestic legislation enacted by the sovereign parliament. The second had to do with the apparent clash between UK legislation and European law and how that clash would be resolved. The third dealt with the availability of

---

[4] Council Regulation (EEC) No. 170/83 of January 25, 1983, established a Community system for the conservation and management of fishery resources (January 24, 27, 1983, pp. 1ff).
[5] See *Hansard*, January 28, 1988, cols. 510, 550.

remedies for the alleged infringement of EU law rights. Let us consider each in turn.

Interim Relief: Disapplying an Act of Parliament. On the first question, the Spanish applicants invoked Community law rights to equal treatment and asked British courts to grant them "interim relief" by temporarily suspending ("disapplying") the application of the UK statute until the merits of their claim could be decided. This question gets to the heart of the United Kingdom's domestic institutional balance. Could a British court effectively strike down – even temporarily – a statute passed by the sovereign parliament? Under the traditional constitutional arrangements, this would have been not only impossible, but unthinkable. In the context of Community law, it was not only conceivable, but the first court to hear the case, the Divisional Court, decided that it was necessary and granted the interim relief. It ordered that the relevant provisions of the Act should be disapplied until the ECJ could decide on the conflict of laws and Community rights questions. The secretary of state for transport appealed, and the Court of Appeal reversed the order. The case then proceeded to the House of Lords.

The law lords faced an "unenviable dilemma" (Lewis 1989: 348). On the one hand, if they found for the claimants and ordered interim relief, all would be well if the ECJ eventually found that the claimants were justified. But if the ECJ found against the claimants, this would harm the Crown and the public, because an act of parliament would have been incorrectly disapplied. If, on the other hand, the UK law lords found against the claimants, only to uphold their case, then the claimants would have suffered irreparable harm.

In an initial decision ([1989] 2 All ER 692) characterized by some as "overly cautious" (Campbell 1990), the court relied on English legal tradition, whereby

... the English courts had no power to grant interim relief in a case such as the one before it.... [I]t held that the grant of such relief was precluded by the old common law rule that an interim injunction might not be granted against the Crown ... in conjunction with the presumption that an Act of Parliament was in conformity with Community law until such time as a decision on its compatibility with that law had been given (*Times*, June 20, 1990).

Uncertain about the continuing validity of this traditional rule in the context of the EU, however, the House of Lords stayed the proceedings and in effect asked the ECJ "whether or not Community law allowed the English courts to do what they could not do under English law, that is to say, to grant interim relief by suspending the operation of an Act of Parliament" (Mackenzie-Stuart 1995: 785). More generally, the Lords asked the ECJ to clarify the conditions under which national courts were either obliged or permitted to grant interim relief by suspending a national law where Community law rights were at issue.

In its judgment, the ECJ recalled its assertion in *Simmenthal* (Case 106/77, *Amministrazionedelle finanze dello Stato v. Simmenthal SpA* [1978] ECR 629, at paras. 22–3) that any national provision that would have the effect of denying courts the full protection of Community law rights was incompatible with EU law and must be set aside.[6] It proceeded to find that a court that would grant interim relief but for a national rule prohibiting it from doing so was "obliged to set aside that rule" and grant the relief (Case C-213/89, *The Queen v. Secretary of State for Transport, ex parte Factortame* [1990] ECR I-2433, para. 21).

In light of this judgment, the Lords granted interim relief in July 1990. In practical terms, this meant that the Lords suspended application of the relevant provisions of the act of parliament insofar as it applied to the fishermen in question until the question of rights could be decided. The ruling had the "on-the-ground" impact of allowing the Spanish fishermen to reregister their vessels and restart fishing in UK waters. Although initial Government assessments suggested that the number of vessels reregistering would be low, estimates climbed and eventually eighty-one vessels, out of about thirty-two hundred total fishing boats licensed to fish in the United Kingdom, qualified for reregistration.[7]

Factortame represents the first time that a British court had suspended the application of an act of parliament, and indeed the term "disapplication" had to be invented for the occasion. In an oft-quoted passage, Lord Bridge rejected claims that *Factortame* threatened parliamentary sovereignty, arguing instead that it was a natural outgrowth of parliamentary sovereignty as expressed in the 1972 European Communities Act. He noted that:

... some public comments on the decision of the Court of Justice ... have suggested that this was a novel and dangerous invasion by a Community institution of the sovereignty of the United Kingdom Parliament. But such comments are based on a

---

[6] The operative part of the judgment, in paragraphs 22–3, may bear reproduction in full:

... Every national court must, in a case within its jurisdiction, apply Community law in its entirety and protect rights which the latter confers on individuals and must accordingly set aside any provision of national law which may conflict with it, whether prior or subsequent to the community rule. Accordingly any provision of a national legal system and any legislative, administrative or judicial practice which might impair the effectiveness of community law by withholding from the national court having jurisdiction to apply such law the power to do everything necessary at the moment of its application to set aside national legislative provisions which might prevent Community rules from having full force and effect are incompatible with those requirements which are the very essence of Community law.

[7] *Hansard*, December 11, 1991, col. 962; Minister of Agriculture, Fisheries and Food (Mr. Curry), *Hansard*, October 17, 1990, cols. 829–30W; *Hansard*, October 19, 1992, col. 93W.

misconception. If the supremacy within the European Community of Community law over the national law of member states was not always inherent in the EEC [European Economic Community] Treaty it was certainly well established in the jurisprudence of the Court of Justice long before the United Kingdom joined the Community. Thus, whatever limitation of its sovereignty Parliament accepted when it enacted the European Communities Act 1972 was entirely voluntary ([1991] 1 All ER 70 at 107j–108a).

Critics, not surprisingly, remained unconvinced. H. W. R. Wade (1991, 1996) characterized the Lords' ruling as nothing short of a "constitutional revolution," going on to decry "how smoothly the courts may discard fundamental doctrine without appearing to notice" (Wade 1991: 4). Constitutional dogma aside, the "disapplication" of an act of parliament was a first, as "There is no room in the classic doctrine of parliamentary sovereignty for the concept of 'disapplication' of statute law" (Harlow and Szyszczak 1995: 651). *Factortame*, these authors continue, "represented a major step towards real acceptance and understanding of the 'new legal order' initiated by *Van Gend en Loos*" (1995, 651).

Conflict of Laws. The second issue concerned the status of the UK Merchant Shipping Act 1988 in relation to European law. If a conflict existed between British statutes and Community rules on freedom of establishment and national nondiscrimination, it would have to be resolved one way or the other. Upon an infringement proceeding initiated by the European Commission, the president of the ECJ issued an interim order in October 1989 that the United Kingdom should suspend the nationality requirements of the Merchant Shipping Act insofar as those legally registered prior to the entry into force of the act were concerned. The House of Commons met the order with outrage, but nonetheless passed the Merchant Shipping Act of 1988 (Amendment) Order 1989 (S.I. 1989/No. 2006) to implement the president's order.[8]

In mid-1991, the full ECJ found the nationality, residence, and domicile provisions of the Act to be incompatible with Community law (Case C-221/89, *R. v. Secretary of State for Transport, ex parte Factortame* [1991] ECR 1991 I-3905). However, the government never responded by adjusting the offensive provisions beyond the adjustments made to the nationality provisions in response to the ECJ president's interim order. In mid-1992, the government was preparing an order, but was clearly chagrined by the need to do so, noting that it would "have the effect of permitting wider European ownership of British registered vessels."[9] In the event, the United Kingdom never introduced new modifications to its illegal legislation, thus keeping itself open to liability for failure to fulfill its Community law obligations.

[8] *Hansard*, October 25, 1989, cols. 997–1018.
[9] *Hansard*, May 11, 1992, col. 17W.

Rights and Remedies. That failure brings us to the final set of issues at stake in *Factortame*, concerning remedies for the infringement of rights. Even after the finding that the 1988 Act was incompatible with EU law, the United Kingdom continued to apply the statute "because of the 'political embarrassment' there would have been in withdrawing it."[10] The issue was crucial because, in the words of the solicitor for the Spanish boat owners, it opened up "for the first time the question of whether individuals have the right to sue the Government for damages. This is a right which at present does not exist in English law, and never has existed, except for cases involving misfeasance by a public official."[11]

This aspect of the case again went through several levels of domestic courts before landing at the ECJ. The ECJ ruled that:

> where a breach of Community law by a member state is attributable to the national legislature acting in a field in which it has a wide discretion . . . individuals thereby suffering loss or injury thereby are entitled to reparation when the rule of Community law breached is intended to confer rights upon them, the breach is sufficiently serious and there is a direct causal link between the breach and the damage sustained" (Joined Cases C-46/93 and C-48/93, *Brasserie du Pecheur SA v. Federal Republic of Germany*; *R v. Secretary of State for Transport, ex parte Factortame Ltd and Others (No. 4)* [1996] ECR I-1029, para. 74).

It then fell to the domestic courts to assess whether the UK's breaches met those three conditions, and thus whether the Spanish fishermen should be compensated. Ruling in 1997, the Divisional Court unanimously held that they did ([1997] Eu.L.R. 475). It adduced four main factors warranting this conclusion. First, discrimination on the basis of nationality was the deliberate effect of the residency requirements. Second, the secretary of state for transport knew that the applicants would sustain losses, as the very purpose of the measure was to prevent them from fishing under UK quotas. Third, the UK government used statutory means "to ensure that implementation was not delayed by actions for judicial review, making it impossible for the applicants to obtain interim relief without the intervention of the Court of Justice." Fourth, the European Commission had opposed the legislation in question and had informed the government of its position. The Court of Appeal unanimously upheld that finding, and on October 28, 1999, so too did the law lords. By early 2001, settlements had been reached with all *Factortame* claimants, at a cost to the British treasury of some £55 million.[12]

---

[10] "Tory Government 'Took Risk' on Fish Ban, Court Told," *Press Association Newsfile*, July 16, 1997.

[11] Quoted in "Euro Court Move to Sue Government over Fishing Ban," *Press Association Newsfile*, November 18, 1992.

[12] *Lords Hansard*, vol. 621, part no. 27, February 8. 2001, col. WA119.

To summarize this rather lengthy discussion of a convoluted series of cases, on each element of the cases, important transformations took place. First, the House of Lords created a term new to English law when it "disapplied" an act of parliament for the purposes of granting interim relief to individuals whose rights had been infringed. More importantly, of course, it effected what some have called a constitutional revolution (Wade 1991), wherein the supremacy of European law over parliamentary statute was definitively established, with European and domestic courts acting as authoritative agents of that transformation. Second, the ECJ found that the relevant provisions of the 1988 UK Act were incompatible with Community law, effectively striking them down against the clearly stated preference of the UK government and parliament. Third, the UK's failure to comply with EU law, and its concomitant infringement of Community law rights, made it liable for damages demanded by injured individuals.

Beyond this, *Factortame* has also spilled over to generate change in purely "domestic cases," which could further heighten its impact. In *M v. Home Office* ([1994] 1 AC 377), the House of Lords established that a *Factortame*-style injunction could be granted against the Crown in purely domestic cases. "The decision," F. G. Jacobs writes, "appears to recognize that it would be anomalous to treat English law rights less favorably than Community law rights. *In this way Community law can serve as a catalyst in the development of judicial protection under national law*" (Jacobs 1999: 242, emphasis added). In addition, as noted in Figure 4.1, references to *Factortame* in UK cases have remained steadily frequent since the litigation began. Overall, then, while *Factortame* is hardly representative of the impact of European law on the British domestic order, it does reveal the many, varied, and substantial ways in which external authority can impinge on long-held pillars of the domestic institutional order in ways that go well beyond legal doctrine.

The Equal Opportunities Commission Case

The case of *R. v. Secretary of State for Employment ex parte Equal Opportunities Commission* ["EOC"] (1994) exhibits many of the same features as *Factortame*, showing more profound reach for external authority on some dimensions and greater limitations on others. At issue were provisions of a UK statute, the 1978 Employment Protection (Consolidation) Act (EPCA), limiting eligibility for redundancy or unfair dismissal compensation. Under the statute, individuals having worked sixteen hours or more per week for a period of two years were entitled to such compensation. Those working between eight and sixteen hours became eligible only after five years, and those working less than eight hours per week were excluded entirely. As a factual matter, women overwhelmingly occupied the disfavored part-time positions, by a ratio greater than four to one.

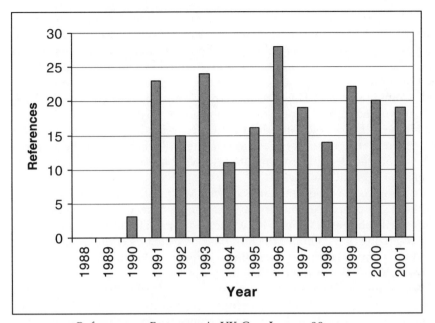

FIGURE 4.1. References to *Factortame* in UK Case Law, 1988–2001
Source: Authors' calculations from searching in Nexis-Lexis Academic Universe, Legal Research, International Case Law, UK Cases, kw = *Factortame*. References to *Factortame* cases themselves were removed. The database was last consulted September 15, 2002.

The UK Equal Opportunities Commission (EOC) felt that these provisions of the EPCA constituted "indirect discrimination" in contravention of EU gender equality laws, and in particular provisions dealing with equal pay and equal treatment as interpreted by the ECJ. The secretary of state did not dispute the disproportionate effect of the contested provisions on women, but argued that the alleged indirect discrimination was in fact a byproduct of measures justifiable on economic grounds. The secretary of state claimed that the contested measures limited costs to business of hiring part-time employees and as such represented a boon to those employees. On this logic, the measure was entirely justifiable on market-competitive grounds. After losing in both Divisional Court ([1992] 1 All ER 545) and at the Court of Appeal ([1993] 1 All ER 1022), the EOC appealed the case to the House of Lords.

"Striking Down" an Act of Parliament. The House of Lords cited the *Factortame* precedent (1990) in holding that the disputed provisions of the 1978 EPCA were susceptible to judicial review for their compatibility with Community law. In addition to confirming the EOC's standing to bring judicial review proceedings, the Lords held quite directly that the contested provisions of the EPCA contravened article 119 of the EU's Rome Treaty and EU directives 75/117 (on equal pay) and 76/207 (on equal treatment). In a move that went well beyond the interim injunction granted in *Factortame*, the Lords quite simply struck down the relevant provisions as incompatible with Community law. They did not see fit to refer the matter to the ECJ. "What is remarkable," notes one commentator, "is the self-confidence of the House of Lords. No longer did the United Kingdom's highest court feel compelled to refer statutory provisions to the ECJ whenever it believed them to be incompatible with Community law. Now it was prepared to override them itself" (Nicol 1996: 584).

Reaction to the judgment came swiftly. Most narrowly, it provided "yet another example of Community law assisting workers where domestic law has proved deficient" (Villiers and White 1995: 573). It did so in a novel way, by recognizing that "a body which fulfills domestic procedural requirements [the EOC] enjoys a public law right to impugn unlawful domestic legislation which is distinct from the directly effective substantive rights conferred by Community legislation" (Moore 1994: 432). It thus "set an agenda for radical changes in the reach of employment protection legislation" (Napier 1994: 396), and promised to have far-reaching effects in other areas of rights, including environmental protection.

Most generally, however, the judgment had profound consequences for the constitutional balance in the United Kingdom. It suggested that "UK courts can use judicial proceedings to strike down Acts of Parliament on the grounds of incompatibility" with Community law (Napier 1994: 396). This goes beyond the "mere" disapplication (temporary suspension) undertaken in *Factortame*. And, while the substantive changes entailed in this judgment were important, so were the means by which the Lords arrived at this result. They went beyond even the purposive interpretation advanced in leading cases *Pickstone* (*Pickstone v. Freemans PLC* [1989], AC 66) and *Pepper v. Hart* (*Pepper v. Hart* [1993], AC 593), where the key determinant guiding the judges was the intent of parliament. In *EOC*, judges assessed the validity of legislation in terms of its social and economic impact. The novelty of this approach can scarcely be overestimated. The validity of the provisions in question had nothing to do with the intent of parliament. Indeed, the majority-Conservative parliament fully intended to maintain the differentiation among full-time and different levels of part-time workers in order to maintain "labor market flexibility" and encourage employment. Instead, the House of Lords found the measures to have a socially undesirable and, under EU law, illegal effect – indirect discrimination against women – that could not be justified on economic grounds. As such, it had to be struck down.

The Times suggests that in taking this approach, "using techniques essentially alien to the English judicial tradition, the law lords were acting as nothing short of a constitutional court in the American manner" (*The Times*

1994). The examination of the substantive merits of an act of parliament was a novel and potentially revolutionary approach for an English judge to take (Mackenzie-Stuart 1995: 787). "If *Factortame* was the revolution," Carole Harlow and Erika Szyszczak summarize, "then the *EOC* case may represent the new legal order" (Harlow and Szyszczak 1995: 651–2).

Legislative Adaptation. The government was clearly unhappy about the judgment. The secretary of state for employment, Michael Portillo, opined that it "clearly gives the relevant European legislation a much wider interpretation than was envisaged when it was originally adopted." He went on to say that "the Government always honor their obligations and accept that the judgment must be acted upon. The House of Lords is the supreme court of the United Kingdom and there is no possibility of further appeal or of reopening the case." Portillo further promised to introduce new regulations intended to comply with the ruling.[13]

Reluctantly, and after nine months' delay, in February 1995 the government enacted the Employment Protection (Part-time Employees) Regulations 1995 (S.I. 1995 No. 31) to give effect to the *EOC* judgment. It removed the differences in statutory employment rights that depended on the number of hours worked, in some ways going beyond the requirements of the *EOC* judgment (Maxwell 1995; McColgan 1996). Now all employees qualify for these rights on the same basis, regardless of hours worked. The change in the regulations extended unfair dismissal protection and a redundancy payment to about 670,000 people, or about 3 percent of all employees.[14] A report completed in May 1997 suggested that the new regulations would cost employers as much as £11.8 million, about half of which would take the form of redundancy payments. For our purposes, it is critical to note that the government strongly resisted such changes, as it felt the original provisions were justified in the interests of a flexible labor market. Succinctly, "a reluctant British government [had] been forced to concede changes in employment protection rights which [were] completely at odds with the Conservative philosophy and policy of deregulation" (Maxwell 1995).

Subsequent Cases. In a fascinating study of the aftermath of the *EOC* judgment in lower courts, Danny Nicol (1996) examines a series of instances in which "bullish" lower courts "go where even the House of Lords feared to tread" in disapplying the contested provisions of the 1978 Act. Many of these went further than the Lords in terms of their definition of pay and in the scope of employment rights with respect to which the hours thresholds were illegal. Although his sample was certainly biased, Nicol examined five cases

---

[13] *Hansard*, December 20, 1994, cols. 1100–01.
[14] House of Commons, Select Committee on Education and Employment, 2nd report, Session 1998/99.

decided between the Lords' judgment in March 1994 and the (February 1995) entry into force of the 1995 statutory amendments, and found that in four of them, lower courts took bold steps to disapply the Act. The cases, he suggests, confirm that "the dismantling of Parliamentary sovereignty has advanced step-by-step" (1996: 589). Subsequent cases give evidence both of extensions of the principles set forth in *EOC* (for example, extending its protections to male workers[15]) and practical limitations on claimants' ability to bring discrimination claims retroactively.[16]

Summary. How can we summarize the *EOC* case? Keeping in mind our characterization of sovereignty as the capacity to exclude external authority, it bears noting that:

... in the Equal Opportunities Commission decision, for the first time ever in the long history of the British Constitution, ... the content and merits of an Act of the United Kingdom Parliament has been analyzed by a British Court and its validity determined by the application of an external standard (Mackenzie-Stuart 1995: 788).

This standard, enshrined in the principle of equal treatment, emanated from European law. "Across the centuries the House of Lords has decided many cases of the greatest constitutional importance," Lord Mackenzie-Stuart continues, "but, because of the principle of parliamentary sovereignty, it has not until *Equal Opportunities Commission* fulfilled the traditional duties of a constitutional court" (Mackenzie-Stuart 1995: 788; *The Times* 1994). What is more, the case gives some evidence of broader and longer-lasting impact on the UK's domestic institutional order.

CONCLUSION

Let us consider more closely the question of UK parliamentary sovereignty in light of European and domestic legal activity. The central aspect of sovereignty highlighted is the capacity to maintain the integrity of domestic authority, represented in the domestic constitutional order. Such a capacity strikes us as more important and certainly closer to the idea of sovereignty than, for example, preserving domestic regulatory standards, protecting certain industries or services, or even protecting certain aspects of the welfare state. All of these goals, however worthy they may be, are part of a realm of policy that is inherently more malleable than the constitutional order. While the constitutional order itself ultimately changes, we visualize it as the bedrock on which the greater relative variability of policy takes place.

[15] *Hammersmith and Fulham London Borough Council v. Jesuthasan, The Times*, March 5, 1998. *Jesuthasan v. London Borough of Hammersmith & Fulham* [1998], 2 CMLR 940.

[16] *Biggs v. Somerset County Council, The Times*, January 29, 1996. *Biggs v. Somerset County Council, Employment Appeal Tribunal* [1995], IRLR 452.

One of the implications of the doctrine of parliamentary sovereignty was the absence of a Bill of Rights – or, indeed, of any "entrenched" rights at all – in the United Kingdom. "Entrenching" rights suggests providing a strong bulwark to change. Insulating such change from parliamentary amendment or overturn would seem necessary, but of course this is precisely what cannot be done within a traditional parliamentary system. Yet, as the EU becomes progressively constitutionalized, it has injected its substance and procedures into the UK's constitutional order. To the extent that the EU enforces, extends, or creates "entrenched rights" – that is, rights that the UK parliament cannot deny British citizens – parliamentary sovereignty must be compromised. Although the extent to which this is happening is not clear – Merle Weiner (1990: 599), for one, holds that the putatively "fundamental right" to gender equality would not exist but for the EU – the negative relationship between rights and parliamentary sovereignty would certainly justify looking more deeply into the enforcement, extension, and creation of rights in the United Kingdom.

Finally, and perhaps most significantly, the extension of judicial review has contributed to the changing relationship between parliament and the judiciary in the United Kingdom, which has profound implications for the UK's institutional order. Several linked aspects of this relationship, all flowing out of traditional conceptions of parliamentary sovereignty, bear mentioning: judicial review, judicial style, and entrenched rights. Historically, the laws of parliament have been supreme, the final statement of the will of the people, and not subject to review by another body. Such review as might occur could only involve administrative action and had to be construed in light of a literal reading of parliamentary statutes, with purposive interpretation generally disallowed. Being supreme, the sovereign parliament could never be frustrated by rights entrenched against the legislative power. While the story is complicated, this relationship is changing, so that parliament now accepts the jurisdiction of the ECJ, along with the supremacy of European law, in ways that implicate each of these dimensions of parliamentary sovereignty and thus the UK institutional order itself.

Through its accession and membership in the EU, the United Kingdom has been constrained to accept the direct effect and supremacy of European law. Discussions about who has the ultimate right to decide are of no help here. The plain fact of the matter is that the United Kingdom has struck a sovereignty bargain (Litfin 1997: 167–204) in which it has traded the autonomy of parliament in return for membership in the EU. That the proximal source of this constraint itself lies with an act of parliament – the European Communities Act of 1972 – hardly changes the reality of these constraints. As a matter of doctrine, parliamentary sovereignty can be salvaged by arguing that only by an act of parliament, is the authority of the ECJ recognized as superior to the UK parliament, and it only takes another act of parliament to undo this delegation of authority (Marshall 1997). True enough! The troops will not leave their barracks in Brussels or Luxembourg to suppress a revolt in Westminster. However, the real "police powers" are not troops but mobile capital, trade, businesspersons, bankers, workers, and consumers. It is not some international version of the national security state that holds the United Kingdom in line. The costs of exit, even selective exit, are high. This disciplining mechanism stands behind the institutionalization of Europe.

In hindsight, this sovereignty bargain seems inevitable. British and European legal orders are progressively enmeshed. They do not move in separate orbits, identify separate issues, and mark off separate jurisdictions. For all practical purposes, they deal with the same subject matter. This commingling of laws requires adjudication as to which level is appropriate and controlling. Thus, we can see that the doctrine of supremacy implies judicial review.

In the final analysis, defenders of parliamentary sovereignty can argue that supremacy of Community law, the direct effect of European legislation, and judicial review are delegated on the basis of the authority in the European Communities Act. This Act can be overturned, thus returning to parliament its traditional idea of sovereignty. But this is the "nuclear option" in the sense that these important relations can be reversed only by renouncing the entire relationship, or something close to it. And, as a more practical matter, "twenty seven years of membership in the European Community has played an important part in exposing the limitations of Parliamentary sovereignty" (Mackenzie-Stuart 1995: 784). "While Britain remains in the Community," a prominent exponent of the traditional (strong) view of parliamentary sovereignty notes, it "is in a regime in which Parliament has bound its successors successfully, and which is nothing if not revolutionary" (Wade 1996: 571). As another author notes:

While some textbook writers continue to maintain that Parliamentary sovereignty [is] unaffected by Community law, the English judiciary has accepted without question that the most fundamental rule of the Constitution – parliamentary sovereignty – has been modified (Jacobs 1999: 245).

The capacity to defend the domestic institutional order against the incursions of external authority constitutes for us one of the primary elements of sovereignty. The nature of the polis – whether it is democratic or not, whether it is a presidential or parliamentary system, what role is played by the courts, and the degree to which private power is allowed to influence the governmental process – is for us central to a conception of sovereignty. The ability to defend a variety of domestic practices, such as treatment of minorities and religious groups, national macroeconomic policy, and trade policy are all important to conceptions of sovereignty. Even closer to the core of sovereignty is the right and the capacity to defend the domestic institutional order, that is, the basic arrangement of institutions and practices that defines the political system. Westphalian sovereignty implies not only legal recognition of others, but recognition despite extreme differences in the nature of the units. The Westphalian ideal is not a leveling device designed to force convergence among countries; quite the contrary, it is a principle for accommodating differences.

Westphalian sovereignty implies the capacity to exclude, if not ICBMs and foreign capital, at least external influences that carry the badge of right and authority. Our exploratory probe suggests that European law represents a source of authority external to the "sovereign" states that comprise the EU. Far from excluding such external authority, as the Westphalian paradigm suggests, the United Kingdom tends to a surprising extent to accept it. Whether this development represents the thin wedge of a more widespread development or a minor blip in geological time remains to be seen, argued, and fought out.

5

Social Citizenship in the European Union

Toward a Spatial Reconfiguration?

Maurizio Ferrera

Since the nineteenth century, the social rights of citizenship have played a crucial role for the process of state and nation building in Europe.[1] Such rights have given rise to wide "collectivities of redistribution" that have strengthened cultural identities, enhanced citizen loyalties to public institutions, and promoted a sharing of material resources throughout the social structure, thus easing civic and political cohesion. The European nation-state is typically a welfare state; the social components of citizenship are no less important than its civil and political components; the right to decide about the forms and substance of social citizenship has always been considered in its turn a crucial aspect of national sovereignty.

The dynamics of globalization and, more specifically, of European integration have been gradually challenging this institutional configuration. In the last couple of decades, the social dimension of national sovereignty has been increasingly undermined by a number of factors. The "right to decide" on social policy matters of each individual state has become less comprehensive and "ultimate" than it used to be. Globalization and European integration have modified the context in which national welfare states operate, offering new constraints and new opportunities to citizens/consumers, producers and delivering agencies, as well as policy makers (in the widest sense). In the debate, the new challenges to social sovereignty are primarily discussed with reference to highly significant, but mainly *indirect*, developments: the increased mobility of capital, the greater volatility of international financial markets and their power to condition domestic choices, the constraining rules of new supranational regimes (typically the European Monetary Union [EMU]), rising migration flows, and so on. In this chapter, I will keep all

[1] A different version of this chapter has appeared in Maurizio Ferrera, 2003, "European Integration and National Social Citizenship: Changing Boundaries, New Structuring?" *Comparative Political Studies*, 36, 6: 611–52. I am very grateful to Chris Ansell, Beppe Di Palma, and two anonymous referees for the precious suggestions received.

these developments in the background and concentrate instead on a number of more *direct* challenges, that is, developments that are weakening two essential traits of social sovereignty in its traditional meaning: 1) the capacity of a state to exert coercive rule on actors and resources that are crucial for the stability of redistributive institutions; and 2) the capacity of a state to bar external authority structures from interfering in their own social space and jurisdiction.[2]

For my analysis, I will draw inspiration from the theory of Stein Rokkan and, more specifically, from his basic argument about the link between boundary building/reduction and internal structuring/destructuring. In full accordance with Stefano Bartolini (1998a, 2000, and Chapter 2 of this book) and Peter Flora (1999, 2000), I find that Rokkan's perspective offers a rich analytical framework for the interpretation of current European politico-institutional developments (including those affecting the sphere of welfare) and for the generation of hypotheses concerning both crosscountry variations and future scenarios.

The first section of the chapter will briefly present my basic theoretical underpinnings. The second section will sketch the development of national welfare institutions from their origin up to the 1970s, discussing their implications in terms of boundary building and internal structuring. The third and fourth sections will discuss the challenges that have emerged in the last couple of decades to the social sovereignty of the nation-state–challenges that are largely exogenous (and mainly connected to the process of European integration), but partly reinforced by endogenous developments as well. The final section will offer some more speculative remarks on the interplay between the transformation of boundaries *around* and *within* European welfare states and their politico-institutional structuring.

BOUNDED STRUCTURING: ROKKAN'S PERSPECTIVE

The notions of "boundaries" and "structuring" are crucial components of Rokkan's theoretical framework on the historical process of state formation and nation building in Europe (Rokkan 1970; Lipset and Rokkan 1967).[3] As is well known, for Rokkan this process took place in the wake of complex dynamics of functional and territorial differentiation in Europe after the fall of the Roman Empire. These dynamics gave rise to two basic sets of structures: cleavage structures and center–periphery structures. Cleavage structures are those sets of fundamental ("obdurate and pervasive") contrasts, rooted in socioeconomic and cultural differences, which have come to divide national

---

[2] For a full discussion of the concept of sovereignty, see Chapter 1 of this book.

[3] Rokkan's theory has been patiently and skillfully reconstructed with a systematic (rather than a chronological) approach by Flora, in collaboration with Stein Kuhnle and Derek Urwin (Flora et al. 1999). For a chronological sketch of the theory and a discussion of Rokkan's distinctive methodological approach, see Mioset (2000).

communities systematically. Center–periphery structures are those systems of relationships and transactions linking the dominant loci of command and control, within relatively "bounded" territories, to their subordinate areas. These two sets of structures have in turn generated a wealth of institutional-organizational forms on both the input and the output side – from interest groups and political parties to executives and administrative agencies. The concept of structuring (that is, of structure formation) connotes the stabilization of all these patterns of interaction through the creation of various rules and norms of behavior, specific coalitions among actors, and the establishment of interorganizational links. In the aftermath of some critical historical junctures, in many countries cleavage structures and center–periphery structures got "crystallized" or "frozen" – that is, they came to be embedded in, and supported by, a dense network of organizations (especially corporate and partisan organizations, but also service bureaucracies), whose main effect was (and still largely is) precisely that of reproducing the structures themselves.

State formation and nation building were slow processes implying the creation of increasingly solid boundaries and the parallel "internalization" (or nationalization) of preexisting structures. Elaborating on Albert Hirschman's work (Hirschman 1970), Rokkan conceptualized this process as a gradual foreclosure of exit options of actors and resources, the establishment of "system maintenance" institutions capable of eliciting domestic loyalty (including the consolidation of what he called the "cultural infrastructure"), and the provision of channels for internal voice, that is, claims addressed to national centers from social and geographical peripheries. The locking in of resources and actors in a bounded space "domesticated" the latter's strategies, focused them toward central elites, encouraged the formation of new organizational vehicles for the exercise of voice and the strengthening of loyalty, and, as a consequence of all this, sparked processes of territorial "system building," that is, the emergence of area-specific, functionally integrated constellations of institutions and actors.

For Rokkan, the notion of space had two dimensions: a territorial dimension and a "membership" dimension, involving sociopolitical and cultural elements. Thus boundary building must be understood in two ways: 1) as the demarcation of physical space through the deployment of effective instruments of territorial defense – primarily military and administrative; 2) as the creation of explicit codes and forms of distinction – for example, citizenship rights – between insiders and outsiders, nationals and nonnationals. Membership (or "social," in a wide sense) boundaries are very important; as Rokkan put it:

(They) tend to be much firmer than geographical boundaries: you can cross the border into a territory as a tourist, trader or casual labourer, but you will find it much more difficult to be accepted as a member of the core group claiming pre-eminent rights of control within a territory (quoted in Flora et al. 1999: 104).

Membership boundaries can also be used to differentiate within the core group itself, establishing barriers or thresholds for accessing political decisions or socioeconomic resources and opportunities. For example the differential voting rights across population strata in the nineteenth century created distinct spheres of membership to the political community, which became the object of harsh and prolonged confrontations. The development of culturally embedded systems of national citizenship, resting on universal civic, political, and social rights, took place in a space of interaction characterized by increasing degrees of social and territorial closure.

Although he never systematically used or discussed the concept in his writings, for Rokkan (in line with the Weberian tradition) "sovereignty" basically meant the capacity of demarcating geographical space and exercising authoritative control on both exit/entries and voice/loyalty dynamics *into* and *within* that space.[4] Since the mid-eighteenth century, the consolidation of such a twofold ability was no easy task – not least for the constant appearance of "boundary transcending technologies" (from the press to underground movements), requiring the deployment of boundary-maintaining counterforces. Toward the end of the nineteenth century, however, in certain parts of Europe the process of bounded structuring gave rise to a novel variant of the sovereign state: a national, democratic, and welfare state that was the most successful political protagonist of the subsequent century.

In his work, Rokkan focused primarily on state formation, nation building, and democratization, analyzing them in the context of growing external closure and the ensuing internal structuration of specific territorial areas. He did not systematically explore the fourth stage or dimension of bounded structuring, that is, the establishment of redistributive arrangements. Yet he recognized that these arrangements played a crucial role in stabilizing the new form of politico-territorial organization that gradually emerged in Europe. This stabilization occurred through the anchoring of people's life chances to state-national institutions, via the creation of explicit entitlements to (a modicum of) material resources. System-specific social rights became new, important ingredients of national membership spaces; their introduction accelerated the fusion between the concept of citizenship and that of territorial identity. The basic duo "cultural identity *cum* political participation" – within a demarcated territory – was complemented with a

---

[4] If we take Stephen D. Krasner's four meanings of the concept (Krasner 1999), what Rokkan had implicitly in mind in his reflections about system building were both Westphalian sovereignty (that is, the exclusion of external actors from authority structures within a given territory – such that domestic authorities become the sole arbiter of legitimate behavior) and "interdependence sovereignty" (that is, the ability of domestic authorities to control what passes through territorial borders). The other two meanings are sovereignty as external recognition, and sovereignty as the ultimate legal right to decide. As argued by James Caporaso and Joseph Jupille (2000), Westphalian sovereignty in particular seems to offer greater analytical leverage over the other three meanings for many questions currently debated about the strains between the EU's and member states' authority.

novel "social sharing" component (Flora 2000), reinforcing on the one hand those feelings of "we-ness" that are a crucial underpinning of the nation-state construct and offering to national elites, on the other hand, new tools for differentiating between insiders and outsiders.[5]

At the beginning of the twentieth century, the welfare state became a distinct institutional order, closely interacting with preexisting or co-emerging orders: the cultural infrastructure, the state decision making and administrative machinery, the party and corporate system, and so on. During the subsequent decades, the fusion among territorial identity, mass democracy, and the welfare state produced very solid and highly integrated political systems, functioning according to distinct internal logics. Of course, these systems maintained several channels of mutual communication, especially in the economic sphere. Looking at institutional developments from a (very) *longue durée* perspective, Rokkan was well aware of the tensions inherently building up between processes of system closure, on the one hand, and the counterpressures for "opening" brought about by crossborder transactions on the other hand. Writing in the 1960s and 1970s, however, he remained rather skeptical about the prospects for European integration – and in particular about the formation of new crosssystem structures "beyond cooperation between corporate agencies."

In the last two decades, however, European integration has proceeded much beyond the stage of a mere open arena of economic transactions and administrative cooperation. Crosssystem boundaries have been extensively redefined, differentiated, reduced, and in some areas altogether canceled. Following Rokkan's framework, we should expect that such changes may have significant consequences for the configuration of internal institutional orders. Developing general hypotheses about the destructuring effects of crosssystem boundary redrawing on these three broad fronts is a very complex analytical task, which falls well beyond the scope of this chapter.[6] Rokkan's theoretical framework can also be mobilized, however, for raising questions and advancing theoretical expectations about the specific theme that interests us, that is, the impact of European integration on national systems of social sharing (see Figure 5.1). To what extent have EU rules affected the territorial and membership boundaries of domestic welfare systems? Is this "rebounding" likely to undermine the institutional foundations (or prerequisites) of redistribution at the national level? Are there symptoms of wider destructuring dynamics – for example, on cleavages and/or center–periphery relations – that are

---

[5] The three basic components of the contemporary European nation-state – cultural identity, political participation, and solidaristic institutions – did not historically emerge in the same sequence everywhere; in many cases (for example, Wilhelmine Germany), social insurance institutions made their first appearance prior to political rights (see Alber 1982; Flora and Alber 1981).

[6] See Bartolini (1998a) for a stimulating exercise in this direction.

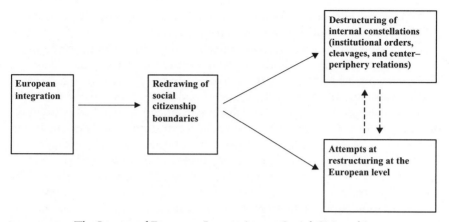

FIGURE 5.1. The Impact of European Integration on Social Citizenship

originated *by* or likely to impact *on* social policy? And if European integration can be looked at as an attempt at system building, following novel modes of bounded structuring and original solutions to the challenges posed by such a process, what are the prospects for a restructuring of social citizenship within this new emerging space?

Keeping such broad questions in the background, our analysis will proceed in four steps. First, we will offer a brief historical survey of welfare state formation, based on the concepts and theoretical links summarized in this paragraph. Second, we will discuss some developments that started to challenge the national closure of social citizenship between the 1950s and 1970s. We will then move to analyze in more depth the tensions that built up during the 1980s and 1990s between the member states and the EU in three relevant sectors: health care, social assistance, and pension insurance. Our fourth and final step will be to return to the Rokkanian framework; building on the empirical findings of the previous steps, we will suggest some possible scenarios and lines of research about the causal sequence charted in Figure 5.1.

THE STRUCTURING OF SOCIAL SHARING: FROM LOCAL ASSISTANCE
TO NATIONAL WELFARE

How precisely did social sharing get structured historically in the European states? Which institutional-organizational forms were created in order to stabilize the new ties of solidarities between social groups? How did such forms interact with the cleavage and center–periphery structures? As is well known, entire libraries have been filled with studies on the evolution of social policy and on its distinct typological trajectories. In this section, I will briefly resketch the story from a Rokkanian angle.

An original European invention, the welfare state emerged as a result of a slow process of policy experimentation, which began with the "liberal break" vis-à-vis conservative paternalism around the middle of the nineteenth century and ended with the establishment of mass social insurance in most countries by the end of the 1920s (Briggs 1961; Rimlinger 1971). Social insurance was a real institutional breakthrough in the history of the European nation-state. Prior to it, the management of social risks was predominantly in the hands of locally anchored institutions. These operated through occasional, residual, and discretional interventions, considered as "dispensations" that society granted to persons often considered as undeserving. Beneficiaries were thus severely stigmatized and very often lost their civil and (to the extent they had any) political rights. The actual delivery of assistance took highly differentiated organizational forms, on a very narrow territorial basis.

Social insurance almost completely overhauled this traditional approach (Alber 1982; Ewald 1986; Heclo 1981; Perrin 1969). Its new objective was to provide standardized benefits, in an impartial and automatic form, based on precisely defined rights and obligations, according to highly specialized procedures and with a national scope; all citizens possessing certain requisites were subject to the new rules. The institutionalization of solidarity through the pooling of certain risks (old age, disability, sickness, work injuries, and unemployment, to name the most important) across the whole population (or large sections thereof) served in this way to strengthen that link between territories, cultural identities, and participatory institutions on which – as noted previously – the European nation-state ultimately rests. The connection between the establishment of social rights and the objectives of political integration and nation building of central elites in many countries – in the face of an increasingly bitter class conflict under capitalism – has been well documented by empirical research (Alber 1982; Banting 1995; De Swaan 1987; Ferrera 1993b; Friedman 1981; Heclo 1974; Zincone 1992).

One of the core traits of the new technique – social insurance – was its compulsory nature. It was precisely the obligatory inclusion of wide categories of workers that allowed the new institution to affirm itself as a powerful redistributive machine, capable of affecting the life chances of millions of citizens. Obligatory inclusion meant that risks could be shared across wide populations, with three big advantages: a less costly protection per insured, the possibility of charging "contributions" (that is, flat rate or proportional payments) rather than "premiums" (that is, payments differentiated on the basis of individual risk profiles, as in policies offered by private companies), and the possibility of granting special treatment (for example, lower or credited contributions, or minimum benefits) to categories of disadvantaged members. In contrast to private and/or voluntary insurance, compulsory social insurance could thus produce not only horizontal redistributions – flowing from the "nondamaged" to the "damaged" – but also vertical ones, from higher to lower incomes (Alber 1982).

The principle of compulsory inclusion lends itself well to being analyzed in a Rokkan-Hirschman perspective. The new compulsory insurance schemes can be seen as very concrete manifestations of that process of institutional differentiation vis-à-vis foreign spaces and parallel internal structuration that characterized the European state system between the end of the nineteenth and the beginning of the twentieth century.

To begin with, the introduction of nationally differentiated systems of insurance added one extra substantive dimension to the external boundaries of the nation-state (that is, its demarcation from other territorial systems). From Westphalia (1648) to Vienna (1815), external boundaries were essentially of a military nature and had only a vague administrative-regulatory component – in the sense that within state territories there remained numerous internal barriers (for example, in terms of labor and even physical mobility) as well as a high degree of legal differentiation (Bartolini 2000b). The right to engage in a work activity of one's choosing only emerged with the dismantlement of the rigid guild systems and corporatist protections (Alber 1982) – the other side of this right being of course the rapid "commodification" of workers in the capitalist labor market (Esping-Andersen 1990; Polanyi 1957). The removal of barriers to free circulation as well as regulatory standardization across the state territory proceeded at an increasingly rapid speed during the nineteenth century, and the establishment of social insurance schemes with a national scope constituted a sort of quantum leap for certain countries in this respect. The first country to ever introduce compulsory insurance was Germany: in 1883 against sickness, in 1884 against work injuries, and in 1889 against old age. The German reforms had a vast international echo. Austria-Hungary was the first country to follow suit (in 1887 against work injuries and in 1888 against sickness). Prior to the turn of the century came Denmark (means-tested national pensions, in 1891), Norway (work injuries, in 1894), Finland (work injuries, in 1895), then France and Italy (work injuries, in 1898). The other countries took off with subsidized voluntary insurance, but shifted to compulsory schemes in the first two decades of the new century. At the outbreak of World War I, only Belgium was missing from the list; compulsory pension insurance arrived in that country in 1924.[7]

The significance of the new social-regulatory component of state borders became evident in the territorial adjustments that followed World War I. For example when Alsace and Lorraine returned to France, both regions had been enjoying for more than two decades the schemes introduced by Otto von Bismarck in the 1880s, which were much more solid and generous

---

[7] See Alber (1982) for a full picture and discussion of the sequence of introduction of compulsory schemes.

than those in place in the rest of the country. This created a pressure for improvements on the French government throughout the 1920s, which led to the establishment of a system of compulsory social insurance in 1928–30 (Baldwin 1990; Hatzfeld 1989; Saint Jours 1982). In its turn, when advancing its claims on the "unredeemed" provinces of Trento and Trieste (still part of the Hapsburg Empire between 1861 and 1919), the Italian government had to promise already in 1916 that in case of "redemption" it would maintain the more generous sickness insurance introduced by the Austrians in 1888 (Ferrera 1993b).

Second, social insurance schemes created new membership spaces internal to the territory of each nation-state. As brilliantly underlined by T. H. Marshall (1950), the extension of social rights was no less significant for the development of modern citizenship than the extension of civil and political rights. In contrast to the latter, insurance membership was typically extended upward rather than downward through the social structure, that is, from lower to higher incomes and from manual to nonmanual occupations (Flora and Alber 1981). At their origins, compulsory schemes only covered employees, and typically only industrial employees earning up to a certain wage. Only Sweden introduced from the beginning (1913) an old-age insurance scheme covering the whole population regardless of income or occupational status. Starting from the end of World War I, all countries began a rapid process of coverage extension. In Britain and Scandinavia, this process developed with just a few big waves of inclusion. In the continental countries, the Bismarckian tradition prevailed, leading to a sequence of differentiated inclusions, typically flowing from industrial employees to agricultural workers, then to the self-employed, and finally to other marginal or inactive categories. It is important to stress that even if occupationally fragmented, the continental schemes rested on a nationwide pooling of risks and standardized rules. Only the more traditional forms of social assistance to the poor remained localized and discretionary – with a gradual decline of salience.

Third – and largely as a consequence of the first two elements – the original establishment and subsequent development of compulsory social insurance became an important element in the internal structuring of all European nation-states, closely interacting with the existing cleavage constellations, with center–periphery relations, and with the wider institutional organizational order. In northern Europe, welfare policies reinforced the state's penetration of civil society and enhanced the latter's loyalty to the state and "nation" via materially substantial, organizationally efficient, and symbolically strong social sharing flows (think of the Swedish notion of a *volkhemmet*, that is, the welfare state as the home of all people). In many continental countries, on the other hand, social sharing arrangements remained characterized by a much lower degree of "stateness" and structured themselves (often at a slower pace) in accordance with preexisting social and/or cultural differentiations.[8] Thus, for example, in the Netherlands, subcultural pillars shaped social insurance virtually in their own image and likeness – the *zuilen* being at their origin confessional organizations with precisely social assistance goals (Therborn 1989) – and it took German occupation to make sickness insurance de facto compulsory. In its turn, the creation of pillar-specific social schemes contributed to freeze the cleavage structure and the *verzuiling* system (that is, the "pillarization" of Dutch society and politics) well into the 1960s. In Switzerland (to mention another extreme case), the federalization (that is, nationalization) of social sharing had to struggle its way upward fiercely against the stubborn resistance of peripheries (that is, cantons) to relinquish sovereignty on this matter. In southern European countries, finally, the structuring of welfare institutions was confronted with a particularly complex set of challenges: economic backwardness, regional differentiations, a harsh church–state conflict (especially in Italy), ideological polarization, and – last but not least – low administrative capacities. These challenges paved the way for the emergence of patronage machines and clientelistic dynamics (Ferrera 1996).[9]

The creation of the new membership spaces via social insurance served to reconfigure (and generally, to strengthen) the sovereignty of the European nation-state, in the sense specified previously. Not only did it enlarge the functional scope of centralized authority, it also offered new means for governing both exit/entry and voice/loyalty dynamics within the territory under its jurisdiction. The creation of new membership spaces within the state opened up various opportunities of entry and exit (or "staying out") on the side of social and political actors, greatly articulating their interaction. The new welfare policies soon became the object of increasing voice activity: voice for entry (on the side of social groups left uncovered), but also voice *against* entry (on the side of social groups who thought they were self-reliant or who regarded social insurance as a "trap of capitalism"). Besides activating voice, the principle of compulsion encouraged in some cases and countries (for example, again the self-employed, or most of the agricultural sector in southern Europe) a second type of response: *hiding* – employing

---

[8] According to Flora (1986), "stateness" refers to the degree of penetration of public institutions into the sphere of welfare, displacing nonpublic institutions such as churches and other intermediary associations.

[9] Rokkan distinguished between various possible channels of citizen influence on decisions for the territorial collectivity: the electoral-territorial (or electoral-numerical) channel, the corporate-functional channel, and also the traditional channel, based on kinship ties and local notables. While social policies became an early target of mobilization via the two former channels, and especially the electoral one, in certain countries the traditional channel continued to play an important role in the formation of social and political coalitions and thus also the internal structuring of the welfare state after the advent of mass democracy.

strategies to avoid membership or eschewing its costs by operating in the underground economy and/or evading contributions.[10]

In the wake of their structural consolidation, in the interwar period and especially after World War II, public insurance schemes turned into relatively autonomous channels for the shaping of social and political interests – channels that were moved and maintained through their own laws of inertia. The famous "freezing hypothesis" that Lipset and Rokkan (1967) formulated in respect to the structural consolidation of European party systems could be fruitfully developed in respect to welfare systems as well. In the latter case, the channeling of interests was driven less by a politico-organizational logic than by an economic and financial logic. The new membership communities created by welfare schemes had to safeguard those chains of redistribution activated by the original institutional choices. For a given insurance scheme, structural consolidation not only meant an organizational strengthening and in some cases a growing political interest in self-expansion, but also the gradual achievement of "actuarial maturation – that is, a self-sustaining equilibrium between contributions and benefits, given the risk profile of the target population. This was especially true for the occupational schemes of continental Europe, which more or less explicitly rested on actuarial criteria and thus incorporated a natural bias against any "path shift." After World War II in both France and Italy, for example, articulated proposals were made to create new highly comprehensive (if not wholly universal) social insurance regimes, but the constellations of material interests around prewar occupational separatism effectively blocked such proposals (Ferrera 1993b; Palier 1999).[11] Policy legacies and institutional feedbacks – which have become central notions in current theories about the new politics of welfare (Pierson 2001) – were already at work in the critical juncture crossed by European welfare systems at the time of their postwar restructurations.

The *trentes glorieuses* (1945–75) were the apex of the national welfare state. The coverage of its schemes reached its "natural" limits (that is, the whole citizenry, at least de jure). The more localized systems of protection were progressively marginalized in their financial size and functional scope. Sophisticated techniques were invented and deployed in order to improve and rationalize the extraction of taxes and contributions, govern redistributive

---

[10] For a discussion of hiding as a behavioral response distinct from both exit and voice, see Laponce (1974).

[11] The preservation of occupational separatism after World War II had of course far-reaching consequences in these two countries, not only for the organization of social protection, but more generally for wider dynamics of social consensus and political legitimation. In Italy, social insurance legislation (often "microlegislation") served the purposes of a strategy of "particularistic attraction" of the middle classes within the social bloc controlled by the Christian Democratic Party (Ferrera 1993b), while in France, professional separatism (and especially the separation between *cadres* and *ouvriers*) promoted forms of legitimation based, precisely, on a *differentiation corporatiste* (Castel 1995; Jobert and Muller 1987).

flows from the center, and deliver benefits and services to the various clienteles. Of particular importance in this respect was the adoption of the "pay-go" system of pension financing, whereby the contributions paid by active workers are immediately used to finance the benefits paid to pensioners. This new technique greatly expanded the scope for intergenerational redistribution.

Finally, alongside the various insurance schemes for the standard risks, new non-contributory programs of general social assistance were created, as well as increasingly articulated health care systems, providing a wide array of medical services. The new programs of social assistance distinguished themselves from traditional public charity to the extent that they were based on rights (for example, to a guaranteed minimum income in case of lack of resources) rather than bureaucratic discretion. Health care systems shifted in their turn the emphasis of social sharing from the provision of cash transfers to the provision of benefits in kind (pharmaceuticals, medical treatments, and so on). This shift made the institutional articulation of the welfare state more complex, because of the new role gained by service providers as relevant actors. It also made the welfare state more popular in general, and the European welfare state more distinct from its U.S. counterpart, which remained much leaner in terms of public health coverage.

Thus in the first three postwar decades, the "social citizenship" attached to state-national institutions displayed its fullest bloom and also its fullest degree of both external and internal closure. For nonnationals, it was rather difficult to enter the solidarity spaces of other states, especially when it came to deriving benefits from them. Under certain conditions, legal foreign workers were admitted into the schemes and thus obliged to pay contributions; but "vesting" rules concerning minimum contributory seniority often barred them from actually receiving benefits (typically pensions). The "principle of territoriality" – a central tenet of international labor law (Pennings 2001) – strictly reserved control over the most relevant aspects of social security in the hands of national governments, putting nonnationals in conditions of systematic disadvantage in dealing with issues of contribution cumulation, transferability, and so on (Cornelissen 1996; De Matteis and Giubboni 1998). More importantly, as a rule, nonnationals were still excluded from accessing social and medical assistance benefits, either directly through explicit nationality requirements or indirectly via "gainful residence" requirements (that is, the possession of legal work permits). Nationals, on the other hand, were virtually "locked in," being subject to the obligation to be members of public schemes. Internally, the level of voice activity and political conflict around welfare policies tended to increase, but the expansion of these programs gave also a big contribution to enhancing citizens' "loyalty" toward their national variant of welfare state. The availability of need-based benefits and "social minima" linked to citizenship contributed to strengthening such loyalty and enhancing general feelings of collective solidarity.

Welfare rights, legitimized through the electoral channel, gave a fundamental contribution for nationalizing the citizenry and accentuating territorial identities. As Rokkan noted:

> ...this sets definite limits to any effort of internationalisation and Europeanisation:... once broad masses of each territorial population have been mobilised through the electoral... channels it will prove very difficult to build up a genuine community of trust across the systems.... Once a population has developed some minimum level of trust in the efficiency and fairness of the territorial government, it is unlikely to favour the transfer of substantial authority from this body to agencies beyond direct electoral control (quoted in Flora et al. 1999: 265).

Survey data seem to confirm Rokkan's expectations: Public social protection is considered a "fundamental achievement of modern society" by vast majorities in all European countries; in most countries, the majority of people think that decisions regarding this matter should remain the preserve of their own national government (Ferrera 1993b).

NATIONAL CLOSURE UNDER CHALLENGE: ENDOGENOUS AND EXOGENOUS PRESSURES

Yet, already during the *trentes glorieuses*, some first cracks started to emerge in these solid institutional compacts, testing the ability of European nation-states to maintain monopolistic control over their social sharing spaces. Two main developments were responsible for this: one of endogenous and the other of exogenous origin.

The endogenous development is connected with the internal differentiation of social insurance and has to do with the creation of the "second pillar" schemes, most notably in the field of pensions. The problem arose already in the 1950s in the northern European countries, which had opted for universal schemes providing relatively low, flat-rate "minimum" or "basic" benefits. In the new postwar climate of greater economic prosperity and social mobility, such schemes were regarded as increasingly inadequate to meet the welfare aspirations of the middle classes. Thus some occupational groups (for example, skilled blue-collar workers and many categories of white-collar employees) started to subscribe to various forms of supplementary insurance, in order to enhance their state pension with additional benefits. Such initiatives, however, posed a number of regulatory and distributive problems, which prompted state intervention.

Not surprisingly, one of the fundamental dilemmas that governments had to face was the issue of compulsion: Was membership to second pillar schemes to be made obligatory – as in the first pillars – or should it be left voluntary? Another controversial issue was the public-versus-nonpublic nature of such schemes. In both cases, what was at stake was the degree of "closure" of this new space for redistribution along the membership axis. Choices on these critical fronts were doomed to have far-reaching implications in terms of allocative efficiency and distributive equity. Less explicit, but equally far reaching, were their "structuring" implications on the overall national patterns of social sharing. Social democratic parties and trade unions strongly favored, for example, the option of compulsory affiliation into publicly regulated collective schemes run by the social partners, which they saw as promising tools for strengthening traditional class allegiances and alliances. Liberals and conservatives, on the other hand, favored freedom of choice and market-based solutions.

Different countries made different choices. The two extreme cases are the United Kingdom and Sweden. In the former country, after a long controversy, in 1958 the Conservative government introduced a bill that established a public supplementary scheme, but allowed workers to "contract out" from it if they so wished, into nonpublic funds (Heclo 1974). This decision planted an institutional seed of high "destructuring" potential for British pension insurance. This seed matured in the 1980s, when Prime Minister Margaret Thatcher promoted a virtual privatization of supplementary pensions and set the United Kingdom on a course quite unique in Europe (Bonoli 2000; Myles and Pierson 2001). In Sweden, instead, the second pillar provision remained firmly in the hands of the state. In 1959 the Social Democratic government decided that all employees would be obliged to enter the new ATP (*allman tillagtpension*, or universal additional pension) scheme offering supplementary benefits on top of the basic universal pension – a highly controversial choice that sparked one of the fiercest political squabbles of postwar Sweden, but also consolidated the public and all-inclusive nature of this country's welfare state (Esping-Andersen 1985; Heclo 1974). The other Nordic countries aligned themselves with Sweden (though in attenuated forms). Somewhat later, continental countries with Bismarckian regimes also had to face the challenge of second pillar insurance: Most of these countries (typically Germany) proceeded with contractual supplementary schemes run by the social partners; France introduced a fragmented system of compulsory *regimes supplementaires* (Guillemard 1986), while in southern Europe the second pillar remained relatively underdeveloped well into the 1980s.

The issue of supplementary insurance did not affect the territorial dimension of social sharing; external boundaries and crossborder controls were not in question. The issue did affect, however, the nature and contours of domestic social membership spaces, creating new institutions and offering new entry or exit options for the various occupational groups. This in turn had significant implications both for voice (that is, conflict) dynamics and for redistributive outcomes. As mentioned, the space for maneuver that Thatcher could exploit to push through her market-oriented pension reform in 1986 can be traced back to earlier decisions taken in the 1950s. In a Rokkanian perspective, changes along the membership dimension of boundaries do matter for structuring dynamics, even within a framework of full national sovereignty/territorial closure.

In the 1960s and 1970s, however, the process of European integration was starting to challenge precisely this framework. As is well known, the expansion of the Common Market and the first steps of institutional supranationalization originated a creeping process of erosion of state sovereignty at large. A more specific development, however, began to weaken directly the external boundaries of national welfare states: the emergence of a supranational regime for the coordination of social security systems.[12] This body of rules specified that the conditions under which entitlements matured in a given national system could be exported or converted into the system of another member state. The regime made sure, in other words, that the new exit options opened by the Common Market were actually matched by corresponding entry opportunities – a true precondition for real exit, a point already well underlined by Rokkan (1973c).

The elaboration of the coordination regime was a rather lengthy and controversial political process. France aimed at a gradual but far-reaching harmonization of social provisions across the European Community (EC), while Germany was in favor of spontaneous mutual adjustments by means of a virtuous "system competition." The compromise was found in the Council Regulation 1408 of 1971 and rested on four basic principles: equal treatment for all EC nationals; the cumulability of insurance periods; the exportability of benefits; and the applicability of a single legislation – the *lex loci laboris* (Cornelissen 1996; Shoukens 1997). The regulation did not substantially affect the sovereignty of the member states regarding membership boundaries. As a matter of fact, this legal provision did not challenge the right of domestic authorities to define and change the content of their social rights. Moreover, the norm for settling conflicts of law – that is, clashes between external and internal rules – was set in favor of the latter: The single applicable legislation was to be that of the host country. The regulation nevertheless weakened social sovereignty along the territorial dimension, that is, in terms of control over external exits/entries: Nationality became an explicitly prohibited criterion and could no longer be used for filtering access into the domestic schemes. Furthermore, the principles of cumulability and exportability meant that states were obliged to let in and out of their borders "bundles of entitlements": imports of entitlements matured under external regimes (such as those from cumulability claims), or exports of entitlements to be redeemed in foreign territories (such as those from claims for payments abroad).

---

[12] Until recently, the coordination regime was seen as a relatively marginal component of "social Europe"; most observers implicitly took as a yardstick for judging the social dimension of the EU the components that were typical of national welfare states (that is, explicit redistributive policies). As noted by Giandomenico Majone already in 1993, however, the very existence of national redistributive institutions set inherent limitations to the establishment of policies of this nature at the supranational level and has pushed the EU to orient its activity in the social sphere toward regulation rather than redistribution (Majone 1993).

Thus, in the background of the national apex of social citizenship (1945–75), the issue of exit options from redistributive spaces was slowly but significantly reopened. With the creation of second pillar insurance, on the one hand, and the establishment of the coordination regime on the other hand, the monopolistic control of the state over both the membership and territorial boundaries of social sharing started to be undermined from within and from without.

The 1980s marked the beginning of a new phase for European nation-states, characterized by a rapidly increasing external "vulnerability" in the wake of multiple dynamics of boundary removal, especially in the economic and monetary sphere. The indirect implications of these dynamics on the autonomy of European welfare states have already been discussed at length by a vast literature, which does not need to be surveyed here.[13] For the purposes of this chapter, it is more important to focus on the *direct* implications connected to the deepening of European integration.

In a well-known study on the EU and national social policy, S. Leibfried and P. Pierson (1995) have suggested an articulated diagnosis about the declining sovereignty (in their terms, legal authority) and autonomy (that is de facto capacity to act) of the member states' social protection systems. This decline has been primarily and directly caused by negative reforms occurring through the imposition of "market compatibility requirements" on the side of the European Commission, the Council of the EU, but especially the European Court of Justice. These reforms are called negative because, aimed as they were at consolidating the internal market, they tended to strike down or at least to attenuate those social regulations that were seen as an impediment to the four freedoms – and especially the free movement of workers and services. More specifically, the gradual expansion of EU regulations – and especially ECJ rulings – have gradually eroded the following:

- *National control over beneficiaries.* In compliance with the freedom of movement, member states can no longer restrict welfare state access to their own citizens only. Workers of other EU countries must be automatically admitted too. In order to avoid controversies over the definition of "worker," the ECJ has itself elaborated through various rulings a wide *notion communautaire* of this concept, extended not only to the self-employed, but also to part-time workers, au pair workers, and even missionary priests (Giubboni 1997).
- *Spatial control over consumption.* On the one hand, benefits paid by each member state (for example, a pension) have become portable across the

---

[13] A useful analytical grid to sort out indirect and direct pressures for change is suggested by Stephen Leibfried and Paul Pierson (2000). For an articulated theoretical discussion of the increasing vulnerability of the welfare state to internationalization and detailed, updated case studies, see Fritz Scharpf and Vivien Schmidt (2000).

whole internal market. On the other hand, the insured of a given national system can increasingly shop around and consume services of other EU systems (for example, in the field of health care) – the so-called passive freedom of service.

- *Exclusivity of coverage on their own territory.* Member states are increasingly obliged to accept the "infiltration" within their territory of other countries' regimes. The most emblematic case relates to the so-called posted workers, that is, workers employed in country *x* who are temporarily sent to work in country *y*, remaining under the jurisdiction of the country of employment.
- *Control over access to the status of benefit producer.* In compliance with the active freedom of service, a state must grant foreign providers access into its national welfare system (for example, for supplementary, second-pillar insurance, or for health care services: see the section "Crossborder Mobility in Health Care" later in this chapter).
- *Control over administrative case adjudication.* Member states must in fact accept that other member states' bureaucratic agencies may determine beneficiary status (for example, being sick or disabled).

As a consequence of these processes, European welfare states have witnessed an increasing erosion of their external boundaries and of their capacity to control them. On the demand side, exit options from national systems have expanded for all workers and their families, in parallel with new entry options in the systems of other countries. On the supply side, the jurisdiction of a national regime has been extended outside its borders in certain cases, national providers can enter the membership spaces of other states, and, more generally, national authorities have seen their capacity to regulate and control restricted. According to Stephan Leibfried and Paul Pierson, all these changes have essentially transformed European welfare states from sovereign to *semi*sovereign entities, irreversibly embedded in an institutional framework characterized by a systematic pro-market bias and by the opacity of a ECJ-led decision-making process.

Leibfried and Pierson (1995) have offered a valuable analytical grid for ordering factual developments, and their diagnosis about an increasingly tight coupling of the Single Market and social policy during the 1980s and 1990s can hardly be questioned. But for our purposes, the nature and implications of the new semisovereign condition of the domestic welfare state need to be further investigated and qualified. The crucial aspect to be assessed is less what national welfare states have surrendered to the internal market (the "lost half" of semisovereignty, as it were) than what they have been able to preserve in terms of boundary control (the remaining half). Has negative integration (and especially the rulings of the ECJ acting as "market police") structurally undermined the institutional foundations of national social sharing, or do such foundations still lie under member-state control? Are there significant variations across different policy areas? And have some areas already reached critical thresholds beyond which boundary maintenance on the side of the state becomes impossible or irrelevant? We will address these questions in the next section.

As noted by Rokkan, in modern European history, the appearance of boundary transcendence options (generally stemming from the expansion of markets) has tended to provoke boundary-maintaining countermoves on the side of state-building (or state-keeping) elites. The last thirty years of social policy developments have been no exception. Member states have not acquiesced without resistance to the erosion of their sovereignty and autonomy originated by the advancement of negative integration. While basically accepting – after the approval of the 1971 regulation – the neutralization of the territoriality principle for workers and employment-related entitlements, member states have shifted the line of defense around three narrower but crucial aspects of their national social sharing systems: 1) the external boundaries of their health care systems; 2) the external boundaries of their social assistance schemes; and, last but not least, 3) the internal boundaries of social insurance (and in particular the issues of compulsory membership and public monopoly). Why have member states chosen to defend these three aspects? Health care and social assistance were less directly related to employment and to the free circulation of workers; the maintenance of state prerogatives could be more easily defended on both doctrinal and practical grounds. Compulsory membership and public monopoly were in their turn essential ingredients of national social insurance systems, thus fighting for their preservation was almost a question of survival. A summary reconstruction of developments on these three fronts is necessary in order to appreciate properly the import of semisovereignty and its destructuring potential for the institutional status quo.

Crossborder Mobility in Health Care

The 1971 regulation included a chapter on sickness benefits, covering both cash transfers and medical treatments. In this latter field, however, the coordination regime was tuned in a very conservative way (McKee, Mossialos, and Belcher 1996). Apart from providing emergency care for transfrontier workers and short-term movers, the mobility of patients seeking care abroad remained subject to prior authorization from competent national authorities (for example, the health funds of affiliation or the National Health Service [NHS] administration) – a filter that the regulation had dismantled in the case of insurance cash benefits. The principle of authorization was challenged rather early, in the late 1970s. Two rulings of the ECJ in 1978 (*Pierik I*)[14] and 1979 (*Pierik II*)[15] opened a serious breech, finding that authorization for treatment abroad was to be granted "when the treatment in question cannot be given to the interested party in the territory of the member state in which he lives" – irrespective, that is, of the coverage rules of the scheme of affiliation and of financial considerations. This ECJ decision risked opening up a syndrome of continental "regime shopping" for the best (and more costly) treatments, with uncontrollable consequences for national systems. Thus the member states reacted swiftly to these judgments and in 1981 forced a restrictive amendment to the regulation. This amendment not only confirmed the need for discretionary authorization, but reaffirmed the principle that only treatments already included in the health care package of the national system of affiliation could receive such authorization (Bosco 2000). In other words, national welfare institutions reappropriated control over eligible benefits – even if their actual consumption could be authorized abroad.

However, the whole issue was reopened at the end of the 1990s, again as a consequence of supranational jurisprudence. In the *Dekker* case[16] (regarding the purchase of a pair of spectacles in Belgium from an insured citizen of Luxembourg), the ECJ ruled that the refusal of Mr. Dekker's fund to reimburse the purchase conflicted with the free circulation of goods. In the *Kohll* case[17] (regarding orthodontic treatment sought in Germany again by an insured party from Luxembourg), the ECJ ruled that the refusal to reimburse conflicted with the free circulation of persons. In both cases, the ECJ argued 1) that member states do have the right to organize their health care system as they like; 2) that nonetheless, public provisions in this field are not exempt from the basic principle of free movement; 3) that the principle of prior authorization to seek treatment in another country under the rules of that country does not prevent reimbursement for the equivalent cost of treatment in the country of insurance; 4) that the principle of prior authorization penalizes service providers established in other member states; and 5) that the requirement of prior authorization (and *a fortiori* its denial) can be invoked only in cases of a serious threat to the financial balance of the domestic scheme or for reasons related to public health (AIM 2000; Hermans 2000).[18]

---

[14] Case 117/77. ECJ 16 March 1978, case 117/77, *Pierek I*, ECR I-825.

[15] Case 182/78. ECJ 31 May 1979, case 182/78, *Pierek II*, ECR I-1977.

[16] Case 33/65. ECJ 28 April 1998, case 129/95, *Decker*, ECR I-1871.

[17] Case 120/95. ECJ 28 April 1998, case 158/96, *Kohll*, ECR I-1935.

[18] In July 2001, the ECJ ruled on two other health related cases: the *Geraets-Smits/Peerbooms* (C-157/99) and *Vanbraekel* (C-368/98) cases. The ECJ basically confirmed its previous orientations, with two important additions: National agencies must specify in advance the criteria that they wish to apply to grant or deny authorization; and patients must be reimbursed in accordance with the legislation of the state in which treatment was received.

The *Kohll* and *Dekker* cases are unquestionably of great importance for the neutralization of territoriality conditions in EU health care systems (Pennings 2001). They have not reestablished the virtually complete recognition of the free movement of patients that had followed from the *Pierik* cases almost two decades earlier. But the national countermove of 1981 has been partly offset by the new judgments, originating a destructuring potential that – as we shall see in the following section – may lead to significant changes in the institutional configuration of this sector of the welfare state, especially in certain countries.

Social Assistance and the Residence Issue

Article 4 of the 1971 regulation excluded social assistance from the material scope of coordination. The rationale behind such provision was that the free circulation of workers required the portability of work-related entitlements, but not necessarily the neutralization of the territoriality principle for social rights unrelated to work (and contributions). Not surprisingly, member states wanted to reserve these rights to their own citizens. The sphere of asymmetrical solidarity (public support based purely on need considerations) presupposes in fact those ties of "we-ness" that typically bind the members of a national community – and them only. But the regulation did not provide a clear-cut definition of social assistance. Thus the responsibility of drawing distinctions fell on the ECJ, which from the very beginning adopted an expansionary orientation, aimed at bringing most of the controversial cases under the notion of social security (as opposed to social assistance) and thus under the scope of coordination. The landmark ruling on this front was the *Frilli* case[19] in 1972, in which the ECJ ruled that whenever claimants have a legally defined position that gives them an enforceable right to the benefit – with no discretionary powers on the side of the granting administration – national authorities cannot treat the benefit as social assistance. This ruling gave nonnationals access to most of those "social minima" linked to citizenship (typically social pensions) that had been created in many countries toward the end of the *trentes glorieuses*.

Again, the ECJ activism in striking down national boundaries in such a delicate area prompted reactions from member states, and a new regulation was approved in 1992 (no. 1247). Its text includes a fixed list of benefits that, for each state, are subject to limited forms of coordination, but it strictly subordinates the fruition of such benefits to residence requirements. Nationals of other EU member states can claim the social assistance subsidies included in the list, but they first must possess legal residence in the host state, and secondly they must "consume" the benefit in the latter's territory, abiding

---

[19] Case 1/72. ECJ 22 June 1972, case 1/72, *Frilli*, ECR I-457.

by the conditionality requirements attached to such a benefit (such as work availability).

In this new regulatory framework, the line of defense on the side of national systems thus shifted to the control over rules of residence. While the various European treaties are based on the principle of free circulation of workers, member states have maintained some important prerogatives in deciding whether someone can legally reside within their territory if he or she is not a worker. Family members do have residence (and benefit) rights and so have persons looking for a job, but only if these persons are receiving an unemployment benefit from the country of last employment and only for up to three months if they move to a different country. Residence eligibility for all other kinds of nonworkers (such as students, pensioners, unsubsidized unemployed, and so on) is disciplined by three directives (nos. 90/364, 30/365, and 93/96) that leave some room for member states to deny eligibility based on economic and other criteria. The host state can, for example, impose a sort of "affluence test," under which would-be residents must give evidence of "sufficient resources" higher than those income thresholds that entitle a resident to social assistance benefits.

As it did for the notion of "employment," the ECJ has recently taken steps toward defining a "Community concept" of residence (Mabbet and Bolderson 2000). In the *Swaddling* case,[20] for example, the ECJ said that the meaning of residence cannot be adapted to suit the unilateral and uncoordinated preferences of the various national systems, while in the *Martinez Sala* case,[21] the ECJ came very close to recognizing a Spanish citizen's right to German social assistance benefits purely based on her status as an EU citizen. But this "Community concept" of residence has still to be formalized; as regards social assistance, member states can still pull institutional levers to close off this sphere of national social sharing.

Compulsory Membership and Public Monopolies Contested

As discussed previously, the core element of the modern welfare state is the principle of compulsory membership within public schemes for the nationals (or residents) of a given territory. It is this principle that gives a solid institutional and financial foundation to national social policy as a key tool for redistribution. How have things evolved on this critical front, in the context of EU market making? Within this battleground, an important distinction must be drawn between the different tiers of insurance.

At the level of "first pillar insurance" (that is, the basic schemes of monetary transfer: the *regimes legaux* in France, the *assicurazione generale*

---

[20] Case 90/97. ECJ 25 February 1999, case 90/97, *Swaddling*, ECR I-1075.
[21] Case 85/96. ECJ 12 May 1998, case 85/96, *Martinez Sala*, ECR I-2691.

obbligatoria in Italy, the *Sozialversicherung* in Germany, and so on), the coercive monopoly of the nation-state has indeed been put in question before the European Court of Justice, but it has been upheld. In a landmark ruling of 1993 (*Poucet-Pistre*[22]), the ECJ established that the freedom of service cannot be invoked in order to exit from compulsory national insurance schemes.

At the level of second pillar insurance, however, the situation has evolved in a different direction. In a ruling of 1995 (*Coreva*[23]), the ECJ specified that public monopoly is not justified when the funded method of financing (as opposed to pay-as-you-go) is used and where benefits depend on contributions and their returns. As second pillar schemes are more geared toward investment, consumers should be free to choose and providers free to sell "the best investment opportunities." In a number of other cases, the ECJ contrasted attempts from the member states to manipulate domestic legislation in order to maintain or introduce obstacles to foreign providers of supplementary pensions and life insurance. In 1998, a directive introduced specific and detailed safeguards for the portability of supplementary pension rights, thus enabling the free circulation of workers affiliated to such schemes.[24] Finally, starting from 1997, a series of steps have been undertaken in order to establish a true "internal market" for supplementary pensions, via the removal of all direct and indirect obstacles to the free movement of covered workers and of service providers, on a common floor of basic prudential rules (European Commission 1997, 1999, 2001).

To summarize, for the internal boundaries of social insurance, the interplay between national and supranational authorities has so far resulted in the maintenance and protection of the central tenet of domestic social sovereignty, but has imposed a cap on it: Residents can be locked in to secure a proper functioning of domestic social insurance arrangements, but only up to the maximum coverage of their existing basic schemes, where solidaristic elements are more evident. Above the cap, however, member states have lost virtually all boundary-setting prerogatives, along both the territorial and the membership dimensions. The previously mentioned regulations of 1971 and 1992 (as well as the 1998 directive on supplementary pension rights) provide for the coordination rules that make these capped territorial/membership spaces compatible with the internal market.

These three brief surveys of case law and regulatory developments lead to some interesting conclusions. The first conclusion is that, far from being a linear, unilateral, and top-down process of erosion, the redrawing of crossstate boundaries in the social sphere since the 1970s has resulted from

---

[22] Case 159/91 e 160/91. ECJ 17 February 1993, cases 159/91 and 160/91, *Poucet-Pistre*, ECR I-637.

[23] Case 244/94. ECJ 16 November 1995, case 244/94, *Coreva*, ECR I-4013.

[24] Directive No. 1998/49 on safeguarding the supplementary pension rights of employed and self-employed persons moving within the Community.

a tug of war between the national and the supranational levels, during which the nation-states have been able in various cases to assert their interests and to claw back prerogatives regarded as critical for their sovereignty. Many boundary-maintaining countermoves on the side of member states have indeed been successful.

The second conclusion is that, far from ruling systematically in favor of the market, the ECJ has in some critical instances defended essential prerequisites for national solidarity (for example, in the *Poucet-Pistre* or *Albany* cases) or struck down national impediments not to the *market*, but to crossborder *redistributions* (for example, the *Giletti et al.* case[25]). In this light, the view of the ECJ as "market police" ought to be partly reconsidered; the issue of reconciling the principle of social protection with that of free movement in a widening market has been taken more seriously by the ECJ than is usually acknowledged.

The final and more general conclusion is that case law and regulatory developments have so far had a differential impact on distinct areas/tiers of national social protection. As regards pensions, member states have been able to preserve effective barriers around the principle of compulsory membership into public schemes in their first pillars (an essential bulwark for domestic redistribution), but have lost considerable ground at the second pillar level. In the field of social assistance, the reassertion of the territoriality principle after 1992 has given back to the member states important prerogatives in determining who can enter the "inner circle" of need-based solidarity. The critical fault line on this front is constituted by residence rules: The formalization of a "Community concept" of residence may in fact undermine national control over entries into this tier of provision. The balance has tilted farther from national control in the case of health care: Together with supplementary pensions, health care currently appears as the sector most exposed to destructuring dynamics.

SOCIAL CITIZENSHIP IN CONTEMPORARY EUROPE:
NEW BOUNDARIES, NEW STRUCTURING?

What do all the described dynamics add up to, in the light of our initial discussion about the structuring of social sharing at the national level? Let us return for a moment to the causal sequence charted in Figure 5.1. The institutional developments discussed in the previous sections indicate that a significant redrawing of social citizenship boundaries has indeed taken place in the last decades, largely (although not exclusively) as a consequence of European integration. Is there a way of capturing the nature and direction

---

[25] ECJ 24 February 1987, cases 379-381/85 and 93/86, *Gilleti et al.*, ECR I-95; ECJ 21 September 1999, case 67/96, *Albany*, ECR I-5863.

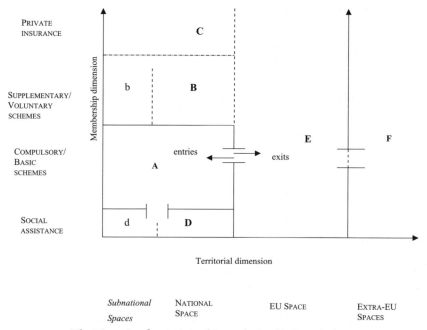

FIGURE 5.2. The New Configuration of Boundaries for Social Sharing

of change in a more systematic fashion? We will try to do this with the help of Figure 5.2, which outlines a space defined by two dimensions:

- A territorial dimension, on which geographical movements occur, physical borders between systems are located, and rules defining what can pass through such borders are of prime importance. On this dimension, the main novelty with respect to the past is the formation of a new space, the EU, next to (or underneath) the traditional space occupied by national systems. Through the four freedoms and the coordination regime, the EU can now legitimately encroach on national social citizenships; this new space is in turn increasingly demarcated by its own external borders and set against foreign territorial units and "third-country nationals": the *extra-comunitari* (as this group is called in the Italian language).
- A membership dimension, on which "movements" across the various layers or pillars of social sharing occur, institutional boundaries between schemes are defined, and rules over who is eligible to what benefits and over who can provide such benefits are of prime importance. On this dimension, the main novelty is the cap imposed on statutory, first pillar schemes and the emergence of an increasingly salient space occupied by supplementary (second pillar) and private (third pillar) schemes – a space that extends beyond the reach of obligatory affiliation and public monopoly on provision.

The intersection between the two dimensions and of their internal partitions generates a number of different subspaces, characterized by different kinds of boundaries. Space *A* is the historical core of social sharing systems; it includes those compulsory and public insurance schemes that still constitute the fundamental pillars of national welfare – as well as a prime source of domestic legitimation for the member states. This space remains relatively protected from external encroachments as far as its internal structuring is concerned: As discussed previously, the EU regulatory framework rests on the *lex loci laboris* principle, while the ECJ has so far upheld the principle of compulsory affiliation and public monopoly as prerequisites for social solidarity. The novelty for this particular space is the opening of a relatively wide gate, through which workers, some other social categories, and certain providers from other EU member states can enter and exit, according to the rules set by the coordination regime, which the ECJ constantly monitors (and often reinterprets).

Space *B* is the new area of second pillar schemes that is particularly important in pensions and health care. Here, as we have seen, endogenous and European pressures have combined to weaken the degree of both membership and territorial closure – hence the broken lines used in Figure 5.2 to demarcate this space both vis-à-vis private insurance and the larger EU space. The primacy of funding as a method of financing, the much stronger link between contributions and benefits, and the high importance of investment decisions have invited a growing tight coupling between this sector and the Single Market. Member states can still maintain some internal and external bounding prerogatives, but the creation of an internal market for supplementary pensions (and plausibly for health care supplementary funds) is only a few regulatory steps away. This market already exists for third pillar schemes (space *C* in Figure 5.2) in the wake of the liberalization of the insurance sector (Mabbet 2000). At this level, only fine-tuning is needed (primarily in the field of taxation) in order to strike down the remaining impediments for a fully free circulation of customers and providers throughout the whole Union.

Space *D* is that of means-tested benefits and services. Here the external wall of national systems is still buffered by member state prerogatives on rules of residence. The gate opened in space *A* allows nonnationals to access social assistance benefits "from above" (through the horizontal gate in Figure 5.2); a worker from another EU country can, for example, claim means-tested noncontributory benefits if he or she meets the requirements set by the host country for its own nationals. But "lateral" access is still barred. In this respect, the EU is not (yet) like the United States or other federal polities, whose citizens are free to settle where they choose.[26] As mentioned,

---

[26] This freedom tends to create "welfare magnet effects" – incentives for "the poor" to shop around for those subfederal units that offer more generous benefits. For a discussion of these issues, see D. Mabbet and H. Bolderson (2000).

steps have already been made toward the definition of a Community concept of residence (the fully federal solution); thus the wall is getting thinner, but it is still there for the moment and has not been challenged by the recently approved Charter of Fundamental Rights (Giubboni 2001). In Figure 5.2, space *D* and space *B* are divided by (incomplete) dotted lines that give rise to internal subspaces (*d* and *b*). These lines are meant to signal the emergence, within many domestic systems, of some internal differentiations based on territory rather than (or on top of) categorical membership. Regional and even municipal responsibilities in the area of social assistance and services are growing everywhere in Europe. In some countries (for example, Italy), regions may soon become the most active level of government for the regulation and even the creation of region-specific supplementary pension and health funds. Decentralization trends are (re)-creating infranational boundaries that – though much weaker than crossnational ones – could lead to new forms of fragmentation and may thus represent a threat *from within* to the maintenance of nationally bounded (standardized and integrated) social rights. In a few countries (such as Italy, Belgium, and Spain), this trend is affecting health care systems as a whole. In these cases, the dotted line of boundary "infranationalization" cut across space *A* as well – to the extent that the latter includes compulsory sickness insurance.

Space *E* corresponds to the "near abroad" of national welfare systems – that is, the EU space from which entries and exits are legitimized by either rights of free movement (especially of workers and services) or by portability rules. Figure 5.2 visualizes this space at the same level as the national space. In reality, what we find next to the latter are all the other EU national spaces. The EU space as such should be considered an underlying floor on which national spaces rest. The formation of this space has been primarily regarded in terms of "market making" and therefore as a source of disturbance and erosion for national solidarity. The ability of the EU to engage in "activist social policy" (that is, affirmation of itself as a source of "market braking" social rights) is limited by those inherent obstacles of "positive" integration that have been identified and analyzed by a vast literature.[27] In our perspective, however, in the midst of its negative and positive rule making, the EU has slowly started to perform two tasks with at least some degree of "structuring" potential. Along the membership axis, it has started to point toward the existence of possible pan-European solidarity publics. The *Frilli* and *Martinez Sala* cases discussed previously can be seen as attempts to stretch the boundaries of redistribution (including its inner core, that is, purely need-based redistribution) beyond individual member states, to the whole EU space. Along the territorial axis, the EU has in turn started to act as boundary builder vis-à-vis the "far abroad" of the member states, that is,

---

[27] On the concept of "negative" and "positive" integration and their application to the analysis of the process of European integration, see Leibfried and Pierson (2000); Scharpf (1996); J. Tinbergen (1965).

non-EU countries. Figure 5.2 includes a space *F*, in which the EU – through its visa, immigration, and asylum policies – is increasingly acting as the legitimate authority for drawing the lines. Of course, the new external territorial boundaries can be crossed following general and/or bilateral rules of access (a "guarded" gate is marked with a dotted line in Figure 5.2). But even when legally admitted, "third-country nationals" do not enjoy, at the moment, the same rights of movement and social protection as EU citizens.[28]

If Figure 5.2 offers an accurate picture of the new boundary configuration of social citizenship in Europe today, what further speculations can be suggested from its "destructuring" and "restructuring" implications (the right-hand boxes of Figure 5.1)? As noted previously, in Rokkan's perspective, the possibility of boundary "transcendence" (that is, the opening up of new exit options) is always likely to have significant destructuring consequences for a given political space; actors' resources and incentives will change, existing social coalitions and political alignments will be challenged, interorganizational links will weaken or break, and old institutions will be destabilized. If new, more external boundaries are created, a wider process of structuring and system building may in turn begin. The scope and intensity of such developments will mainly depend on two elements: first, the range and distribution of the new exit options, and second, the profile of the existing structural constellations. From Rokkan's own pioneering research and from a vast subsequent literature, we know that through processes of institutional freezing, these constellations can become very solid over time and highly resistant to change. Being the historical core of the modern welfare state, space *A* (and to some extent also space *D*) in Figure 5.2 definitely shows many features of frozen landscapes: Its internal fabric has close links with both the cleavage structure and the center–periphery structure and it is crowded with deep-rooted and interlocked organizational networks. Thus it should not surprise that such space has succeeded in remaining largely protected from external encroachments.

The space of supplementary insurance (space *B*) is instead of more recent origin and thus much less crystallized than space *A*. It is thus plausible to expect that destructuring dynamics will hit at this level first. The social reach and economic salience of the sector is quite considerable. In the field of pensions, for example, it is estimated that around 25 percent of the Union's population is now covered by occupational schemes. Around 5 million European individuals aged fifteen and over reside in a member state different

---

[28] A proposal to reform the Regulation (EEC) no. 1408/71 relating to the coordination of social security systems was prepared by the Commission (COM 1998/779) and sent to the European Council (COD 1998/0360). On December 3, 2001, the Council adopted the parameters for the modernization of Regulation no. 1408/71 and submitted the conclusions to the European Council in Laeken (December 14–15, 2001), which eventually endorsed them.

from that of their origin; the number is increasing and the enlargement will certainly contribute further to this trend. The value of funded pension assets as a percentage of the EU's GDP is also rather substantial: 20.3 percent for second pillar schemes, and nearly 50 percent more for third pillar schemes (European Commission 1997, 1999). The share of private expenditure represents in its turn between a quarter and a third of total expenditure for health care in most countries – a big potential market for supplementary forms of insurance. These data indicate that at this level of provision, there is a wide potential basis for interest articulation and aggregation, both via electoral and corporate channels. The relevant actors will not only be the trade unions and business and professional associations, but also the service providers themselves: insurance companies, provident funds, and mutual societies. Economic and political pressures are likely to build up for changing existing institutions and creating new ones, and perhaps in the future for challenging the traditional mix of statutory and supplementary provision.

In Figure 5.2, the internal design of the national space is a mere exemplification. In reality, each individual welfare state has its own mix of layers and pillars of different size and scope. Given the wide variation in structural profiles, we should expect that the potential destructuring (and reconfiguration) of European welfare systems will take place in different forms and degrees of intensity. This expectation is very much in line with the perspective of Rokkan and his constant effort to contextualize general trends and hypotheses according to specific "typological-topological" variables. A detailed contextualization of the destructuring hypotheses stemming from Figure 5.2 cannot be offered in this chapter. We can, however, advance the suggestion that destructuring pressures on national systems will be filtered by two main critical factors.

The first factor is the *institutional status quo at the national level*. In the field of pensions, what seems important is in particular the extant division of labor between basic and supplementary schemes, on the one hand, and the extant mix of public and private provision. In those countries where first pillar schemes are small and the middle classes *already* enjoy extensive exit options (such as the United Kingdom), the impact of the developments illustrated in the previous sections will not make much of a difference in politico-institutional terms. At the other end of the spectrum, in those countries where basic schemes play the dominant role and supplementary schemes only a marginal one (for example, Italy's pension system), such developments constitute, for the moment, only a distant source of disturbance. Stronger incentives for the expansion of second pillar provision might accelerate the consolidation of the new pillar (thus helping to improve the bleak financial prospects of hypergenerous basic schemes), but the latter will also be shaped by the emerging supranational regime and a Europewide market of pension funds – for example, forcing an institutional bias in favor of voluntary membership and individual choice. The highest potential for destabilization is probably to be found in the "Scandinavian model." As mentioned previously, the Nordic systems designed their second pillar in analogy with the first, by forcing all employees to enter the same public supplementary schemes. The original designs have been subsequently modified and fine-tuned several times since the 1950s and 1960s, and recent assessments of the state of affairs in the face of globalization and European integration indicate that the Scandinavian model is alive and well – financially and politically. These assessments do recognize, however, that the institutional balance is gradually shifting away from the tradition of "full universalism," giving way to a more "plural" landscape in which nonpublic and nonnational options will play a greater role in the social protection of citizens. Where this might lead in terms of institutional design and – more importantly – in terms of distributive outcomes is hard to predict at this stage, with speculative evaluations ranging from serious preoccupation (Hagen 1999) to moderate optimism (Alestalo and Kuhnle 2000).

In the field of health care, what is important about the status quo seems to be the internal organization of the statutory insurance system. The impact of recent ECJ case law is likely to be more direct on those systems that are based on a plurality of occupational funds (Belgium, France, Luxembourg, Austria, Germany, and the Netherlands), especially if these funds operate through ex post reimbursement (as in Belgium, France, and Luxembourg). The impact should remain more limited in those countries that have a national health service (the United Kingdom, Ireland, the Nordic countries, and southern European countries). But even in such systems, we might expect some destabilizing consequences. The idea that reimbursement is always due in case of territorial exit may undermine cost-containment strategies introduced at the national or subnational level; it may challenge the logic of functioning of national health services resting on in-kind provisions (especially their rationing policies); it may by implication lead to claims for reimbursement also in cases of partial exits, such as exits into the private market of the same country, thus strengthening the position of private providers. Some of these concerns (already vocally expressed in the policy debate prompted by the ECJ rulings) may sound exaggerated. But as suggested by Leibfried and Pierson, "the health area will be a first Europe-wide testing ground for the turf struggle between national welfare states and the Community plus the market, as represented by private insurance, producers etc." (Leibfried and Pierson 2000: 283).

The second critical factor that will "filter" national dynamics of institutional destructuring is the *changing constellation of cleavages and center–periphery relations*. We have already underlined – following Rokkan – that the original architecture of European welfare states closely reflected the cleavage and center–periphery structures that were active at the moment in which mass social insurance was introduced. The hypothesis discussed in this chapter is that these original architectures may have now begun a process of (partial) unfreezing, in the wake of both exogenous and endogenous pressures. We know that national cleavage and center–periphery structures have in their turn undertaken a process of transformation, with the incipient emergence of new subnational, crossnational, functional, and crossfunctional interest coalitions (Bartolini 2000a; Ferrera 1993a; Mair 1998). It is therefore plausible to expect a "mutual attraction" between the two processes and an ensuing reconfiguration of European social protection in which new social sharing institutions will tend to match with the new cleavages. Will this reconfiguration retain recognizable territorial boundaries, possibly emphasizing subnational lines of demarcation – a development in line with Bartolini's argument in Chapter 2? Or will social membership differentiation reconfigure itself within the Euro-polity container with a less marked territorial dimension and in response to new emerging structures of opportunities – a development more in line with Sidney Tarrow's argument in Chapter 3? It is hard to say at this moment; a more accurate reconnaissance would be needed in order to take sides based on some empirical evidence. What can be tentatively said is that there seem to be more signals of a reconfiguration along territorial rather than crosslocal, functional lines. Two trends in particular are worth mentioning.

The first is the increasing role of regions (and in some cases even provinces and municipalities) as basins of reference for social policy. This is clearly the case of social services and assistance – an area in which subnational units have gained prominence not only in implementing national policy with certain margins of choice and discretion, but also in setting autonomous standards and even in establishing distinct territorial schemes, often with "exclusionary" clauses for nonresidents. A similar trend is emerging in other policy areas: active labor market policies and, at least in certain countries, health care. With the reforms of the 1990s, for example, the Italian National Health Service is increasingly being transformed into a system of health care regions (Maino 1999). This first trend thus points toward a creeping *subnationalization* of certain areas of social protection, that is, a reconfiguration along infrastate borders, reviving or strengthening political units that often existed before the nation-state.

The second development is the emergence of new forms of regional cooperation across established state borders. On this front, the pioneering policy area is health care – not surprisingly, given the institutional developments previously illustrated (Hermans 2000). The EU has not only provided the legal framework for these new forms of cooperation, but also relatively substantial material incentives. The INTERREG initiative launched by the EU in 1992 to promote interregional cooperation offers, for example, financial grants to promote projects in the "Euroregions," that is, regions situated along state borders – which make up about 50 percent of the EU territory and absorb about 10 percent of its population. Many of these projects concern the pooling of health care facilities for the residents of neighboring transfrontier regions (Coheur 2001). The numbers involved in such projects are still relatively low, both in financial terms and in terms of actual beneficiaries. But new collectivities of social sharing are forming that cut across old state borders, yet are territorially defined and bounded.

It is true that we can observe also some signs pointing in the alternative direction – that is, the appearance of a demand for transnational, sectoral membership spaces. For example, in Brussels several multinational enterprises are actively lobbying to create a space for crossborder schemes reserved to their employees: the so-called pan-European pension institutions (European Commission 2001). The incentives emerging in spaces *B* and especially *C* in Figure 5.2 might soon change the structure of opportunities for transnational welfare entrepreneurs. But no specific organizational form has seen the light yet. Thus the signs pointing toward deterritorialized functional reaggregation are relatively weak at the moment.

All the described trends toward *national* destructuring will interact with developments at the *supranational* level, that is, the further evolution of EU rules; and with this we touch the last box shown in Figure 5.1. It should be clear from our reconstruction that European integration has produced a gradual shift from uncoordinated social sovereignties to coordinated semisovereign welfare states, increasingly subject to the constraints and to the *Eigendynamik* of supranational governance. Some institutional restructuring at the EU level has already taken place; turf struggles over what level of government has the right to do what (what benefits and what services are provided, and how are they defined) are bound to become more frequent and more delicate in the coming years. Among the crucial issues are the following: Will the principles of compulsory affiliation and public monopoly for basic schemes be retained? How rapidly will a harmonized EU regime for the market of supplementary benefits (especially for pensions and health care) be created, resting on a close coordination (if not harmonization) of tax regimes?

In the wake of this latter development, the supply at the European level of comprehensive, market-based alternatives to national provision could rapidly reach a critical mass, capable of significantly accelerating destructuring developments. One scenario that is frequently evoked in the debate is that of "Emu-winner" strata (higher income groups and informed consumers) responding to stronger incentives to opt out of public/national schemes (or actively demanding such options), choosing the "best investment" for themselves and leaving "losers" to fall on increasingly lean basic schemes and means-tested assistance (Hagen 1999). But there might be other, less gloomy scenarios. As noted by M. Alestalo and S. Kuhnle (2000), the possibility of exit does not necessarily lead to massive exit. In most European countries, cultural norms and institutional rules and dynamics do not make a U.S.-style "dualization" of society very likely. And there might be ways of creating new virtuous circles between public and private, on both the demand and the supply side (especially in the field of health care; see Ferrera and Rhodes 2000). It must also be kept in mind (as noted previously) that supranational jurisprudence need not rule in all cases and systematically in favor of more competition and individual choice. While it seems relatively safe to predict, in general, more moves down the road of supranational social governance, characterizing these moves as a one-way road to outright marketization and residualization of the so-called European social model seems at this stage to be an exaggeration.[29]

Especially after the quantum leaps of the 1990s, European integration has now fully entered the phase of system building. Clashing with preexisting (and largely frozen) systems, this process is deemed to produce lasting structural strains, and a long time may elapse before new institutional solutions capable of enhancing and safeguarding crosssystem integration are found and put in place.[30] Due to their deep embedding into the framework of the nation-state, European welfare systems will encounter many delicate dilemmas in their transition toward new multitier and multilevel configurations. A full-fledged reconstruction of social citizenship at the European level appears today so unrealistic as to render the question of its actual desirability a nonissue. But the landscape charted in Figure 5.2 shows that things are moving and some ideas have started to circulate about the introduction of modest but symbolically significant social rights attached to EU citizenship as desirable corollaries to free movement rights (such as a universal minimum income guarantee).[31] For all those who attribute prime importance to equality and solidarity, the rise of exit options and its destabilizing potential on national social contracts is mainly looked at with preoccupation and suspicion. But as Rokkan noted in his early commentary to Hirschman (Rokkan 1973c), exit can be a potent generator of positive (that is, virtuous) institutional innovation. Scenarios are still open, and if structures do count, it is actors who ultimately decide.

---

[29] I use here the notion as conceptualized by Alec Stone Sweet and Wayne Sandholtz (1997).

[30] For an interesting discussion of the EU as an "imperfectly integrated political order," see J. P. Olsen (2000).

[31] See the debate about the "Euro-stipendium" (in *Journal of European Social Policy* 11, 4) that followed the article by Philippe C. Schmitter and M. W. Bauer (2001).

6

Islands of Transnational Governance

Alec Stone Sweet

This book considers the changing relationship between territory and political authority, thereby focusing attention on the sovereign state and the issue of its continuing vitality. In the introduction, Christopher Ansell notes that, along with other factors, the "internationalization of markets" and the "development of new technologies" may have accelerated a "retreat of the state." As the world has shrunk – that is, as physical space imposes fewer constraints on trade, travel, and other forms of global communication – the classic techniques of rationalized state rule (public, authoritative, territorially based regulation of social exchange) have been undermined. In this chapter, I examine the construction of a system of private governance for international commerce.[1] I conceive of governance generically, as the mechanisms through which the rule systems in place in any social setting are adapted to the needs of those who live under them (Stone Sweet 1999). In its heyday, the so-called Westphalian state constituted the center of gravity for regulating trade, including trade across borders. Governance was largely hierarchical, authoritative *government*, or the administration of agreements between governments. Today, traders increasingly govern themselves, and the institutions that traders and their lawyers have created are substantially insulated from, while being parasitic on, state authority.

The Westphalian state, at least in its ideal typical form, provides a model of political organization that resolves fundamental questions concerning the relationships among boundaries, territory, jurisdiction, citizenship, and nationhood. It does so by equating state sovereignty with the internal control and external autonomy of national governments. Among other things, sovereignty implies the organizational capacity to police borders and determine what moves in and out. It implies that the state's law and organizations

---

[1] This chapter was originally prepared for the workshop "Boundaries, Territory, and the State," held at the University of California, Berkeley, in 1999. Parts of the original draft have been published in Martin J. Shapiro and Stone Sweet (2002: ch. 5).

authoritatively govern the activities of those who live or act within state territory. And it implies that the state is only legally constrained in its relations with other states by rules upon which it and other states have agreed.

The Westphalian state may never have actually existed. Conceptually, political control, however exclusive (an actual or an asserted state of affairs), and sovereignty (a purely juridical concept) are not one and the same; empirically, they need not be related at all. In this chapter, I argue that sovereignty and control are detaching from one another rapidly, at least with respect to transnational commercial activity. In the past three decades, a growing and increasingly cohesive community of actors – including firms, their lawyers, and arbitration houses – have successfully created a transnational space.[2] The space is comprised of a patchwork of private jurisdictions, of rules and organizations without territory, an offshore yet virtual space. These are islands of private, transnational governance.

The chapter is divided into two sections. In the first, I discuss, in a abstract way, obstacles to the emergence of a stable network of traders engaged in relatively long-range, impersonal exchange. I focus on three generic problems faced by any trading community: commitment, transaction costs, and institutional choice. In the second section, I examine three quite different regimes that have governed transnational commercial activity: the medieval law merchant, the Westphalian state system, and – my principal focus – the new *Lex Mercatoria*.

THEORETICAL CONSIDERATIONS

Let's begin by positing the existence of a pool of actors who would engage in trade with one another if it were profitable. I assume that these individuals are strangers to one another, in the sense that no pairing of them has had prior dealings, and no pairing shares a comprehensive normative system, such as a common culture or another institutional structure, to guide their relations.

There are good theoretical reasons to believe that extensive networks of impersonal exchange will emerge, and institutionalize as stable commerce, only if a set of linked problems can be overcome. These problems, which are present in all commercial settings, are all the more acute for strangers who wish to trade with one another. First, although our pool of potential contractants share, *a priori*, a common interest in constructing trading relationships

---

[2] The transnational space described in this chapter must not be confused with the supranational space constituted by arenas of governance within the European Community (EC) or European Union (EU) (see Sandholtz and Stone Sweet 1998). The latter is public space, constructed by and from the jurisdiction of the member states, and the sovereignty claims (such as, the supremacy of EC law) are delimited by state boundaries. The former makes no sovereignty claims.

with one another, they may nonetheless fail to do so if temptations to renege on exchange commitments remain powerful. Second, transaction costs are almost always higher for long-distance than for local trade. Most important for us, existing institutions, by which I mean the rules and organizational practices governing interactions in a specific social setting, may not favor the expansion of private commerce outside of the local boundaries drawn by these rules. That is, separate systems of parochial rules may impose, rather than reduce, transaction costs on long-distance trade. Third, to the extent that our pool of traders does exchange with one another, issues concerning collective agreements about the nature and meaning of contractual instruments are inevitably raised. Actors will need to choose or develop rules of contract, as well as techniques for resolving contractual disputes. As with trade-relevant institutions more generally, how such systems of governance are organized and operate will help to shape both the nature and scope of impersonal exchange into the future.

Problem 1: Cooperation and Commitment

The prisoner's dilemma (PD) game captures certain core elements of the situation confronting strangers who would exchange with one another, namely, a strategic choice context in which the dominant move is to cheat. To the extent that traders in our pool fail to live up to their contractual commitments, dyadic exchanges will tend to be one-shot deals. To the extent that this is so, conditional strategies, such as tit-for-tat (Axelrod 1986), do not emerge, and the trading system is stillborn.

Where contractants are not strangers, a pool of potential traders enjoys ongoing, face-to-face relations with each other within a shared normative framework, collective action problems and prisoner's dilemmas are more easily overcome (Hardin 1982; Taylor 1976). If communities are small and cohesive enough, social order can be constituted as a public good, and profitable individual exchange relationships can be sustained, without the prior construction of public authority or the state (Stone Sweet 1999: 160–1; Taylor 1982).

Game theorists make a related point in models of n-person, iterated PD games, and in elaboration of the Folk theorem (Fudenberg and Maskin 1986; Kandori 1992). Cooperation can be achieved by individuals, and diffuse within a group, if each player possesses some knowledge about the preferences of other players (Schofeld 1985) or there exists some means of assessing individual reputations for trustworthiness (Kreps and Wilson 1982; Milgrom, North, and Weingast 1990).

The individuals in our pool know that they can make themselves better off through exchange. At the same time, trader X recognizes that cheating trader Y can be advantageous if Y abides by the contract made (the prisoner's dilemma). On the other hand, *given adequate information about the past behavior of potential contractants*, X may choose not to cheat. Instead, X may figure that cheating Y today would make it more difficult to find new trading partners tomorrow, to the extent that cheating damages one's reputation for trustworthiness. Once any group of traders establishes trustworthy reputations with each other, they will only trade among themselves. And traders who fail to establish good reputations will be punished by being excluded from the arrangement. This solution, of course, depends entirely on the organization of information and monitoring capacities, a collective good that, given the myriad costs involved, may or may not be generated by the traders themselves.

Similarly, a group could seek to impose rules, that is, to create an institutional solution *ab initio*. Assume that, within our pool, a group of traders adopts the rule, "one must not cheat," along with a set of corollaries designed to give it life and agency. Like all norms, the rule would provide behavioral guidance, generate common expectations, and facilitate the monitoring of compliance. Nevertheless, the establishment of a new norm, being itself an act of cooperation, is subject to the same potentially insurmountable obstacles that all such efforts face. This is the prisoner's dilemma again, in the guise of an institutional design game (Tsebelis 1990: ch. 4). Further, once this or any rule has been established, problems do not go away. The critical test of a norm's robustness, or legitimacy, occurs when the social interest embodied in the norm comes into evident conflict with the private interests, or interest-driven objectives, of any given trader. In such a case, an individual may well choose to behave in contravention of a norm, especially if the probable outcome of conforming to it would be to leave that individual worse off. So, even after norms have been created, the linked problems of how to ensure compliance and to punish noncompliance persist.

Of course, if we assume that the social interest has been clearly expressed, that some mechanism of letting everyone know who is and who is not a cheater has been put into place, and that everyone will eschew trading with cheaters, cooperation will be the likely outcome. But assuming such things does not explain them.

Problem 2: Transaction Costs

Now let us assume that our pool of long-distance traders has established a regime bounded by robust norms that stigmatize cheating. All potential contractants share a commitment to the rule that trade promises shall be made and kept in good faith (in this sense, they are no longer quite "strangers" to one another). Our traders face a second set of problems: relatively high, and potentially prohibitive, transaction costs. Following Douglas C. North (1990, 1991), I understand the costs associated with any dyadic commercial exchange in a broad way to include all of the expenses incurred to complete that exchange.

If the potential gains to be had from long-distance exchange are out-weighed by these costs, or are smaller than the gains to be had from local exchange, trade will remain local. Relative to local trade within longstand-ing communities, the transaction costs of long-distance trade are likely to be far higher. Two parties to any commercial contract face bargaining costs, which increase if no common language, common understandings of how to measure the relative value of goods, or common currency or payment system exist. Contracting costs are transactions costs, and they are higher where a secure system of property rights and enforcement mechanisms has not already been established. Further, expenses related to the transport of goods, communications, insurance, letters of credit, other financial instru-ments, and the payment of agents (middlemen) will almost always be less avoidable, and the outlays higher, for long-distance, as compared to local, exchange.

For most of human history, most commercial activity has not been long-distance and impersonal, but rather local or autarkic. The models typically employed by economists to explain the logic of impersonal exchange – increased specialization through comparative advantage, and growing inter-dependence within and between markets – rests on a set of assumptions that ignore transaction costs. On the one hand, individuals and firms possess per-fect information (an assumption that bundles together, makes anonymous, and then denies the real significance of a long list of such costs); on the other hand, the only real constraints on trading activities, and the only structural determinants of outcomes, are the distribution of tastes for consumption and natural endowments.

North (1990) has argued that differences in national economic growth and development, whether measured crossnationally or across time within the same state, are due in large part to the relative capacity of institutions (such as, contract law) and of governmental organizations (such as, courts) to respond to the needs of those willing to engage in impersonal exchange, most importantly by lowering the costs of such exchange. In North's account, which relies on complex feedback mechanisms that manifest themselves in lock-in and path dependence, either a virtuous or a vicious circle is possible. Where institutions themselves impose higher transaction costs, impersonal exchange is stifled and economic growth is stunted. The question of whether or not a community can construct or adapt institutions capable of respond-ing to the needs of traders is therefore critical to the successful consolidation of a cosmopolitan trading system (across localities or regions in a given national territory, or across state boundaries). Exactly how institutions are constructed also matters. Traders can be expected to adapt their own prac-tices to institutions that are in place, thus reinforcing them. And they will seek to evolve new institutions, or abandon trade altogether, if they find their activities governed by dysfunctional rules. Finally, there are individual ac-tors who are advantaged by maintaining local hindrances to outside trading, and whose behavior and interactions have been tailored to these local rules, thus making the institutional setting more resistant to changes desired by cosmopolitans.

Problem 3: Institutional Choice and Governance

Finally, let us assume that our pool of traders has found ways to overcome the basic hindrances to long-distance trade discussed to this point: Traders enter into contracts in good faith, expecting that the benefits from exchange with one another will exceed costs. The third problem our group faces is one of institutional choice. How shall the new trading regime be governed?

In a world of competing sovereigns, where jurisdictions may overlap (medieval Europe) or where jurisdiction constitutes and more or less maps onto territorial boundaries (the Westphalian world), long-distance traders may have a choice of arrangements to govern their interactions. If they do have choice, they may decide to assign an already existing set of authoritative institutions to their contract. Or they may decide to build their own institutions and organizations in order to consolidate their regime. There is little social science theorizing about, and still less theoretically inspired empirical attention paid to, how such decisions are made or their consequences (but see the important paper by Mattli 2001). Nonetheless, I would emphasize the following three points.

First, our pool of traders cannot avoid the problem of institutional choice. Some (at least rudimentary) system of governance is required if an extensive network of long-distance exchange is to be constructed. For reasons already discussed, our traders require principles to govern their activities, such as rules of contract. Further, even if traders enter into agreements fully expecting to meet their own obligations, the contracts themselves are never complete. Most agreements of any complexity are "relational" contracts. The parties to an agreement seek to frame their relationship broadly, by agreeing on core commitments, but otherwise fixing outer limits on acceptable behavior and establishing procedures for completing the contract over time (Milgrom and Roberts 1992: 127–33). Just as important, contracting within our pool of traders generates a massive social demand for third-party dispute resolution, to settle conflicts involving interpretation of and compliance with agreements (Stone Sweet 1999). In the absence of rules of contract and organizational capacity to resolve disputes, our traders face fearsome uncertainties that may keep them from building and sustaining exchange relationships.

Second, our traders may choose to select an existing local (that is, national) regime on efficiency grounds, since startup costs are low or nonexistent and the organizational infrastructure is already in place. The downside is that courts do not simply behave as neutral third parties, vis à vis the contracting parties and their negotiated instrument. They also bring to bear on the proceedings the interests of another party, that of the regime itself

(Shapiro 1980). In resolving disputes, judges typically enforce the law of the regime. In the case of national courts, judges engage in norm enforcement, boundary maintenance, and social control, through their interpretation of the sovereign's statutes and through their own rule making (as registered in case law). For long-distance traders, local statutes and preexisting judicial precedent may not be well adapted to their activities. Instead, national regimes may impose, rather than reduce, the transaction costs of transnational commercial activity.

Third, despite the evident costs of creating their own body of principles to govern contracts, and of establishing an organizational (third-party) means of resolving contractual disputes, our traders may nonetheless seek to do so, primarily to enhance their own autonomy vis à vis preexisting jurisdictional authority. In escaping the control of national jurisdiction, for example, the traders can hope to create a more flexible regime adapted to their own specific needs. Yet in constructing a new system of governance, they face a dilemma inherent in all institutional design, namely, how best to keep it operating in light of their priorities. Unintended consequences are to be expected. Those who design new legal systems, for example, regularly find themselves in worlds that judges have constructed, to the extent that judges do their jobs effectively. Yet these worlds were hardly imagined, at the ex ante constitutional moment, by the designers (Stone Sweet 2000; Stone Sweet and Caporaso 1998).

TRANSNATIONAL EXCHANGE AND GOVERNANCE

My focus in the rest of this chapter is on the renaissance of the Law Merchant during the last decades of the twentieth century. I nonetheless begin by summarizing, for comparative purposes, how the problems surveyed in this chapter's first section were resolved prior to the emergence of the Westphalian state and then by the Westphalian state.[3]

The Medieval Law Merchant

The Law Merchant – or *Lex Mercatoria* – is a multifaceted term that serves both to draw boundaries around a community and its practices, and to denote a legal system. It describes the totality of actors, usages, organizational techniques, and guiding principles that animate private, transnational trading relations. And it refers to the body of substantive law and dispute resolution rules and procedures that govern these relations. I will use the term in the second, more narrow, sense. In doing so, I assert that the Law Merchant possesses meaningful (if not absolute) autonomy from traditional

[3] These first two accounts grossly simplify what are enormously complex histories and realities.

public sources of law, such as national statute and public international law. This view, which is rapidly gaining more and more adherents, provokes deep controversy among scholars, arbitrators, and municipal law judges (Berger 1999; Berman and Dasser 1998; Booysen 1995: 45–7; Carbonneau 1998b; Jin 1996; Rensmann 1998; Yu 1998).

The Medieval Law Merchant (MLM), which emerged and institutionalized between the eleventh and twelfth centuries, comprised a relatively comprehensive, relatively efficient legal regime for trade beyond "local" borders. This legal system was constructed and operated by the traders themselves. The functional logic of the MLM is straightforward: It enabled merchants to escape conflicts between various local customs and rules, and to avoid submitting to the authority of judges attached to preexisting jurisdictions (the courts of feudal manors, city states, local gilds, the church, and so on). By the close of the twelfth century, the MLM governed virtually all long-distance trade in Europe and, through middlemen and their codes of conduct, at critical points along the great Mediterranean and Eastern trading routes (Greif 1989, 1993).

The MLM regime was "voluntarily produced, voluntarily adjudicated, and voluntarily enforced" (Benson 1992: 15–19). The regime embodied certain constitutive principles, including: good faith (promises made must be kept); reciprocity, and nondiscrimination between "foreigners" and "locals" at the site of exchange; third-party dispute settlement; and conflict resolution favoring equity settlements. In practice, the MLM required traders to use contractual instruments, which were gradually standardized, and to settle their disputes in courts staffed by other merchants (experts, not generalists). Traders and their merchant judges placed a premium on quick judgments, and deemphasized adversarial procedure. The function of dispute resolution was not so much to declare a winner and punish a loser, but to resuscitate the contractual agreement and cajole the parties to get on with their business.

The effectiveness of the MLM depended critically on reputation effects, and the general fear of being ostracized from the trading community. As Paul Milgrom, North, and Barry Weingast (1990) have it, the crucial problem facing medieval long-range trade was not the infrequency of relations between any two traders, but the "costliness of generating and communication information" about the histories of potential trading partners. In their model (see also Greif, Milgrom, and Weingast 1994), the MLM acts as a kind of information clearinghouse about trading relations, making of reputations a transferable good, or "bond," within the community of traders. The MLM also provides a forum for third-party dispute resolution, reinforcing the "reputation system." Because the results of the merchant judge's decisions are recorded, traders' past compliance with decisions can be monitored. The Nash equilibrium of the incomplete information, n-person PD, is that no player honors the contract. The institutional setting supplied by the MLM, however, creates the conditions necessary for constructing social order without a coercive state apparatus, by making promises self-enforcing and by placing future contracting in the shadow of the law.

Milgrom, North, and Weingast recognize that to gather and disseminate relevant trading information and to provide dispute resolution are costly organizational undertakings, but they nevertheless imply that the MLM was a uniquely efficient solution to the traders' problem. While one could take issue with this part of the analysis and conclusion, it would seem to make little difference whether the MLM was the most efficient regime possible, as long as it performed more efficiently than existing institutional alternatives. However, it does warrant emphasis that, in addition to the costs of paying those who run the system, the substance of a third-party's decisions themselves may generate future costs of transacting and dispute resolving, if decisions are treated as having some precedential status. We have good reasons to think that third-party dispute resolution will generate something akin to a precedent-based discourse on trade and contracting, that is, that giving reasons for decisions is a practice that will be basic to the functionality of arbitration (North 1990; Stone Sweet 1999), but Milgrom, North, and Weingast ignore this possibility and its consequences. I will take up the question, with respect to the new Law Merchant, in the following section.

The Westphalian State

Until well into the fifteenth century, the Law Merchant provided the institutional underpinning for most long-distance exchange in the trading world. As early as the twelfth century in England, and thereafter on the continent, governments of states consciously sought, first, to emulate the main features of the MLM and, second, to subordinate the merchant's regime to state control. New statutes, designed to "move merchants into royal courts, and/or make merchant's courts less desirable" (Benson 1992: 19), absorbed large parts of the merchant's law into the state's commercial law.[4] At the same time, the European state gradually weaned itself from its more rapacious practices, such as repudiation of public debt and confiscations of property (Veitch 1986). By the close of the sixteenth century, the private commercial law of the nation-state and the state's law courts had reduced the significance and scope of the Law Merchant, while never quite replacing it. During the nineteenth century, which witnessed waves of nation building (and nationalism), extensive market integration, and huge reductions in transaction costs (due to improvements in transportation and communication, and to the emergence of modern banking and insurance practices), the salience of national regimes to transnational commercial activity was at its zenith.

Thousands of volumes have been written about how national judges resolve conflicts involving transnational business deals. In a world of sovereign

---

[4] Important innovations include the possibility of appeal.

states, each of which supplies its own authoritative law of contract and fora for dispute resolution, it is not always obvious and may be a point of contention as to which body of legal rules is meant to govern a transaction or a dispute that arises from it. Due to the complexity of the topic, and to the basic normative incoherence of the solutions at which judges have arrived, there is little point in going into great detail, beyond the following remarks.

For one or more reasons (which can fall within dozens of categories), a legal dispute may arise that involves the law of two or more jurisdictions. If that dispute comes before a national judge sitting on a law court of, say, state X, that judge may choose to assign the law of nation-state X to the case, and then proceed to resolve the dispute accordingly. Frequently, however, the national law of the presiding judge is very obviously not the appropriate law. The parties may have solemnly agreed, for example, that the contract law of nation-state Y would govern their relationship; the material dispute may involve business that was concluded according to very specific commercial rules provided by the law of two or more other states (rather than X's); and the business may have been, or was meant to have been, conducted outside of the territory of state X (and Y). In such cases, our judge must determine which legal system will provide the substantive rules to bear on specific aspects of the dispute, and then proceed to settle the case.

These practices go by two names, "private international law" and "conflict of laws," which, for our purposes, are synonyms. I use the word *practices*, because conflict of laws has virtually no substantive content (although it is often portrayed as a branch of law). The private international law is, rather, a set of *techniques* or *doctrines* that are employed by the municipal law judge to enable the resolution of certain kinds of disputes. These techniques first developed in Italian city-states (twelfth–fourteenth centuries), France (fourteenth–sixteenth centuries), and the Netherlands (seventeenth century), and, with the expansion of markets and trade, became widespread across Europe and North America in the nineteenth and twentieth centuries (Lipstein 1981).

Transnational actors today consciously work to avoid conflict-of-laws problems in national courts, because such problems generate uncertainty and other costs. They can do so in two main ways. First, they may incorporate specific national rules and procedures directly into their contract, in choice-of-law and choice-of-forum clauses (Farnsworth 1985). An American firm is likely to prefer this solution, as long as the law chosen is American. Traders may also allow their lawyers to select the law with which the latter are most familiar. And it may be that, for some kinds of business, there is a substantive advantage for one or both contracting parties to selecting one, rather than another, national law and forum.[5] The second technique is to

---

[5] This logic probably explains a great deal why a big part of the "globalization of freedom of contract" (Shapiro and Stone Sweet 2002: ch. 2) is the Americanization/Anglicization of transnational business.

avoid national law altogether, by explicitly referencing the *Lex Mercatoria* in choice-of-law clauses, and arbitration houses in choice-of-forum provisions (see the following section).

Institutional Failings. In the early-modern period, when regional – let alone national – markets were not well integrated, state building, market formation, the elaboration of codes of commercial conduct, and the construction of legal systems were tightly linked activities. For long-range merchants, there were obvious advantages to adapting their own activities to those of the state, including enhanced security and enforceability of agreements. Nonetheless, as transnational activity expanded, especially in the nineteenth century, it put pressure on states to recognize and adapt to the special needs of long-distance trade. The development of conflict-of-laws techniques represents one crucial way in which state organizations adapted.

State-supplied institutions probably reached their functional limits no later than the 1950s, prompting transnational commercial society to reinvent itself and, at the same time, to construct a new social order. In fact, institutions provided by the state system have lost their dominance and are now being gradually displaced.

Transnational actors' priorities remain autonomy, security, certainty, and efficiency, but actors increasingly came to believe that they could, on their own, do better than states. The indicators of dysfunction in national regimes are clear enough. On the one hand, as Lawrence Newman (1998: 1) puts it, "litigation means entanglement with a judicial process that is time-consuming, possibly biased in favor of locals, and perhaps even corrupt." Yet even assuming that judges will always do their best to be as efficient and fair as possible, the various national commercial codes and laws of contract are deeply entrenched, slow to change to inputs from more cosmopolitan environments, and have a lock on too many judges' imaginations. Further, conflict-of-laws techniques are in deep crisis. In the absence of such techniques, judges simply nationalize transnational disputes, which would be unacceptable to traders. Yet the use of such techniques may produce even worse outcomes for traders. In private international law adjudication, judges must decide which foreign law to assign to the case, according to a complex set of criteria including policy considerations, which normally leads the litigants to solicit advice (another significant transaction cost) on the relative advantages of various regimes.

Once judges have decided to apply the law of a jurisdiction other than their own, they have to behave as if they were judges trained in another national legal system. In essence, they "jump into the dark," and hope they can land upright. In the past two decades, a substantial literature has appeared showing that existing conflict-of-laws techniques lead to wholly unpredictable decisions, even within the same jurisdiction. In Klaus Peter Berger's (1999: 9–31) survey of the contemporary literature, conflict of laws is characterized variously, but always contemptuously: "an inveterate evil," "a murky maze," "creative chaos," "alchemy," and a "dismal swamp filled with quaking quagmires and inhabited by learned but eccentric professors who theorize about mysterious matters in a strange and incomprehensible jargon." Friedrich Juenger (1998: 277) bluntly states that, for proponents of the *Lex Mercatoria*, "it is a happy coincidence that at this time in the United States legal history the conflict of laws lies in shambles." Finally, litigation means waiting in line for a judge and then suffering the delays imposed by procedure, whereas the trading environment can change in a matter of weeks or even hours.

Not surprisingly, transnational economic actors increasingly take for granted the notion that national regimes make it more, not less, difficult for them to achieve efficiency and predictability in their relations with one another.

The New *Lex Mercatoria*

In the past three decades, transnational commercial activity itself has generated more and more of its own institutions. The trading community now commonly sees national legal systems as constituting an obstacle to doing business, and thus seeks to avoid them. With the help of lawyers and academics, this community is now engaged in the effort to "unify" or standardize contract law, and various standardized, a-national model contracts are in fact being intensively used. A system of private, competing transnational arbitration houses has emerged, providing traders with a range of alternatives to litigating their disputes in state courts. In consequence, national courts and legislators have adapted, most notably, by gradually but inexorably reducing the scope of their authority to regulate contracting and arbitration.

Transnational Contract Law. It has become easier and increasingly common for traders to select the new *Lex Mercatoria*, rather than national law, to govern their relationships. By doing so, they gain maximum control over their own relations. This control and the centrality of the *Lex Mercatoria* as a mode of governance are partly enabled by the "creeping codification" (Berger 1999; Ferrari 1998) of transnational commercial law. As this law is codified and used, its autonomy from national and public international sources of law is enhanced.

Projects to unify and codify transnational contract law have proliferated in recent years. The most important of these, which are run by independent institutes of practitioners and academics, have produced draft commercial codes of global and regional reach. Beginning in the 1970s, for example, the International Institute for the Unification of Private Law (UNIDROIT) began work on what would become the UNIDROIT Principles of International Commercial Contracts, which purports to be a comprehensive code for international commerce (Berger 1999: chs. 3–4; Bonell 1998).[6] The code (adopted by the Governing Council in 1994), organized in 7 chapters and 119 articles, deals with the fundamental notions of contract, including *pacta sunt servanda*, good faith and fair dealing, validity, interpretation, performance and nonperformance, choice of law and forum, and so on. Significantly, the institute decided not to submit the code to governments or to intergovernmental bodies, for fear that rounds of treaty negotiations would lead to changes and the reassertion of the priorities of states rather than traders. In Europe, various projects designed to unify European private law have been put forward (discussed by Berger 1999; Bussani and Mattei 1997/98; Ferrari 1998; Lando 1998), including the European Civil Code, which emerged in the 1990s and which has been submitted to European Community (EC) governments and the European Parliament. Although actual practice has outpaced such efforts, what is important is that the UNIDROIT and European codes are increasingly being referenced expressly as the controlling law underpinning transnational contracts.

Opponents of the *Lex Mercatoria* have questioned whether general principles constitute law, at least as they understand law in their own national context. General principles, by their very nature, are abstract, if not vague; but abstractness has its advantages. National contract law, when read as black-letter law, suffers from the same alleged problems. But codified private law has already been substantially "completed" by judicial lawmaking, which is partly what makes it ill adapted to the needs of modern business. Further, general principles of contract are functional for traders in that they give wide latitude to private arbitrators to tailor arbitration to the specific needs and wishes of the parties. After all, through contracts, parties create their own law; the *Lex Mercatoria* is meant to provide an institutional foundation for this law, not to replace it.

Last, these projects can substantially lower the bargaining and transaction costs of doing transnational business, relative to contracting under domestic law. Not only can traders avoid the myriad costs that inhere in using national law, including bargaining stalemates wherein neither party agrees to assign the contract to the specific national jurisdiction preferred by the other party. They can also easily access lawyers and contractual instruments that now comprise and occupy the virtual space of the transnational community. The

---

[6] The inspiration for the UNIDROIT project was the unification of U.S. contract law that took place through the American Law Institute's (ALI) Restatement of the Law of Contracts, as published first in 1932 and updated thereafter. The ALI's restatements, which appear in the form of black-letter law, both codify existing law (including settled case law) and creatively push solutions to unsettled questions, against a background of conflict-of-laws pathology. Like the ALI, UNIDROIT uses both comparative methodology and a functional analysis of problems of and solutions to achieving codification. The U.S. example, due to the federalist nature of American private law, is functionally equivalent to, and a microcosm of, the present transnational situation.

International Chamber of Commerce (ICC), for example, sells inexpensive model contracts in the form of a booklet and floppy disk; the software allows the contracts to be customized to meet specific needs. The introductory remarks to the ICC's model international sale contract bluntly states: "parties are encouraged not to choose a domestic law of sale to govern the contract" (International Chamber of Commerce 1997: 6).

Transnational Dispute Resolution. Traders want dispute resolution that will enforce, as the controlling law, the rules traders have selected themselves. Further, because traders want to maximize their autonomy, including at the dispute settlement stage, they are attracted to arbitration. As Juenger has it, "the tendency to keep transnational commercial disputes out of the courts, and thereby beyond the reach of local laws, is nearly universal" (1998: 266). Higher levels of transnational activity have pushed arbitral practice to organize and to formalize; and as the institutionalization of global arbitration of private commercial disputes has proceeded, the autonomy of the *Lex Mercatoria* has, again, been enhanced.

The "transnationalization of arbitration" story has a similar plot, many of the same characters, and much the same ending as the story just told about contracts. In the 1950s, UNIDROIT produced a Draft Uniform Law of Arbitration. This project was followed by UN Commission on International Trade Law's (UNCITRAL's) Model Law on International Commercial Arbitration of 1985. While there are differences, both are model codes meant to unify national rules concerning arbitration, through adoption as national legislation. Both emphasize what transnational businesses most desire from the *Lex Mercatoria*: the freedom of the parties to contract; the choice of arbitration and their arbitrators; arbitral discretion in tailoring the law to the case; procedural fairness on terms acceptable to the traders themselves; and restricted national judicial review of arbitral awards.

Some states have in fact adopted parts of these (and other) model laws in their own internal reforms of codes governing commercial transactions, reforms all but required by the explosion of global trade (see the following discussion). As important, the trading community has increasingly treated these rules as themselves part of the customary law governing their relations *(Lex Mercatoria)*.

In any case, the number of arbitral centers that handle transnational business disputes has grown at an astounding pace. In 1910, there were ten arbitration houses; there were over one hundred by 1985; today there are more than one hundred and fifty. For the biggest houses – the American Arbitration Association, the London Court of International Arbitration, and the International Chamber of Commerce – activity has tripled in just the past twenty-five years. The ICC, for example, processed 3,000 disputes during the 1920–80 period, but decided 3,500 during the 1980s alone. By the end of the 1990s, the annual number of filings of arbitral cases had reached 500.

The global scope of arbitration has also expanded. Walter Mattli (2001) gathered data on the national origin of parties to ICC arbitration cases since 1971. In the 1974–85 period, nearly 60 percent of the parties hailed from Western Europe, while less than 4 percent came from Latin America and the Caribbean, Central and Eastern Europe, and Asia. In Mattli's most recent period (1996–7), the share of business given to the ICC by West European firms declined to below 50 percent, whereas companies from Asia now make up 9.5 percent of parties to arbitration, Latin America and the Caribbean 11.5 percent, and Central and Eastern Europe 7.1 percent. Mattli also analyzed data on the regional basis of ICC arbitrations. About 70 percent of all disputes are interregional ones, wherein the firms involved originate in different regions.

From the point of view of traders, arbitration in an established house like the ICC makes good sense. In addition to the advantages already discussed, an arbitration can normally be completed within six months, and the price of the service can be selected according to the size of the financial stakes at issue or the desired complexity of the arbitral procedures.[7]

The Nation-State Adapts. The rise of the new *Lex Mercatoria* raises deep questions about the nature of law, and about the relationship of law to state power. Simplifying a very complex set of issues, traditionalists tend to portray the *Lex Mercatoria* as a set of practices enabled by states. Over time, states have granted, within realms constructed through treaty law and national statute, more rather than less contractual autonomy to transnational economic actors, while retaining ultimate regulatory authority over these practices. Underlying this view is a theory of law according to which only public authority – the commands of a sovereign – can produce law, or confer upon private acts legal validity. In contrast, proponents of the *Lex Mercatoria* argue that state authorities have largely "relinquished their authority to regulate" transnational contracting and arbitration, permitting both "to function autonomously," in what is, in effect, an "a-national" way (Carbonneau 1998: 293).

Traditionalists tend to focus less on what traders, their lawyers, and arbitrators are actually doing, and more on the linked problems of validity and enforcement of contracts and arbitral decisions. Their strongest argument for the continuing relevance of national law and courts to transnational commercial activity is straightforward: Traders need the coercive state for enforcement purposes. Through various international instruments, the most

---

[7] Even assuming relatively complex, adversarial proceedings, litigation is likely to be more expensive for the parties. As of 1999, ICC arbitrators were typically paid at least $300/hour, but rarely more than $400. A three-member panel would typically cost the parties about $100,000 in arbitrators' fees for a moderately complex matter. The ICC's own fee, which is billed separately, is capped at $65,000.

important of which is the 1958 New York Convention on the Recognition and Enforcement of Foreign Arbitral Awards, states have agreed to limits on the reach of their own jurisdiction in order to resolve collectively a host of collective action problems associated with soaring trade and the popularity of arbitration. The New York Convention is a short treaty, with narrow but important purposes. It provides that states "shall recognize" the validity of arbitral agreements, and that states shall, through their courts, enforce arbitral judgments subject, *inter alia*, to the exceptions of "inarbitrability" and "public policy."[8] Today, some 110 states have ratified the Convention.

Clearly the development of the *Lex Mercatoria* has been spurred by ratification of the New York Convention. Its broad function has been, in Thomas Carbonneau's words, to "eradicate systemic hostility to abritration . . . stemming from the view that arbitration amounts to a usurpation of judicial adjudicatory authority" (1998: 392). At the same time, the nation-state has adapted far more to the *Lex Mercatoria* than vice versa, going far beyond the black-letter dictates of the Convention. A broad pattern of ongoing "sovereign acquiescence" to the construction of the new Law Merchant has emerged (Carbonneau 1992: 119).

While I will turn to the specific situations in Europe and the United States shortly, three trends deserve emphasis. First, in the national law of most advanced industrial states, the recognition and validity of a contract, before a national judge, are now presumed, even if the contract law in question has no relationship to the law of that judge's jurisdiction. Second, national legislative provisions and judicial case law concerning arbitration have been dramatically transformed, in ways that enhance the autonomy of the Law Merchant. To take three examples, arbitral clauses are today commonly treated as separable from the main contract,[9] the scope of judicial review of arbitral awards has been radically reduced,[10] and issues of *Kompetenz-Kompetenz* have been largely resolved in arbitrators' favor.[11] Third, the public

---

[8] Article 6 V.2 of the Convention states that:

> Recognition and enforcement of an arbitral award may also be refused if the competent authority in the country where recognition is sought finds that: (a) the subject matter of the difference is not capable of settlements by arbitration under the law of that country; or (b) the recognition or enforcement of the award would be contrary to the public policy of that country.

[9] National legislation increasingly accepts what is known as the "separability doctrine," according to which the validity of the arbitral clause is not affected by the legal nullity of the contract of which it is a part. In essence, the doctrine forecloses moves by one of the parties to the contract to avoid arbitration by pleading the contract's nullity.

[10] That is, the legal validity, in national law, of arbitral awards is presumed.

[11] *Kompetenz-Kompetenz* refers to the formal competence of a jurisdiction to determine its own jurisdiction, or the jurisdiction of another organ. Modern arbitration statutes and case law largely accept that the arbitrator possesses the authority to fix the scope of its own jurisdiction, subject of course to the will of the contracting parties.

policy and inarbitrability exceptions to the recognition and enforcement of arbitral awards, contained in the New York Convention and thus in most national statutes, are being constructed narrowly by national courts and, in some countries like the United States, no longer have any practical relevance.

Before I proceed, a broader point deserves emphasis. Islands of transnational governance are not found everywhere, or at least not in the same form and intensity. Instead, they depend for their emergence, survival, and effectiveness, in part, on certain necessary background conditions. Most important, arbitration houses flourish in "international zones of liberalism" – those areas characterized by relatively stable forms of (a) political democracy, (b) rule of law and judicial independence, and (c) market-based economic organization. They are unlikely to emerge in zones of illiberalism, or to develop fully as robust systems of governance in mixed zones.[12] As briefly discussed (see Mattli 2001), companies from outside of Europe and North America have gradually been drawn to arbitral centers in the industrial West. But the legislatures and courts of states in Asian and Latin American have been more reticent to facilitate arbitral autonomy.

In the United States, the law on international commercial arbitration is entirely a matter of how the federal courts have interpreted the New York Convention, which the United States ratified in 1970. In this case law, American judges have appeared anxious to support arbitrators vis à vis disgruntled parties, and to reduce the scope of substantive review afforded the latter in American courts. The leading cases show the courts to be favoring the wider interests of transnational society rather than the specific interests of American business in any given case, even when public policy considerations raised by the dispute could be interpreted as overlapping with national security interests. Two examples will suffice to make the point.

In 1974, the Court of Appeal for the Second Circuit decided litigation involving a challenge, by an American company, Parson's Overseas, of an ICC arbitral tribunal decision to award an Egyptian company some $350,000 for breach of contract (U.S. Court of Appeals, Second Circuit [1974]. *Parsons and Whitmore Overseas Co. v.* Société Générale de l'industrie du Papier. 508 F.2d 969 [2d Cir: 1974]). The dispute involved failure, on the part of Parson's, to complete the construction of a paper mill in Alexandria, Egypt, a mill that the company had also agreed to manage for the period of one year after construction. In May 1967, as building was in its final stages, Arab–Israeli relations rapidly deteriorated, and the American company decided to evacuate its workers; the Six-Day War erupted a few weeks later. When Parson's subsequently decided to pull out of the project definitively, the Egyptian company

---

[12] The underlying logic of this assertion, which applies to public international regimes and organizations as well, has begun to be theorized (see Moravcsik 1997; Slaughter and Stone Sweet 1995; Stone 1994).

activated the arbitration clause of the contract, and an ICC tribunal found in its favor.

Parson's sought to have the award vacated on public policy grounds and, indeed, the dispute had policy implications. The U.S. Agency for International Development had agreed to finance a portion of the mill's construction, but financing was terminated with the U.S. government's decision to break diplomatic relations with Cairo. Parson's argued that U.S. foreign policy "required" it, "as a loyal American citizen, to abandon the project." The court dismissed this argument with a broad statement of policy of its own:

We conclude that the Convention's public policy defense should be construed narrowiy. Enforcement of foreign arbitral awards may be denied on this basis only where enforcement would violate the forum state's most basic notions of morality and justice.... To read the public policy defense as a parochial device protective of national political interests would seriously undermine the Convention's utility. This provision was not meant to enshrine the vagaries of international politics under the rubric of "public policy."

American courts have hardly wavered in their support of foreign arbitrators since. In 1990, for example, a federal district court forced an American company, Sun Oil, to pay a $20 million ICC award to a Libyan company, although Sun's inability to perform its contractual obligations stemmed from decisions taken by the U.S. government in pursuit of its antiterrorism policy (U.S. District Court [1990] *National Oil Corporation v. Libyan Sun Oil Co.* 733 F. Supp. 800 [D. Del 1990]). The dispute involved Sun Oil's decision to cease its participation in an oil exploration program in Libya, after the U.S. State Department prohibited travel to that country on U.S. passports. Shortly thereafter, the U.S. government banned imports from Libya, including of oil, and exports of goods and technical information, and Sun Oil's application for a license to export data and technology to Libya was denied. After Sun refused to abide by the ICC tribunal's decision, the Libyan company asked American courts to enforce the award.

The district court sided with the Libyans. The court rejected Sun Oil's claim that to affirm the award would effectively "penalize Sun for obeying... its government," and weaken "the ability of the U.S. government to make and enforce policies with economic costs to U.S. citizens and corporations," flatly declaring that "'public policy' and 'foreign policy' are "not synonymous." The court admitted that "Libya itself is not a signatory to the Convention... and [that] if the tables were turned,... a U.S. company would not necessarily be able to enforce an arbitral award against a [Libyan company] in Libyan courts." But, the court continued, "Libya's terrorist tactics and opportunistic attitude towards international commerce are simply beside the point."

The Supreme Court has pushed even further, all but abolishing the role of American courts in regulating what arbitrators do. In *Mitsubishi Motor*

Corp. v. Soler Chrysler Plymaith (U.S. Supreme Court [1985] 473 U.S. 614), the Supreme Court recognized the authority of arbitrators to interpret and apply American statutes when these can be shown to affect the rights and claims of one or more of the parties to the dispute. In *Mitsubishi*, the Court refused to review the merits of an award of the Japan Commercial Arbitration Association, an arbitration that turned in large part on how the arbitrator would apply U.S. antitrust laws to resolve the conflict. Declaring that arbitration represents an autonomous system of dispute resolution available to the parties, the Court went on to assert its functionality and underlying legitimacy:

By agreeing to arbitrate a statutory claim, a party does not forego the substantive rights afforded by statute; it only submits to their resolution in an arbitral, rather than a judicial, forum. It trades the procedures and opportunity for review of the courtroom for the simplicity, informality, and expedition of arbitration.

... As international trade has expanded in recent decades, so too has the use of international arbitration to resolve disputes arising in the course of that trade. The controversies that international arbitral institutions are called upon to resolve have increased in diversity as well as complexity. Yet the potential of these tribunals for efficient disposition of these legal disagreements has not yet been [fully] tested. If they are to take their place in the international legal order, national courts will need to "shake off the old judicial hostility to arbitration" ... and also their customary and understandable unwillingness to cede jurisdiction to a claim arising under domestic law to a foreign or transnational tribunal. To this extent, it will be necessary for national courts to subordinate domestic notions of arbitrability to the international policy favoring commercial arbitration.

Since 1970, it appears that U.S. courts have only twice refused to enforce foreign arbitral awards, and then only in part (reported in Stewart 1992: 191–2).

In Europe, national adaptation to the *Lex Mercatoria* is most visible in legislative revisions to the relevant code law (commentaries and assessments in Drobnig 1998; Hill 1997; Lörchner 1998; Rubino-Sammartano 1995). In the 1990s, the parliaments of England and Wales, Germany, and Italy adopted statutes extensively revising the law on arbitration, whereas the French regime was reconfigured in the 1980s. Reforms have been in one direction: to deregulate international commercial arbitration by enhancing the autonomy and a-national character of the Law Merchant. While there remain important technical differences, the new statutes treat international arbitration more liberally than they do domestic arbitration, confer upon the contracting parties a wider scope to choose procedures and the controlling law of contract and arbitration, codify a doctrine of separability (refer to footnote 9 in this chapter); recognize at least implicitly the *Kompetenz-Kompetenz* of arbitrators as well as their capacity to resolve conflict of laws issues (see footnote 11 of this chapter); and reduce the grounds for judicial review of awards to a bare minimum. In France, the new code aligned itself with ICC priorities (Carbonneau 1992: 121), even placing the *Lex Mercatoria* on "equal footing" with national and international sources of law as legitimate bases for awards (see Delaume 1995: 9–10). "The common thrust of the recent European statutory law," Ulrich Drobnig (1998: 195) writes, "elevates arbitration to the status of a true alternative to the traditional court system for dispute resolution."

There are at least three underlying motivations for deregulation. First, legislators and judges find it in the national interest to encourage transnational commerce. Second, court systems are overloaded. Providing for the autonomy of private international law arbitration drains much complex litigation for which national law is less and less relevant. Third, there is now international "competition for the 'business' of . . . international arbitration," and liberalizing is essential to attracting this business (Drobnig 1998: 196). In updating their own codes, German and Italian legislators claimed to be working to make their systems as hospitable to arbitration as that of France and the United States.

The states of Latin America have adapted much more slowly and less completely to the rise of arbitration and to the demands of traders for more contractual autonomy. By most accounts, the dominant factor is a legacy of suspicion created by previous experiences with state-to-state arbitration, mostly involving the United States (for example, international boundary arbitrations between the United States and Mexico). These suspicions have been formalized as the Calvo Doctrine: Any foreign national "seeking redress for alleged grievances suffered in a Latin American country . . . agree[s] to accept the remedies proffered by local law and courts (Luis Sigueiros 1998: 220). For our purposes, the doctrine means that foreign companies may not be afforded greater legal protection, nor may they enjoy different rights, than those afforded and enjoyed by Latin Americans. In many states in the region, hostility to arbitration is justified in terms of national sovereignty, which is in turn defined as the national interest in relation to the perceived dominance of the United States. That the latter has used military force for the benefit of U.S. companies operating in the region, including to protect them from the reach of national laws, gives a concrete urgency to sovereignty claims.

Ratification in Latin America of the major treaty instruments on the enforcement of arbitral awards (the New York Convention and the Inter-American Convention) is spotty; even where implemented, national judges are often loathe to narrow exceptions to the judicial duty to enforce awards, say, when the recognition or enforcement of the award would "be contrary to public policy." That said, in recent years, "a better understanding of arbitration is beginning to prevail, accompanied by a belated but firm awareness of the needs of international commerce" (Luis Sigueiros 1998: 221). National courts are today rarely willing to review the merits of arbitral rulings, for example. In the past five years, Brazil, Paraguay, Costa Rica, Panama, Uruguay, and Venezuela have all revised legislation concerning arbitration, modeled for the most part on the new European statutes. The underlying logic of change seems obvious. It is easier for Latin America, and other regions, to embrace arbitration to the extent that (a) houses of arbitration, like the ICC, resolve commercial disputes in ways that do not merely reflect the relative power of states, and (b) more powerful states have renounced national judicial control over arbitration. Put differently, the more a-national the arbitral system becomes, the more obvious it is that arbitration is designed to serve the trading community, rather than state power per se, and the less relevant are classic sovereignty concerns.

The Institutionalization of the Lex Mercatoria. In a brief account such as this one, little is lost in emphasizing functional logic – such as relative institutional efficiencies – as a major impetus of the construction of the new *Lex Mercatoria*. The institutionalization of arbitration as a system of governance, however, is a somewhat different matter. By institutionalization, I mean the process through which arbitral practices are consolidated as stable rules and procedures. The growing popularity of arbitration houses, as substitutes for national courts, has pushed arbitrators to maximize values other than the parties' private right to contract. Most important, they are increasingly moved by considerations of legal certainty – arbitrators prefer the word *justice* – not simply for the parties involved in a specific case, but also for future contractants and disputants. In other words, arbitrators are becoming – if with some hand-wringing and residual reluctance – lawmakers for traders.

To be sure, the arbitral concern for justice can be expressed in the language of efficiency, that is, as yet another drive to reduce transaction costs. Producing just and fair decisions, after all, helps to elicit compliance from the losing party, and to reduce the animosity of national judicial systems to the exercise of arbitral power, if enforcement becomes necessary. The less acute are compliance and enforcement problems, the more the house will attract more business, and the more their clients will be socialized into the *Lex Mercatoria*. In this way, everyone in the system is made better off. To achieve just results is to enhance legal certainty; and legal uncertainty is one of the reasons national systems (with their arcane conflict of law methods) had come to be avoided in the first place. A great deal could be said about these issues, but one point is clear: The balance between (a) procedural efficiency and (b) predictability of outcomes (that is, a concern for justice and legal certainty) is being recalibrated to the advantage of the latter. The more arbitrators care about justice, and particularly about using their decisions to help them obtain diffuse and prospective justice, the more arbitration will be judicialized (Lillich and Brower 1992); and the more arbitration mimics litigation, the more costly it will be to maintain the system.

Judicialization is proceeding along three linked dimensions. The first concerns who arbitrates. Whereas a single arbitrator was once commonplace, parties today typically demand three panel members, as "additional as-surance that [they] will not become victims of a single arbitrator's folie" (Newman 1998: 5). This is all the more true for relatively high-stakes dis-putes. Further, as arbitration has increased in popularity, bigger (in terms of money) and more complex (in terms of the contractual instruments) cases have been filed. Arbitration houses have had little choice but to replace the once-ubiquitous trade generalist with the technical expert, and to develop more formal and complex procedures to deal with the demands being placed on them (Dezelay and Garth 1996).

Second, arbitral procedures are developing quickly, including notions of discovery and other rules governing the submission of evidence. Partly this is a product of increasing adversarialism, as lawyers use the techniques of litigation to gain advantages, or level the field, in arbitral settings. Partly this is, again, related to a concern for justice. An arbitrator concerned with producing the fairest possible decision can hardly allow one or both of the parties to hide relevant facts, or selectively reveal evidence, or lie outright. The logic associated with procedural fairness in judicial settings reappears in the arbitral setting, all but naturally. As Newman (1998: 4) has it, "the recent trend ... has been to add more complex procedures, thereby providing the parties with greater assurance of a just result."

Third, and I consider this to be the crucial move, the *Lex Mercatoria* is now being built through precedent. It is a matter of dogmatic orthodoxy in positivist jurisprudence (Hart 1994; MacCormack 1978) that judicial dis-cretion can be counted as a virtue to the extent that judges actually use their discretion to enhance legal certainty (that is, to reduce normative indeter-minacy). They do so by developing and applying rules to govern their own decision making. The most important of these is the famous principle of formal justice: Like cases will be decided similarly. Arbitrators today are be-having according to the dictates of this model, and self-consciously so. They work to generate just decisions, but they are also careful to insist that deci-sions in equity are possible only if anchored in general principles. Further, if their clients act in ways that introduce adversarial legalism to the pro-ceedings, then arbitrators may be all but required to justify their decisions, that is, to adopt a nascent "giving reasons" requirement (see Shapiro and Stone Sweet 2002: ch. 2). Arbitrators need to defend their own reputations for fairness, vis à vis the parties to the dispute before them[13]; they also have a corporate interest in making the law that governs international commerce clear, transparent, and available to future disputants. Giving reasons for their decisions, and publishing them, allows them to do both.

---

[13] As Newman (1998: 5) puts it, "A reasoned award is one of the only protections the par-ties have against decisions born of caprice, bias, or intellectual indolence.... The practice of rendering awards without explaining them is not suitable for complex international matters."

Today, more and more decisions are being published, and certain kinds of decisions are treated by subsequent litigators as having precedential value.[14] The published rulings of arbitral panels sitting for important, high-profile disputes may be full of dicta, which the panel has designed to make general points about general principles; they do so to help codify the *Lex Mercatoria*. The doctrine of *stare decisis*, once only implied, is now explicitly invoked (see Berger 1999: 57–74, 214–20). Carbonneau (1998b: 16–18) refers to the steady emergence of an "arbitral common law," tailored to the needs of specific types of traders, through case-by-case dispute settlement. Unsurprisingly, the question of whether the creation of appellate instances for the arbitral system is being actively debated (Seventh Geneva Global Arbitration Forum 1999).[15]

The dynamics of the process should be obvious. The system can enhance legal certainty only by adding more cumbersome procedures and by delegating more lawmaking powers to the arbitrator-judge. Decentralized governance begins to take on the features of centralized government.

CONCLUSION

The story told here appears to be the most extreme case of the unbundling of state authority and territory presented in this book. At the same time, this history is not a marginal case. Rather, core relationships between states and markets have been reconfigured. The rise of the new *Lex Mercatoria* shows how globalization can be formalized as a system of governance, replete with all of the institutional trappings that the notion of governance implies. This new system, it bears noting, is parasitic on state sovereignty. On the one hand, it has been constituted by actors actively seeking to avoid submitting their activities to the state's jurisdiction. On the other hand, national courts and public international law remain in place, to be used selectively as needed. At most, traders, their lawyers, and arbitrators "rely on national courts as local outposts of the . . . system" (Pechota 1998: 263). Given present realities, it is difficult to see how the state's authority over international commerce, in the Westphalian sense of authority, could be reasserted. Instead, the sovereign has ordained that the sovereign shall no longer rule.

---

[14] Important decisions are regularly published in various specialized journals, often with commentaries by eminent arbitrators and scholars.

[15] The development of practices associated with judicialization and precedent in the *Lex Mercatoria* is strikingly similar to what took place in the pre–World Trade Organization (WTO)/General Agreement on Trade Treaty (GATT) regime (see Stone Sweet 1999).

7

Regional Integration and Left Parties in Europe and North America

Gary Marks and Ian Down

Regional regimes – authoritative arrangements facilitating economic integration in a particular region – have sprouted across the globe in recent decades. More than fifty such arrangements currently exist, among them the European Union (EU) and the North American Free Trade Agreement (NAFTA). They are an important – perhaps the *most* important – form in which competencies, formerly the preserve of sovereign states, have been rebundled. Yet there is no sign of convergence in the policy scope and institutional depth of such regional regimes. In this chapter, we argue that such variation has a decisive effect on their political support. So, to extend Sidney Tarrow's line of argument in Chapter 3, rebundling of authority may shape group support and opposition as well as the strategies that groups adopt to achieve their objectives.

Our focus is on mainstream left political parties in the member states of the EU and NAFTA. Political parties are vital in building regional regimes. When Jean Monnet built his Action Committee for the United States in Europe from the mid-1950s, he sought above all to gain the support of socialists and unions, because he regarded these groups as critical to the future of European integration. He realized that the European Community was a political, not merely a functional, project, and that its future would depend on the support it could muster from political parties and mass organizations (Duchêne 1994: 285ff). The European project was carried out by states, but Monnet was too canny to restrict his political canvassing to national governments – in any case, national governments in Europe are, above all, party governments.

The same consideration motivates Ernst Haas' approach in his classic book, *The Uniting of Europe*. The first indicator of integration, according to Haas, is whether "interest groups and political parties at the national level endorse supranational action in preference to action by their national government" (Haas 1958: 9). Political parties at the national and supranational levels feature more prominently than any other kind of group in Haas' analysis of integration processes.

Monnet and Haas realized that regional regimes have distributional as well as Pareto optimizing consequences. The argument that trade increases economic growth in the aggregate is unconvincing for groups who fear that they will lose. Yet, as both Monnet and Haas stressed, regional regimes can do more than facilitate economic integration. The logic of regional regime creation is fundamentally different from that of globalization. Regional regimes are not merely attempts to deepen economic internationalization. Or, to be more precise, they are not *necessarily* attempts to deepen economic internationalization. They may come to have a capacity for authoritative regulation, and this, we argue, is decisive for the support they receive.

To evaluate how the character of the regime influences left parties as they support or oppose regional integration, we first need to consider the economic consequences of regional integration. Economists have long analyzed the dynamic consequences of trade for previously protected factors of production, including labor, and it seems fair to suppose that the consequences of regional integration for labor may sway the positions of left parties on the desirability of regional integration. We begin, therefore, with the expectations of neoclassical trade theory for the relative scarcity (and therefore the price) of labor in response to regional integration.

Our second step is to refine these expectations by considering some economic consequences of regional integration that are not captured by neoclassical trade theory. We find, however, that an economic accounting of the net benefits or losses arising from regional integration is blind in one eye. It accurately predicts opposition to NAFTA on the part of mainstream left parties in the United States and Canada, but it goes badly wrong for European social democratic parties, most of which support, rather than oppose, European integration.

To make sense of left support for regional integration in Europe, we contend that one must investigate the regional regime itself. To what extent does the regime create a capacity for authority that can help left parties achieve their goals? Some regional regimes offer something beyond market integration – a capacity to regulate markets, to "rebundle authority" – and this, we hypothesize, exerts a powerful influence on left party support.

FACTOR INCOME EFFECTS

The reduction of barriers to trade is theorized to have distributional consequences for factors of production in a society, and to the extent that such factors coincide with political parties, it is plausible to believe that they will determine party support or opposition to regional integration.

Our analysis here is based on one assumption and one analytical choice. The assumption is that mainstream left political parties pay serious attention to the distributional consequences of regional economic integration for labor when they decide to support or oppose further integration. While the class basis of left parties has become more diverse in recent decades, these parties remain sensitive to the fate of labor. European social democratic parties are historically rooted in the class cleavage that divides skilled and unskilled workers from the owners and managers of firms, and while the lines between these groups have become blurred as white-collar employment has grown, social democratic parties continue to draw support from labor, broadly conceived. The Democratic Party in the United States and the New Democratic Party in Canada, like mainstream left parties in Europe, are entrenched among trade unions and are strongest among poorer, less privileged socioeconomic groups whose main source of income is labor, not ownership of capital.

Our analytical choice is to take the factor of production – rather than the sector – as the unit of interest aggregation. Both are utilized in the trade theory literature (Hiscox 2001; Verdier 1994: 7), but for our purposes, a factor approach makes most sense. Political parties in general, and left parties in particular, are distinguished by their factoral location more precisely than they are by sector. Moreover, regional integration is an ongoing process of increasing economic openness. While sector models assume fixed sector-specific portfolios and thus capture short-run interests, regional integration can be considered a long-term, essentially unidirectional, process. In the long term, the relevant characteristic of economic actors is their factoral location (Magee, Brock, and Young 1992).

The Stolper-Samuelson (1941) extension of the Heckscher-Ohlin theorem provides a basis for predicting the effects of regional integration on factor incomes. The theorem posits the now-familiar argument that returns to factors possessed by a country in abundance, relative to the rest of the relevant trading area, will increase with market integration. Conversely, returns to factors that are scarce in a given country relative to the rest of the relevant trading area will decrease with market integration.[1] In short, economic integration reduces rents generated by protection for the locally scarce factor (Alt and Gilligan 1994). A factoral approach suggests, therefore, that left parties will oppose regional integration in countries where labor is relatively scarce, and that left parties will support regional integration in countries where labor is relatively abundant.[2]

We use Edward Leamer's (1984) formula for calculating a country's relative labor abundance:

$$(L_I/L_{RR})(GDP_I/GDP_{RR}) - 1$$

---

[1] While Stolper and Samuelson (1941) discuss the effects on factor incomes of changes in tariff levels, as Ronald Rogowski (1989) and Jeffrey Frieden and Rogowski (1996) stress, the argument holds for any exogenous change in the costs of crossnational economic transactions.

[2] We assume a two-factor model, based on labor and capital and ignoring land. As Rogowski (1989) notes, land is of questionable relevance in the contemporary developed world given the declining size of the agricultural sector and the increasingly capital-intensive nature of agricultural production.

TABLE 7.1. *Labor Abundance in European Union and NAFTA Member Countries*

European Union						
Labor-Scarce Countries	**1988**	**1996**	**Labor-Abundant Countries**	**1988**	**1996**	
Austria	−0.1	−0.2	Greece	1.8	1.0	
Belgium		−0.1	Ireland	1.3	0.5	
Denmark	−0.2	−0.3	Italy	0.2	0.1	
Finland	−0.4		Portugal	2.0	1.1	
France		−0.1	Spain	0.4	0.6	
Germany	−0.1	−0.2	United Kingdom	0.2	0.1	
Luxembourg		−0.4				
Netherlands	0.1	−0.1				
Sweden	−0.3	−0.2				
NAFTA						
Labor-Scarce Countries	**1988**	**1996**	**Labor-Abundant Countries**	**1988**	**1996**	
USA	−0.2	−0.2	Mexico	6.3	5.6	
Canada	−0.1	0.1				

Note: A negative score indicates relative labor scarcity; a positive score indicates relative labor abundance. The factor endowments of countries that were not members of the EU are calculated relative to member countries in the relevant year. We have no theoretical expectation for countries on the margin between abundance and scarcity. We have treated all scores between 0.05 or −0.05 as being on the margin, and these cases are left blank in the table.

Source: IMF International Financial Statistics Yearbook, 1998

where L_I = total population in country I, L_{RR} = the sum of the populations of the member states comprising the regional regime, GDP_I = gross domestic product of country I, and GDP_{RR} = the sum of the gross domestic products of the member states comprising the regional regime.[3] We estimate this for each country relative to all other countries in the regional regime. A negative score indicates relative capital abundance, a positive score relative labor abundance.

Table 7.1 presents data on the factor endowments of EU and NAFTA member countries in 1988 and 1996. Labor is abundant in Greece, Ireland,

---

[3] Leamer (1984) makes use of gross national product (GNP) rather than gross domestic product (GNP). We opt for GDP because it reflects wealth generated within a country and hence a country's capital endowment. The use of GNP data does not significantly alter our results, except in the case of the United Kingdom, which becomes only marginally labor-abundant by virtue of its substantial overseas investments. We also utilize the Special Drawing Rights (SDR)–national currency unit exchange rate, in order to compare national GDP with regime GDP. We use the SDR exchange rate to minimize the impact of currency fluctuations on the calculation of labor abundance. Nevertheless, use of the dollar-national currency unit generates almost identical results.

Italy, Portugal, Spain, United Kingdom, Canada (1996), and Mexico, and scarce in Austria, Belgium (1996), Denmark, Finland (1988), France (1996), Germany, Luxembourg (1996), the Netherlands, Sweden, the United States, and Canada (1988). According to Stolper-Samuelson, regional economic integration will increase the price of labor in the former set of countries as the relative abundance of labor diminishes, and will decrease the price of labor in countries where it is relatively scarce.

Does this affect left party positioning on regional integration? Our data on party positioning is derived from expert surveys conducted by Leonard Ray (1999) for political parties in the EU and by ourselves for parties in Mexico, Canada, and the United States. We examine the positioning of left parties at two time points, 1988 and 1996, on a seven-point scale, ranging from −3 (strongly opposed to regional integration) to +3 (strongly in support of regional integration).[4] Left parties in labor-abundant countries score on average 2.02, while left parties in labor-scarce countries score 1.23. The difference between these means is significant at the 0.05 level.

However, there is much greater left support for regional integration in Europe – but not in North America – than one might expect on the basis of Stolper-Samuelson income effects (in only six of twenty-two labor-scarce countries do left parties oppose regional integration). Both the Democratic Party in the United States and the New Democrats in Canada are skeptical, but they are followed by only two European parties, the Finnish and Swedish social democrats in 1988. All other mainstream left parties in labor-scarce EU countries support regional integration. How can one explain this?

Perhaps regional economic integration harbors additional benefits for labor in Europe that escape factor comparisons. A more precise accounting of the net effects of regional regimes would include the benefit of trade for economic productivity, which is, after all, the main economic rationale for setting up a regional regime. However, as we discuss in the next section, international economic integration has serious negative consequences for the

---

[4] Eight to ten experts for each country evaluated the position of the leadership of each political party on European integration (in the case of EU parties) and on NAFTA (in the case of parties in the United States, Canada, and Mexico). The reliability of these expert judgments, indicated by the standard deviation as a proportion of the scale range, is comparable to the reliability of estimates produced by previous expert surveys. As reported in Ray (1999), the standard deviation of the expert judgments for EU political parties decreases slightly each year, dropping from 0.97 for evaluations of 1984 to 0.82 for evaluations of 1996 (on a scale from 1 to 7). The validity of our data can be established by comparing the EU party estimates for 1988 with Eurobarometer survey data for spring 1988, and party positions derived from party platform data collected by the Comparative Party Manifesto project (Woldendorp, Keman, and Budge 2000). Principal components factor analysis indicates that one underlying factor accounts for most of the variance in these three indicators. Differences in factor loadings suggest that Ray's expert survey data come closest to the underlying party positions (loading = 0.95), while the Comparative Party Manifesto data are a near second (loading = 0.93), and the Eurobarometer data third (loading = 0.87).

welfare state, the institutional position of labor, and the stability of employment – all of which escape a Stolper-Samuelson account. If this is correct,
there is even less reason to expect left parties in labor-scarce countries to
take a positive view of regional integration.

FACTOR MOBILITY EFFECTS

Neoclassical economic theory suggests that international economic liberalization increases the *substitutability* of labor irrespective of its effects on the
price of labor (Rodrik 1997). Trade increases the extent to which manual and
nonmanual workers can be substituted across national borders. It therefore
flattens the demand curve for labor (as well as shifting it to the left or right).

This has some far-reaching consequences. First, it leads to greater volatility in workers' earnings and hours worked. If employers can move jobs from
one country to another, a change in the price of labor in any particular country has a larger effect on demand in that country than if labor were not
substitutable. Hence, economic internationalization gives rise to greater job
insecurity for workers. It makes their working life more precarious.

The creation of an integrated European market brings workers in labor-
scarce countries into direct competition with workers in labor-abundant
countries. This weakens unions in labor-scarce countries. It is more difficult
for them to increase wages without endangering jobs, and to the extent
that workers perceive union power to be declining, union membership may
fall (on union membership, see Golden, Wallerstein, and Lange 1999).[5] If a
regional regime encompasses a mix of unionized and nonunionized firms, this
results in additional pressure on unions. Unionized firms will fiercely resist
union pressure for better working conditions if some of their competitors
are nonunionized.

Third, labor will have to shoulder a greater share of the costs of social
spending, including outlays on work conditions and benefits (Rodrik 1997;
Scharpf 2000a). Regulatory competition arises to the extent that firms are
able to locate where costs are lowest, yet maintain access to their home
markets. Increasing corporate taxes may squeeze mobile firms out of the
country, and may even lead to declining total tax yields. The result, as Fritz
Scharpf observes, is that:

...the terms of trade between capital, labor, and the state have shifted in favor of
capital interests, national powers to tax and to regulate have become constrained,
and governments and unions wishing to maintain employment in the exposed sectors of the economy must seek for ways to increase productivity, rather than for
redistribution (2000b: 224).

---

[5] *Ceteris paribus.* Institutional factors, such as the Ghent system of union administration of
unemployment insurance, may operate in the other direction

In short, the effect of economic openness is to undermine the postwar bargain between capital and labor, in which the government provides a generous welfare safety net and wages grow roughly in line with productivity in return for labor quiescence in employers' control of production.

Regional economic integration gives rise to a dilemma for the left: Increasing capital mobility imposes greater costs on labor at the same time that it reduces the capacity of the state to ameliorate those costs. The opportunity cost of raising taxes to maintain social insurance increases as the mobility of capital increases. An increase in taxation on capital is likely to provoke capital flight and thereby reduce economic growth. Governments may be pressured to cut welfare just as the demand for it increases (Stephens, Huber, and Ray 1999). By making it easier for international capital to locate in the country that provides the most favorable conditions and rules, economic integration increases the substitutability of labor across countries, pressures employers to demand labor flexibility, and fosters regulatory arbitrage. The negative consequences of regional integration will hit hardest in labor-scarce countries.

These considerations raise the bar for those who would argue that, despite Stolper-Samuelson, labor in labor-scarce countries benefits economically from greater market integration with labor-abundant countries. How, then, can one explain strong left party support for regional integration in the labor-scarce countries of Western Europe?

REGIME EFFECTS

Our response is that one must go beyond neoclassical economic theory to examine the *political* character of regional integration. Regional integration has the potential to be much more than market making, and in the European Union this potential is partially realized. European integration began as an experiment in supranational institution building alongside the effort to deepen economic cooperation among national governments. Those who dreamed of a federal European state have been disappointed, but a system of multilevel governance has been created. Significant levers of authority have been established at the European level that go beyond those necessary to facilitate market integration. To the extent that European integration provides the left some useful means to regulate markets at the European level, so, we hypothesize, social democratic parties will support regional integration.

In this respect, the European Union contrasts sharply with NAFTA. Table 7.2 evaluates the scope and depth of authority at the regional level in Europe and North America. While individual scores set out in Table 7.2 are open to debate, the overall contrast between the EU and NAFTA is beyond doubt. NAFTA today exercises much less authority than the European Economic Community (EEC) did in its first year of existence, in 1958.

TABLE 7.2. *Issue Arenas and Levels of Authority in the EC/EC and NAFTA: 1950–2000*

	EC/EU					NAFTA
	1950	1957	1968	1992	2000	2000
I. Economic Policy						
1. Goods/services	1	2	4 (3)	4	4	2
2. Agriculture	1	1	4	4	4	2
3. Capital flows[a]	1	1	1	4	4	2
4. Persons/workers[b]	1	1	2	3	4	2
5. Transportation	1	2	2	2	3 (2)	1
6. Energy[c]	1	2	1	2	2	1
7. Communications	1	1	1	2	3 (2)	1
8. Environment[d]	1	2	2	3	3	1
9. Regional development[e]	1	1	1	3	3	1
10. Competition	1	2	3 (2)	3	3	1
11. Industry[f]	1	2	2	2	3 (2)	2
12. Money/credit	1	1	2	2	4 (5)	1
13. Foreign exchange/loans	1	1	3 (2)	2	4	1
14. Revenue/taxes	1	1	3 (2)	2	3 (2)	1
15. Macroeconomic[g]	1	1	2	2	4 (3)	1
II. Social/Industrial Policy						
1. Work conditions	1	1	2	2	3	1
2. Health	1	1	1	2	2	1
3. Social welfare	1	2	2			1
4. Education/research	1	1	3 (2)	2	3 (2)	1
5. Labor-management relations	1	1	1	1	3 (2)	1
III. Legal-Constitutional Policy						
1. Justice/property rights[h]	1	1	1	3	4 (3)	1
2. Citizenship[i]	1	1	1	2	3	1
3. Participation	1	1	2 (1)	2	2	1
4. Police/public order[j]	1	1	2 (1)	1	2	1
IV. International Relations/ External Security						
1. Commercial negotiations	1	1	3	5	5	1
2. Economic-military assistance	1	1	1	2	4 (2)	1
3. Diplomacy/IGO membership	1	1	2 (1)	2	4 (3)	1
4. Defense/war	1	1	1	2	3 (2)	1

Code:

1 = *All policy decisions at national level*

2 = *Only some policy decisions at supranational level*

3 = *Policy decisions at both national/supranational level*
4 = *Mostly policy decisions at supranational level*
5 = *All policy decisions at supranational level*
Notes:
[a] Category not in Lindberg and Scheingold (1970). Schmitter (1996b) estimates for 1950–68.
[b] Category not in Lindberg and Scheingold (1970). Schmitter's (1996b) estimates for 1950–68.
[c] Category not in Lindberg and Scheingold (1970). Schmitter's (1996b) estimates for 1950–68.
[d] Defined as "exploitation and protection of natural resources" in Lindberg and Scheingold (1970).
[e] Category not in Lindberg and Scheingold (1970). Schmitter's (1996b) estimates for 1950–68.
[f] Called "economic development and planning" in Lindberg and Scheingold (1970).
[g] Called "counter-cyclical policy" in Lindberg and Scheingold (1970).
[h] Category not in Lindberg and Scheingold (1970). Schmitter's (1996b) estimates for 1950–68.
[i] Category not in Lindberg and Scheingold (1970). Schmitter's (1996b) estimates for 1950–68.
[j] Called "public health, safety and maintenance of public order" in Lindberg and Scheingold (1970).
Source: EC/EU 1950–68: Lindberg and Scheingold (1970: 67–71). Source for estimates, EC/EU 1992–2000, Schmitter (1996b: 125–6). Estimates for 1992 and 2000 are based on projections from existing treaty obligations and obligations undertaken subsequently. Schmitter's scores were based on judgments provided by Geoffrey Garrett, Peter Lange, Gary Marks, Philippe C. Schmitter, and David Soskice in March 1992. Scores in parentheses for 1968 represent *ex post* revaluations in March 1992 of the original scores in Lindberg and Scheingold (1970) by Garrett et al. Scores in parentheses for 2000 represent *ex post* revaluations in March 2000 of the original scores in Schmitter (1996b) by Liesber Hooghe and Gary Marks (2001a). Scores for NAFTA 2000 are those of the authors of this chapter.

   After the Maastricht Treaty (1993) and the Treaty of Amsterdam (1997), the EU has come to share authority with national governments in several policy areas relevant to the mainstream left, including social, cohesion, environmental, and employment policy. The expectation is that monetary integration will give rise to serious pressures for the creation of a fiscal policy to counter asymmetries of response to exogenous economic shocks within the Union. Decision making in the EU has become more open to democratic (and, therefore, social democratic) pressures. The European Parliament has come to play a progressively larger role in decision making with the introduction and generalization of the cooperation procedure after 1986 and, from 1993, the codecision procedure. In the year 2000, around 80 percent of all legislation before the Council of Ministers was handled by qualified majority, not unanimity (Hooghe and Marks 2001a). Interest groups, including trade unions and a variety of social movements, have mobilized directly at the European level (Imig and Tarrow 2001; Wessels forthcoming). The European Union is no longer the preserve of national governments operating in a business-dominated climate. On the contrary, the EU has become a contested polity in which a social democratic project for regulated capitalism competes with neoliberal demands to intensify regulatory competition (Hooghe and Marks 1999).

It should nevertheless be noted that the European Union is limited for social democratic purposes in several respects. First, the European Court of Justice (ECJ) is institutionally biased away from *positive* regulation – regulation to achieve social objectives – and toward *negative* regulation, that is, the elimination of barriers to market integration (Scharpf 1996, 1999). Second, the weakness of a European identity poses a formidable bar to serious redistribution at the European level. It is simply not conceivable to re-create the national welfare state at the European level. Third, deep-seated differences among member states in the way they organize their economies make it difficult to envisage a social democratic brand of capitalism across the EU as a whole. Finally, social democrats who wish to deepen European governance must contend with a widespread perception that the EU is wasteful, intransparent, and undemocratic.

The result is an ongoing debate among social democrats about regulated capitalism at the European level (Pollack 2000). To the extent that European regulated capitalism is deemed infeasible, it makes more sense to defend national freedom of action than to press for European regulation. Social democrats have certainly been pulled in different directions on key issues of fiscal and tax policy (Kulahci 2002). But the main thrust of social democratic strategy has been to extend European regulation in piecemeal fashion on a broad front. Since the mid-1980s, social democrats have campaigned for increased powers for the European Parliament, more majority voting in the Council of Ministers, the creation of a "Social Europe" with more stringent health and safety rules, environmental regulations, workers' rights to information, equal pay, and gender rights (Hix 1999; Ladrech and Marlière 1999). The manifesto of the European Socialist Party (PES) for the European parliamentary election of 1999 contrasts its support for "market economy" with its rejection of a "market society." It goes on to list areas in which more European cooperation would be desirable, including employment policy, transport and telecommunications, social policy, foreign policy, and efforts to constrain tax competition (Party of European Socialists 1999). While the EU is no panacea for the deficiencies of the national state, it nonetheless serves social democratic objectives.

This line of argument has implications for variation among European left parties across time and across countries:

- As the EU has deepened over the past decades to become more than a market-making regime, so one would expect social democratic parties to tilt toward support. This difference should be evident in the span of time for which we have data on party positioning: 1988, three years after the Single Market Act, and 1996, three years after the Maastricht Treaty.
- The decision to join (or leave) a regional regime is fundamentally different from the decision to deepen (or retrench) an existing regime. If entry is on the agenda, a party will evaluate the net benefits of membership

against national autonomy. Once a country is de facto locked in, then the decision becomes one of comparing the relative benefits of different levels of integration. Given what we have argued in this section, we have a substantive expectation: Once a mainstream left party recognizes that there is no escape, it may wish to create a regional polity that can regulate as well as deepen markets. Left parties will either try to avoid regional economic integration altogether or they will seek to endow the regime with a greater capacity for authoritative social democratic regulation.

EVIDENCE

We have developed, in onionlike fashion, a set of expectations about how left parties respond to regional integration. We began by assessing the implications of neoclassical and institutional economic theory for labor, and we have concluded by theorizing that left parties respond to the regional regime itself and the extent to which it provides them with opportunities to achieve some of their goals.

Figure 7.1 applies these hypotheses to twenty-one political parties at two time points. We bifurcate our universe of left parties in three stages. The scores after each party indicate, for successive time periods, the level of party support for regional integration in 1988 and 1996.

First, we divide left parties according to whether labor in their country is relatively scarce or relatively abundant compared to other countries in the regional regime. Our expectation is that left parties will support regional economic integration if labor in their country becomes more scarce and will be opposed if labor becomes more abundant. As noted, the mean score for left party support of the regional regime in labor-abundant countries is 2.02, while that for left parties in labor-scarce countries is 1.23.

Our second bifurcation captures whether the regional regime has some capacity for positive market regulation. This distinguishes powerfully among left parties in countries where, according to Stolper-Samuelson, labor will become less scarce as a result of economic integration. One branch, at the extreme left of Figure 7.1, contains the U.S. Democratic Party and the Canadian New Democratic Party. These are, by far, the most anti-integration parties among the parties we examine, with a mean score of −1.38 on our seven-point scale. Labor in the United States and Canada is scarce relative to Mexico, and NAFTA offers no offsetting authoritative capacity. Regional integration in NAFTA is market integration and nothing more, and left parties in the United States and Canada fear the distributional consequences.

Left parties in the labor-scarce countries of the European Union, by contrast, regard regional integration as the creation of both a multilevel polity and a market economy. The EU intensifies the distributional pressures posited by Stolper-Samuelson and penalizes less mobile factors of production. But

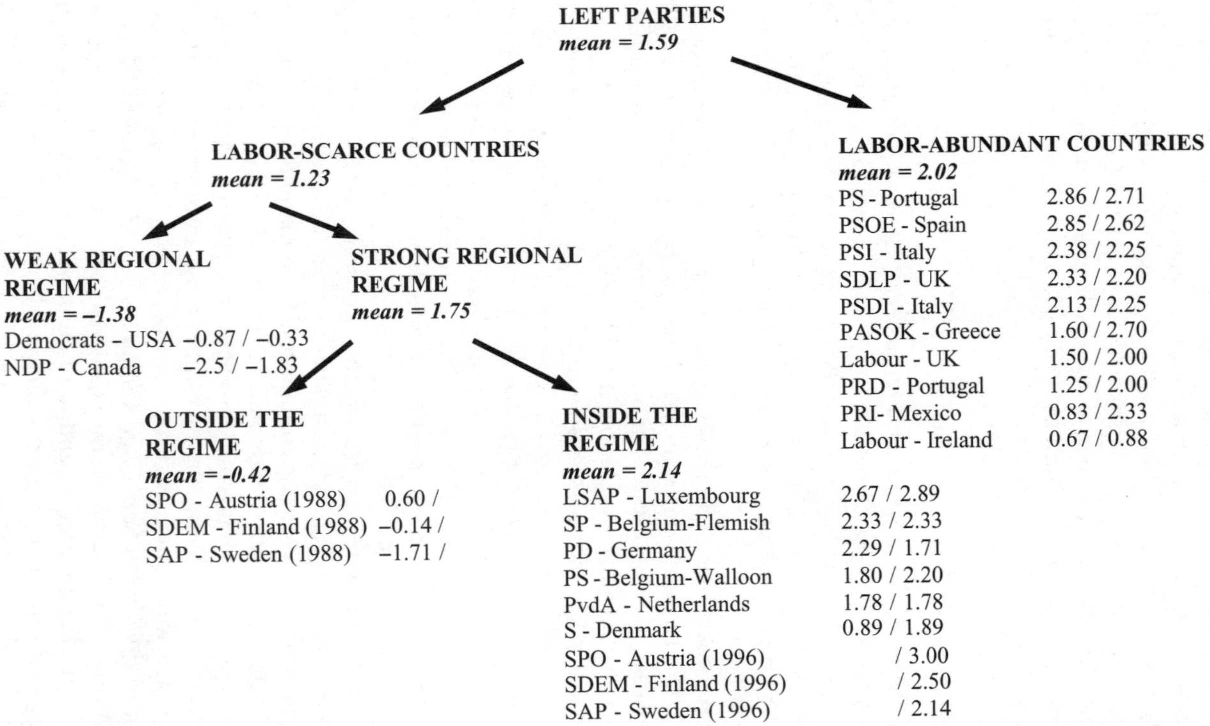

LEFT PARTIES
mean = 1.59

LABOR-SCARCE COUNTRIES
mean = 1.23

LABOR-ABUNDANT COUNTRIES
mean = 2.02

PS - Portugal	2.86 / 2.71
PSOE - Spain	2.85 / 2.62
PSI - Italy	2.38 / 2.25
SDLP - UK	2.33 / 2.20
PSDI - Italy	2.13 / 2.25
PASOK - Greece	1.60 / 2.70
Labour - UK	1.50 / 2.70
PRD - Portugal	1.25 / 2.00
PRI - Mexico	0.83 / 2.33
Labour - Ireland	0.67 / 0.88

WEAK REGIONAL REGIME
mean = -1.38

Democrats - USA	-0.87 / -0.33
NDP - Canada	-2.5 / -1.83

STRONG REGIONAL REGIME
mean = 1.75

OUTSIDE THE REGIME
mean = -0.42

SPO - Austria (1988)	0.60 /	
SDEM - Finland (1988)	-0.14 /	
SAP - Sweden (1988)	-1.71 /	

INSIDE THE REGIME
mean = 2.14

LSAP - Luxembourg	2.67 / 2.89	
SP - Belgium-Flemish	2.33 / 2.33	
PD - Germany	2.29 / 1.71	
PS - Belgium-Walloon	1.80 / 2.20	
PvdA - Netherlands	1.78 / 1.78	
S - Denmark	0.89 / 1.89	
SPO - Austria (1996)	/ 3.00	
SDEM - Finland (1996)	/ 2.50	
SAP - Sweden (1996)	/ 2.14	

Note: The scores in brackets after each party and country refer to the parties' position on regional integration for the years 1988 and 1996 respectively. Orientation was measured on a scale of –3 to 3, from "strongly opposed" (–3) to "strongly in favor" (3).

FIGURE 7.1. Left Parties and Regional Integration (1988 and 1996).

it may also open up possibilities for continental regulation. On the strong regime side of the fork in Figure 7.1, left parties in labor-scarce countries (mean = 1.75) are almost as favorably disposed to regional integration as left parties in labor-abundant countries.[6]

The third, and final bifurcation taps the difference between membership and prospective membership of a regional regime. A left party in a prospective member state is faced with a take-it-or-leave-it decision: whether to enter the regime or remain independent. The choice will depend on the anticipated impact of membership on social democratic achievements at the national level. How developed are social democratic policies and institutions at the national level? How viable are such achievements if the country joins the regime? How viable are they if the country does not join?

Figure 7.1 reveals a sharp contrast between left parties that are outside the regional regime and can hope to escape regional integration altogether (mean = −0.42), and those that are inside the regime and have to choose between more, or less, integration (mean = 2.14).[7]

Social democratic parties outside the EU, in Austria and the Scandinavian countries, had a lot to defend in the mid-1980s. These countries were at the top of the social democratic/neocorporatism league. The European Union was predominately a market-making enterprise. Most social democrats were fearful of membership. While some social democrats argued that social democracy was, in any case, vulnerable and that a Europeanwide platform for regulation was the best option available, the majority defended the status quo.

The calculus for social democratic parties changes once membership is seen to be irreversible. Social democracy pursued outside the EU appeared a chimera after the debacle of "socialism in one country" in France in 1982–3. In his electoral program for the 1980 presidential election, François Mitterrand proposed to increase France's room for maneuver in the EU by reducing trade to 20 percent of French GDP by 1990. The policy was unsustainable under the pressures of international currency and capital markets, and after 1983 Mitterrand and the majority of socialists in France and in other EU countries came to believe that the only realistic alternative was to deepen, rather than marginalize, the EU (Cole 1996). The issue became one of how to extend the possibilities for EU-regulated capitalism while defending social democratic institutions at the national level from corrosive EU policies, particularly negative court judgments. By the mid- to late 1980s, most social democrats in established EU member states came to the conclusion that the European Union was the "only game in town," and adjusted their policies accordingly.

---

[6] A difference of means test is significant at the 0.01 level.
[7] Again, a difference of means test is significant at the 0.01 level.

CONCLUSION

Regional regimes are institutional means to facilitate trade. But they can be more than this, as the European Union attests. The European Parliament, which has the authority to veto the bulk of legislation in the EU, cannot be satisfactorily explained as a functional means to lower trade barriers. From an economic standpoint, the European Parliament is an inefficient institution in that it *increases*, rather than decreases, transaction costs of decision making. Similarly, a significant share of policy making in the EU is oriented not to market making, but to market regulation. In Europe, democratic principles – and the democratic class struggle – do not stop at national borders, but are extended into the European arena. NAFTA, by contrast, is exclusively a trade-facilitating regime, and it lacks the authority to do more.

We have sought to understand "(un)bundling of authority" as a political process that gives rise to explicable patterns of support and opposition. Exit opportunities arising from regional integration, analyzed by Stefano Bartolini in Chapter 2, are heavily biased toward those with mobile resources, and as a result, regional integration has palpable distributional consequences. At the same time, the kind of regime that is built, often as a result of many choices with unpredictable effects (as Guiseppe di Palma stresses), may provide some measure of authoritative *re*bundling.

In this chapter, we presented a layered theory of left party response to regional integration. We began with a neoclassical model of returns to factors. This allowed us to predict party positioning in NAFTA countries, but not in the European Union. When we broaden the analysis to include factor mobility and its consequences, the puzzle deepens. Given the negative effects of lowering trade barriers for the least mobile factors of production, and in particular labor, why should mainstream left parties favor regional integration?

To answer this question one must pay attention to the character of the regional regime itself. To what extent does it provide a platform for realizing left goals? To what extent does the regime provide some means for controlling international economic pressures? Regional regimes can shape as well as intensify globalization if they have some capacity for authoritative regulation of market activity, as appears to be the case in the European Union. Since the late 1980s, social democratic parties throughout the EU have supported the regime, and by 1996 these parties had a higher average level of support than those in any other major party family (Marks and Wilson 2000).

When a regional regime is simply a means to lower market barriers, the left has a difficult choice. The groups that protested the pure market focus of the WTO in Seattle in December 1999 wished to broaden the scope of that regime to include regulation of child labor, job safety standards, the environment, and freedom of unionization (*Economist*, December 4, 1999: 25–6). They wanted, in other words, to rebundle market transactions with certain kinds of authoritative regulation. They wished to extend and deepen the WTO, creating in the process a putative world government in an effort to "democratize" international trade. But they also wished to block the negotiations and to eliminate the WTO itself.

The implication of our argument is that there is no paradox here. One finds the same response on the part of the left in the United States and Canada with respect to NAFTA. The AFL-CIO and Canadian unions have repeatedly sought to introduce social and organizational concerns into the framework of NAFTA. In addition, many groups have campaigned for environmental standards. The failure of such efforts has led to root and branch opposition to NAFTA, and a massive and successful effort on the part of labor to block "fast track" legislation that would facilitate extending the regime to other countries (*Financial Times*, November 12, 1997).

Social democratic parties in Western Europe faced the same dilemma in the process of European integration. From the start, social democrats realized that the creation of a single market would diminish their room for maneuver in national states, and many wished to escape or reverse the process (Griffiths 1993). But as European integration progressed, the costs of exiting the regime increased. Enhancing a capacity for authoritative regulation of market activity at the European level – creating an "organized space," in the words of former European Commission president Jacques Delors – became a more realistic goal and one that most social democrats came to support.

PART III

EUROPE–U.S. COMPARISONS

8

The European Union in American Perspective

The Transformation of Territorial Sovereignty in Europe and the United States

Sergio Fabbrini

The evolution of the European Union (EU) seems to epitomize the transformation of contemporary politics. To use the words of Christopher Ansell in his introductory chapter to this book, in Europe it is evident that "the mutually reinforcing relations between territory, authority, and societal interests and identities can no longer be taken for granted." Although formally still sovereign, the (Western) European nation-states have witnessed a migration of a considerable degree of their own individual sovereignty both toward the supranational EU and the subnational regional and local governments. A silent divorce between sovereignty and authority has been practiced. The decisional power over a growing number of traditionally domestic policy issues has been transferred from the single nation-states to the network of European Community institutions. Of course, the single nation-states are part of those institutions, but their individual representatives participate in collective decision making that dilutes their influence and power. The authority over decisions they have to bring back home is shared with other nation-state representatives, community officials, and members of the EU parliament. Moreover, those decisions are the outcome of a political process that has features of fragmentation, porosity, and indeterminacy unknown to domestic political processes.

On this basis, it has been rightly said that the EU indicates the crisis of the Westphalian state (Caporaso 1996). In international relations literature, a Westphalian state refers primarily to the "institutional arrangement associated with a particular bundle of characteristics – recognition, territory, exclusive authority, and effective internal and transborder regulation or control" (Krasner 1999: 227). It is much less clear what a Westphalian state means from a comparative politics perspective. Nevertheless, in Europe, at least, it was often assumed that only specific organizational arrangements make possible the exercise of that exclusive authority: that which implies a concentration of decision-making resources at the center of the state. From this perspective, it is inevitable to consider the evolution of the EU as a substantive challenge both to the *external* and *internal* faces of the sovereignty of single European nation-states. Although historical sovereignty never corresponded to its theoretical model, it is nevertheless unquestionable that the single European nation-states registered a dramatic decrease in their capacity both to exclude *outside* authorities from their own decision-making process and to centralize the *inside* resources necessary for carrying on that process. The European nation-state is enmeshed in an institutional cobweb with features of a compound polity unknown to domestic institutional arrangements.

In sum, Europe has moved from a plurality of distinct nation-states to a continental-sized integrated polity, which from one side has destructured the traditional model of the Westphalian state, and from the other has promoted a polity in which the relations between authority and territory are no longer clearly settled. The EU has a growing authority, but not sovereignty in the traditional sense, and its authority is not supported by centralized institutions or procedures. As Alberta Sbragia (2002) has pointed out, the EU acquired powers over those domestic policies that in federal systems were tenaciously controlled by the federated states, while it left to the member states the powers in foreign and military policy that elsewhere were successfully claimed by the federal state. Of course, the EU's experience has no equivalent in the modern history of democratic countries. It is the first time in history that established nation-states have decided to pool a growing part of their own sovereignties into a larger institutional container. Nevertheless, the institutional outcome of this process and the functional logic that supported it appear much less unusual if one does not consider that the nation-state developed in Europe as the only or predominant type of institutional organization of democratic sovereignty.

In fact, historically, Westphalian sovereignty was interpreted in radically different ways, internally, in Europe and in the United States of America. If both the European nation-states and the American state achieved the recognition of their external sovereignty, nevertheless they organized in opposing ways the internal authority structures through which that sovereignty was exercised, or better, through which groups of rulers compete for the exercise of power over the ruled within the territory of the state. Whereas European rulers chose to operate within a unified organization of sovereignty, their U.S. counterparts operated within a fragmented organization of sovereignty. Such a fragmentation is proper for a polity in which the relations between authority and territory have to be continuously redefined. In this sense, the United States is a "compound republic" by design (Ostrom 1987), because its founders decided to promote a system of multiple separation of powers where the boundaries between institutions and territorial units, to use Giuseppe Di Palma's words in his postscript to this book, are "a matter of negotiation and jurisprudence, driven by shifting interests and interpretations."

This is why we need to compare the process of nation-state building and development in Europe and the United States in order to better locate, analytically, the transformation of the European state model. As necessary as this comparison is, very few attempts have been made so far. Yet, Europe is facing institutional and conceptual challenges that the United States tried to resolve all through its history. And yet the United States, pressured by its domestic transformations and external responsibilities and powers, has made significant attempts, in the post–World War II period, to neutralize the decision-making incoherence attributable to its compound nature. It is not my interest here to investigate the degree of compatibility between the United States and the EU. Rather, my aim is to show how the EU might be interpreted as a specific institutional solution to the problems of "political compoundness" already experienced in the United States. For this reason, I will compare the political development that led to the institutionalization of radically different authority structures in Europe and the United States. On this basis, it will be easier to understand why the EU differs much more from the political experience of its member states than from the U.S. experience. If this is true, then Europeans may derive useful analytical indications from the U.S. experience of political development. The United States past and present might still help Europeans to better envision their future.

THE EUROPEAN PROCESS OF TERRITORIAL BUNDLING

There are many influential theories of European political development (that is, of state and nation building). Two of the most significant theories (and, for my purpose, the most useful) in comparative political analysis are Charles Tilly's *exogenous* approach and Stein Rokkan's *endogeneous* approach. If it is true that Tilly's later approach (Tilly 1990) "places a very heavy emphasis upon class and class conflict as the motor force propelling state development" (Page 1995: 13), nevertheless it is also true that his general approach (Tilly 1985, 1975) is based upon interstate conflicts and wars as the driving forces for state organization. As Hendrik Spruyt (1994: 30) notices, "Tilly explains the variation between types of organization by differential responses to the functional demand of waging war." On the contrary, Rokkan is more interested in the internal sources of political development, which may vary from case to case, but that nevertheless involve the rulers' need to consolidate and extend their own power in a given territory. Although both approaches are interested in European political development, it is noteworthy that both of them did not consider the U.S. experience, even as a reference case. This could be understandable in Tilly's approach, with its emphasis on the role of the international system in forging the European states from the seventeenth to nineteenth centuries. That system, in fact, could not exert much pressure on the American colonies and thus the U.S. republic, given their geographical and political isolation from Europe. But the U.S. case is also analytically marginal and theoretically peripheral in Rokkan's approach, although the endogeneous approach might have benefited from a comparison with it.

If we want to bring the United States back in the comparison, then we need to deal first with Rokkan's approach. In Rokkan's approach (Rokkan 1999, 1973a, 1973b, 1970, 1968; Rokkan and Meritt 1968), there are different paths to European nation and state building. If the state coincides with the territorial bounding of sovereignty, this process had different modalities of development. In general, modern European nation-states are to be considered the outcome of the long-drawn-out transformation of the feudal structure inherited from the disintegration of the Roman Empire. The state-building process occurred in different ways, because it was influenced by the different quality of four variables, which combine cultural and economic factors. These variables helped Rokkan build his conceptual map of Europe, based upon two axes of differentiation: the East-West axis, which differentiates between the highly monetized economy in the West and the agricultural economy in the East; and the North-South axis, which differentiates between the local (national)–oriented Protestant cultures of the North and the supranational orientation of the Catholic culture in the South:

[For Rokkan] the North-South axis is central to the process of nation building, that is to say in defining processes of allegiance to or identification with national political organization. The East-West axis is crucial to the understanding of state formation – the creation of institutions of political authority (Page 1995: 12).

The question Rokkan raises is why the European nation-states developed more easily and first at the peripheries of the western Roman Empire, then in the latter's heartland, with its vast network of cities and local units and differentiated secular and religious authorities. Reporting on a paper of his own presented for the UNESCO Program on "Comparative Cross-National Research" in 1973, Rokkan explained that "his model" is based on

...four sources of variations in the structuring of territoriality defined political organizations: (1) the distinctiveness, the consolidation and the economic, political, and cultural strength of the *territorial centre*; (2) the cultural distances of the *peripheries* from the centre and their economic and political resources for resistance against integration and standardization; (3) the internal strength and the external resources links of *cross-locally organized subcultures* such as churches, sects, castes; (4) the internal strength and the external resource links of *cross-locally organized economic units*, such as merchant leagues, credit networks, international corporations (1973a: 18, italics in the original text).

Although Rokkan's approach is still the object of an intense debate (Flora 1999), it seems plausible to argue that for Rokkan these variables were crucial because they produced different incentive structures for the central elites who wanted to maximize their own power aspirations. The nature of the various types of variables, in other words, implied different cost/benefit calculations for the central elites in pursuit of territorial bounding. The calculations also offered different coalitional strategies to the elites. If state building is a process that (mainly) neutralizes (individual, groups, or area) free-riding and defection options, then the four variables may explain much about the chances for success of strategies of territorial bounding. Where, with the spread of the Protestant Reformation movement in northern Europe, it was possible to fuse the secular and religious realms and to create a local language of social communication (to replace Latin), then an important barrier was raised to prevent individual, group, or territorial exits from that given polity. At the same time, the exit options were much more difficult to circumscribe, whereas the territory was organized around a network of economically independent trading cities, connected to their own surroundings with land ownership divided into small estates.

Thus, it is not by chance that the sovereign territorial state developed in the periphery of the old Roman Empire (such as France, Britain, and Spain), whereas in the core of the Roman Empire, with its dense network of independent cities, alternative institutional organizations of power arrangements developed, like the city-leagues (in the German and Dutch areas) and the city-states (in the Italian center-north). In this sense, there were different routes of state building, because there were different power relations between the center's and peripheries' elites. In the heartland of the Roman Empire, the richness of city networks and the differentiation of secular and religious authorities strengthened the resistance of those groups and individuals opposing integration and standardization from the center. This is in contrast to the other territories on the peripheries of the Roman Empire, where the city networks were weak and where the differentiation between secular and religious authorities disappeared in favor of the formation of national (Protestant) churches. A national church helped the process of vernacularization and thus stimulated the process of linguistic unification (or homogeneity) of a given territorial area. Says Rokkan:

The great paradox of Western Europe was that it developed a number of strong centres of territorial control at the edge of the old empire: the decisive thrusts of state formation and nation-building took place on the peripheries of the territory left without effective control by the disruption of the Western Roman Empire (1973b: 90).

In sum, "for Rokkan, centre-periphery structures are the essential features of the *territorial* structure of political systems, evolving in the processes of territorial expansion, political centralisation, and population concentration" (Flora 1999: 6, italics in the original text). For him, structures are the configuration of variables that offer different resources, in different periods of time, to the political actors. The structures represent distinct time periods because his analysis is not only synchronic, but also diachronic. The concept of *timing* becomes crucial in this regard, because the political actors may pursue different strategies in the different sequences of the territorial organization of sovereignty. As Peter Flora stresses:

...the concept of *timing* is systematically bound up with Rokkan's model building through his distinction between four fundamental developmental processes of territorial political systems: state formation in the narrower sense, nation-building, democratisation, and the establishment of the welfare states. Taken together, the features of these individual processes and the way they combine over time make up nation- or type-specific *developmental paths* or *trajectories* (1999: 18, italics in the original text).

Thus, for Rokkan, territorial centralization features in Europe depended on structural conditions that involved the power relations between the center and both crosslocally organized subcultures and crosslocally organized economic units. The sovereign, territorial state developed where the center enjoyed clear supremacy over the periphery. This state also developed where there was no cultural distance between the center and the periphery, and where, crosslocally organized subcultures and economic units could neither mobilize resources against the center nor obtain an internal cohesive authority structure. In these conditions, central elites could create a system of alliances with peripheral elites, in order to extend their own jurisdiction to a given territory, or better, extend their own power within that jurisdiction. Moreover, the original pressure for territorial centralization in the form of the state came from within the territory itself, although its consolidation was helped by the subsequent external development of a competitive interstate system.

Other alternative forms of territorial organization, like the city-state and the cities' league, were available when the state started to develop. But the territorial state prevailed because of its greater capacity to mobilize societal resources. Those resources were necessary, in the first place, to face internal challenges, and only subsequently to confront external challenges. As Hendrik Spruyt precisely stresses:

Sovereign authority proved to be more effective in reducing economic particularism, which raised transaction and information costs, and it created a more unified economic climate. Central administration provided for gradual standardization of weights and measures, coinage and jurisprudence. Undoubtedly this was a lengthy process.... But... the dominant political actor, the king in France, the king-in-parliament in England, had vested interests in limiting defection and freeriding and in furthering the overall economy. The greater autonomy of urban centers in the Hansa (league) and the Italian city-states made such objectives more difficult to achieve (1994: 185).

The increased resources acquired through the state organization thus helped the rulers' strategy of consolidation and expansion of their own territorial power, thus soliciting mimicry on the part of the threatened neighboring rulers. Success guarantees emulation.

Once the state had won, then the new rulers needed to look for a new cultural (or ideological) legitimation of their own power. The nation, as a community of belonging to a stock of shared experiences and predispositions, was the outcome of this process. Of course, with Rokkan, one has to distinguish between earlier and later state building in Western Europe. To be sure, the earlier state building, represented by the French experience, implied the formation of the state before the same definition of a nation; or better, the successful building of the state created the strategic conditions for the identification of a given nationality. Later state building, as in Italy and Germany, shows exactly the opposite process. The state was created to represent an already defined nationality, although the state building was the condition for the latter's recognition. Here territorial bounding came about more under the pressure of an already-established state system than as an endogenous process of public authority centralization. Between these two cases, moreover, we have the creation of the consociational states (like Switzerland, the Netherlands, and Belgium), which escaped from the superimposition of state and nation, regardless of the timing that led to that superimposition. In the consociational states, we have a compact of different nationalities, or better, a state without a (single) nation but with many (single) nations. After all, these states developed in the broad buffer zone of Europe located between northern Protestantism and the southern counter-Reformation – that is, in the area most exposed to the religious conflicts of the seventeenth and eighteenth centuries.

Thus, with these caveats, it is plausible to argue that the experience of the oldest European states "suggests the priority, temporal as well as logical, of the state and the system of states to the formation of European nations and the rise of nationalism." But:

... [this idea] that in Europe the state has been the matrix and agent of the nation needs to be qualified in two ways. In the first place, it applied historically more in the western and northern parts of the continent than in the south and the east.... [In the second place], even in the west and north of Europe, a dominant or core ethnic population formed the basis of both state and nation" (Smith 1995: 49).

The end result of these differentiated processes was, nevertheless, the diffusion of a model of territorial sovereignty based upon a state organization connoted by a concentration of public authority in a specific central institution, be it the king, then the king in the parliament, and then, finally, only the parliament.

THE AMERICAN TRAJECTORY TOWARD SOVEREIGNTY

The elites pursuing the strategy of territorial sovereignty in the American colonies had to operate on the basis of different cultural and economic premises. The disintegration of British rule left a territory constituted by unusual (from a European view) features. On the cultural side, in America there was neither the overlapping of the secular and religious realms (which greatly helped the process of state building in Protestant Europe) nor the competition between the secular and religious authorities (which greatly hampered the process of state building in Catholic Europe). America came to define itself as a polity of Protestants, rather than as a Protestant polity. The plurality of Protestant sects and the fierce theological competition among them induced the central elites to distance the two realms, allowing religious pressures to develop at the civil level and not at the political level. And if America had only one standard of language communication, contrary to the several standards that connoted Europe, that standard never achieved the mythic status of the national language, given that it was (after all) the language of the colonial power. "In some general way, the political culture of the country as a whole was English and Protestant, but this culture was never firmly established either in the symbols or the substance of law and policy. Nor did the immigrant groups assimilate entirely in the dominant culture" (Walzer 1996: 9).

On the economic side, America was much closer to the European trading belt than to those areas that fostered the earlier process of state building. The colonization process encouraged the creation of differentiated networks of trading cities, with growing areas of land distributed to a free peasantry, which proved highly unfavorable to any attempt at centralization. In the same way, as Michael Walzer makes clear, the creation of the American polity was never able to produce a condition of no exit. The exit options, for individuals and groups, was always there, even well beyond the end of the Civil War in 1865 (although the Civil War halted the exit options for territorial units). Neither religious or language barriers nor economic or territorial constraints were operating. The enlargement of the polity (which was continuous for the first century of the new republic) challenged any attempt to constrain the exit options. In fact, "the *rural-land frontier . . .* lasted from the beginning of settlement in the seventeenth century to the end of the nineteenth century on the eve of World War I" (Elazar 1994: 55, italics in the original text).

Nor was America ever a nation of nationalities like the European consociational states. To be sure, since the very beginning, the American colonies organized themselves as separate territorial entities, but they shared the same religious and linguistic background. In a way, the United States started its experience as a compact of states, not greatly different from other territorial compacts (like the city leagues of postfeudal Europe). The Articles of Confederation (of the period 1781–7) were an attempt to celebrate constitutionally the principle of territorial consociation that resembled the consociational compact of Switzerland before 1848. This *first* American constitution reflected a strong corporate idea of territorial organization, in the sense that the new polity was intended as an outcome of a pact between distinguished and separated territorial communities, rather than between rulers and ruled. [I]n the Articles of Confederation...the Congress had no authority over individuals: Congress could act only through the states themselves (Dahl 1976: 87). The corporate idea of territorial organization also influenced the institutional design of the *second* constitution, the one defined in the Philadelphia Constitutional Convention of the summer of 1787. This influence passed through those who opposed the second constitution (the Anti-Federalists), in the name of the idea "of each state as having 'individuality'" (Beer 1993: 384). In fact, this individuality was recognized in the design of the new Senate, where all the states had the same two representatives, regardless of their demographic size. The federal Senate, thus, "could be considered a victory for the principle of corporate representation" (ibid.). After all, it is well known that "the Federalists borrowed significantly from the Articles of Confederation" (Ackerman 1991: 93).

Though the Hansa league was able to prosper for centuries in continental northern Europe, the league of American colonies lasted only for a few years. Some years ago, William K. Riker (1964) argued that this was due to the pressure applied by the main European powers (Britain, France, and also Spain) that were still involved (at the end of the eighteenth century) in the American continent and wanted to curtail the ambitions of the new American republic. In this competitive context, it was implausible to preserve domestic interests and promote the expansion of those interests in a vast and promising territory without any form of more centralized public authority. For other scholars, the failure of the American league was instead primarily due to the challenges raised by an increasingly differentiated internal society beginning to display, more often than not, in a crude way a socioeconomic contraposition of interests. In this regard, Shay's rebellion is considered a turning point.[1] Thus, de jure, in less than one decade, America experienced two different roads (the confederal and the federal) to the definition of a national public authority, whereas in the European territorially consociational states, the move from the former to the latter took centuries.

But even the new federal solution did not provide the model to solve decisively the question of double representation (of territorial communities and individuals) in a large republic. In fact, de facto, the two options (or roads) continued to coexist, notwithstanding the Civil War, with their alternative strategies of organizing the relation between public authority and territory. The two options took the form of a permanent confrontation between two highly coherent and largely diffuse theories of republican government: the compact (confederal) theory and the national (federal) theory. This confrontation ultimately encouraged a reciprocal influence whose institutional

---

[1] In 1787 in Massachusetts, "debt-ridden farmers who were facing foreclosure demanded that the state legislature issue more paper money...and [led by Daniel Shays] took up arms... when the legislature refused" (Lipsitz and Speak 1989: 63).

outcome has been a *compound republic* – a political system of multiple and overlapping jurisdictions, with a variable combination of self-government (by the states) and shared government (between the federated states and the federal state) (Ostrom 1987). Within constraints, the constitution allowed the representatives of the federal state and the federated states to negotiate continuously the distribution of public authority on the republican territory.

TERRITORIAL SOVEREIGNTY IN AMERICA

For several reasons, it is plausible to argue (as Riker himself suggests) that in America the pressure upon the confederation and then upon the federation was supported (in any case) by the same need that supported state territorial bounding in Europe: to limit defection and free-riding and to further the overall economy, as Stefano Bartolini argues in Chapter 2. Yet this pressure was constrained by less compelling structural conditions than in Europe. Given the polycentric feature of the development of the previous colonial period, America did not have a territorial center in the European sense. There was a prominent elite (the Virginian), but this elite never gave up its local roots in order to advance its national role. At the same time, although the cultural distance between this elite and the elites of the other former colonies was quite limited, the economic and ideological distance was (on the contrary) quite extensive. In each state, especially in the southern ones, there were entrenched crosslocally organized subcultures and economic units. In fact, since its inception in 1789, the federal constitution was constrained by a sectional conflict over slavery as well as over incompatible socioeconomic state systems (trade versus plantation).

The second constitution could not avoid recognizing this sectional divide if it wanted to guarantee its own recognition by the main political actors. Thus, the constitution tried to conjugate two different (and until then considered as opposing) principles of sovereignty: one based upon individual preferences, and the other based upon state interest. A separated system of organization of the public authority was the outcome (Fabbrini 1999b). This system was separated both vertically (between the states and the federal institutions) and horizontally (between the president and the Congress, and the latter between two chambers charged to represent respectively individual electors and territorial units). Moreover, since 1804, all the main political and institutional actors have recognized the ultimate role of the judiciary in establishing the boundaries of the vertical and horizontal separation of powers of the rulers operating within the authority structure of the republic. But of course, through the power of judicial review, the judiciary has become a policy-making actor in its own right. If it is true that the second constitution strengthened the capacity of the central rulers to guarantee the external sovereignty of the republic, nevertheless that constitution continued to constrain internally the exercise of sovereignty to a degree unthinkable in Europe. It constrained that exercise through the institutionalization of a fragmented sovereignty, one based on the diffusion of lawmaking authority among different rulers, some endowed with electoral and others with nonelectoral legitimacy.

Although federal in form, the constitution preserved a mixed regime. A protected equilibrium was institutionalized between the two principles, represented by the strong bicameral nature of the new public authority: the Congress. For a large part of the nineteenth century, separation of powers was basically intended as separation *within* the main institution of the separated powers (that is, the legislature). Within the legislature, the separation of powers was thought to make the sectional divide or territorial conflict of the country governable. The political role of the president was severely constrained: He acted more as a head of state than as a head of government. After all, the Electoral College through which he came to be elected had been designed to keep his election within the states' boundaries, rather than to let that election promote a national constituency. One has to wait for the democratization of the Electoral College in the second half of the nineteenth century, with the election of the president's selectors in a competitive race between party lists, to see the first steps toward the nationalization of presidential elections. In sum, the United States of the nineteenth century was federal in form, but with strong confederal features. Congressional government was federal government through states' representatives, rather than European-style parliamentary government. There was no national institution to challenge the power of the Congress as patron of the states' interests. After all, as V.O. Key, Jr., stressed, "territorial differentiation and conflict in extreme form may pose for the politician the problem of manufacturing a formula for the maintenance of national unity. Only once did the American politicians fail in this endeavor" (1964: 233).

If the new constitution extended the federal jurisdiction over the entire American territory, that jurisdiction overlapped with the states' jurisdictions protected at the federal level by a Senate representing the states' legislatures (in fact, until 1913, the federal senators were selected by the states' legislatures). However, the same federal jurisdiction promoted by the House of Representative continued to be largely defined by the states' interests. Sectional conflict, in fact, was the main source of Congressional activity. "Sectional conflict was revealed most regularly and consistently in the halls of Congress. There ... sectionalism pervaded the less public and more informal political processes of the committee chambers, cloakrooms, and the Committee on the Whole" (Bensel 1987: 9). Thus, the overlapping of jurisdictions was necessary to guarantee the corporate compact along with individual preferences. Inevitably, this overlapping had two correlated outcomes. First, it forestalled the development of a process of verticalization and centralization of public authority at the federal level. Second, the overlapping of jurisdictions left a longstanding ambiguity about the exit options at the states' level.

Regarding the first outcome, the United States is an unusual case (in European terms) of a nation that developed without the support of a state. Of course, "[a] unified legal order was effectively maintained, but the distinction between state and society was blurred. The official realm of government, so clearly demarcated in Europe, seemed to blend inconspicuously with American society" (Skowronek 1987: 6). The judiciary was crucial in promoting the legal order, as well as the parties in designing the legislative terms of the latter. "The success of the early American state came to depend on the working rules of behaviour provided by courts and parties" (ibid.: 24). Thus, the United States contrasts with all the European experiences. For earlier state builders, such as France, the nation-building process was supported by a previously achieved state authority. The consociational countries did not have the state, but neither did they have a nation. For later state builders, like Germany and Italy, their national identity, before the creation of the territorial state, was an ideological construct without precise territorial references. The United States is a case of national sovereignty neither protected by a central state nor authorized by separated national entities. "*Nationality* identity in America . . . preceded the formation . . . of the institutional framework of the American nation, and even of the national territory" (Greenfeld 1992: 402, italics in the original text). In fact, once that institutional framework was put in place, the conflict concerned the proper location of the national identity, more than its definition, which was taken for granted

Regarding the second outcome, it is plausible to argue that the very same constitutional design that America invented to deal with the problem of a compound republic made the United States unable (at least for a long period of the twentieth century) to come up with the threat of territorial defection. If it is true that "regional strife has a weapon not available to other groups – secession" (Schwartz 1974: 107), it is also true that in America the use of that "weapon" was ambiguously guaranteed by the constitution. In fact, until the Civil War, the southern states continued to entertain the idea of secession, and they needed a dramatically bloody war to dismiss that idea. But, of course, if the end of the war settled the impossibility of secession, nevertheless its very conclusion deepened the already profound sectional divide of the country. The U.S. postwar republic became largely defined by a geographical cleavage, which started from a cleavage between those favoring and those opposing a "stronger national union," and ended up in a cleavage between different territorial-economic interests. Thus, in the twentieth century:

. . . the comparative lack of religious or ethnic rivalry between the American regions has meant that the sectional stress in the United States has usually been grounded in economic competition. [That is,] sectional stress is political conflict over significant public decisions in which a nation is divided into two or more regions, each of which is internally cohesive and externally opposed to the other[s] (Bensel 1987: 4).

Thus, the political development of the United States was permanently constrained by a territorial cleavage, which was based both on an institutional contrast between different interpretations of the republic (confederal versus federal) and on a sectional divide between different socioeconomic structures (land-based economy versus commercial economy). This territorial cleavage implied that for the republic to be governed, a permanent combination of the institutional and policy interests of the actors representing it was necessary.

DEMOCRATIZATION IN AMERICA AND IN EUROPE

In his examination of European political development, Rokkan (1973a: 29) stressed the challenges faced by territorial leaders in their attempts to consolidate territorial sovereignty. They had four tasks to perform, says Rokkan. First, these leaders needed to form a boundary-defining state and develop an administrative machinery for the control of transactions within the territory or across the boundary (territorial incorporation). Second, they needed to build institutions of socializiation in order to create – through linguistic standardization, religious unification, and educational penetration – a specific political identity within that given territory (territorial legitimacy). Third, the leaders needed to institutionalize channels of participation, representation, and opposition (democratic incorporation). Fourth, they needed to create territorial economic solidarity through measures for the equalization of benefits and opportunities both across regions and across strata of the population (democratic legitimacy).

Each task corresponded to a specific phase of territorial development, and each implied a set of different potential partners or different potential opponents. Of course, the transfer from one phase to the other was never linear and gradual, given that the transfer implied the destructuring of previous coalitions and the construction of new ones. Old coalitions tended to persist, thus constraining the definition of new political alliances to achieve the new task. This complex process of coalition rebuilding inevitably slowed the movement from one phase to the other, or better (in some areas) ended in cumulating tasks proper to one phase with those of a previous or subsequent phase. In other words, in Europe, the process of territorial consolidation was anything but uniform. Central territorial elites were able to overcome the four thresholds of territorial consolidation through conflicts and compromises that generated different institutional outcomes. Of course, each threshold represented a decision-making point for the central elites, but the institutional solution found for the previous threshold ended up constraining the institutional solution defined for the following threshold.

Nevertheless, one can argue that, in the European experience (of course, ex post, because history appears efficient only after specific events have happened, as Di Palma argues in the postscript to this book), a detectable chain reaction starts with the state, passes through the nation, and ends up with democracy. To stick with Rokkan's approach, the first two thresholds were overcome *before* the second two. Or, better, the thresholds concerning state and nation building were consolidated before achievement of the thresholds involving the diffusion of democracy. In other words, the state arrived not only before the nation, but also before democracy. Thus, from a European point of view, it does not make sense to talk of democracy before the previous identification and mobilization of the nation. It was the active definition of the nation, connected to a specific territory protected by state authority, that created the opportunity structures for those actors interested in the achievement of democracy. European nationalism was both the forerunner of democracy and its adversary. It is true, in general, that national identity tended to reduce individual and social differences within the nation, emphasizing the sense of a unitary body of preferences. In this sense, nationalism prepared democracy through its promotion of shared values. But that preparation took time – and, more often than not, blood. Democracy arrived after nationalism asked people to die for the nation. Equality in the grave often seemed to be the prerequisite of equality in voting.

This process of territorial consolidation was anything but uniform in Europe, because the different coalitions that made it possible to achieve one threshold ended up constraining the subsequent coalitions activated for achieving the other threshold. Nation building was thus constrained by the nature of the previous process of state building and democracy building by the nature of the previous processes of nation-state building. In Europe, democracy was obliged to grow within the conditions imposed by those who already controlled the state and by those who constructed the concept of national identity. Its antihierarchical and egalitarian biases thus were largely tamed by the already-established power structures of the nation-state (Lipset 1996). Also, the main actors of the process of democratization, the political parties, gradually assumed organizational features imitating the institutional features of the nation-states, and became as centralized as the latter. Notwithstanding democracy, sovereignty maintained its unified organization. A new regime took place with the liberal and political revolutions of the second half of the nineteenth century, but that regime of statist democracy preserved a relation of institutional continuity with the previous regime of statist nationalism (Rose 1996).

The process of territorial consolidation followed a quite different path in the United States. This was not only because the boundary of federal authority was an open question until after the Civil War, but especially because the timing of territorial consolidation was completely different in the United States than in Europe. Here resides a double crucial distinction between the two Western political systems experiences: First, in America, the state arrived after the nation; second, in America, the processes of nation building and democratization were synchronic, and not diachronic as in Europe. This fact explains why in the United States nationalism has been a permanent supporter of democracy, whereas in Europe it frequently risked being a challenger.

It was the constitution (a procedural document soon backed by the ten principled amendments of the Bill of Rights) that crystallized the already existent national identity of America. If it is true, as John Jay wrote in the *Federalist n.* 2, that the Americans were "one united people – a people descended from the same ancestors, speaking the same language, professing the same religion, attached to the same principles of government" (quoted in Beard 1964: 39), it is also true that this united people became conscious that it existed only through a sequence of political acts from the Declaration of Independence in 1776 to the federal constitution of 1787. "This is the genuinely American spirit of constitutionalism: the making of the constitution is the act of founding the nation" (Preuss 1996: 21). Through the second constitution, the American nation started to identify itself as peculiarly different from other nations, also because the constitution allowed it to be divided in a multiplicity of localities and states and then in a plurality of ethnic and religious groups of immigrants, but nevertheless offered to all an opportunity of inclusion:

Only procedure united these countless pieces. . . . the results were stunning: equal but separate, separate but joined. . . . [Electoral] democracy was essential to America's complex 19th century process of nation-building. . . . Where European cultures invoked ancient traditions and folk spirits to unite their nations, American culture called on democracy, which occupied the heart of America's romantic nationalism. By midcentury, popular understanding made America and democracy synonymous (Wiebe 1995: 82–3).

Thus, in America, there were the apparent paradoxes (from a European point of view) of the democratic thresholds being consolidated coterminously with the nation, but long before the consolidation of the federal state thresholds. The institutionalization of channels of participation, representation, and opposition was largely implemented in the 1830s. And alternation in power between different political options had taken place since the very beginning of the new federal republic, that is, in the presidential elections of 1800 with the success of the Jeffersonian Democratic-Republicans against the Hamiltonian Federalists. Those thresholds were overcome in the context of a polity that continued to be "radically decentralized." A low level of taxation was the key factor in keeping the central government small. Throughout the nineteenth century, apart from the period of the Civil War, the ratio of government expenditure to gross national product (GNP) was routinely one-fifth or one-sixth that of the major European nations, according to several reports (Mann 1993). In sum:

America's 18th century political heritage encouraged pulls away from the center: states resisting national power, assemblies serving constituent interests, locally rooted legislatures guarding the right to initiate – or, more likely, not to initiate – new tax laws. Unlike the Jacobin legacy for France, republican ideology in America merely deepened the distrust of a national mobilization (Wiebe 1995: 70).

As it happened in Europe, but this time with an inverse effect, the coalition of interests that favored the growth of democracy constrained the opportunities of the subsequent coalition to develop a "stronger union." Thus, the existence of a democracy intended as protection of decentralized interests largely constrained the options of those national rulers who wanted to promote the interests connected with centralization. In the United States the states could long entertain the idea of exit, whereas in Europe the exit option was quite soon neutralized by the central rulers, because the idea of exit was properly protected by democracy in the first case, whereas in the second case the peripheries did not have any procedural protection. Moreover, the institutional achievements of the democratic process not only postponed the state-building process, but also conditioned its features once it started. In fact, the development of a federal administrative machinery able to control economic as well as civil transactions within the national territory came only at the end of the nineteenth century and at the beginning of the twentieth century. It was the progressive reform period that triggered the creation of a civil service based upon merit and not party spoils. And, moreover, it was the gigantic industrial and territorial transformations of the post–Civil War that required new techniques of economic and social regulation:

The close of the frontier, the rise of the city, the accentuation of class divisions, the end of isolation – these changes raised demands for national governmental capacities that were foreign to the existing state structure and that presupposed a very different mode of governmental operation (Skowronek 1987: 9).

Thus, only in the twentieth century has the United States (at the national level) fully overcome the two thresholds of territorial and democratic legitimacy. In fact, the building of institutions of socialization was traditionally a task (and a power) for state (peripheral) elites, and not for national (federal) elites. The educational system was organized at the level of the states, each pursuing its own cultural or sectional predisposition. Of course, the linguistic standard was uniform throughout the federal territory, but that did not prevent the institutional pursuit of different interpretations of the culture connected to that standard. In fact, the creation of territorial economic and social solidarity was long intended to be the duty of the states, although the federal state did play an important role with the veterans program introduced in the aftermath of the Civil War (Skocpol 1992). Thus, in general, the two crucial legitimacy thresholds were overcome long after the national consolidation of democracy and the state, whereas in Europe they were instrumental to guaranteeing the passage from the territorial to the political phase of development (that is, from the statist to the democratic phase). In sum:

Democracy was firmly established in America before a concentration of national governmental controls was demanded. . . . In America a new kind of state organization had to be fashioned through a highly developed electoral democracy to meet the governing challenges of the industrial age (Skowronek 1987: 9–10).

TERRITORIAL AND PARTISAN CLEAVAGES IN EUROPE AND AMERICA

To Rokkan and Seymour Martin Lipset (1967), the European party systems of the twentieth century appeared as the frozen expression of the structure of cleavages that emerged in European politics in the wake of the national and industrial revolutions. The first revolution triggered a conflict between center and periphery interests and thus between state and church interests. The second revolution encouraged an opposition between land and industrial interests and thus between capital and labor interests. The main European political parties of the twentieth century were the heirs of those conflicts, the expression of these cleavages, and the representatives of the coalitions expressed by those historical transformations.

In America, contrary to Europe, the national revolution did not pass through the conflict between center and periphery and/or between state and church, but between a coalition of colonies and their "corrupted" motherland. In this sense, the United States is the first new nation of the modern era, because it was born from a struggle against an external power rather than from a struggle to overcome an internal divide (Lipset 1979). That birth made it possible for the United States, to become a nation without the lead of a center. In fact, the United States of the nineteenth century never had truly national parties, or better, those national-based organizations that emerged after a conflict with the representatives of local organizations. U.S. national parties were (and still are) confederations of state and local parties, vehicles for the promotion (or the defense) at the national level of state and local interests. Moreover, the United States became a nation without the need to tame a rival religious authority. Its sectarian origins encouraged a pluralism of faiths that put the United States in a different path from the one pursued by both Protestant and Catholic Europe. In the United States, nationalizing a church was impractical, because there were too many candidates for the job. Nor did she need to face the shadow of the Catholic Church, because the very foundation of America derived from the search for "a city upon the hill" located as far as possible from that shadow. The solution had been the drastic separation of the civil and religious spheres.

Thus, the United States never witnessed the rise of religious parties with their lay counterparts. Of course, religious groups were and are traditionally active in U.S. politics. Indeed, in some states they proved themselves able to acquire a powerful influence in political affairs, controlling legislatures, mobilizing citizen action groups, and conditioning newspapers and media networks. Nevertheless, at the national level, they never played a distinct role, partly because they had to enter larger coalitions if they wanted to be recognized and accepted or if they wanted to be influential. The same Industrial Revolution of the second half of the nineteenth century pitted the commercial interests of the Northeast against the land interests of the southern plantation elites, more than it pitted the economic interests of capital against those of labor. In sum, in the United States, the conflict between capital and labor, which was particularly crude at the turn of the last century, took a quite different *political* form than in Europe. That is, it did not produce class or socialist parties, because that conflict exploded in a different material and institutional context than those of Europe.

To paraphrase Bartolini's argument in this book, this conflict did not materialize in a European-style party system because of the exit options available to individuals and groups. Internal migration and the possibility of westward expansion at the height of industrial transformation diluted the pressure for class confrontation. The permanent appeal of the exit options reduced the potential impact of the voice strategies – an impact that Europe experienced in the aftermath of state bounding. The United States of the nineteenth century was not tortured by the religious and class conflicts that tortured Europe in the same period – conflicts that resulted in the cleavages that structured the European party systems in the following century. It seems plausible to argue that the possibility of individual and group exits helped to prevent the formation of both class and religious parties, that is, the traditional European voice parties. Thus, after the Civil War, the only unavoidable cleavage remained the territorial one. And, in fact, this sectional cleavage overshadowed the social and the religious cleavages.

Partisan politics thus intertwined with the territorial interests of the states and with economically homogeneous geographical regions. Parties were important actors in electoral and institutional politics, but they were constituted by different attitudes than the European parties:

Americans of the late nineteenth century were deeply attached to their party-labels . . . links with economic class divisions always existed, though less clearly than elsewhere. [But], each major-party label had strong . . . embittered sectional associations and also considerable reinforcement from ethnic and religious divisions (Epstein 1986: 249).

Thus, the class cleavage proper of the Industrial Revolution could not generate the party systems it generated in Europe. Materially, this failed to occur because individual members of the working class always had the chance to pursue individual exit options (to move westward or to change business), contrary to workers in Europe. Institutionally, the cleavage failed to generate such party systems because capital was, for a long period, also state-based. Federalism meant also exit options for capital, which could move from one state to another, thus making the nationalization of conflict difficult (Lowi 1978).

Of course, the possibility of institutionalizing a European-style party system was also powerfully limited by the fact that, in America, democracy arrived before, not only the state, but also before modern capitalism. White and male workers were individually integrated in the political system, before they could develop a collective conscience. And, in any case, their granted individual integration neutralized a potentially enormous pressure to the process of class formation. Once the worker was a citizen as an individual, he did not need to organize with others in order to conquer his citizenship. In the United States, in fact, as early as 1824, almost fifty years before mass male suffrage began to be regularly established in most of Europe, all but three U.S. states extended the right to vote to almost all adult white males. Moreover, the distribution of government jobs to faithful party workers, starting with the presidencies of Andrew Jackson and Martin Van Buren, in a institutional context of a radically decentralized polity, helped to diffuse the democratic belief that government was open to all and not just to a few (as in Europe). And of course, without a socialist party, there was no need for the capitalist and religious parties that Europeans built to counteract socialists.

Weakened from below by the relative fluidity of class and religious cleavages and constrained from above by the institutional separation of powers, U.S. parties were never able to develop the kind of organizational structures that could support the activity of permanent political mobilization. Neither Republicans nor Democrats had truly national extragovernmental organizations, and their national committees had (and continue to have) the structure of a confederal coalition of state and local parties (Epstein 1986: 123). At the same time, the parties' Congressional caucuses were traditionally more coordinating devices than ideological committees, given that the sectional divide often tended to overlook the partisan cleavage. And the presidential party appeared only every four years during the national convention for the selection of the party candidate. Thus, nineteenth century American politics featured strong party organizations, but the localities were their privileged field of action. "As local agencies, political parties energized the community.... In a nation of mobile people, parties called out to the community's shifting population with a steady drumbeat of appeals ... bringing them out to the polls on election day ..." (Wiebe 1995: 78).

Decentralization was crucial to this process, because it created the favorable conditions for mobilization. But what united this decentralized party system?

What gave heterogeneity its wholeness in the 19th century, what created unity . . . out of this diversity, was the single moment of general election. Here democratic culture came full circle. At the beginning it was the franchise that defined each white man as the equal of every other. . . . At the end it was using those same badges of sovereignty that transformed otherwise scattered, suspicious men of every type of persuasion into one governing People (Wiebe 1995: 82).

In sum, as Supreme Court Justice David Brower wrote in 1900, "the voting booth is the temple of American institutions" (quoted in Walzer 1996: 59). But the voting booth was located in the states, and its national effects were controlled by the states' representatives. Nothing comparable happened in European politics. With the institutionalization of the voting booth, parties started to grow, appealing primarily to national constituencies, socially or religiously defined. Of course, certain European countries witnessed the formation of territorial cleavages, but their political impact was gradually overshadowed by the growing nationalization of electoral politics induced by political parties interested in mobilizing a constituency expression of entrenched classes and religious communities.

FROM WASHINGTON TO BRUSSELS

The U.S. compound republic could prosper in the nineteenth century because of very fortunate conditions. The courts filled the void of federal authority, and the external sovereignty of the republic was rarely seriously challenged (and in any case it was silently protected by the British navy). But the context changed drastically at the turn of nineteenth century. The impetuous industrial development of the country and its subsequent international projection activated formidable forces asking for a nationalization of the country, or better, for a more active intervention of the federal state. The need, first, to regulate the internal industrial economy and society and, second, to promote the geopolitical/geoeconomic interests of the country in the international realm started to strain the separated institutions of the United States. This process of nationalization fully developed in the second half of the twentieth century. Thus, after a century of Congressional primacy, the United States registered in the twentieth century a significant constitutional change without a formal constitutional amendment: "the replacement of Congress by the president as the central governing institution" (Lowi 1988: 33). Also, after a century of states' primacy, the United States enhanced the role of the federal center with New Deal policies. In fact, the two processes supported each other.

The challenges of economic transformation and international involvement had pressured central (federal) rulers to look for more-centralized institutional answers. The capitalist transformation's challenge was met with a promotion by the federal government of a growing number of policies. The states became the terminal of federal activism; if they wanted federal money for their policies, they had to respect very detailed federal guidelines or regulations. The international involvement required by the challenge of World War II was met by centralizing the decision-making power on foreign and military policies within the presidency. The National Security Act of 1947 institutionalized a foreign policy establishment close to the president, who was weakly constrained by the separation of powers. The modern presidency inaugurated by Franklin Delano Roosevelt became gradually the home for a personal president (Lowi 1985) able to act in the international arena independently from the other separated rulers. Thus, the international involvement of the country triggered by the cold war confrontation gave the federal government the ideological justification that it never previously had to oversee the states, and gave the president the justification that the executive branch had never previously had to lead the Congress. In terms of authority relations, the territorial sovereignty of the nation-state became much less fragmented than in the past. The pressures of the cold war demanded what the constitution intends to impede: the centralization of decision-making powers. It seemed the revenge of Tilly's approach, because post–World War II America developed a formidable central security and military apparatus largely controlled by the president. But it was revenge within institutional limits.

In fact, on the foreign policy side, the military defeat in Vietnam and the resignation of President Richard M. Nixon following the Watergate scandal triggered a mobilization of interests and institutions opposed to presidential centralization. The Congress regained significant influence in the field of foreign and military policy, while the credibility of the presidency collapsed to a similar degree. Since the 1970s, presidential leadership was continuously weakened, regardless of the party of the sitting president. The terrorist attack of September 11, 2001, does not seem to have had the effect of shifting influences back to the presidency, but federal centralization has been successfully halted. Fiscal stress and ideological change in the 1970s gave important political resources to political leaders within the states who questioned the expansion of federal power. Thus, a swing took place from the centralization of the 1950s and 1960s to the decentralization of the following three decades. After all, "American federalism is at once a system of law and a structure of power. It has both a juristic and a behavioral aspect. [The point is that] our juristic federalism does not unambiguously determine our behavioral federalism" (Beer 1993: 23–4).

In sum, the American compound republic continued to allow an alternation from phases of centralization and presidentialization to others of decentralization and Congressional activism. If confrontation with the external world pressured the United States to centralize internal authority relations, nevertheless the constitutional structure of a fragmented sovereignty continued to protect the fluidity of internal relations, granting ample room for maneuvering to those rulers and territorial units that had a stake in opposing centralization and presidentialization. The net effect of these contradictory pressures has been the formation of a "new political (dis)order." That is:

... government policies are made in response to a greater number and variety of conflicting and substantially independent interest groups. . . . Political institutions . . . are weaker than before. . . . The new order, then, is more *fragmentation* and less *integration* (Dahl 1994: 1–2, italics in the original text).

If it is true that the institutional and political structures of individual European nation-states are still different from the institutional and political structures of the United States, this is no longer the case if the latter are compared with the institutional and political structures emerging within the EU. In fact, the EU has the features of a compound republic, meaning a polity structured around a separation of powers both vertical (between Brussels and the member states) and horizontal (between the European Council, the European Commission, and the European Parliament). Of course, there are other democratic polities with vertical separation of powers (such as the federal countries of Canada, Germany, Austria, and Belgium), but none of them has also a horizontal separation of powers (they are parliamentary democracies, such as in the case of Austria, whose president is popularly elected). The only other exception, apart from the United States, is Switzerland, which has both levels of separation. But, of course, size matters.

Thus, in terms of institutional structures, the United States and the EU are based on subsystems endowed with their own bases of authority (the member states versus the Community institutions); both have a diffusion of decision-making powers among the central institutions (President-Senate-House versus Commission-Council-Parliament); both institutionalize (or try to institutionalize) a double representation within their own legislative bodies (the Senate representing the states through their electors and the House representing the individual voters versus the Council representing the member states' interests and the Parliament elected by individual voters), although those legislative bodies have different resources of influence; both have a powerful and independent judicial body (the Supreme Court versus the European Court of Justice); and both have regulatory agencies independent from electoral institutions (the Federal Reserve and the Independent Regulator Commissions (IRCs) versus the Central European Bank and the European agencies) (Majone 1996).

Of course, similarity in institutional configuration does not mean comparability in power resources. In terms of the political process, both the United

States and the EU seem to prize interest group pressures more than electoral mobilization, along a pluralist model that was traditionally found in the United States. In fact, within the European Union:

... policy outcomes become less predictable; majorities become more difficult to mobilize. The power of public coercion is blunted, but so is the capacity of the state to overcome private exploitation. The most accurate *appellation* for this system in interest intermediation is *pluralism* (Schmitter 2000: 22 of ch. 3, italics in the original text).

Although some important differences exist, "pluralism idealizes important elements of the American experience with democracy, [and] the EU manifests some of the very same characteristics that make the US the archetypical pluralist system" (Coultrap 1999: 127). It seems plausible to argue that, at the EU level, this evolution toward pluralist policy making is connected to the fact that political parties appear to be much less able at the EU level than at the nation-state level to aggregate preferences and to delineate public policies. Within the European Parliament, parties are more confederations of national or subnational parties, as the U.S. parties traditionally were and are, than programmatic agencies of social mobilization. Interest groups can move, as Bruce Cain argues in Chapter 9, from one "shop" to another, looking for the better offer.

Moreover, in Europe, as an effect of both the structural transformation of economies and cultures and institutional displacement of the decision-making resources from the national to the continental arena, traditional class and religious cleavages tended to wane as driving forces of the structure of the party system. On the contrary, sectional or geographical cleavages, concerning both the legitimacy of the EU as a decision-making body and the distributor of the resources it controls, are becoming the sources of the birth and development of new partisan actors and of the structuring of new divisions within the party system. "Were he alive, Rokkan would certainly acknowledge that the [parties'] contemporary salience is not what it was (at the national level) during the heroic founding epoch of the late 1800s and early 1900s.... This, I suspect, holds even more for the EU" (Schmitter 2000: 24). As Bartolini argues in Chapter 2, the decline of the salience of those cleavages increases the relevance of territorial and sectional cleavages, as has been the case in the United States. In sum, "as one well-informed observer has put it: 'Brussels is getting closer to Washington than to Bonn, Paris or London'" (see Schmitter 1999: 21).

CONCLUSION

To compare similar cases does not mean to assimilate them. Quite the contrary. As Stephen Skowronek rightly said of the experience of the turn of the twentieth century, "The development of the national government did not

portend a 'Europeanization' of America, nor, for that matter, did the democratization of Europe portend its 'Americanization'" (1987: 10); the same can
be said of the experience of the turn of the twenty-first century. The evolution of the EU toward a compound polity does not mean its Americanization,
nor is the continuous attempt of America to neutralize the incoherence of its
compound nature a Europeanization.

If it is true that the evolution of European politics from a national to
a continental scale brought with it an institutional organization of public
authority with many features similar to the institutional organization of territorial sovereignty operating in the United States, then it is plausible to assert
that the EU has something to learn from the political experience of the other
shore of the Atlantic (Fabbrini 1999b). In particular, the EU might surmise
that compound polities are intimately fragile institutional and conceptual
constructs. In fact, the U.S. compound republic was institutionalized thanks
to very fortunate material and cultural conditions, among them its basic isolation from world affairs. Nevertheless, it had to face the most dramatic civil
war ever seen in a democratic country. In any case, when the institutional
equilibrium of the compound republic started to be structurally challenged
in the twentieth century, especially with the military stretching of the country
in world affairs, the United States could meet those challenges with a constitution unquestionably revered by all sections of the country. As Di Palma
argues in his postscript to this book, the efficient secret of U.S. politics is
its liberal constitutionalism. U.S. political development might be interpreted
as a permanent dialogue on how to interpret the normative frame within
which to carry social and political interactions. "Conceptions of authority
and of purpose have been interconnected in American thinking about government from our early days.... The concern with the institutions of authority
has continued to characterize American constitutionalism" (Beer 1993: 379,
383). If this constitutionalism constrained the search for more rational answers to external challenges, it nevertheless preserved the conditions that
made possible the survival of U.S. compoundness.

The EU, on the contrary, is not the outcome of a constitutional design,
although it gradually became a constitutionalized regime. The EU seemed
to emerge from historical contingency and by the need of European nation-
states to preclude a third continental civil war. Of course, global development
in the last decades of the twentieth century have further fostered the reasons
for supranational integration. The EU offered to each member state an opportunity to better protect its own interest from globalization or to better
promote its own interest in a globalized economy. Moreover, the EU could
also preserve its compoundness because of its isolation, as a polity, from
world affairs. It was U.S. military might, this time, that protected Europe's
isolationism. Although no external strains have yet challenged its internal
institutional equilibrium, it remains to be seen how this equilibrium will
react to pressure for the EU to take a more active international role. As it

happened in the U.S. experience between the 1930s and the 1970s, that pressure will probably require a more precise definition of its internal authority structures, but this time without the guidelines of a formal constitution. And here resides the problem for the EU. Because, if it is true that a constitution-making process has been activated at the EU level with the Laeken decision of December 2001, it is also true that:

The massive shift in scale, the greater heterogeneity of identities and interests, the wider range of development levels and, most of all, the unprecedented process of gradual and voluntary polity formation all conspire to make the contemporary outcome of a constitutionalized Euro-polity much less predictable than the earlier national efforts (Schmitter 2000: 8).

For now, it is only plausible to argue that if it is known that the United States started from a formal constitution and thus developed through a constitutionalization of the political process by the courts, it is much less known whether the constitutionalization of the political process of the European Union that has been brought about by the European Court of Justice since the 1960s (Stone Sweet and Caporaso 1998; Weiler 1999) will end up with a formal constitution accepted by all EU member states. It remains that the United States has been successful in pursuing the strategy of *e pluribus unum* because it has been since its inception a political republic, constituted through and protected by the constitution:

Perhaps the adjective "American" ... points to the citizenship, not the nativity or nationality, of the men and women it designates. It is a *political adjective*, and its politics is liberal in the strict sense: generous, tolerant, ample, accommodating – it allows for the survival, even the enhancement and flourishing of manyness (Walzer 1996: 26, italics added).

It remains also that the EU has to deal with very different, and more complicated, conditions. Nevertheless, it seem undisputable that the U.S. experience may offer useful insights for better focusing some of the problems that the EU will have to resolve in order to develop.

9

Is the Democratic Deficit a Deficiency?

The Case of Immigration Policy in the United States and the European Union

Bruce E. Cain

There are many parallels between U.S. and European Union (EU) immigration trends and policies despite the clear and important differences in their decision-making institutions. Among the common problems these two entities face are the following: a global economy that promotes (or perhaps requires) a freer migration of capital and labor; fluctuations in the economic cycle that alter the perceived value that immigrants make to national economies at given points in time; greater racial, national, and cultural diversity in the immigrants and refugees who seek entry into the United States and Western Europe; political backlash from the far right against the growing presence of third-country migrants and cooptation of their issues by more mainstream, center-right parties; changing patterns of foreign migration from single male sojourners to permanent resident families; the failure of official border controls to stop the flow of illegal immigrants and false asylum applicants; and mounting pressure from cosmopolitans who deplore both the direct and indirect racial discrimination that these policies have spawned and who hold out an ideal of a borderless, prejudice-free international community that directly challenges traditional concepts of national sovereignty and citizenship. But for all these similarities, there are also important differences in how the United States and Europe have handled these new challenges, and some of this variation can be traced to institutional factors.

To pose the democratic theory question most abstractly, the issue is whether particular institutional arrangements bias the attainment of responsive and efficient immigration policies in predictable ways. Some definitions are needed at this juncture. The term *responsive* is here defined as a policy that represents the majority of a polity's constituents' wishes without violating basic, agreed-upon fundamental rights as embodied in national or supranational constitutions, or in international treaties. *Efficiency* refers to the proper functioning of the market to provide sufficient labor to meet the needs of an advanced economy. The relevant questions then are: 1) To what degree do U.S. and EU immigration policies meet these criteria? 2) Do these policies deviate from these criteria in systematic and predictable ways? 3) Finally, do institutional incentives explain the observed variations in their immigration policies?

Posing the institutional question in this way does not presume that institutions by themselves determine immigration policies. Policies are a function of both the preferences of voters and interest groups and the context of institutional structures. Therefore, depending upon the distribution of voter preferences in a country or area, it is possible for very different institutional structures to have very similar immigration policies, and vice versa, for similar structures to produce very different policies. The former (that is, similarity in policy despite differences in structure) is the case presently with respect to the EU and U.S. policy on undocumented immigrants. Both have taken steps in the last fifteen years to restrict the flow of undocumented immigrants and refugees despite very different mechanisms for making such decisions (Cornelius, Martin, and Hollifield 1994). This convergence is even more remarkable if we bear in mind that EU policy in this area is really determined by national governments that have an even wider variance in institutional structure, and yet still exhibit a fairly uniform concern with the problem of false asylum seekers (Fassmann and Munz 1992; Papademetriou and Hamilton 1996; Pettigrew 1998; Ucarer and Puchala 1997).

While institutions do not completely determine policy, they are the source of decision-making incentives and constraints that make certain immigration policies more or less likely. This can happen in various ways, such as by fixing the threshold of consent needed to pass legislation, multiplying the number of veto points, or varying the degree of constraint that court-enforced rights play in policy making. Specifically, my thesis is that the EU decision-making structure biases immigration policy in a direction that will make the expansion of immigrant labor very difficult if and when economic conditions favor expansion. By contrast, the U.S. decision-making structure favors expansion, even under unfavorable economic conditions. Under unfavorable economic conditions, however, the bias of the EU is less evident since it tends to produce an outcome that is both majority-preferred and economically efficient. Indeed, the so-called democratic deficit problem, a topic of great controversy in the EU, really does not apply to EU immigration policy under present conditions in Europe. The democratic deficit in this policy area will likely be realized when economic and labor conditions require more immigration in order to preserve growth and prosperity.

The first section of this chapter examines the democratic deficit argument in some detail and suggests that while parts of it seem correct, other parts do not. In particular, the issue needs to be reformulated more clearly, and some new distinctions need to be made. Secondly, the EU decision-making structure with respect to immigration policy will be compared with that of the United States with an eye toward the relative biases of both. Lastly, returning to the EU democratic deficit problem, I will argue that if and when a true democratic deficit emerges with respect to immigration policy, this might prove to be an important event in the evolution of the EU insofar as the goal is to build upon economic cooperation toward a stronger political union.

THE DEMOCRATIC DEFICIT AND EU IMMIGRATION

A common argument in the literature is that the democratic deficit in the EU's current governance structure as it relates to the core issue of citizenship leads to an increasingly restrictionist and discriminatory policy toward non-EU refugees and immigrants (see especially Papdemetriou 1996; Sorenson 1996). Since Western Europe has not encouraged or received large numbers of legal economic immigrants since the mid-1970s (Fassmann and Munz 1992), the most important immediate issues concern refugee policy: the responsibility of European nations for taking legitimate political refugees (those that meet the stringent definition of the 1951 UN Convention on the Status of Refugees), and the problem of dealing with those who use refugee status for economically motivated reasons. Since the mid-1980s, there has been a dramatic and unprecedented increase in the numbers of persons requesting asylum in EU nations. By the early 1990s, there were more than three times the number of asylum seekers into the member states than there had been in 1985 (Sorenson 1996: 91). There are now also large numbers of illegal immigrants in Europe (Sorensen 1996: 90). Hence, while legal immigration has dropped considerably, migration still occurs in significant numbers.

In response to the rise in asylum seekers, the EU member states have adopted a number of restrictive measures. Some nations have adopted stricter visa requirements for individuals who come from refugee-producing states. Others have imposed carrier liability on flights and ferries that take people on board who do not have proper documents. Lists of safe countries from which individuals have no need for asylum have been drawn, and many refugees have been assigned a "temporary status," giving the state the right to expel them when conditions appear to have improved sufficiently. Policies and agreements fashioned at the EU level are primarily concerned with formal control procedures for limiting access and not with harmonizing migration law per se. For instance, the Dublin Convention (1990) represents an attempt by the Immigration Group to deal with the growing problem of asylum abuses. In an effort to put an end to "asylum shopping," this agreement designated a single member state to examine a refugee application, depending upon a number of criteria. Similarly, the Convention on the Crossing of External Borders (1991) attempted to tighten controls over third-country nationals by more explicitly setting out the definition of external frontiers and the conditions for crossing them.

The harshest critics of current EU refugee policies believe that the EU structure is responsible for an excessively exclusionary and racially biased policy. The argument goes as follows: EU immigration and migration policy has been forged within an intergovernmental framework (Convey and Kupiszewski 1995; Geddes 1995; Papademetriou 1996; Philip 1994; Sorensen 1996). The Trevi Group, the Working Group on Immigration (1986) that grew out of the work of the Trevi Group, the Schengen Agreement (1984), the Dublin Convention (1990), and the External Frontiers Convention (1991) are all examples of intergovernmental agreements that exhibit three features. First, they cede power on immigration matters to the national governments, and each state has formally equal power in the form of a national veto. Second, neither the European Parliament nor the European Court of Justice can override the decision making or implementation of intergovernmental decisions in this area. And lastly, the negotiation process in this area tends to be secretive and unaccountable.

Added to the general perception that European "economic integration involves a technocratisation of still more policy areas and issues without direct democratic control" (Sorensen 1996: 122) and that citizens feel locked out of participating in EU decision-making processes, the modus operandi of immigration and refugee policy making only reinforces the general democratic deficit problem. In the words of one scholar:

Parliamentarians meanwhile have begun to get increasingly anxious about the opaque and uncontrolled decision-making processes by which many of the new decisions at EC level on citizen rights, asylum and refugee policy, and immigration matters are made.... The problem of lack of control over the decision-making processes arises from the sensitivity of many of the issues (inviting secrecy of discussion) and the conduct of negotiations on an intergovernmental basis where the negotiators are not accountable to EC institutions, nor frequently to national parliaments. In practice, national parliaments have been presented with deals done by ministers and officials behind closed doors and have been required to approve such deals without amendments because each is a delicate intergovernmental compromise. (Philip 1994: 8).

Another related critique argues that the democratic deficit is even greater for the ethnic and immigrant minority groups who live in EU countries. In the words of Andrew Geddes:

...a central feature of the Union is that many decisions are taken in intergovernmental forums which often meet in secret, about whose activities remarkably little is known and which are distant from the people of Europe in both a political and geographical sense. This participatory gap – an important aspect of the democratic deficit – is compounded for people from ethnic and immigrant groups in the EU (1995: 197).

In other words, the problem of political response is even greater for ethnic and immigrant groups who would like to counter the anti-immigrant backlash in Europe, but find that they are hindered from doing so by being in the minority and having few political rights. Even if such groups were to achieve such rights, intergovernmental modes of decision making remove the issue one step further from any arena in which they can have impact.

Finally, a third criticism holds that EU intergovernmentalism leads to a restriction bias that may ultimately prove to be both inefficient and unfair as previously defined. In his book, *The Exclusive European Citizenship*, Jens Magleby Sorensen argues the intergovernmental structure presented nations that wanted more liberal immigration policies with a dilemma:

> ... between being flooded by new immigrants or making their migration and immigrant policies as strict as the strictest member state. Thus when migration issues had to be coordinated between the member states, the tendency of national migration laws has been the erection of stricter and less attractive migration and immigrant policies. A highest common denominator approach will become the standard for the region (1996: 146).

In other words, the cooperative dilemma that arises when the member nations separately make decisions about residency and citizenship combined with the unit veto nature of intergovernmental negotiations empowers nations that favor more restrictive policies – they cannot be outvoted by a more moderate majority and forced to compromise.

To unravel this a little more, there are two factors in this immigrant aversion bias. First, there is the problem of the national veto, which empowers the restrictionist outlier in collective decisions, and second, there is the implicit prisoner's dilemma that prevents individual nations from being too generous in their acceptance of immigrants or refugees. With respect to the veto, giving European nations the right to veto or not sign on to an agreement constrains agreements in important ways (Scharpf 1988). Since nations are not equally populated, from a purely majoritarian perspective, nation-based negotiations do not necessarily lead to decisions that a referendum of all the individuals in Europe would approve by a majority. Nations that prefer highly restrictive policies can veto proposals to make Third World immigration or asylum seeking easier across the EU member states. This point of course applies to all movements away from the status quo, and not just expansionist outliers. A unit veto or supermajoritarian system requires virtual or total unanimity in order to initiate change. Since the status quo in Europe is highly restrictive to begin with, the inertia of the system makes it hard to liberalize immigration policies.

The other component of the restriction bias is the implicit prisoner's dilemma between nations that want to have more liberal immigration policies and those that do not. In the integrationist ideal, labor flows freely to the areas that have the most demand. In theory, when demand wanes in a given area, labor will cease to migrate into that area and will instead go elsewhere.

But in practice, often labor either cannot go elsewhere (if there is no free movement across borders) or chooses not to go elsewhere for noneconomic reasons (for example, because the package of political and social rights is not favorable). Hence even when a nation wants to live by liberal trade ideals, it cannot do so if other EU nations do not cooperate. This then causes the more liberal nation to pursue a more restrictive policy than it might otherwise. Similarly, with respect to refugee policy, a nation that wants to live up to humanitarian ideals will feel more reluctant to do so if the refugees that the nation accepts are prevented from moving elsewhere within the EU or if for want of other alternatives it must absorb more than its fair share. It is characteristic of these cooperative games that risk-averse players often choose suboptimal outcomes for fear of being taken advantage of, and this logic reinforces the restrictionist bias created by the intergovernmental form of agreement.

While this is a powerful and convincing analysis of EU immigration policy, a few aspects of the democratic deficit critique seem a bit muddled. First, with respect to accountability and secretiveness, the question is really one of democratic oversight over the actions of elected and unelected members of the state. This is a problem for all democracies, including the United States. The evidence that democratic oversight is uniquely bad in the area of immigration policy is lacking. Military negotiations and treaties are every bit as sensitive as immigration issues, and they are also often presented to national legislatures as take-it-or-leave-it propositions because of the intricacy of the negotiations and the multisidedness of contemporary international conflicts. If the democratic deficit is worse in Europe than in the United States in this specific sense (and the evidence on that point is lacking), it is not simply an EU deficit per se but also a national deficit by default – that is, the fact that the most critical immigration and migration decisions have been ceded by default to national governments means that the deficit lies partly in the national structures themselves. As such, this is really an inherited democratic deficit problem, not a newly created one. Because European nations tend to have stronger state mechanisms and central administrative structures, bureaucratic controls are less directly electoral than in the United States. From another vantage point, this has also meant that European nations have enjoyed certain advantages in governance as well. As democratic theory so often warns, institutional choices are about trade-offs in advantages and disadvantages.

The restriction bias produced by the national veto and the prisoner's dilemma of cooperation on immigrant policy is a serious structural issue. But ironically, there is actually little evidence that the democratic deficit matters much in this area under current conditions, although it might under different, more favorable conditions. Currenly, the EU's restrictive policies, it could be plausibly argued, are responsive and efficient as previously defined.

They are reponsive in the sense that they are likely the same policies that would be chosen by the European electorate on a referendum vote or if the matter were given over to the European Parliament.

There is no evidence that a majority of Europeans want to admit larger numbers of non-EU refugees except in response to very specific refugee crises (such as the British seeking to relieve the plight of the Kosovars). Reviewing data from seven Eurobarometer surveys, Thomas Pettigrew observes that the percentage of Europeans who believed that there were too many "non-EU foreigners in their country" rose dramatically between 1988 and 1991, with clear majorities in Belgium, West Germany, France, and Italy. There was also a rapid increase in the numbers of Europeans who wanted to restrict the rights of non-EU nationals (Pettigrew 1998). Some argue that "in no West European country can politicians or political parties gain votes by favoring new immigration or immigrant voting rights" (Lahav 1997; Messina 1990). While the emergence of anti-immigrant forces has given rise to some transnational political organizing on the part of immigrant groups (Ireland 1991), the calculus of democracy inevitably favors voting majorities over nonvoting minorities. Moreover, it is unlikely that Members of the European Parliament (MEPs) would choose any differently if it were in their power. Survey evidence indicates that MEP attitudes on immigrants are forged by the same ideological and partisan factors that drive members in the national legislatures (Lahav 1997). Hence, even though national government policy making and supranational policy making theoretically could yield very different outcomes, that is not what is happening here.

While there is some concern about the details of particular policies and about nonelected officials controlling elected ones, the simple fact is that there is no deficit in the most important sense that the European majority is deprived of policies that the majority prefers. To put it another way, there may be a procedural deficit in the sense that the process is not sufficiently democratic (in the sense of being consultative or connected to elected officials), but there is not much evidence of a substantive policy deficit (in the sense of immigration policies that lack majority support). One might also argue that in the short run at least, the current immigration policies in Europe are probably efficient in the sense that the demand for the labor that is being excluded has been relatively low since the mid-1970s. This, of course, might change over time, and efficient short-run labor policies might not be so efficient in the long run.

Indeed, the true motivation for the democratic deficit argument as it applies to immigration policy seems to be an integrationist vision or a cosmopolitan ideal that finds restrictionist policies objectionable on other, broader grounds. To the integrationist, the heavy reliance on intergovernmentalism is a step back from progress toward a politically unified Europe. However, the assertion that restrictive immigration policy derives from the intergovernmental structure is both unproven and disingenuous. One suspects that structure is being blamed for what preference has produced. Without placing a normative value on European preferences, the widespread reluctance to absorb more non-EU populations seems to be what is really driving current policies in Europe. As indicated earlier, structure alone does not determine policy, and structure may not matter at all when preferences are configured in a sufficiently high level of consensus. That apparently is the present situation in the EU with respect to immigration.

Cosmopolitans have a slightly different take. They rightly see that national control over the citizenship and immigration policy area makes it hard to develop universal social and political rights. This is an admirable goal, but until there is indeed a consensus that these rights should be universal, cosmopolitans have to accept that what the majority in Europe wants is fair by definition. The harsh reality is that the ideals of liberal trade and cosmopolitan rights are flawed in application. Labor does not simply move in efficient ways toward areas of demand and away from oversupply. Workers put down roots, and labor flows become sticky. This stickiness has external costs to the communities in the form of education costs, social security benefits, medical care expenses, and the like. This means that immigration and openness toward refugees is not always cost effective, and hence other values have to be traded against economic self-interest. Similarly, beyond the most basic rights to life and freedom, nations and cultures vary significantly in the obligations and opportunities that constituents demand as rights. Pretending that there is harmony on these matters when none exists does not necessarily facilitate their evolution.

Hence, the standard story about the democratic deficit in the EU seems to be right in some parts and wrong in others. There is a restrictive logic to the current structure, but it is not clear that the policies that Europe is currently pursuing are more restrictive than a majority of European voters or a European Parliament would prefer. There are problems of secretiveness and unaccountability in the negotiations over immigration and refugee status, but they can be traced partly to oversight problems in the national governments, and are in that sense inherited from national structures, and not simply attributable to the EU. Later, I will argue that a true democratic deficit is more likely under different conditions, and that far from lamenting it, integrationists should welcome it since it will be a more effective motive for greater European integration. But first, in order to lay the groundwork for that argument, I will review the U.S. structure for handling immigration and highlight what I consider its pluses and minuses.

THE BIASES OF THE U.S. DECISION-MAKING STRUCTURE

If the EU structure tends to produce a bias toward restrictiveness, what is the comparable bias of U.S. governmental structures? The sheer numbers of foreign population in the United States dwarfs the other Organization for Economic Cooperation and Development (OECD) countries: In 1991, there were 19 million in the United States as compared to close to 6 million in West Germany, 3.5 million in France, 1.7 million in the United Kingdom, and 896,000 in Italy (Money 1994). On a per capita basis, however, the United States falls more in the middle of the range at 7.9 percent, lagging well behind Australia at 22.8 percent and Canada at 16 percent. Even more significantly, the trend line on U.S. legal immigration is a relatively steady upward drift. By comparison, the trend line in other OECD countries that have accepted large numbers of immigrants, such as Germany and Australia, is much more cyclical (Money 1994: 4–5). Can this difference be attributed to institutional sources?

On the assumption that structural differences may account for differences in immigration policy, it is illuminating to contrast U.S. and EU decision-making structures. More than in the EU, immigration decision making in the United States is multilayered. In the EU, the nation-states control both the borders and the allocation of goods and services to non-EU immigrants/refugees, while the EU Community facilitates the coordination of those policies. In the United States, the federal government controls the borders, but the states and local governments provide the critical social services for immigrants such as emergency health care, schooling, and police and fire protection. This explains why immigration policy can sometimes be controversial at the state government level. For example, Proposition 187 – the 1994 ballot measure in California that would have denied nonemergency state and local services to undocumented immigrants – was an attempt by a state electorate to mitigate the effects that federal immigration policies were having on California by denying state services to immigrants, and thereby making settlement in California less attractive to prospective immigrants (Colino 1995; Johnson 1995; MacDonald and Cain 1998; Schockman 1998). As it has turned out, the federal courts have constrained a state's ability to use social policies in this way, but even so, the point is that immigration policy is not simply dictated by the federal government.

This points to a second difference: the greater role the U.S. courts play in significantly constraining immigration policy in at least two ways. First, they have used the Fourteenth Amendment and fundamental rights doctrine to limit the ways that the U.S. government can treat immigrants and refugees, and second, any attempt to return to a Eurocentric immigration policy would likely be struck down by the courts. In *Plyler v. Doe* (457 U.S. 202 [1982]), the U.S. Supreme Court ruled that children of undocumented immigrants could not be denied a free public education, based on a Fourteenth Amendment guarantee of equal protection for members of a suspect class (that is, the children) and the assertion of a fundamental right to education. Similarly, any attempt to revert to pre-1965 standards for legal immigration with quotas favoring white Europeans would run afoul of statutory and constitutional protections against racial discrimination. These legal precedents significantly limit the options available to governments, and in particular make certain kinds of restrictive immigration policies impossible.

With respect to international law, however, the United States and Europe may be becoming more similar. Consider, for instance, how the United States handled Albanian refugees in the wake of the NATO bombing of Kosovo. Faced with the crisis of a half-million Kosovars fleeing their homes and seeking safety in neighboring Macedonia, Albania, and Montenegro, the United States along with Germany, Turkey, Norway, Greece, and Canada agreed to accept twenty thousand refugees to ease the pressure on Albania. However, it did so in a manner that critics charge was "calculated to deprive the ethnic Albanians of the rights which they would be entitled to under the 1967 Protocol Relating to the Status of Refugees ratified by the United States in 1968" (Musalo 1999: 2). By proposing to place the refugees on the U.S. naval base in Guantanamo Bay, as they had the Haitian refuges following the 1991 coup of Jean-Bertrand Aristide, the United States could keep the Kosovars off U.S. territory, thereby denying them the right to apply for political asylum in the United States.

The reality, say critics, is that while the United States is widely regarded by many countries as a leader on refugee issues, it clearly has adopted strategies in recent years to minimize its obligations under international law. This is very similar to the strategies the British (who have a much worse international reputation on refugee matters) have recently adopted to discourage false asylum seekers. Faced with a large and growing backlog of asylum cases and the fear that the benefits of the British welfare state might be a powerful allure to would-be refugees, the British government has restricted benefits (such as replacing cash welfare benefits with food vouchers and not giving asylum seekers a choice of where to live), speeding up the claims process and making it harder for refugees to get into Britain (for example fining airlines for carrying passengers without proper documents).

Third, U.S. decision making is more majoritarian than the EU system at present. As noted earlier, the EU makes immigration policy largely through intergovernmental negotiation, and the national units are not equally sized. Hence, it is possible (although it is not currently the case) for national negotiations to produce immigration policies that the majority does not prefer. That can also happen in the United States, but it is harder. With the exception of the U.S. Senate, "one person, one vote" has replaced territorial representation, and the House and the president are strongly influenced by majoritarian pressures.

This majoritarian influence is somewhat greater at the state than the federal level. In addition to the U.S. Senate (the only violation of the "one person, one vote" principle the Supreme Court allows), the federal system offers multiple veto points in the organization of the U.S. Congress and supermajoritarian rules (for example, to break a filibuster and to overturn a presidential veto) that empower nonmedian interests and representatives

(Brady and Volden 1997; Krehbiel 1998). The states mostly mimic the federal government structure with division of power between three branches (with the exception of Nebraska), but many states supplement their representation with direct democracy mechanisms such as the referendum and the popular initiative. This has both the direct effect of causing majority policies to succeed at the ballot box when they cannot pass through the state legislatures and the indirect effect of pressuring legislatures to pay closer attention to median voter positions (Gerber 1996).

With these comparisons in mind, let us return to how democratic deficits affect U.S. immigration policy. Leaving the court constraint aside for the moment, the prospects for the kind of democratic deficit to which the EU is vulnerable are somewhat less in the U.S. case. This is particularly true at the state level, where median voter pressures are favored in various ways, as discussed earlier. Moreover, since states do not have unit veto power, any territorial or state-centric attempt either to block departures from the status quo or initiate new policies put forward in the House or Senate must win significant support from representatives from other states. To put it another way, it would be harder for any outlier state that prefers greater restrictions on immigration to prevent the liberalization of national immigration policy unless it had either majority support in the House, or by the logic of pivotal politics, the support of at least a third of the Senate to sustain a filibuster. The same point applies to the liberalizing state outlier.

Second, the U.S. structure solves part of the prisoner's dilemma that EU nations face. In the European case, all nations might be better off with a free-flowing labor supply across borders, but nations that open their borders when others do not face the prospect that they will be saddled with the social costs of unwanted immigrant labor during economic downturns. By having one and only one border policy for all in the United States, and guaranteeing free movement within the states for immigrants and nonimmigrants alike (although the Carter Administration's refugee program tried to limit movement for specified periods of time), there is no cooperation dilemma concerning the border. But the multilayered nature of decision making in this area still leaves states with a second and related cooperation dilemma in the sense that if one state's social policies are too favorable, they might attract more than their fair share of immigrants and refugees. Clearly, this was an issue that Proposition 187 and welfare reform sought to address. By constraining the most restrictive states in terms of what they can refuse to offer immigrants, the courts have de facto limited the effects of this cooperation problem somewhat.

Finally, with respect to the democratic deficit problem that might arise through the secretive and unaccountable implementation of immigration policies by executive agencies, the Congress provides oversight into the administration of immigration policy by the Immigration and Naturalization

Service (INS). By both casework intervention and Congressional hearings, the INS is closely monitored by U.S. elected officials.

The upshot of all these factors is that the U.S. legislative policy is more likely to be based on majority opinion than EU policy. Having said this, two factors limit the responsiveness of immigration policy to shifts in majority opinion. First, an enormous amount of policy inertia is built into the U.S. system. Quite apart from the drag that federalism and the division of power place on policy making at all levels, the decentralized nature of Congressional decision making and the multiple veto points that interest groups and individual legislators have in the U.S. system serve to slow down and stop many new initiatives. It takes a great deal of consensus to overcome these inertial pressures.

But the most important democratic deficit in the United States with respect to immigration policy making comes from the courts. Whereas in the EU it is theoretically possible for nations to create policies through intergovernmental agreements that are not preferred by a majority of EU voters, court decisions can bias U.S. policies against the median. Whereas in Europe those who want a more liberalized immigration and refugee policy complain about national control, in the United States those who want a more restrictive policy object to the courts' constraints on policy making. Since the federal courts are more insulated from majoritarian pressures and are less accountable to the people, they create yet another kind of democratic deficit. But this takes us to the critical question of whether a democratic deficit is necessarily a democratic deficiency.

VENUE SHOPPING, INSTITUTIONAL REFORM, AND DEMOCRATIC DEFICITS

The discussion to this point reveals that at least three different types of democratic deficits arise with respect to immigration policy, and that at least two of these help to explain the characteristic biases in U.S. and EU immigration policy. The first type is a deficit caused by the failure of delegation oversight: A democracy (or a union based on democratic principles) delegates the details of immigration policy (the issuing of visas, the policy for handling of problematic asylum cases, and so on) to administrative officials (especially unelected ones), but then has to hold them accountable. This entails finding out the specifics of what those officials have done and making them responsive to the wishes of the citizens. As suggested previously, all democracies struggle with this problem, particularly with respect to technical issues. A growing literature in American political science places the delegation aspects of modern democracies in the framework of principal-agent models (McCubbins 1985). These situations are often characterized by informational asymmetries in which the agent knows more about the details of a given issue than the principal.

To hold agents accountable, it is important to find ways to inform principals about actions that affect them and to design mechanisms (usually electoral) by which principals can bring consequences to agents when they do not like the consequences of the actions that agents have chosen (that is, mechanisms of accountability). In the U.S. system of checks and balances, the agency that deals with immigration (the INS) is ultimately accountable to both an elected president and legislature. The drawn-out saga of Elian Gonzalez nicely demonstrates the degree to which Congressional oversight checks (or interferes with, as the case may be) the INS. Had the Congress not itself been divided over the benefits of giving the boy permanent residency or citizenship, it could have taken the matter out of the hands of the INS in one Congressional act. Or, to take another aspect of this example, the Republican-led Congress has taken upon itself the task of investigating the child's seizure to discover whether excessive force might have been avoided, demonstrating that the downside of accountability can be politicization – that is, using immigration disputes for partisan political advantage. But one at least cannot say that the INS was operating in an unexamined, unconstrained policy-making vacuum.

The EU's involvement in immigration and refugee issues is necessarily limited to issues of cooperation in policing borders. The understandable unwillingness of European nations to surrender their control over basic decisions of national membership pushes any democratic deficit problems with respect to the core issues of immigration and refugee policy back to the national arena. The accountability of national agencies on these issues is a matter of national institutional structure. But as European nations have come to deal with common problems of enforcing borders and trying to reconcile the principle of free labor movement for EU citizens with the national concerns for controlling non-EU migration, immigration has slipped into the least accountable and visible realm. The first type of democratic deficit seems to be most applicable to the EU. However, it is hard to see that this type of deficit necessarily contributes to any particular policy bias per se. In principle, it could serve the interests of liberalizing immigration as much as limiting it.

The second type of democratic deficit is judicial and international treaty constraint, limiting the freedom of the United States and Europe to close their borders to legitimate political refugees and preventing American states from denying fundamental rights and services to undocumented immigrants. This becomes a democratic deficit when the courts overturn the will of the majority in a particular state or country. The best illustration of this is the court action in preventing the implementation of Proposition 187, the California measure that would have denied nonemergency benefits to undocumented immigrants. This deficit type is more prevalent in the United States because of the checking role that the courts play in the structure of U.S. government. As noted before, the rights orientation of the U.S. courts contributes to a liberalizing bias in U.S. immigration policy. In theory, international treaties also protect the rights of political refugees, and in this way constitute a liberalizing constraint, but both the United States and EU nations have devised ways to limit their responsibilities in this area.

The third type of democratic deficit is the mediation of constituent preferences through subnational or formal group representation. This is a deficit in the same sense as the other two types, because the policy that emerges from mediated representation can vary from the majority will. Of course, all republican forms of government as opposed to direct forms of democracy can suffer deficits for any number of reasons – for example, the influence of lobbyists or special interests on representatives, miscalculation on the part of elected officials, party pressures, and so on. However, within the context of EU immigration policy, mediation can become problematic when national constituencies make policy for a multinational entity. Aside from the fact that the European member states are unequally populated, the delegation to nations in the EU introduces a prisoner's dilemma cooperation dynamic that favors a more restrictive policy.

The assumption in the literature is that democratic deficits are undesirable. Clearly, they can be, but deficits are not always deficiencies, for two reasons. One has already been mentioned – the existence of a deficit does not always mean that the policy chosen is different from what would be chosen if the deficit did not exist. This gets back to my point that policy is both a function of preference as well as institution. There is no evidence that Europe has adopted current policies that are more restrictive than what they would have adopted if the matter had been decided by referendum or even by the European Parliament. However, a different configuration of preferences might change things. Assume for the moment that the economic growth rate in Europe greatly increases and birthrates within the EU countries remain low. Several scholars have observed that natural population increases (births over deaths) have decreased throughout Western Europe at the same time that the economic economy has expanded, creating a potential labor shortage in the future (Munz 1996; Thraenhardt 1996). The amount of free-flowing labor across EU countries has been relatively small, perhaps because the "increasing industrialization in the peripheral countries of the EC" has leveled economic development and pay (Werner 1994: 160). But insofar as the supply of labor from third countries is motivated by a relatively low level of pay in the origin country, we can expect it to be high in the future. If the demand for imported third-country labor returns to pre-1973 levels, then the pressure for liberalization could build. Under those conditions, the EU's restrictive bias would become more problematic. Nations that wanted to expand their pool of immigrant labor might want to solve the prisoner's dilemmas associated with liberalized immigration, and to initiate more harmonized labor-expanding policies without the threat of a single member veto.

To play this scenario out further, one might predict that liberalizing forces, led by business elites, might venue shop (take the issue to the forum where they are most likely to succeed) and ultimately take their case to the European Parliament if they felt that support and the prospects of winning there were greater. The strategic choices of elites might lead eventually to a general acceptance of the principle that immigration was no longer simply a matter of national interest but was properly a European matter. Policy preferences would end up driving institutional change. This policy-driven scenario is similar to the "benefits of decisional reallocation" scenario of Gary Marks, Liesbet Hooghe, and Kermit Blank, who suggested that European nations might surrender control in instances when "the political benefits may outweigh the costs of losing political control or there may be intrinsic benefits having to do with shifting responsibility for unpopular decisions or insulating decision-making from domestic pressures" (Marks, Hooghe, and Blank 1996: 349).

Clearly, this scenario of shifting power from the nation to the EU leaves out many of the cultural preconditions of closer, future political union. This does not imply that the sense of "we-ness" and trust that develops when people grow accustomed to an arrangement is unimportant. But based on the history of institutional change in the United States, it is important to acknowledge that it is often driven by frustrated majority policy preferences. However much it upsets classical notions of constitutionalism, all too frequently the real impetus for institutional change is to overcome policy obstacles by shifting to a more favorable policy venue. A corollary observation is that when the shift is in a majoritarian direction, it is often hard to reverse unless there is a massive breakdown in the unity of the larger electorate. When that happens, a minority seeks to change the rules so that it can prevail – hence separation or at least decentralization.

It is hard to say whether the conditions leading to greater union on immigration and citizenship matters will arise in the near future. But there is a second, and even more important, consideration, which is that democratic deficits may not be deficiencies in the sense that deficits may actually be valuable in some policy areas if the goal is responsiveness and efficiency as previously defined. The assertion that the unmediated majority should prevail on issues assumes: 1) that the majority will not trample on the basic rights of minorities; and 2) that the majority will choose policies in its best interests. Few, if any, would dispute that these conditions are sometimes violated. Many of the institutions that are perceived to be democratically deficient can also be perceived as checks against the breakdown of these two majoritarian assumptions: The U.S. courts cannot protect minority rights by themselves, and administrative officials often make technical choices that are beyond the expertise of the average voter.

Since the situation in the EU is so far from a tyranny of the EU electoral majority (or even the European Parliament), this might seem like a purely

American problem. That is a fair objection, but my point is only that the concepts that political scientists bring to EU discussions need to build a balanced perspective of democratic deficits or they might put in force democratic expectations that are ultimately destructive. In this sense, the United States is an object lesson.

The history of political reform in the United States in a nutshell is the story of a populist drift – the gradual but progressive shedding of most forms of indirect and territorial representation in favor of more direct and egalitarian representation. This has put the courts in a more visible role of checking majoritarian excesses. With respect to representation, there is some degree of substitution going on in the United States, with the courts substituting for the territorial and indirect protections of the original eighteenth-century structures of representation. Perhaps, if the EU follows a similar course, a strengthened EU court system will be called upon to do the same.

To flesh this argument out some, the history of political reform in the United States has been toward more openness (extending the franchise and opening up the workings of government to more external scrutiny) and more unmediated majority control. Hence, political parties have been weakened (the direct primary system, the end of patronage, and so on), territorial bases of representation have been abandoned to the extent the constitution allows (for example the "one person, one vote" doctrine), direct democracy has been introduced in twenty-three states, and indirect representation has ended except in specialized local boards (for example, the direct election of U.S. Senators). The two major twentieth-century reform movements in the United States have been the Progressive and the Populist. Progressives (both in the pure historical sense of the Progressive movement and the more generic sense of those who follow in that tradition) seek to check the mediation of the popular will by political parties and business interests by supplementing the representative system with direct democracy, campaign finance and lobbying reforms, and political party regulations. Populists increasingly reject any form of mediation, including by representatives themselves, and seek to give more power to the people directly (hence, term limits, the popular initiative, and so on). While these two movements diverge on some important points (see Cain and Miller 1999; Persily 1998), the joint product of their influence and efforts has been the removal of Madisonian filters and the handing over of more power to the electorate directly.

This has placed the courts in the role of checking decisions made by electorates that might have been headed off in the past by party leaders or more insulated representatives. This is particularly important in immigrant issues, for several reasons. First, nativist fears rise and fall with economic cycles, and decisions taken in panic at the trough of a cycle might not be in the best economic interests of a country (the efficiency condition). Second, because immigration issues often conflate with racial discrimination issues, majority reactions to temporary immigration crises might lead to policies that violate basic rights.

Eventually, European courts may come to play a similar role, but in the interim, the best protection for immigrant rights might be the decentralized way that these decisions are currently made. With many nations making separate decisions about immigration and refugee policy, there is always the possibility of outlier countries that will be sympathetic to letting in noncitizens. A truly uniform EU policy without sufficiently strong court checks might be able to close off doors to immigrants and refugees in the future more effectively than is possible under the current EU arrangements. Purely responsive policies are not necessarily fair. Antimajoritarian features can sometimes be more preservative of rights. In this sense, democratic deficits are not always deficiencies.

10

Territory, Representation, and Policy Outcome

The United States and the European Union Compared

Alberta M. Sbragia

The United States is a federal system with a strong federal government, whereas the European Union is an entity with characteristics found in both polities and international organizations. Although a theoretical dispute rages between those who would use international relations theory (Moravscik 1998) and those who would use concepts drawn from comparative politics to analyze European integration (Hix 1994; Hooghe and Marks 2001a; Kohler-Koch and Eising 1999; Sandholtz and Stone Sweet 1998; Sbragia 1992), it is now clear that both approaches have utility depending on the features of the European Union being examined. The European Union is simultaneously an international organization, an international regime, and a semipolity with some federallike features.

The 'semipolity' is shaped in many ways by the fact that it is intertwined with an international organization. As Andrew Hurrell and Anand Menon point out:

> ... traditional comparative politics explanations of actor strategies in policy-making cannot deal with a central motivation of much EU policy making – namely the management of unequal state power and the desire to tie certain states within a structure from which they have the option to defect. (1996: 392).

Such management of unequal state power is calibrated in all the institutions of the European Community (Sbragia 1993), but it is most explicitly addressed in the Council of Ministers with its differential votes and different rules for different types of policy-making procedures. As Fiona Hayes-Renshaw and Helen Wallace argue, the Council of Ministers "is the forum for reconciling the distinctive purposes and powers of the member states with the needs for recurrent and disciplined joint action . . . its attributes resemble the traditional features of conventional international organisations" (Hayes-Renshaw and Wallace 1997: 2–3). Within the Community's legislative process, it has been (until the widespread use of codecision) the ultimate decision maker.[1]

In the United States, the ultimate decision maker in the legislative process is the bicameral Congress. From a comparative U.S.–EU perspective, a striking difference between the two systems lies in the system of territorial representation. In the United States, the governments of the federation's constituent units have no formal representation (although electorates within those units do), whereas in the European Union the governments of the constituent units (the member states) themselves act as the ultimate decision makers within the Council of Ministers. In the United States, the periphery is in fact the state governments qua governments while in the EU the term *periphery*, with its connotation of a strong center, does not apply (Sbragia 1993). In William Riker's terms, the United States is a centrally directed federalism, whereas the EU resembles a "peripheralized" federalism. In other words, the United States makes federal decisions "exclusively through the machinery of the central government," whereas in the EU the member states have a "constitutional right to take part in central decisions" (Riker 1987: 137).

Does it make a difference to policy making and to policy outcomes that the two systems differ along that dimension? Much of the literature on the EU implicitly or explicitly argues that the system of member-state bargaining characteristic of the Council leads to very slow decision making, lowest common denominator decisions, and generally suboptimal policy outcomes worsened by the "democratic deficit." Deadlock within the Council is so frequent that analysts have explained policy change only by arguing that "the use of subterfuge... has become second nature to... policy makers" (Heritier 1997: 171).

Critics of EU decision making seem to use an often implicit comparative referent – that of some ideal federal state in which decisions are made expeditiously, at a high level of regulation, and with full democratic participation by interest groups and social forces. Those features of the Council that are making it an international organization – rather than a federal institution – are viewed as largely responsible for its decision-making deficits. The view of the Council as problematic is especially widespread when the Council is adopting legislation with the decision-making rule of unanimity.

Would the EU be more likely to arrive at decisions more quickly if it were a federal state? The question of whether even a strong federal state characterized by the extraordinary cultural and economic diversity of the EU would in fact be able to make decisions more rapidly, more efficiently,

---

[1] Under the codecision procedure, both the Council and the European Parliament must agree on a piece of legislation. Either institution can veto the proposed legislation, in which case the proposal dies.

and more openly and produce optimal policy outcomes is rarely asked. It is precisely that question which this chapter seeks to explore by comparing decision making and policy outcomes in the EU and the United States in the area of air pollution, a policy area that imposes differential costs and involves fierce lobbying by producer interests.

The politics of air pollution are extremely contentious in both the EU and the United States – but is the difficulty the EU has experienced in arriving at agreement in the Council of Ministers due to the fact that the Council still resembles an international organization in which member-state governments can very effectively defend their interests? Is the Council of Ministers, understood as a legislature, less effective at the making of air pollution policy than is the U.S. Congress? In other words, does EU air pollution policy suffer in comparative terms from having an institutional decision maker that resembles an international organization as well as a conventional legislature?

Given that national governments make decisions at the level of the EU, and given that in the United States, the governments of the states are excluded from central decision making and therefore less able to defend their territorial interests, a logical assumption is that a federal government would find it easier to impose differential costs than would an international organization.

One would expect that the system with a central government independent of the states would find it easier to impose differential costs on actors in those states than would the entity in which the member-state governments are embedded within the decision-making apparatus. In the latter case, one would expect that governments would be able to defend the interests of producers forcefully against regulation whereas in the former case, interest group representation would be comparatively less effective. Yet this chapter argues that such is not necessarily the case.

This chapter begins with the assumption that we can compare the U.S. Congress with the Council of Ministers. Although, as Hayes-Renshaw and Wallace point out, the Council of Ministers has rarely been compared to other legislatures (Hayes-Renshaw and Wallace 1997: 8), I argue that it is precisely through such a comparison that we can begin to isolate the impact of different ways of representing the periphery. Although it is possible to discuss the difference between the EU as an "international regime with an international organization," and the American federation in broad conceptual terms, it is difficult to draw conclusions about how policy outcomes might be related to such differences without careful empirical analysis. Through a fairly close analysis of how the key decision-making institutions within those two systems operate within the same policy area, we can begin to understand what difference it makes that the EU resembles an international organization in that its constituent units make the decisions for the center whereas the United States is a full-fledged federation.

INSTITUTIONAL DECISION-MAKING RULES

The Council of Ministers operates by policy area, so that legislation concerning environmental protection is considered, debated, and negotiated by the Council of Environment Ministers. National environment ministers make up the Council of Environment Ministers while other national ministers, such as finance ministers, do not participate. Such segmentation by policy area differentiates the Council from such national institutions as the Cabinet in the United Kingdom, and often allows national ministers who might be relatively weak in national governments to exercise considerable policy latitude in Brussels.

The Council of Ministers operates either through unanimity or through the use of a supermajority. In the latter case, under the rules of qualified majority voting, one-third of the member states can form a blocking minority. (Sixty-two out of eighty-seven votes are needed for adoption.) The use of unanimity has been viewed as the clearest expression of the Union's intergovernmental dimension, and the point is often made that such a decision rule leads to policy outcomes that represent the lowest common denominator. Such an argument has usually been made without comparing the policy outcomes made under the rule of unanimity with policy outcomes in that same policy sector in the United States. The United States is a particularly useful case, not only because it has few cases that can be used for viewing the EU in comparative perspective but also because the United States was widely viewed as an environmental leader during the 1970s and the 1980s.

In the bicameral U.S. Congress, both houses (the House of Representatives and the Senate) are elected by constituencies defined by territory. Members of the House are elected within Congressional districts, while Senators are elected in statewide races. Thus, each representative and each senator defines his or her electoral constituency by territory. Both the House and Senate are veto players, as both agree on a piece of legislation before it is sent to the president. In the case of a presidential veto, both houses must vote by a two-thirds majority to override that veto. While the House is a majoritarian institution, with each state's delegation being determined by population, the Senate is not (each state, regardless of population, is represented by two senators). Because of the rules regarding cloture (banning filibusters), which requires a three-fifths vote, in practice sixty votes are required to pass a piece of legislation (Tsebelis 1999: 592).

Amendments from the floor can significantly change a bill reported by a committee; the committee's approval is essential to have the committee report the bill to the floor. Once the bill gets to the floor, however, the committee no longer has a veto (Bailey 1998: 193). If the committee was united, however, it is less likely to face significant revision. If there was a significant number of dissenters, amendments from the floor are far more likely to change the bill. Thus, dissenters within a committee who lost the intracommittee battle can regroup and reconstitute themselves as a "veto player" on the floor during the vote by the entire House or Senate.

TERRITORY AND ECONOMIC SPECIALIZATION

Traditionally, a distinction has been made between "territorial" and "functional" politics (Tarrow, Katzenstein, and Graziano 1978). The former referred to the political representation of interests defined by territorial boundaries, and the former largely referred to the interests of producers (firms and trade unions). Functional politics was embedded in the notion of corporatist politics, in which producer associations and umbrella trade union organizations were fairly centralized and had regularized relationships with governments in the field of economic policy. These functional interest groups covered the entire national territory and therefore were not tied to localized territorial boundaries.

This distinction is problematic when applied to the U.S. case. The economic structure of the United States is such that sectoral politics and territorial politics are often entangled. As Paul Krugman has pointed out, "to a remarkable extent, manufacturing industries within the United States are highly localized" (Krugman 1991: 350). The implications of such regional economic specialization for the representation of territory within the United States are so significant that it is worth quoting Krugman at some length:

...many industries are indeed highly concentrated geographically. The automotive industry offers a useful benchmark. It is a famously localized industry....half of the employment is still in the traditional automotive district of Southern Michigan and neighboring regions of Indiana and Ohio. So we might expect motor vehicles to be an exceptional industry. But it isn't. It is just slightly above the median. The point is not that automotive production is not highly localized – it is. But so are a lot of other industries...Hartford is an insurance city, Chicago the center of futures trading; Los Angeles the entertainment capital; and so on....And arguably technology is moving in a direction that will promote more localization of services (1991: 58, 66).

If one looks at the United States through the lens of economic geography, the periphery is defined as those regions that do not form the core of either the services or manufacturing areas. As Krugman puts it, "Idaho is part of the periphery" (Krugman 1991: 71).

When he turns to Europe, Krugman becomes really interesting if we think about his findings in relation to the dynamics of representation within the Council of Ministers: "European nations are less specialized than U.S. regions...in terms of the economic roles they play, U.S. regions are more distinct than European nations..." (Krugman 1991: 76; see also Brulhart 1998). If one compares the American Midwest and the South and Germany and Italy (in effect comparing a "traditional heavy industrial producer with a traditional light, labor-intensive producer"), the results are very important for the argument developed here. The Midwest has no textile industry, while Germany still has a significant textile industry; Italy, for its part, produces far more machinery than does the American South (Krugman 1991: 77). If we compare the auto industry in Europe with that in the United States, Krugman again finds significant differences:

...the US [automotive] industry is far more localized [than the European]. In essence, the US industry is a Midwestern phenomenon, with only a scattering of assembly plants in other parts of the country. The European equivalent would be a concentration of half the industry within 150 kilometers of Wolfsburg (1991: 78).

On the other hand, the EU is far more divided than the United States when it comes to purchasing power: "Interregional income differentials within Europe are much larger than within the United States, and they are closely associated with geographical position" (Krugman 1991: 93–4).

REGULATORY POLICY AND TERRITORY

Theodore Lowi's well-known typology of different types of public policies made a distinction between regulatory and redistributive policies by arguing that redistributive policies had a much broader impact (Lowi 1964: 691). However, Lowi did not consider the territorial implications of regulatory policies. Current analyses of regulatory politics in both the United States and the EU do not focus on the territorial implications of such policies either. Rather, they note the dispersed cost of such measures and the fact that they therefore require very little expenditure on the part of governments (Majone 1992, 304–5).

Keeping Krugman's findings in mind, however, it becomes clear that certain types of regulatory policies could actually have redistributive consequences for those territorial units characterized by economic specialization. If a sector (such as autos) is going to be severely affected by proposed regulation, it can be conceptualized as a redistribution away from that sector. At the very least, that sector will be hurt. And that means that the region within which the sector is localized will also be hurt. One would hypothesize that, absent very strong party discipline, regulatory policy affecting a selected sector will be strongly resisted by the representatives of political units in which that sector is localized. In that instance, territorial and sectoral politics will converge, intensifying the conflict and making agreement very difficult.

On the other hand, the very fact that industry is so localized can make it more difficult for affected industries to mobilize widespread support for their position in Congress. If ways can be found to circumvent or defeat the "veto players" defending the sector, legislation can in fact be passed. Such was the case when the 1970 Clean Air Act, with its requirement that pollution from auto emissions be severely cut, was adopted (Cohen 1992: 16). On the other hand, if legislation were to affect several "dirty" industries, a greater number of representatives would resist, again making agreement more difficult.

AIR POLLUTION POLICY AND TERRITORY

Air pollution policy is precisely the kind of regulatory policy that, given the economic specialization of American regions, will affect a sector and a region simultaneously. Functional politics and territorial politics are very likely to be the same. "Dirty coal" in the United States tends to be regionally concentrated as are the power plants that use it, for example. Automobile production, as Krugman points out, is also concentrated. The comparatively high degree of economic specialization that characterizes American regions reinforces the territorial nature of Congressional environmental debate. Thus, those producer interests (industry and trade unions) that have an interest in shaping regulations in certain ways are territorially concentrated rather than being scattered throughout Congressional constituencies. In a similar vein, the damage produced by acid rain is also territorially concentrated.

Although industry and environmental groups certainly coalesce at the national level, the voting and bargaining patterns are typically regionally defined. During the bargaining leading to the Clean Air Act of 1990, especially those provisions involving acid rain, the regional dimension became very clear. The same happened with the 1977 amendments – the high sulfur "dirty coal" producing states' representatives in Congress accepted universal scrubbing, which would allow high sulfur coal to continue to be used in power plants.

Given the regional concentration of industrial or extractive activity likely to be regulated by legislation, that Congressional representatives from those regions not surprisingly are very sensitive to the costs imposed by regulation. Costs imposed on producers are likely to affect employment in the region; at the very least, they represent an "opportunity cost" in the form of foregone further investment and expansion. And the costs of environmental regulations can be high. In the period 1975–86, over $560 billion was spent on environmental protection by both public and private actors. The private sector paid about 60 percent of the total bill (Rosenbaum 1991: 81).

CONGRESSIONAL VETO PLAYERS, TERRITORY, AND ECONOMIC SECTORS

Territorially defined constituencies are central to the dynamics of Congressional policy making. Although the political parties within both the House and the Senate are very significant for certain types of issues, they are much less important when territorial and sectoral interests converge. In those cases, it is very likely that, all things being equal, constituency interests will trump party affiliation. Party can be important not so much in determining the voting of specific members but rather in the role played by the party leadership within the institution. The leadership can be important, as we will see, in fashioning or preventing compromises, expediting or preventing legislation from reaching the full House or Senate, and bringing pressure on reluctant members to agree to the compromise.

Constituency politics, however, do not exist within a vacuum. Rather, they are institutionalized within the committee structure. The U.S. Congress is composed of committees that have been so powerful that Congress has been characterized as a "kind of confederation of little legislatures" (quoted in Rosenbaum 1991: 83). The chairs of committees are key to understanding the committee's activities. Environmental policy is so horizontally cross-cutting that very large numbers of committees and subcommittees claim some jurisdiction. In the early 1990s, water policy, for example, was considered by over seventy committees and subcommittees (Rosenbaum 1991: 83). Certain committees are key in the adoption of selected pieces of legislation. It is those committees that can be viewed as "veto players." Although most such committees would be concerned with environmental protection in some form or other, the Appropriations Committee can also play an important role if the committee chair has a particularly powerful interest in the environmental legislation being considered.

The role of such committees can be either that of defending the status quo or of providing the policy entrepreneurship to change that status quo. Amendments to existing legislation can be initiated by a committee that under other conditions would be a defender of the status quo. Veto players can act as policy entrepreneurs and vice versa depending on the issue at stake. Thus, proposed legislative changes within Congress can involve a conflict among committees – some of which are acting as policy entrepreneurs in favor of change while others are acting as veto players (either defending the status quo or trying to achieve an outcome as close as possible to the status quo). Committees and subcommittees that previously had had no jurisdiction can use a crisis to claim a new jurisdiction – for example, after the energy crisis of 1973, the energy committees "began to claim parts of the air pollution brief" (Bailey 1998: 175), and the links between chlorofluorocarbon (CFC) emissions and the depletion of the ozone layer allowed committees concerned with space and the atmosphere to become involved in air pollution legislation. Thus, new entrants into the "committee market" are to be expected once a new dimension of environmental damage becomes prominent on the policy agenda.

Although committees are still very powerful, they now have to contend with a party leadership that has successfully increased its own power. As the power of the latter has increased, the power of committees has waned. The leadership is certainly a veto player. In the House, the power of the speaker has expanded to such an extent that his support is crucial if legislation is to proceed. Finally, the representatives voting during a floor vote are also amending legislation with far less hesitation than in the past. Once the leadership brings a measure to a floor vote, those who opposed the measure during the process can still mobilize enough votes to force the adoption of significant amendments.

THE TERRITORIAL DIMENSION

The territorial dimension divides Congressional representatives within the same party. During the debates concerning what eventually became the 1977 amendments to the Clean Air Act, Democratic Party representatives from districts with severe air pollution problems tried to increase the stringency of regulations. Leading the fight to relax standards were Democratic Party representatives from districts in which the auto industry was dominant. The auto industry in fact was defended by a bipartisan contingent from Michigan; economic/producer interests become synonymous with territorial interests, and a system of representation based on territory then defends the territorial "twin" – that is, producer interests. In Christopher J. Bailey's words, "no secret was made of the fact that the purpose [of various legislative maneuvers]...was to protect the automobile industry" (Bailey 1998: 193). In fact, the 1977 amendments postponed the deadlines for compliance with auto emission standards.

The issue of acid rain perhaps most vividly illustrated the territorial divide in Congress:

Politicians from northern and northeastern states gave graphic accounts of the damage apparently caused by acid rain...while those from the coal-producing states of Appalachia and the Midwest argued that there was insufficient evidence to implicate soft coal as a cause of the problem. (Bailey 1998: 211).

No formula was found that could bridge the divide between regions, between the coal producers and those who suffered from the pollution caused by that same coal, or between lobbyists for industry and lobbyists for the environmental movement (Kraft 1990: 115). The regional divide continuously stymied attempt after attempt to regulate "dirty coal" and the utilities in the Midwest that used it. Representatives feared the loss of Appalachian coal mining jobs and higher electricity prices throughout the Midwest. Although the 1977 amendments mandated scrubbers be built on existing power plants, high sulfur coal was protected (Ackerman and Hassler 1981).

Although the Clean Air Act of 1970 was amended and extended by the 1977 amendments, no proposal for further changes gained enough support to be adopted until 1990. Thus, thirteen years of gridlock characterized air pollution policy. In the Senate, the Northeastern Republican committee chairs who wanted stronger controls were stymied by the Republican leadership in the Senate, which opposed them, while in the House the committees (all controlled by Democrats) representing different territorial interests fought each other to a stalemate. Subcommittee chairs who favored stronger regulations

were stymied by committee chairs who did not, and so on. Those seeking
to relax standards could not gain control of enough committees to win, and
those seeking tighter controls either did not control all the committees or
were stopped by the leadership. The status quo prevailed as the veto players
stopped change in either direction.

Interestingly, the one group that was indeed able to make changes represented areas in which the steel industry was dominant. The so-called
steel caucus managed to break the gridlock to some extent. Its members
(both Democratic and Republican) from steel-producing areas (Pennsylva-
nia, Ohio, Illinois, and West Virginia) were successful in passing legislation
in 1981 that lightened the regulatory burden on the steel industry (Bailey
1998: 218). Although the powerful steel industry had resisted complying
with environmental laws, in general it was viewed as facing very tough foreign competition. Unemployment in the industry was very high, and plant
closings that occurred in the Middle Atlantic states had received a good deal
of publicity (Landy, Roberts, and Thomas 1994).

In the House, the chief protagonists of the more general story of gridlock were John Dingell, representing a district on the outskirts of Detroit,
who became chair of the House Energy and Commerce Committee in 1981,
and Henry Waxman, who became the chair of the Health and Environment Subcommittee within the Energy and Commerce Committee chaired
by Dingell. Given that Waxman represented Los Angeles, Dingell thought
Waxman "wanted already distressed Detroit and the rest of the nation to
pay the bill to clean up Los Angeles" (Cohen, 1992: 31). As the battles
dragged on, it became very clear that Dingell was going to use his chairmanship to gain "more leverage to assure support for his views in one area –
chiefly, protection of the auto industry – by making concessions elsewhere"
(Cohen, 1992: 34). Waxman, for his part, learned how to use the threat of
floor votes to get what he wanted when he was stymied by Dingell. Floor
votes could be used to veto what Dingell's committee wanted (by significantly modifying the legislation that the committee reported to the full
House).

In the Senate, the Republican's control of the Senate in 1980 led to the
Republican senator from Vermont, Robert Stafford, taking over the chair of
the Environment and Public Works Committee. Not surprisingly, the New
Englander was a zealous proponent of stringent regulation – far more so
than had been his Democratic predecessor, a senator from the coal state of
West Virginia. The committee had a disproportionate number of senators
from New England and strongly supported clean air legislation. However,
the Senate's Republican leadership refused to schedule bills reported out of
committee for floor action. As Richard Cohen points out:

According to leaders and Reagan administration officials, the committee had become
a captive of the environmental lobby and it had lost touch with other legitimate

viewpoints, especially those in the Midwest. Another key fact was the strong-willed opposition to acid-rain and other environmental controls by [Robert] Byrd [from West Virginia], who was Democratic leader throughout the Reagan years (Cohen 1992: 37).

After the Democrats recaptured the Senate in 1986, George Mitchell from Maine took the chair of the Environmental Protection Subcommittee. Mitchell decided he had to deal with Byrd, the veteran and very cunning defender of Appalachian "dirty" coal who had been a key actor in preventing the adoption of acid rain legislation during the Reagan years. Through Byrd, he began at one point negotiating with the president of the United Mine Workers. He also began to work with senators from the West – where low sulfur coal is mined. However, after Mitchell became the new majority leader in 1989, his subcommittee chairmanship went to Max Baucus, a senator from Montana, a western low sulfur coal state, who had very little sympathy for the United Mine Workers union from the East.

A new piece of legislation, finally passed in 1990, was hailed as a milestone. It is perhaps not surprising that a good deal of the credit for the legislation went to Mitchell, who was then Senate majority leader and later went on to gain fame as the negotiator who played a key role in bringing peace to Northern Ireland. Whether it takes someone of such legendary political skill to fashion air pollution legislation in the United States is an open question. Certainly, the legislative history of the Clean Air Act of 1990 makes clear the difficulties intrinsic to overcoming the veto points in the U.S. Congress. And it makes clear that the position of the president is terribly important in prodding Congress to come to an agreement.

It was the administration of George Herbert Walker Bush that managed to put together a new coalition, one that bypassed the constituencies protected by Byrd and representatives from the coal states. The new coalition on acid rain regulation was defined in regional terms:

The potent new axis included the Western states, which had relatively clean coal-burning and did not want to pay the cost for Eastern states to meet their standards; both Eastern and Western producers of low-sulfur coal, who would benefit when coal users were free to choose which fuel they preferred; advocates of less intrusive government interference in the marketplace; and the Northeastern states, which were the original proponents of control. The big losers were the United Mine Workers, which had its greatest presence in high-sulfur coal mines, and the Midwest states, whose utilities have relied on high-sulfur coal (Cohen, 1992: 57).

President George Bush was particularly committed to environmental protection and saw such an initiative as helping the prime minister of Canada (Canada suffered from acid rain rooted in Midwestern utility plants as much as did New England). The process used in formulating the administration's bill showed a sensitivity to different interests. Rather than being drafted primarily by the Environmental Protection Agency (EPA), the bill was drafted by a team including White House officials, representatives from the Office of Management and Budget, and the Department of Energy as well as the EPA. The centrality of energy issues as well as economic issues allowed a new coalition to be formed in Congress (Bryner 1995: 115).

Most interesting from our point of view, however, was the extraordinary complexity of the process that led to a final agreement. Intricate agreements and compromises had to be fashioned – so much so that Barbara Sinclair argues the dynamics involved in adopting the Clean Air Act of 1990 exemplify "unorthodox lawmaking" (orthodox lawmaking refers to the "a bill becomes a law" diagrams found in now out-of-date textbooks) (Sinclair 1997).

This sketch of the problems of making air pollution policies signals the problems that the U.S. Congress faces in trying to fashion policies that regulate powerful yet highly localized industries. Economic specialization combined with the institutional fragmentation of both the House and Senate and with the power of both industry and environmental interest groups render lawmaking extraordinarily difficult. In the end, the negotiations that resulted in success were carried out in the "back rooms" of Congress:

...the Mitchell-sponsored talks were conducted behind closed doors and they spurned roll-call votes that would have revealed the legislative divisions. Mitchell believed, probably correctly, that senators would not get down to hard negotiating on environmental issues so long as they were in the public spotlight, where they might make statements that a political opponent could use against them (Cohen 1992: 88–9).

In a similar vein, negotiations in the House were nearly all behind closed doors – and often in the middle of the night. As a former representative put it, "behind closed doors, lobbyists don't know everything that is going on" (quoted in Cohen 1992: 131).

Clearly, agreement on the costs to be imposed on territorially concentrated industries is not likely to be constructed under conditions of transparency and openness. The fact that the governors of West Virginia, Michigan, California, and Maine were not present at the negotiations hardly seems to matter. Senator Byrd organized the coal-state senators, Senator Mitchell safeguarded the interests of those New England states damaged by acid rain, Congressman Dingell laid out the strategy for the auto industry, and Congressman Waxman represented the interests of one of the smoggiest districts in the country. Environmentalists, unions, and industry groups lobbied fiercely, but in the end, it was the elected officials who made the trade-offs and decided who would be the winners and the losers. Winners and losers were largely chosen in secrecy. Back rooms rather than the Senate or House floor were the key negotiating fora. Territorial interests, sectoral interests, and secrecy were all intertwined as elected officials engaged in lawmaking.

VETO PLAYERS, TERRITORY, AND THE COUNCIL OF MINISTERS

The account of U.S. policy making outlined in this chapter would not strike a student of American politics as particularly unusual. Functional and territorial interests, when they converge, are likely to trump party discipline and render policy making extremely difficult. Yet, if it were to have occurred in the European Union, analysts would bemoan the lack of efficiency in decision-making structures, the lack of transparency and democracy in the European Union, and the concern with narrow parochial (national) interests.

What is striking about the making of air pollution policy in the European Union, however, is that while it has undoubtedly been a difficult process, the Council of Ministers has been able to arrive at compromises and adopt legislation far more easily than has the U.S. Congress. Legislation addressing the issue of acid rain and vehicle emissions was agreed to far more quickly than was the Clear Air Act of 1990. Those attributes that the U.S. Congress adopted to make the compromises that ultimately led to success – secrecy, bargains, and side payments – have been intrinsic to the way the Council of Ministers works.

The kind of interstate bargaining that the Council of Ministers takes for granted can in fact be far more effective in producing policy outcomes than the kind of political dynamic that characterizes lawmaking in the U.S. federal legislature. The features of an international organization that still permeate the Council of Ministers can, perhaps especially when confronted with very contentious issues, help avoid the kind of long-term deadlock found in the U.S. Congress.[2]

It is impossible to compare the Clean Air Act of 1990 to any single piece of air pollution legislation adopted by the EU. The various components of the Act have been dealt with in several different pieces of EU legislation. Nonetheless, it is possible to compare how the Council of Ministers in the EU treated two key issues addressed by the Act: acid rain and emission controls for small cars.

In the case of acid rain, geography plays a role similar to that which it played in the United States. The British, the largest exporter of pollutants

---

[2] The legislation considered here was adopted before the European Parliament acquired codecision-making powers under the Maastricht Treaty. The legislation addressing acid rain (the Large Combustion Plant Directive) was adopted under the rule of unanimity so that all national governments in the Council had to agree to the legislation. The directive on small car emissions was adopted under the so-called cooperation procedure in which the Parliament could amend the Council's position if the European Commission supported the Parliament. The Parliament's position could then be overturned by the Council only if it unanimously rejected the Parliament's legislation. If the Council could not unanimously agree to overturn the Parliament's version of the legislation (and thereby return to its original proposal), the Council faced the choice of either killing the legislation completely or accepting the version that the Parliament had adopted.

in Western Europe, were roughly in a situation analogous to that of the Midwestern American states – that is, British air pollution was borne by strong winds away from Britain. Germany and the Netherlands were roughly in the position which the American New England states found themselves in: They received the acid rain created outside their national boundaries.

In 1982, the German government, worried about the death of its forests, gave a high priority to the issue of acid rain and began to urge European Community action on the issue. The issue was first highlighted by the Social Democratic Party/Free Democratic Party coalition government, and the Helmut Kohl government that came to power in December 1982 continued to give the issue priority at both the national and European Community level. In 1982, the Large Combustion Plant Regulation was adopted at the national level in Germany. At the EC level, the Large Combustion Plant (LCP) directive, which set emission limits for sulphur dioxide and nitrous oxides, was proposed by the Commission and supported by the German presidency in December 1983 and was adopted by unanimity in June 1988.

During the five-year period, between 1983 and 1988, various proposals were rejected, especially by the British, Spanish, Greeks, Italians, and Irish (Boehmer-Christiansen and Skea 1991; Héritier, Knill, and Mingers 1996: 186ff; Zito 2000: 61–4). The British, who had emerged as the key opponent of the various drafts of the proposed directive, gradually changed their position as a result of international and domestic political pressures (Héritier et al. 1996: 191–5). In 1988, the British and the Germans were able to agree on the formula for sulphur dioxide reduction, and a complex bargain was then struck that involved a number of air pollution–related issues.

One of the key elements of that bargain was the question of emission controls on small cars. Legislation on that issue was separate from that on acid rain, but the political dynamic led to the Council considering both issues simultaneously. Emission controls on small cars would have a differentiated impact on auto producers. If strict controls, known as U.S. 83 standards, were to be adopted at the EU level, only catalytic converters would have the capability to meet such standards. German manufacturers would be advantaged because they had begun to use that technology (partially because of their exports to the U.S. market, which required such converters). If standards were set at a lower level, a technology such as "lean burn," which was being developed by auto producers outside of Germany, would be feasible. Furthermore, since the directive in question concerned small cars, auto producers in France, Italy, Britain, and Spain would be particularly affected by the level of stringency chosen.

Anthony Zito's description of the final bargain gives a sense of the complex "package deal" that the Council of Ministers negotiated in June 1988 with Germany holding the presidency. Given the complexities of the issues and nature of the compromises that had to be struck, it is not surprising that the

Council of Ministers did not adjourn until 4 A.M. The Council, in addition to negotiating the LCP directive:

...also sought to untangle the small car emissions dispute, an item of major importance for the Germans and other automobile producing countries. Great Britain, France, Italy and Spain opposed the idea of fitting the expensive catalytic converter equipment that Germany favored. France, with the support of Great Britain, offered Germany a deal knowing that acidification and the LCP directive were Germany's highest priority. If Germany accepted a looser emission standard for small cars, the British and French would accept the latest version of the German proposal [for the LCP]. The prospect of leaving the Presidency with neither essential agreement forced Topfer [the German environment minister] to concede (Zito 2000: 64; see also Bennett 1992: 129–30).

The period in which the Council was able to adopt legislation on acid rain from power plants seems very short when compared to the thirteen-year period in which the U.S. Congress fought over the acid rain issue. Interestingly, the auto emissions part of this bargain was overturned because of action taken by the European Parliament in April 1989. The Parliament voted in favor of strict U.S. 83 standards, and the result was that in June 1989 the Environment Council did in fact adopt U.S. 83 norms. Thus, the policy outcome of the decision-making process was not only that both acid rain from power plants and emissions from small cars were dealt with in a six-year period but that both the LCP and the auto emissions legislation were much "greener" (that is, more environmentally progressive) than would have been predicted in the early 1980s (Boehmer-Christiansen and Weidner 1992; Sbragia 1996; Tsebelis 1994; Turner 1988).

In the case of the legislation on power plants, the fact that the Council could negotiate such a complex bargain in the relatively short space of five years is striking. The number of actors was much smaller than in the U.S. Congress. Once the British and Germans came to an agreement, the rest of the negotiations proceeded rather quickly. That dynamic contrasts with the dynamic within the U.S. Congress, in which no coalition could strike a bargain that was comprehensive and fundamental enough to shape subsequent bargaining.

CONGRESS AND THE COUNCIL OF MINISTERS COMPARED

In comparing the U.S. Congress and the Council of Ministers, three differences stand out. The first is that Congress, as a legislature within a traditional nation-state, adopts legislation that is generally uniform in its requirements. That is, controls are applied across the territory of the United States. The Council of Ministers, as a forum for interstate bargaining, is able to adopt legislation that differentiates across the member states. Thus, the LCP directive mandated a 40 percent reduction of sulphur dioxide from existing power plants by 1993 for the Federal Republic and the Netherlands but only a 20 percent reduction for the United Kingdom (Haigh 1996: 163; Zito 2000: 65). Such precise territorial differentiation would be nearly impossible in the United States. The intergovernmental format within the Council allows such bargains to be made, which in turn allow the adoption of legislation by consensus. In the United States, the institutional structure of the Congress itself and the way interests are mobilized would make the adoption of legislation by consensus impossible.

Secondly, the kind of bargaining that takes place within Congress is fundamentally different from that which takes place within the Council. Members of Congress represent local constitutencies and are not swayed by the views of voters who do not reside in their district. Given the fixed nature of economic interests in a constituency, it is unlikely that a legislator will change his or her position due to new influences. Whereas the British began to change their position because the electric companies were going to be privatized and would have to attract private investors (who hate regulatory uncertainty), it is unlikely that a representative would need to worry about an equivalent situation in his district. Therefore, the only way to adopt complex legislation is to construct a coalition among members whose voters and campaign contributors, for a variety of reasons, will support a given piece of legislation.

By contrast, the bargaining within the Council of Environment Ministers is carried out by ministers and, at a lower level, by diplomats supported by civil servants (Jordan 2002). In other words, the executive branch of the national governments is involved and national parliaments are excluded. Such executives are far more likely to be receptive to the pressures of other governments than are members of Congress to each other or to the desires of anyone outside their own country. The evolution of the British position on acid rain is difficult to imagine occurring within U.S. Congressional districts, given the convergence of territorial and producer interests in the latter. It is not accidental that all democracies have kept legislatures largely out of foreign affairs. The representation of a territorially defined electoral constituency involves fundamentally different dynamics from those embedded in the representation of a national position in an international setting. Diplomacy is the art of representing a territory at the international level, but it is quite different from representing a territory within a national legislature.

Thirdly, the very fact that ministers represent an entire nation rather than a limited constituency allows them to make the trade-offs, to decide the winners and losers, which any single legislator is likely to find impossible to do. The fact that, as Krugman points out, the EU is not as economically specialized as are American regions makes the possibility of such trade-offs easier. If only one or two large member states had auto producers, the incentive to trade off more stringent controls on power plants against more lenient emission standards for automobiles would not have existed.

GENERAL CONCLUSIONS

The purpose of comparing the U.S. Congress and the EU's Council of Ministers was to assess, in very rough and exploratory terms, the widespread view among scholars of European Union politics that the Council of Ministers finds it exceptionally difficult to adopt legislation. If one compares the Council to the decision-making institutions in the member states, that view is usually quite valid. But the European Union as an entity is of course a far more complex territory to govern than is any of its individual member states. While an EU-U.S. comparison is far from ideal, it does at least allow us to compare the EU with another entity characterized by a large and diverse population and governance based on territorial representation.

Viewed in that light, the Council of Ministers is an institution that is surprisingly good at arriving at compromises and developing a consensus broad enough to adopt legislation. Whether or not the regulations imposed by the Large Combustion Plant Directive were as stringent as those adopted by the Clean Air Act of 1990 in the area of acid rain is a different (albeit very important) question. What is important for the argument made here is that the Council was able to arrive at a consensus in an area in which the American political system had found it exceedingly difficult to formulate any consensus.

The fact that the Council of Environment Ministers was the decision maker undoubtedly helped the process of consensus building. After all, ministers for the environment do have a stake in focusing on environmental protection even if economic interests must be defended. By contrast, the members of Congress from Detroit may well have absolutely no commitment to environmental protection. The policy segmentation by which decision making is carried out in the EU is an important factor in understanding how functional and territorial interests converge. The regulations imposed by the LCP would likely have been quite different if ministers of finance and economic affairs had been negotiating the directive rather than those ministers specifically concerned with environmental protection.

In the EU, the segmentation of the Council allows functional interests such as environmental protection to be somewhat more insulated from competing functional interests such as those represented by producer groups than is the case in the United States. In the Congress, coalitions had to be constructed by bringing together representatives of those economic interests (low sulphur coal producers) that stood to gain from environmental regulation and those who wanted cleaner air. In the Council of Ministers, the trade-off was made by environment ministers who accepted looser emission auto standards in order to obtain tighter restrictions on power plants. Territorial representation was important in both cases, but in the EU, the fact that the ministers concerned could make trade-offs across the sectors in very explicit ways helped advance the decision-making process. In the Congress, by contrast, equivalent trade-offs had to be made in the end (with elected officials hiding from lobbyists), but the process whereby such trade-offs could be realized was a far more torturous one than in the EU.

In both systems, functional and territorial interests intersect in air pollution policy. Yet an organization like the Council, which operates by many of the same rules as an international organization and is segmented by policy area in terms of its jurisdiction as well, seems better suited than the U.S. Congress to arrive at decisions that must accommodate very different viewpoints within that policy area. At the very least, the experience of the EU in dealing with acid rain in particular raises the possibility that the Council of Ministers is actually quite an effective decision-making institution if compared to the American alternative. Governing a very diverse territory is not easy, and when territorial and functional interests both converge and conflict, as occurs when environmental protection and producer interests each find territorially based champions, decision making will be protracted and difficult. Yet the Council of Ministers, when viewed in comparative terms, is a rather successful decision maker.

PART IV

CONCLUDING THOUGHTS

II

Territoriality, Authority, and Democracy

Christopher K. Ansell

As described in the introduction to this book, our collective inquiry was partly prompted by John Gerald Ruggie's provocative description of the European Union (EU) as the world's first "postmodern polity" and his argument that this new state of affairs was a consequence of the "unbundling of territoriality" (Ruggie 1993).[1] Ruggie suggested that modernity transformed the "multi-perspectival" feudal world, with its parcellized authority and overlapping jurisdictions, into the "single-point perspective" modern world with its "territorially defined, fixed, and mutual exclusive enclaves of legitimate domination." As Ruggie puts it, "The chief characteristic of the modern system of territorial rule is the consolidation of all parcellized and personalized authority into one public realm." The EU represents the reemergence of parcellized authority and overlapping jurisdictions in a postnational (and hence postmodern) framework.

Our group agreed (and who does not?) that territoriality – the consolidation of political authority into "territorially defined, fixed, and mutually exclusive enclaves" – is a core constitutive principle of modern political organization. Indeed, territoriality is like the air we breathe – something upon which we utterly depend and yet largely take for granted. The "unbundling of territoriality" does not simply pose a challenge to sovereignty. We are familiar with those types of challenges. A weak state may have its sovereignty violated by a strong state, and even strong states do not fully control their borders. Yet the *organizing principle* of territoriality remains intact. States still strive to be sovereign. The power of Ruggie's analysis was his suggestion that the constitutive principle was itself being transformed. And the EU was there to reveal the future.

[1] My thanks to the Triple Rock discussion group for its help in revising an earlier draft. Sincere thanks also to the University of Michigan's Interdisciplinary Committee on Organizational Studies for allowing me to present an earlier version of this conclusion.

How should we characterize the EU as a political institution? It seems too complex, too powerful, and too extensive to be simply described as an international organization. Yet it also seems too fragmented, weak, and disjointed to be a state. If we interpret this awkward new political institution in light of a trend toward globalization and a presumed weakening of national sovereignty, we are apt to conclude that there has been a rupture with the institutional status quo. If we then conclude that the EU does not obey the same organizing principles as do the institutions that have preceded it, we may then reach the conclusion that it represents a novel institutional form for a new age. We will, in turn, expect it to behave in distinctive and perhaps unprecedented ways and to require a different kind of analytical apparatus to understand it.

In this concluding chapter, I want to both draw on what we have produced in this book, and to point beyond it, in order to confront directly this issue of how to characterize the EU. I will concur with Ruggie that the EU is a novel institutional form. However, in contradistinction to Ruggie, I want to argue that this novelty lies in the fact that the EU is a hybrid of rather conventional institutional forms: an intergovernmental organization, a confederation, and a federation. Hence, I will argue that many aspects of the EU can be interpreted in wholly conventional – or, if you will, modern – terms. Nevertheless, the novelty of the EU lies in the extensive interpenetration of these conventional forms and in the institutional accommodation that allows this hybrid to work.

This description of European integration raises the question of change. We might, for instance, argue that this hybrid is ultimately unstable and interpret the current situation as a process of transition from intergovernmentalism to federalism. In this transition, we would expect federal institutions gradually to supplant intergovernmental arrangements. Such a process appears to capture the general long-term trend of European integration, but tends toward teleology as an analytical perspective. A second possibility is that this hybrid arrangement is relatively stable. Movements toward federation will be counterbalanced by the pull of national sovereignty. Consequently, this hybrid arrangement may be a stable institutional equilibrium.

In the remainder of this chapter, I establish the idea that the European Union is a hybrid of an intergovernmental organization, a confederation, and a federation. I link this claim to the nature of territoriality and the character of institutional competences (authority) with which the EU is endowed. I then examine some of the institutional accommodations that sustain this hybrid.

THE TERRITORIAL STATE

In this section, I want to delimit my concepts of intergovernmentalism, confederalism, and federalism vis-à-vis the ideas of territoriality and authority that have been prominent in this book. The discussion broaches the subject of whether the EU can be thought of as a state, and if so, what kind of state.

As a constitutive organizing principle of the modern state system, territoriality should be thought of as the corporate organization of a territory. A corporate group is a collectivity, defined according to some criteria, that acts and represents itself as a single person or entity. A corporate group is therefore an "agency" that acts in the name of the unitary will of the collectivity. Hence, a corporate group necessarily has an authority structure and an executive structure (what Max Weber called its "binding order" and its "administration," respectively) that allows it to act in such a manner. The modern state, as Weber would suggest, can be defined in terms of the corporate organization of territory. Or, as Gianfranco Poggi writes, quoting an Italian jurist: "the state does not *have* territory, it *is* territory" (Poggi 1990: 22).

To understand the range of state forms, it is necessary to define corporateness as a variable ranging from weak to strong. The overarching difference between weak and strong corporateness is the degree of symbolic and functional unity of the collective.[2] Weak corporate groups are more *compound* organizationally than strong corporate groups. The distinction is useful in analyzing the EU, because if the EU is a state, it is certainly a compound one, as are all federations. A federation is a compound corporate group whose members are also corporate groups. Federal representation is based, in part, on representation of lower-level corporate groups (states) at the federal level. While not all federal organizations are territorially based, a federal state is one in which the member "states" and the federal "state" have a territorial basis.

Is the EU a territorial state? The description of European integration as "variable geometry" is revealing. Variable geometry is a phrase used to describe the overlapping functional arenas in which member states can "opt in" or "opt out" of European institutions depending on their particular interests. The Schengen Accords and Monetary Union are classic examples of functional arenas in which different subsets of EU member states participate. Variable geometry is an excellent example of what Ruggie means when he describes the EU as a "multi-perspectival" polity. Variable geometry, at best, reveals weak territoriality. Strong territoriality would not permit this voluntarism and would require uniform participation of all territorial subunits.[3]

---

[2] For a more extensive discussion of the structural and symbolic integration of corporate groups, see Chapter 2 of my book on the French labor movement (Ansell 2001).

[3] Philippe Schmitter describes two forms of polity – *consortio* and *condominio* – that he distinguishes from either a confederation or a federation. He defines them as follows: "the consortio assumes a fixed and irreversible set of member states within defined territorial boundaries, but with varying policy responsibilities." In a condominio, "both territorial as well as functional constituencies would vary" (Schmitter 2000: 17). This distinction suggests an interesting progression: (1) a set of functional international organizations, each with a distinctive set of

On this basis, Virginie Mamadough (2001) describes the territoriality of the EU as less fixed and less exclusive than that of the nation-state. Nevertheless, the EU does have a territorial dimension. Legal acts and regulations, for example, apply to the entire territory of the EU. This territoriality, however, is still primarily derivative of the territoriality of member states in that they implement and administer these directives. EU borders are also derivative of member-state borders, though market integration has clearly reduced internal borders.

STATES AND COMPETENCES

This description of weak and strong corporateness can be more fully articulated by describing variations in the organization of authority and the integration of governing structures. With respect to authority, a *functional competence* is one in which an institution has only a narrowly delineated authority, with only limited grants of power necessary for fulfillment of a particular function. Typically, national administrative agencies and international organizations exemplify functional competence. *General competence*, in contrast, is a multipurpose grant of power over a range of subsidiary functions that are conventionally organized into executive, legislative, and judicial "powers." Legislatures have general powers to "legislate" (to set policy and establish laws); executives have the general power to "execute" the law; and the judiciary has the general power to interpret and enforce law. General powers, in turn, may be separated or fused.

While states certainly have functional competences (for example, the post office, the tax agency, and the ministry of education), I argue that a necessary condition of being a state is the exercise of general competences. By this definition, the early-nineteenth-century American state was indeed a state in that it exercised general competences (legislative, executive, and judicial power) over federal territory, despite the fact that it organized only minimal functional competences. In contrast, international organizations with well-developed functional competences are not states in that they lack general competences.

The broad trend suggested by Ruggie's work is the growth of specialized competences (parcellization) at the expense of states' general competences. In this book, a number of chapters point in this direction. Most strongly, Stefano Bartolini's chapter suggests that the hierarchical control of national centers over domestic peripheries is weakening. Maurizio Ferrera's chapter on welfare reform suggests vertical disaggregation of functional authority as

members; (2) a set of functional international organizations from the same territorial pool, but with each organization having a distinctive subset of members from that pool; and (3) a set of functional international organizations, each with the same membership set drawn from the same territorial pool.

welfare states undergo subnational regionalization. Although not included in this book, my own contribution to the project that produced this book described the upward delegation of some regional development competences to the EU and the downward delegation of other regional development competences to subnational regions (Ansell 2000). The James A. Caporaso and Joseph Jupille chapter describes the weakening of the horizontal fusion of powers in Britain with the emergence of judicial review. Alex Stone Sweet describes the creation of new private legal competences at the international level – the emergence of an international *Lex Mercatoria*.

Ruggie sees the EU as a product of the unbundling of state authority. However, the direction of change is not strictly toward functional parcellization. In fact, European integration is a dramatic example of the bundling of functional competences and their upgrading into general competences. This process began with the creation, under the European Coal and Steel Community (ECSC), of a Common Assembly, a Council of Ministers, a High Court, and a High Authority. In 1957, two additional communities – the European Economic Community (ECC) and Euratom – were created, and the three communities were brought together as the European Communities. A single European Parliament (EP) and a single court – the European Court of Justice (ECJ) – were created for the three communities. Each of the communities, however, retained their own commissions and councils until 1967, when they were merged into a single commission and council. The new Parliamentary Assembly expanded the powers of the Common Assembly, but remained largely consultative. Its members were appointed by national legislatures until 1979. The 1987 Single European Act strengthened the Parliament's power to amend legislation. The Maastricht Treaty, ratified in 1992, further consolidated functional competences under general powers by creating the EU to replace the previous communities and to incorporate the European Councils and Summits. It also further expanded the European Parliament's veto power over legislation.[4] The treaty also clarified the horizontal limits of this general competence, describing two "pillars" (foreign policy and security; internal affairs and justice) that would remain intergovernmental (and not under the jurisdiction of the ECJ).

If a state is defined by having general competences – legislative, executive, and judicial powers – then the EU is a state. These general competences are still quite limited in many respects, particularly when considered in relation to the enormous functional complexity of EU institutions. However, as argued earlier, the territorial dimensions of this state are still weak and derivative. Indeed, this juxtaposition of extensively developed functional competences and weak territoriality give credence to Ruggie's suggestion that the

---

[4] As Amie Kreppel writes of the European Parliament: "In the nearly thirty years following the first significant increase in its powers (the 1970 Budget Act), the EP has been transformed from a consultative assembly to a true legislative body" (Kreppel 2002: 89).

EU might be seen as a novel kind of nonterritorial state. Yet I believe it is more revealing and accurate to see the EU as a hybrid between intergovernmentalism and a federal territorial state. From this perspective, the EU is still novel. It is much more horizontally integrated than any other intergovernmental system (with the possible exception of the United Nations), while it has less territorial integrity than even a very compound state like Switzerland.

FEDERALISM AND CONFEDERALISM

The EU began as an intergovernmental organization (though as Ernst Haas established in his celebrated 1958 treatise on European integration, an unusual one) and is still characterized in a great many respects by intergovernmentalism. Briefly, intergovernmentalism suggests that states cooperate to establish international organizations by treaty, which typically must be ratified by domestic institutions. These international organizations are endowed with or delegated specific functional competences. Hence, the relationship between states and international organizations is conceived of as a principal–agent relationship. Decisions are made through bargaining between states as corporate entities, with each state retaining its veto power over final decisions (which is equivalent to the state retaining its national sovereignty). States act as the exclusive gateway of interest representation.[5]

Since there is little controversy about the fact that the EU still has intergovernmental features, I focus this discussion on the more controversial claim that the EU has federal and confederal dimensions. This claim obviously requires a preliminary consideration of what these terms mean. I begin with the concept of a federation. Building on my earlier discussion, I suggest that federalism implies at least two levels of government, with government at both levels organized around a set of general competences.[6] This

---

[5] This intergovernmental logic has been forcefully argued in the European case by Andrew Moravcsik (1998). The logic presumes that the state has a monopoly over external representation and is hence analogous to the logic of a two-level ("nested") game.

[6] The association of federalism and general competence is rarely explicit, but I would argue that it is presumed. Perhaps the most commonly cited definition of federalism is William K. Riker's:

A constitution is federal if (1) two levels of government rule the same land and people, (2) each level has at least one area of action in which it is autonomous, and (3) there is some guarantee (even though merely a statement in the constitution) of the autonomy of each government in its own sphere (1964: 11).

The idea of general competence is implied by the description of two levels of "government" and in the use of the term "constitution" rather than treaty. It is also implied in the idea of the "autonomy of each government in its own sphere," since autonomy requires the articulation of "powers." Ronald Watts defines a federation as:

... a compound polity combining constituent units and a general government, each possessing powers delegated to it by the people through a constitution, each empowered to deal directly with citizens in the exercise of a significant portion of its legislative, administrative, and taxing powers, and each directly elected by its citizens (1998: 121).

definition suggests that even when specific grants of sovereignty are pooled at the level of an international organization, the relationship is not necessarily a "federal" one. The possibility of EU federalism also depends on the upgrading of competences (horizontal bundling).

Like federations, confederations also organize general competences at two levels of government.[7] However, in a confederation, decisions made at the higher level of government are made through a representative process controlled by its corporate members (for example, different member states). These decisions may be binding on members and the confederal level may enforce collective decisions by imposing sanctions on recalcitrant members. But two conditions delimit confederal authority. First, its decisions have no form of legitimation independent of the voting procedures of its corporate members; second, although its decisions are binding for individual citizens, it has no authority or capacity to intervene directly to sanction or administer these decisions. The relationship between the confederal level and citizens remains an indirect one, exclusively mediated by the member states.

Federal states typically retain channels of indirect corporate representation of citizens. However, a critical transition occurs. In a federation, the federal level of government has a direct relationship with citizens. This means that these citizens must provide direct as opposed to indirect legitimation to federal authority, and that the federal government must have the capacity to intervene directly with citizens in the affairs under its direct control. The difference between a confederation and a federation can also be stated in such a way that draws on my concept of territoriality as the corporate organization of territory. In both confederations and federations, member states are represented as *corporate actors* in decision-making processes at the

---

[7] For two good discussions of confederalism and federalism in the EU, see Frederick K. Lister (1996) and John Kincaid (1999). Murray Forsyth distinguishes a confederation from an intergovernmental organization (IGO) as follows:

A treaty of [a confederal] union founds a body that possesses personality, but it is more than merely the technical, "legal" personality of the typical international organization.... The personality formed by [this] union is an original capacity to act akin to that possessed by the states themselves ... it is a profound locking together of states themselves as regards the exercise of fundamental powers (1981: 33).

However, confederation is a midway case between international organizations and federations in terms of the scope of general competences. Both international organizations and confederations may have councils that govern them. But Lister suggests that:

The main difference between IGOs and confederations in this respect is that the latter have been entrusted with certain sovereign powers: Their joint councils are thus involved in a decision-making of crucial importance for their member states. These bodies are the legislative counterparts of the national parliaments of federal and unitary states (1996: 42).

Executive and judicial functions are generally quite weak in confederations, these competences being reserved for member states. However, some confederations have executives and courts.

confederal and federal levels. In confederations, corporate representation is the *exclusive* mode of representation. In federations, corporate representation becomes one mode of representation alongside individual representation. To the extent that it has its own distinctive bases of legitimation, the federal level becomes a corporate group itself (a unity that transcends its own internal pluralism).

In judging the EU by these criteria, we see that it has some features of both a confederation and a federation. For the most part, representation in the EU is dominated by the corporate representation of member states through the Council of Ministers. But although the powers of the European Parliament are limited, it is now directly elected. Hence, the EU has a measure of direct legitimation.

In the shift from intergovernmental to confederal to federal status, we also see a shift in the voluntary nature of membership. Intergovernmental treaties and organizations certainly place constraints on exit from membership. However, they are clearly voluntaristic organizations. The narrow functional competence of these organizations facilitates exit, since exit threatens only a narrow range of commitments. Other memberships and treaties (between the same parties) can proceed unharmed. The voluntarism of confederations is somewhat more blurry, but still largely voluntaristic (Lister 1996: 37). Exit is made more difficult by the multipurpose nature of the organization. In such an organization, members cannot so easily pick and choose the competences with which they will comply. Nevertheless, exit remains possible. The confederal level has no direct claim over citizens; hence, a confederation is more fundamentally decomposable than a federation. When one moves toward a federation, the federal level develops a vested interest in the internal affairs of its members. Decomposability declines, and we should expect it to decline more sharply as the competences of the federal power increase in scope.

In the case of the EU, we have already discussed variable geometry and the ability to "opt in" or "opt out." Yet to opt in or out of EMU or the Schengen Accords is not the same as exiting the EU in general. Since no member has tried to exit, the voluntarist basis has not been tested. Secession would in all likelihood be permitted, but it becomes more and more difficult to imagine.

Federations are certainly multiperspectival polities in the sense that Ruggie suggests. Their multiperspectival nature is indicated by the way that they imply a form of dual authority and identity. Citizens are members of and are represented through two sets of overlapping territorial institutions. They have rights and obligations in both simultaneously. Moreover, at the federal level, both corporate and individual representation operates, typically producing dual legislative chambers (bicameralism). Though still very weak, a distinctive European citizenship is in the early stages of formation, as Maurizio Ferrera's chapter describes with respect to social rights. The EU also has an emerging bicameralism (the Council of Ministers and the European Parliament) and possibly an unprecedented tricameralism (the Committee of Regions).

General competences are jealous of their powers. Hence, dual authority creates strong incentives and demands to delineate jurisdictions between respective powers. Typically, in federations, these jurisdictions are delineated by strong constitutions. Judicial review is then necessary to protect the constitution. Such review typically implies the creation of a separate federal court system that can safeguard this constitutional order through judicial review. Constitutional law scholars typically interpret the ECJ as among the most "federal" of EU institutions, and they see a process of treaty constitutionalization resulting from the ECJ's judicial independence.[8] The move toward legal federalism is indicated by national court acknowledgment that EU law trumps national law.[9] It is also apparent in the formation of independent judicial review at the European level. However, many features of the ECJ better reflect confederal rather than federal arrangements. For instance, European judges are selected from among national judges nominated by member states. Moreover, each member state is represented on the ECJ. And national courts are treated as "coordinate" rather than inferior courts. Leslie Friedman Goldstein (2001) argues that the lack of member-state resistance to ECJ rulings can be attributed to the veto power that national governments have over EU legislation and constitutional review.[10]

Confederations have, as Lister puts it, a raison d'etre – a joint interest that binds member states together. However, this interest is conceived of as a joint or mutual interest of the respective member states. By contrast, federation implies the definition of a distinctive federal interest that transcends these individual interests. This federal interest entails the claim that for certain purposes the federal territory must be managed or regulated as an integrated territory. Such a claim, in turn, clearly requires independent legitimation by a federal constituency that transcends member-state constituencies. A concomitant of the articulation of a distinct federal interest is the move away from the consensus-based position, in which each member holds a veto over confederal policy, toward a majoritarian position. "Qualified majority

---

[8] Leslie Friedman Goldstein provides a nice summary of this process:

> What is unusual about the European Court of Justice is that, beginning in the early 1960s, its judges took a treaty and turned it, as well as any rules adopted under its authority, into judicially enforceable, higher law – law that takes precedence within each member state, even over subsequent national legislation or constitutional provisions to the contrary. In effect, the ECJ transformed this international treaty into a higher-law constitution and thus transformed the EC into a nascent federated polity (Goldstein 2001: 16–17).

[9] Lister argues that confederations typically rely on arbitration rather than courts of law for resolving disputes between members (1996: 42).

[10] Essentially, her argument suggests the consociational nature of the EU legal system.

voting" was first introduced by the 1987 Single European Act, and later treaties have expanded its use to a wide range of issue areas.

In traditional federations, a distinctive federal interest was typically claimed for defensive reasons. Such defensive federations are more than military alliances or pacts in which countries agree to utilize their respective militaries for collective defense. A federal conception of defense requires a unitary conception of the territory and a federal military. Here we see Ruggie's description of a shift from a multiperspectival to a single-perspective. Hence, we should expect that one form of jurisdictional regulation in a federation should be the differentiation of functions attributable to the territory as a whole from those attributable to its member states. This is precisely the sort of discourse we see in discussions about subsidiarity in the EU, although the EU does differ from traditional defensive federations. Since the beginning of the European Coal and Steel Community, European integration has been conceived of in terms of the integration of economic rather than military space. The conceptual shift from common market to single market in the Single European Act indicates the movement toward a unified single-point perspective on economic territoriality.

BETWIXT AND BETWEEN: INSTITUTIONAL HYBRIDITY AND ACCOMMODATION

Although intergovernmentalism and federalism are conventional analytical frameworks for understanding the structure of political institutions, I have argued that the novelty of the EU lies in its hybridity. Certain institutional features of the EU are best described in intergovernmental terms, while others are more confederal or federal. While debate framed in terms of intergovernmentalism versus federalism is certainly relevant to the broader macroinstitutional evolution of the EU, it overlooks something that this analysis of hybridity helps to highlight: the creation of a set of largely informal institutions that manage and accommodate the tensions and interpenetration among intergovernmental, confederal, and federal features of the EU. In very general terms, this institutional accommodation of hybridity has depended upon the creation of increasingly dense transnational networks that rely on deliberation, learning, and mutual adjustment. Although such informal institutions are present in all complex organizations (see, for instance, Chisholm 1989; on the EU, see Jabko 2001), these informal institutions have become an increasingly prominent aspect of European integration. Since these informal institutions are enormously complex, varying widely across issue domains, this section simply provides a very broad outline of them.

The most general way of describing these informal institutions is to indicate the shift, noted by both scholars and practitioners, toward describing European integration in terms of "governance" (Jachtenfuchs 2001; Scott and Trubek 2002). The focus on governance reflects the deepening density and complexity of institutional interaction in the EU (Fligstein and Stone Sweet 2002; Pierson 1996; Wessels 1997, 2001).

As is now widely acknowledged, informal governance of these dense and complex transactions increasingly takes place through networks (Ansell 2000; Héritier 2001; Kohler-Koch 1999), committees (Joerges and Vos 1999), epistemic communities (van Waarden and Drahos 2002; Zito 2001), and other forms of interinstitutional linkage (Christiansen 2001). These networks, committees, and epistemic communities bridge both the vertical (multilevel) and horizontal (intergovernmental) tensions created by institutional hybridity.

As the governance model suggests, these interinstitutional links are processes as well as structures. Hence institutional accommodation has been accompanied by an intensification of social interaction, information flow, and communication. This intensification has been described in terms of the intensely deliberative nature of EU governance (Joerges 2002; Joerges and Neyer 1997; Neyer 2003). Others have described the deepening "logic of information" in the EU (Culpepper 2002). This deliberative logic appears to be at work even in the most intergovernmental institutions and policy domains (Falkner 2002; Puetter 2003).

A third feature of this institutional accommodation is that certain institutions become the arenas in which the various pushes and pulls of EU institutions can be accommodated. Although primarily conceived as an intergovernmental institution, for example, the Committee of Permanent Representatives (COREPER) has become one such institutional location that acts as a mediator between national perspectives and community perspectives. It is an institutional arena in which the frictions between intergovernmentalism and federalism are managed. As a result, it has developed the features of networked deliberation described previously (Bostock 2002; Lewis 1998, 2000).

A fourth feature of this institutional accommodation is that European and national institutions have gradually become more self-conscious about the logic itself. The most important example of this self-consciousness is the introduction of the "Open-Method of Coordination," with its emphasis on mutual adjustment and learning (de la Porte 2002; Hodson and Maher 2001; Mosher and Trubek 2003).

This description of the features of an accommodation of the tensions of institutional hybridity raises a larger question about the character of institutional change in the process of European integration. As posed in this section, the tension between intergovernmentalism and federalism is managed through informal accommodation. These informal accommodations, however, can create their own tensions. The recent case of food safety is illustrative. The harmonization of food standards has a long history at the European level and is a classic example of what has been called comitology (Joerges and Vos 1999; Rhinard 2002). Under comitology, experts and ministers from different member states meet in joint committees to work out common EU positions and the technical details of harmonization. This process is seen as a particularly advanced form of intergovernmentalism, which Christian Joerges and Jurgen Neyer (1997) call "deliberative supranationalism." However, following the scandal and public outcry over the handling of mad cow disease, the comitology system was seen as contributing to the invisibility of decision-making processes. In response, a new European Food Agency was created to enhance the transparency of scientific expertise, and the oversight role of the European Parliament was expanded. These institutional transformations can be seen as a move in the direction of greater federalism. Nevertheless, as Giandomenico Majone has argued, the new agency is not (and should not be) a European Food and Drug Administration. It will (and ought to) retain a distinctive element of intergovernmentalism (Majone 2000).

The food safety case illustrates the continuing tensions in the construction of the EU. Deliberative networks, as represented by comitology, provide a means of managing the tensions between intergovernmental and federal institutions. Although deliberative, this very form of accommodation is subject to the criticism of being elitist, technocratic, and nontransparent (Eriksen and Fossum 2002). Such criticisms go directly to the heart of claims that the EU suffers from a democratic deficit. To further understand the tensions generated by hybrid institutional arrangements and the informal accommodations that manage them, it is necessary to investigate this broader issue of democratic representation.

INTERESTS AND IDENTITIES

To analyze the forces pulling Europe between intergovernmentalism and federalism, we must shift our attention from state to society. How does the mobilization of societal interests and identities propel the European integration process? I will try to approach these questions in a way that parallels the analytical framework I have described previously.

To begin, we can draw a parallel between functional and general competences and interests and identities. The general competence of the state has its parallel in the societal realm in an "omnicompetent" identity – national citizenship. Citizenship is a legal status bearing general rights and obligations of membership in the national state, and it is, in theory, the fount of popular sovereignty. Functional competences parallel interests that are typically narrower (though in some cases broader) than these national identities. Both omnicompetent national citizenship and narrower interests are typically mobilized by institutions and organizations. Elections are the institutional manifestation of the omnicompetence of citizens, and political parties are the organizational vehicle for mobilizing and representing citizens (political parties obviously mobilize specific interests as well, but they generally do so in the context of mobilizing many such interests). Functional interests are mobilized through interest groups, which may be more or less narrow in their representative claims.[11]

While this is the textbook view of political representation, it provides a convenient starting point. It enables us to think about the balance between an intergovernmental, confederal, and federal Europe. For both intergovernmentalism and confederalism, interests and identities are mediated through the state. Functional competences at the international level tend to encourage the mobilization of narrow interests and identities within nations, though these interests and identities are *in theory* channeled through the much more general authority structures of national governments. In an intergovernmental world, states themselves may act more like interest groups at the international level than like omnicompetent citizens. In this book, Sidney Tarrow makes such a claim about the emergence of regional lobbies in Europe when he argues that the EU coopts regions into acting like interest groups. The more general the competences of international organizations (for example, the move toward confederation), the more states are themselves constrained to act in a more omnicompetent fashion – in essence, as corporate citizens in a confederal system. This in turn leads them to seek more general sanction from their own citizens (perhaps through referenda).

Interests and identities may crosscut national borders. Tarrow examines transnational interest mobilization in his contribution to this book (and elsewhere). He argues that interests and identities do join up across member-state borders, although national mobilization remains primary. We might add to this picture the long-held neofunctionalist claim that the state monopoly on external representation is routinely violated. Functional interests can intervene directly with intergovernmental institutions rather than working through states.[12] Indeed, we might imagine the following interaction among transnational mobilization, direct representation, and the autonomy of European institutions:

• The more autonomous European institutions, and the more general their competences, the more that interests and identities will attempt to engage them directly.

[11] Semantically, I have associated "identities" with general competences and "interests" with functional competences. This is partly a convenience. But we also know that there are broader identities – particularly regional or ethic – that are quite encompassing, but narrower than national identity. The semantic distinction will be useful in drawing out some of the consequences of European integration.

[12] On the creation of European lobbying groups in light of processes of European integration, see Neil Fligstein and Stone Sweet (in Stone Sweet, Sandholtz, and Fligstein 2001). Christoph Knill (2001) argues that European interest groups became stronger during the 1990s, replacing membership based on national association with mixed membership (national associations and individual firms) and increasing crosssectoral (horizontal) integration through the creation of alliances and umbrella groups.

- The more national interests want to engage directly with European institutions, the more it will make sense to form alliances with interests and identities in other nations.
- The more directly that national and transnational interests engage European institutions, the more autonomous and powerful European institutions will become.[13]

Among the authors in this book, Bartolini, for instance, doubts the cohesion of "crosslocal functional interests" (in this case, transnational mobilization). Tarrow argues that transnational mobilization is only one form of mobilization and expects shifting alignments that will counterbalance movement in a federal direction. Chapter 7, by Gary Marks and Ian Down, however, offers more support for this dynamic. The authors argue that the European labor movement has evolved toward a pro-integration stance as the powers and competences of the EU have increased.

We can also examine the future of integration from the perspective of citizenship and electoral representation. As described previously, federations imply independent legitimation of federal institutions and the creation of a distinctly federal constituency. In informal terms, this means the development of a distinctive European identity that will coexist with prevailing national identities. Lister describes the dualism of federalism succinctly:

People living in federations usually have double allegiances and loyalties to the nation and to the region or homeland with which they identify themselves with their federal state. Since the central and regional governments both operate directly upon the people, each citizen is subject to two governments (1996: 20).

Survey analysis suggests that European identity is still significantly weaker than national identity, but that it can often coexist comfortably with national identity.[14]

In addition to identity, debates about the democratic deficit in Europe often note that federalization implies the creation of a European "public" – the development of European dialogue that transcends strictly national dialogue. It is also argued that federalization would require European citizenship and political party institutions that can effectively mobilize this citizenship at

---

[13] For evidence of this argument in the case of the development of the early-twentieth-century American state, see Daniel Carpenter (2001).

[14] Liesbet Hooghe and Marks (2001a) find European identity to be relatively weak compared to local, regional, and national identity, when 1991 and 1995 survey data is analyzed by country. However, they find that 30 percent of the individuals surveyed identify as strongly with Europe as with their nation. At the same time, they find a relatively small group of respondents who see national and European identity as opposing one another. See also Jack Citrin and John Sides (2003) and Kees van Kersbergen (2000). Joachim Schild (2001) finds the coexistence of multiple identities on the decline in France, and particularly, Germany, in the 1980s and 1990s. This decline appears to be the result of the increasing politicization of the European integration project.

the European level. The relative weakness of a European identity, public, citizenship, and political parties amounts to the commonly heard argument that the European Union lacks a *demos*.[15] While correct in a static sense, this claim misses the movement toward the creation of a European *demos*. For example, the Maastricht and Amsterdam treaties marked the first steps toward the definition of a formal European citizenship (Hoskyns and Newman 2000).

In addition to the weakness of a European *demos*, the democratic deficit is also attributed to the weakness of the European Parliament and European elections, the lack of a formal constitution (currently in the process of being rectified), and the unaccountable nature of the Commission and the Council (vis-à-vis Parliament).[16] To address this debate in more specific terms, it is useful to distinguish four models of democratic representation: parliamentarism, consociationalism, corporatism, and pluralism.

- In the classic Westminister model of parliamentary democracy, a strong fusion of powers and parliamentary sovereignty encourage the creation of "responsible parties" as the dominant mode of democratic representation.
- For consociationalism, a few overlapping (as opposed to crosscutting) cleavages dominate politics. Subnational identities (for example, religious, ethnic) rather than functional interests are the basic constituencies of politics. Democracy operates through grand parliamentary coalitions premised on the security of mutual vetoes, which encourage negotiated consensus. Consociationalism leads to strong integration at the elite level, but reflects segmentation at the mass level.
- Like the consociational model, the corporatist model also encourages a consensual form of democracy. However, functional representation, organized through peak associations, is the primary form of interest intermediation. These peak associations are more aggregated, cohesive, and

---

[15] Wolfgang Merkel, for example, argues that the EU lacks an integrated party system, truly European interest groups, sufficient voter turnout for European elections, a common language, and a Europeanwide mass media (in Anderson 1999). Carlos Closa (in Weale and Nentwich 1998: 176) writes:

It is, however, scarcely even possible to disagree with the diagnosis that the prerequisites for EU democracy are largely lacking: there is no "Europeanised" party system, no European association or citizens' movements, no European media. The biggest obstacle, however, seems to be the absence of a common language, so that political discourse remains bounded by national frontiers.

He then goes on to argue, however, that this is an "organicist" perspective on citizenship. He argues that EU citizenship must be far more political or "liberal" if it is to develop at all and a national *demos* is an inappropriate standard. Michael Zürn also argues that we should think of a liberal and civic notion of *demos* as, in part, a product rather than a precondition of democracy (in Greven and Pauly 2000).

[16] This summary is based on a more detailed description by Michael Greven in Greven and Pauly (2000: 37).

disciplined than pluralist interest groups and can therefore act in a manner equivalent to "responsible parties."

- The pluralist model also focuses attention on functional interest representation. In the pluralist model, however, the separation of powers encourages the mobilization of more fragmented and less cohesive interests. Pluralism suggests a "veto democracy" in which functional interests mobilize relatively independently of party representation and engage in "venue shopping" (shifting institutional arenas in search of favorable treatment). The model suggests a form of highly competitive, but negotiable, democratic politics and presumes a society rift by multiple, crosscutting social cleavages. A civic republican version of this pluralist model, first described by Alexis de Tocqueville, emphasizes the role of associations in promoting political participation and a civic culture.

Which of these democratic models is appropriate to the circumstances in Europe?[17] We arrive at the importance of the comparison between the United States and the EU. As Sergio Fabbrini argues in his chapter, the EU is developing more along lines suggested by U.S. political development than by the political development of European states. This point has important implications for thinking about the democratic deficit. If we measure European democracy against the yardstick of parliamentary democracy, we inevitably find it wanting.[18] It has neither the degree of institutional integration nor the degree of citizenship and identity achieved by European states. And if the standard itself is unreachable, institutional reforms designed to correct the democratic deficit may produce undesirable outcomes.

The liberal pluralist model may offer a better model of how to think about the democratic deficit in Europe. Guiseppe Di Palma develops this argument in his postcript, building on Bruce Cain's chapter and on John Coultrap (1999).[19] Cain argues that veto politics, with its countermajoritarian effects, may have important functional benefits in immigration policy and does not

[17] We can also take the mirror image of this democratic theory question and ask about resistance among member states to the strengthening of federal institutions. For example, what happens if the pluralist, corporatist, consociational, or responsible party model is operative at the local level? Bernard Wessels and Achim Kielhorn (in Katz and Wessels 1999) argue that corporatist member states and states with strong parliaments (that is, a responsible party model) tend to be more resistant to the transfer of competences to the European level.

[18] Jean Blondel, Richard Sinnott, and Palle Svensson (1998) argue against using the standard of an electoral mandate – epitomized by the Westminster model – as the basis for reforming European democracy. Frank Decker similarly argues that parliamentary democracy is the "wrong yardstick" (Decker 2002: 270).

[19] Albert Weale contrasts the countermajoritarian and majoritarian theories of democracy as applied to the EU (Weale and Nentwich 1998). Richard Katz and Wessels (1999) argue that a pluralist model may indeed prevail, but it will not solve the fundamental problem of democratic legitimation. See also Katz (2001). Adrienne Héritier suggest some modest mechanisms of legitimacy in a European polity that falls short of full democratic legitimation (1999).

necessarily accentuate the democratic deficit. Di Palma similarly raises the issue of efficiency when he refers to "experimentalism" and "problem solving" as being at the heart of a constitutionalized international regime. He is raising the point that national responses to problems may no longer be efficient even if they are democratically sanctioned.

Many factors suggest that Europe is headed in a pluralist direction. The functional competences of intergovernmentalism, for instance, encourage a narrow functional mobilization of interests. Moreover, these interests are likely to be organized along pluralist rather than corporatist lines, if only because European interest groups face the same intergovernmental-confederal-federal tensions that states do. While noting that European institutions have sought to institutionalize a more corporatist system of representation, Wolfgang Streeck and Philippe Schmitter (1991) argue that this attempt has largely failed and that pluralism prevails at the European level. Tarrow's description of "shifting alignments" certainly suggests pluralist relations at the European level. Observers have also generally emphasized that social cleavages at the European level are likely to be far more heterogeneous than at the national level.[20] Furthermore, to the extent that the EU moves toward more general competences, it is certainly much closer to a U.S.-like separation-of-powers regime than to a European fusion-of-powers regime. Chapters by Cain on immigration policy and Alberta Sbragia on environmental policy in the EU and the United States certainly suggest the usefulness of applying the "veto" model to European politics. Multiple "venues" at the European level are likely to increase the opportunities for interests and identities to mobilize outside of national party frameworks, hence weakening national party control. And, by the same token, this same dynamic of expanded venues should limit the ability of European-level interests and identities to be mobilized around a strong "responsible party" framework. The weaknesses of the European *demos*, Parliament, and political parties are seen as contributing to the weakness of the responsible party model.[21]

While the pluralist model appears more likely to prevail than the responsible party model or the corporatist model, an argument can also be made in favor of the consociational model (Chryssochoou 1994, 1997; see also

[20] Merkel summarizes the point:

> With these [national] states, societal cleavages are overlapped and reconciled by shared communication *(Kommunikationsgemeinschaft)*, shared experiences *(Erfahrungsgemeinschaft)*, and a deeply felt sense of national identity. This is not the case at the European level, where diversity intensifies segmentation and exclusion. European society, assuming it exists, is much more heterogeneous, segmented, and conflictual than even the national societies of Switzerland, Belgium, and the Netherlands – segmented societies that require special consensual democratic structures and procedures (Anderson 1999: 56).

[21] For a relatively optimistic analysis of the responsible party model in light of an analysis of the 1994 European elections, see Hermann Schmitt and Jacques Thomassen (1999). A companion volume is less optimistic (Katz and Wessels 1999, esp. 241–2).

Bogaards 2002). The pluralist model fails to give adequate weight to the strong national identities that everyone expects to persist even into a "post-national" future. These national identities are unlikely to behave like simply another pluralist interest group. Moreover, they coincide with the strong national vetoes that still dominate many EU institutions. A number of EU features, for instance, suggest a consociational design. For example, two features of the ECJ that Goldstein (2001) describes as critical in preventing resistance to EU laws read like a textbook of consociational principles:

- "Supermajority decision-making (Council of Ministers), or the appearance of it (ECJ) at the center, such that federal rules appear to be the product of consensus."
- "Equal representation of member states on federal decision-making bodies" (ECJ).

These consociational features are closely associated with confederal structures. Michael Tsinisizelis and Dimitris Chryssouchou (in Weale and Nentwich 1998) argue that the political framework for European integration ought to be "confederal consociationalism." Moreover, the elite networks associated with comitology reflect the type of elite integration envisioned by the consociational model.

Nevertheless, consociationalism fails to confront the tensions related to *indirect* representation at the European level. The argument about the democratic deficit is, in my opinion, an argument about the indirect nature of European representation – and hence the limits of both intergovernmental and confederal institutions. The stronger EU institutions become and the more general their competences, the more that EU citizens will demand direct representation at the European level. Moreover, it appears unlikely that this demand can be satisfied exclusively through elite or interest group representation. From the perspective of popular sovereignty, such forms of representation are regarded as insufficiently transparent or accountable.

I return now to the broader claim that the EU is a hybrid of intergovernmentalism, confederalism, and federalism. By analogy, it may be less useful to fret over which democratic model best captures the essence of EU politics and to examine instead the ways they may be forced to coexist. For intergovernmentalism, democratization of the EU is really a non-issue. As an intergovernmental organization, democracy operates at the level of the nation-state. Democratically elected national governments aggregate domestic political interests and legitimately represent them at the European level (Moravcsik 1998). As described previously, confederal forms of government have a strong affinity with consociational forms of democratic legitimation, emphasizing the continued importance of national (as opposed to European) publics and identities. The federal model for Europe is broadly compatible with parliamentary, pluralist, or corporatist models. The parliamentary model would emphasize the trend toward a strengthened European Parliament, political parties, and citizenship as precursors to a responsible party model (Kreppel 2002). The corporatist model would point to the growing cohesiveness of European interest associations and to strategies of institutions like the European Commission to produce consensual interest intermediation (Knill 2001). The liberal pluralist model would emphasize the unmediated representation of national and transnational interests at the European level and the constitutionalization of a separation of powers regime.

While it is reasonable to argue about which of these models explains the most variance, an analysis of the EU as a hybrid grants each of these models some normative and empirical merit and shifts our attention to how their juxtaposition produces tension and accommodation. What does politics look like when national executives remain critical (but no longer monopolistic) intermediaries in the representative process at the EU level, where national identities are powerful organizers of public opinion, and where European interest associations and political parties are increasingly cohesive and the European Parliament increasingly relevant? Is there a parallel to the intensification of informal institutional accommodation described previously?

Ansell, Craig Parsons, and Keith Darden (1997) describe the shifting alignments between regional, national, and European actors that operate as subnational and European actors gain relative autonomy from national governments. These shifting alignments, they argue, tend to produce a dynamic balancing between intergovernmental and federal dominance on regional policy matters. In this book, Tarrow develops a similar but much more general argument about "relational" mechanisms he calls brokerage, object shift, and scale shift. Each of these relational mechanisms, he argues, presents the possibility for shifting political alignments that crosscut the "composite" institutional terrain of Europe. Tarrow's conception of shifting alignments is not unlike the veto politics described previously.[22] However, his emphasis on relationships that align political actors within and across institutional jurisdictions better illustrates the hybrid nature of political mobilization in Europe. In similar terms, Christoph Knill (2001) argues that the need for coordination across multiple arenas in the EU has created a demand for "interface actors" that mediate between heterogeneous interests. In conjunction with the role of the Commission in producing coordinated policy responses from interest associations, he notes that the dynamic of interest mobilization across multiple arenas produces a "competition for cooperation" that offsets the importance of veto politics.

---

[22] In a study of Belgian interest mobilization, Jan Beyers (2002) finds that interest associations mobilizing for access to Belgian policy networks are the same ones actively mobilized for European access. Franz Pappi and Christian Henning (1999) find that national farm associations work through both their national ministries and their European peak associations.

Do these "betwixt and between" societal institutions exhibit the type of intensive deliberative qualities described earlier? On this point, the literature is more hesitant. Erik Oddvar Eriksen and John Erik Fossum (2002) argue that the Charter Convention does embody some aspects of a transnational deliberative network. Alex Warleigh (2000) finds variable evidence that European nongovernmental organizations (NGOs) are able to act as "credible ambassadors" for EU citizenship when they mobilize in broad policy coalitions.

A parallel question about citizenship can be posed. Building on Stein Rokkan's emphasis on territorial boundaries and Albert Hirschman's argument about the trade-off between exit and voice, the theoretical framework Bartolini develops in this book might be used to emphasize the organic relationship between the civic and the nationalist qualities of citizenship. Ferrera (in Chapter 5 of this book) uses such a framework to argue that the development of "social citizenship" and national welfare regimes was closely associated with territorial closure. By contrast, recent discussions of postnationalism – notably by Jürgen Habermas – suggest that nationalist and civic identities are not inherently bound together (Habermas 1992). In fact, their separation might leave behind the more particularistic traits of nationalism. Without being able to adjudicate between these contrasting positions, the analysis developed here might point toward an investigation of what happens when the relationship between national and civic (or social) citizenship is partially but not completely differentiated. In fact, Ferrera's analysis of social citizenship demonstrates something very much like a hybrid arrangement. He argues that compulsory "first pillar" welfare schemes, which presume national membership, have been upheld by the European Court of Justice. However, voluntary "second pillar" schemes have become linked to European market integration, and the ECJ and member states have, to quote Ferrera, "lost virtually all boundary-setting prerogatives, along both the territorial and the membership dimensions."

CONCLUDING COMMENT

Ruggie is correct in calling attention to the novel institutional character of the EU. Yet I have argued that this novelty arises from the EU's hybrid nature as a blend of intergovernmental, confederal, and federal institutional arrangements. Ruggie is also right to call attention to the weak territorial base of the EU and to note that this is novel if we judge it as a *state*. It is unsurprising, however, if we judge it as an *intergovernmental institution*. The multiperspectival variable geometry we see in the EU must be considered in conjunction with significant movement toward a unified territorial space (single-point perspective). Monetary integration, for example, reflects *variable* geometry *and* the shift toward a *single* market.

As a hybrid institution, the EU does raise questions about the direction of change. Is this hybridity stable? Or is this hybridity a transitional stage in the development of the EU from an intergovernmental system to a federation? As Di Palma writes in his postscript, "Social scientists are not philosopher kings but rather roosters announcing, yet not thereby conjuring, the sun." The direction of change is difficult to predict and history is not inclined toward efficiency. Hybridity does create deep tensions – the most important of which is captured in the term "democratic deficit" – that must be addressed if the EU is to be a viable form of governance. However, hybridity has also prompted the creation of forms of institutional accommodation – notably, deliberative networks – that seek to manage the tensions produced by the clash of different logics of political representation and administration. Although these institutional accommodations present their own problems, they pose an alternative path of institutional evolution. This analysis suggests we consider the deepening of institutional accommodation to be an alternative – or at least a complement – to the more conventional conception of European integration as an evolution from an intergovernmental to a federal system.

Postscript

What Inefficient History and Malleable Practices Say about Nation-States and Supranational Democracy When Territoriality Is No Longer Exclusive

Giuseppe Di Palma

This book focused attention on the restructuring of the territorial bases of public authority and societal interests in the contemporary Western state. We employed two analytical tracers. Stefano Bartolini provides the first, Sidney Tarrow the second. Bartolini employs an exit-voice decoder to highlight the subversion of state-centered territorial order, leading to new forms of territorial representation. Tarrow's attention to the relational, exchange, and opportunity strategies available to institutional actors takes us one important step forward. The underlying forces that unpack the state-territorial container, which Bartolini traces, may be insufficient to map how authority and interests will be reshaped: whether around new territorial venues, functional concerns, or both. Thus, exit-voice analysis benefits when cast in an opportunity structure. Together, Bartolini and Tarrow give us a map to visit the contributions to the book.

Christopher Ansell's introduction uses the map to point out the contributors' shared attention to the restructuring of authority and interests. Personally, I am particularly struck by those parts of Bartolini's and Tarrow's analyses that, together, suggest the open-ended, contingent, still unfathomable direction of restructuring. At the same time, I am reminded that, within the modern Western state, territoriality is bundled with sovereignty and by way of it with democracy. Hence, to raise issues about territoriality and its restructuring is to raise empirical and normative issues about democracy.

I therefore revisit the book by way of a postscript. Revisitation involves introducing a foundational set of arguments as to why we cannot speak conclusively to the shape of restructuring and the way it may order relations between authority and societal interests. It also involves addressing the issue of democracy when territoriality is no longer exclusive. My arguments bear first on the proper understanding of change as a dissynchronic composite process. They then bear on whether relations between authority and societal interests will remain, despite restructuring, within the democratic framework, or whether democratic relations are only conceivable within an exclusive sovereign territorial state.

We might impute the protracted uncertainty and apparent inefficiency of the processes of restructuring, the difficulties in forecasting and conceptualizing new structures, to theoretical shortcomings. Are we not up to the task? As social scientists, we are additionally concerned with the processes' presumed costs in democratic accountability and effectiveness: Is democracy possible only within the Weberian modern state? Are citizens and interests best empowered by their own states? I suggest a reading of the book that mitigates these normative and empirical-conceptual concerns. I do it by emphasizing in the first section of this chapter that, even when impressing us as assuredly historical, almost all change is inefficient. It is better seen as processually open-ended, discontinuous, composite, and incremental. In the second section, I focus at greater length on the special role that ideas, as practiced identities, play in nonlinear change. The final section raises the issue, empirical and normative, of democracy beyond the nation-state.

THE INEFFICIENCIES OF HISTORY

Much modern social science sees history as efficient. The term is evocative but vague and treacherous, especially when dealing with the world relevant to this book – the world that sovereign institutions inhabit.[1] The notion that history is efficient is rooted in a set of broadly cast ideological and socioscientific dispositions. As an ideological disposition, it does not need social science. A comfortable belief in human progress will do. Still, the belief can claim scientific credentials because we can cast it within the long-range developments of early-modern Europe: the economic and scientific revolutions, the Enlightenment, hence modernity as progress.

I submit that efficient history, history as the just-so outcome of weighty objective forces or rational templates, is an oxymoron. Many facts run interference. One is the very fact that both structures and agents impinge on change. And they impinge in open combinations capable of multiple equilibria of variable duration. True, in Karl Marx's much abused dictum, men make their own history, but do not make it "as they please," that is, out of metaphorical whole cloth. However, by the same dictum, the cloth at hand does not fashion itself. Therefore, on one side, the design of, say, a united Europe may be inconceivable outside the structural and historical conditions that marked Europe in the last century. On the other side, the dictum does not designate the tailor or his or her fashion. Further, the limits imposed on the tailor by what is at hand, the stock and quality of cloth available,

---

[1] A critical discussion of the efficiency of history is in James G. March and Johan P. Olsen (1984, 1998).

make room for improvisation, reflectivity, *creativity*. To use jargon skeptical of efficiency, actors avail themselves of existing repertories. And by tinkering, they may enrich them. Subjective factors – of inventiveness, learning, persuasiveness, or for that matter of standing pat – defy linearity.

Agency and structures may not interact in a linear fashion – where sequentially arranged factors affect others down the line – but rather in a cascading one, moving at speeds that are variable yet possibly converging toward serendipitous results. We may speak here of different temporalities. James G. March and Johan P. Olsen observe:

Temporal order provides an alternative in which linkages are less consequential than temporal. Things are connected by virtue of their simultaneous presence or arrival... [A]ttention to problems seems to be determined as much by the time of their arrival as by assessments of their importance (1984: 743).

Different temporalities suggest that change starts in piecemeal fashion, and when the pieces come together, they do so under conditions that are in part fortuitous, in part crafted on the advantage of fortuitousness. The observation is prompted by the critical comments by Karen Orren and Stephen Skowronek about the conception of order and change prevailing in the study of American history (1995: 297). Within this conception, institutions and policies, either in linear fashion or at critical junctures, are erroneously constructed as guided toward complete convergence by the efficient coordination of history. Orren and Skowronek suggest, instead, that specific institutional and policy areas exhibit specific receptivity, or resistance, to external change. Receptivity and resistance are conditioned by the sectoral relevance of pressures, but also by the particular mechanisms that institutions and policies mobilize. Policy and institutional areas, each with their own practices and temporal orders, communicate with each other, but they do so in the presence of those practices and orders. This means that actors are often subject to the tyranny of small choices confined within institutional and policy domains where actors attend to routines and everyday maintenance.

It is within these confined tyrannies and their temporalities that change may yet occur. Even when change is momentous, it seems therefore imprudent to divide political history into well-ordered periods, where change is a neat transition from one institutional and policy order to another one (say, from feudalism to absolutism), sealed and delivered by the irrevocability of history or the prefigurations of its midwives (Rose 1990). It is wiser to move from the opposite view: Different temporal orders coexist, each with its own propensities to engage with the others and to respond to change. Hence, retrospectively, major change is not thereby necessarily linear and comprehensive. Hence, also, it seems unwarranted to refer to specific episodes of change as unfortunately disharmonic or retarded. Rather, different institutional temporalities make it so that institutions tend to "abrade against each other and, in the process, drive further change" (Orren and Skowronek

1995: 307). Here, change is piecemeal in two senses: in that it may originate at different times in different domains, and in that, like Lucretius' atoms, it may weave among paths rather than speeding down regulated highways. What other trajectories of change it may thus bump into and possibly instigate on its journey, when, with what consequences for its own and other journeys – these are fairly open matters, beyond the ordering reach of chaos theory.

The weight of so-called inefficient events and the Lucretian perspective help account for the fact that there is often a gap between the scale of effected changes and that of individual causes. Major changes may often result from circumstantial accumulation (not at all overdetermining) of smaller events and the abrading of confined choices. James M. Caporaso and Joseph Jupille's chapter on the European Court of Justice (ECJ) and the reshaping of the UK institutional order offers a good example of the piecemeal, happenstance way that relatively confined institutional steps may feed into broader institutional change. The authors point to an imbalance of scale between circumstantial contextual causes and consequences that alter long-standing constitutional setups. Because of the imbalance, the consequences are unanticipated (although not thereby unwelcome) both by the social scientist and by the practitioners. The imbalance is between the European Court of Justice's declared doctrine of direct effect and the deep alteration that the doctrine appears to have produced in the ingrained practices of British parliamentary sovereignty. A larger unanticipated effect of the ECJ's doctrine is the slow transformation of the Rome Treaty and following treaties from international compacts into what Alec Stone (1994) calls a supranational constitution. But the British case does not just illustrate how the inefficiencies of history are part and parcel of change. It also highlights one source of inefficiencies – namely, the fact that institutional identities (Britain's constitutional/parliamentary identity) are not assigned and do not live by eternal fiat. They rest on how persuasively they continue to be practiced. As such they are malleable, rendering history malleable within some degree of freedom, which is the topic of the next section.

Actually more revealing, as to the inefficiencies of history, than the current European story is the story of how the modern Westphalian state came into being. Gary Marks writes: "[S]tate building [resembles European integration] in its lack of a master plan ... [S]tate building was a conscious process of political engineering. Yet it was not engineering according to some external master plan" (1997: 26). Indeed engineering went on for centuries, but it was neither comprehensive nor exactly aware of its ultimate outcome. Westphalia was a tipping point (Gladwell 2000), a decisive moment in which different temporalities happened to converge into a contagiously critical mass. Eventually, Westphalia lent its name to an ideal type: the Weberian/Westphalian modern state. But the type was constructed retrospectively.

Bruce Cain, in his chapter on immigration policies in the United States and the European Union, takes us one step further. He offers one reason why new institutions are not born whole from a comprehensive institutional design. Rather, new institutions are likely to emerge as validated practices, deemed appropriate for the supervening policy needs of specific policy sectors. Extrapolating from the history of institutional change in the United States, Cain argues that, in matters of immigration, any transfer of institutional powers from member countries to the European Union will be driven by changes in policy preferences. Preferences drive institutional change. However much it upsets classical notions of constitutionalism, the impetus for institutional change is to overcome policy obstacles by shifting to a more favorable policy venue. Over time, in turn, emerging institutional practices may prove adept at and facilitate the adoption of new tasks and expanding purposes. But to do this, institutions must be able, as they go along, to pin down or invent and then to justify a new policy area or policy style.[2] Such seems to have been the story of state building. It is the story of building up and *upon* institutions; a story that, with significant variations, may recur in other realms of change; and a story that is best assembled from inside, with the retrospective narrative care that many stories of *virtù fortuna* deserve.

True, constitution making, institutional engineering, and institutional borrowing came to assume a central role in the career of the modern state, but only subsequently. Their lateness resides in the simple fact that the specialized institutions of the modern state became visibly consequential and available for constitutional engineering only as their practices congealed. Constitution making became common across states, standardizing constitutional models and institutions, when there were models and standards to be imitated. Only then did a regulatory area of policy making come into being: the area of constituent policies, as Theodore J. Lowi (1972) calls them, regulating how substantive policies should be made and how decisional institutions should be structured. Another reason for lateness can be teased out of Cain's mantra about venue shopping: The adoption of institutional solutions does not rest only on their visible availability. It also rests on whether they might address or perhaps redefine a particular policy preference. This leads me to a preliminary reflection on institution building in European integration. There are no unassailable models to borrow from, no bags of tricks from which to pull existing solutions. The reason is that the solutions do not come from but rather contribute to institutions. And even when actors dare, even when they are ready to learn and not just adapt and survive, even when intentionality

---

[2] March and Olsen comment:

Nation-state builders started with instrumental motives, such as winning wars or collecting taxes; over time they discovered that they had built the foundations for strongly institutional states.... The existence of capabilities is converted into an inclination to discover goals the capabilities might serve..." (1998: 966–7).

drives them, the contours of their imagined institutional change cannot prefigure, save happenstance, a distant outcome that possibly has never before been practiced. In particular:

- As I will argue in the final section of this chapter, it is imprudent to think that the European Union will be filled with institutions similar to those that marked the modern democratic state (representation, parliaments, elections, majority or consociational rule, and popular accountability).
- The search for a new European order started as a search for ways of addressing old and new policy issues by bending the mold of territorial sovereignties. Hence the search is characterized by a slow move away from the tested rules of intergovernmentalism. To the extent that the rules and institutions originally adopted reflected intergovernmentalism, they were progressively joined or replaced by rules not yet congealed in a final set of institutional practices. Many of the most important rules are closely designed to regulate a specific policy domain, in ways that in turn indirectly affect the quality and the tempo of policy choices.

It is with these two considerations in mind that I read the following excerpt from an op-ed piece on the Maastricht Treaty, authored by Mario Monti, European commissioner and former rector of Milan's Bocconi University:

Let us not stop at institutions. . . . Let us suppose that instead of Maastricht, a treaty had been signed. It says nothing on the EMU [European Monetary Union] or on public finances, but recognizes one or two features of 'formal' political integration: direct popular election of the president and members of the European Commission, full legislative powers for the European Parliament, curtailment of the powers of the Union's Council of Ministers. In that case, we would have today (and it would be very positive) the institutional instruments to conduct democratic politics, as if we were an integrated continent. But the continent would still be fragmented. How could we really pursue common policies equally appropriate for, and acceptable by, the citizens of [countries so disparate in their policy practices and in their performance] . . . ? Maastricht was important, in my opinion, because it gave us the single currency; but more important because, with the single currency, it has given us a constitution, a body of rules that, ostensibly financial, carry a civic substance. Today, a "culture of stability" is taking roots. . . . The euro, even before its adoption, has also changed the way we make policies. The choices are starker, more transparent and sincere. With a ceiling on national deficits, what we give to some we must take away from others. . . . This, it seems to me, reestablishes the "primacy of politics" (*Corriere della Sera*, May 3, 1998, my translation).

I close this section by returning to the inefficiencies of history. I suggest that those inefficiencies confront social scientists with intellectual challenges we should not short-circuit. To impose linear schemes on how change in territorial sovereignty will and should unfold and how institutions will finally shape up is not just premature; it will likely take us in the wrong direction.

Sensitivity to the open-ended, nonlinear quality of ongoing changes in sovereignty and territoriality is offered by the two theoretical chapters in this book, by Bartolini and by Tarrow. Significant differences in their approaches are analyzed in Ansell's introduction. But despite their differences, the following commonality is worth stressing: Both authors construe their theoretical contributions by an open-ended focus on political actors' calculus and strategizing. Bartolini employs Stein Rokkan's and Albert Hirschman's powerful logic of exit versus voice to lay out the numerous ways in which private actors can avail themselves of the emerging options for territorial exit offered by globalization and European integration. As they challenge domestic authority, these options also allow for dispersed sites of territorial relocation. Tarrow draws rather on political exchange and political opportunity models to push Bartolini one open-ended step further. Bartolini's exclusive emphasis on exit gives privileged attention to territorial transfer of interests at the expense of the state. Tarrow's processual emphasis on models of political exchange and multiple opportunity structures sees a restructuring along functional rather than territorial lines. Further, says Tarrow, the changing coalitions made possible by a spectrum of opportunity structures may be local or transnational, but may also stay centered on the state. But the point I wish to stress here is that, given their agential emphasis on options and opportunities, both authors reject univocal outcomes.

Finally, this section's observations about the limits of comprehensive aspirations and ambitious visions in early state building as in the present restructuring of territorial authority are not meant to deny the significance of these institutional transformations. Rather, these observations invite us to contextualize visions and aspirations and to revisit a series of fundamental questions about the role that ideational forces generally play in processes of change: what *kind* of ideational forces, how comprehensive, steady, and consequential? I believe that this book's contributions see the issue of ideational forces as something more than a matter of the relative weight of utilitarian versus ideational explanations – a question that has framed in part the European debate between intergovernmentalists and supranationalists.[3] They more interestingly see it as a matter of understanding how ideas become relevant and how relevant they become.[4] This is the topic of the following section.

---

[3] Besides, the distinction between utilitarian and ideational explanations does not easily hold. Utilitarian motives are not "naked," they are always rooted in and justified by culturally specific notions of appropriateness. See *infra*.

[4] In a statement that maps out much of my terrain, March and Olsen write:

[It is not] possible to describe the evolution of international political orders in terms of any simple notions of intentionality and design.... As individuals, groups, organizations, and institutions seek to act intelligently and learn in a changing world involving others similarly trying to adapt, they create connections that subordinate individual intentions to their interactions.... Expectations, preferences, identities, and meanings are affected by human interaction and experience. They coevolve with the actions they produce (1998: 968–9).

IDEAS AS PRACTICED IDENTITIES

What kind of place do ideas occupy? John Gerald Ruggie, inspired by John R. Searle's (1995) work on "constitutive rules" and "collective intentionality," offers a vivid response. Reflecting on European integration, Ruggie writes:

Some ideational factors simply do not function causally in the same way as brute facts or the agentive role that neo-utilitarianism attributes to interests . . . [Ideational] factors fall into the category of *reasons for actions*, which are not the same as *causes of actions*. Thus the *aspiration* for a united Europe has not *caused* European integration as such, but it is the *reason* the causal factors . . . produced an outcome that is historically *so* and not *otherwise*. Absent those "reasons," however, and the same "causes" would not have the same causal capacity (1998: 869, emphasis in the original text).

In Searle's vocabulary, ideational factors are constitutive. Ruggie's insight is an important epistemological opener, but it demands specification. In a comment on Ruggie's insight, Ernst Haas avers: "Constitutive norms require the consent of the relevant community. . . . They cannot arise merely in the mind of the philosopher who then observes how real-life actors gradually come to agree with him" (2000: 454). Central to specification is how embedded ideas become what we may call the *practiced identities* of their carriers. The authenticity of ideas, to carriers and others, and their durability rest on usage more than on legal-institutional utterance. Furthermore, ideas, norms, and rules need not arrive fully developed. Haas concludes: "New constitutive norms, however, may evolve piecemeal and incrementally from regulatory rules deliberately changed by the actors who are not even conscious of creating new orders" (ibid.). Here, successful usage is cumulative, recursive, and channeling. It clusters into modes of action that depend on, and reciprocally articulate and sustain, values, beliefs, views of the world, and therefore identities (Swidler 1986). This perspective defines political actors precisely by what they behold and practice. And it supplies new lights on how to approach the place of ideas and carriers in the early formation of the modern state and in its present unbundling and rebundling.

One such light is cast on the identity of the relevant actors in the process of European regional integration. Some of the participants in the debate between intergovernmentalists and supranationalists frame the question as bearing on the role of states versus European institutions. The debate usually amounts to a test of whether states or supranational institutions carry more weight. The same debate is at times framed as a tug of war between innovative, ideationally driven, "genuinely" European institutions (the Commission, the Court of Justice), and national governments beholden to largely fixed, self-referential domestic perspectives. True, sovereign European states go by their own practiced identities and epistemic resources. True, these identities are intensely self-referential. Therefore, state sovereignty carries a cautionary tale as to how far the rebundling of a spatially differentiated world-system can travel. I will return to the cautionary tale shortly. Still, precisely because they live by practice, identities, albeit rooted, are not unshakable. Alexander Wendt emphasizes: "The sovereign state is an on-going accomplishment of practice, not a once-and-for-all creation of norms that somehow exist apart from practice" (1992: 413). Viable practices need more than lawfully required compliance. They need acceptance by the context in which they are engaged (Krygier 1999; Selznick 1992). If novel behaviors emerge, they will be tentative at first. But if they slide into recurring alternative practices, they may be harbingers of cognitive dissonance. In turn, dissonance rewards a reorientation of past practices and a redefinition of identities (Di Palma 1990; Rustow 1970). Thus, by viewing states' and other actors' identities as ongoing practices, normative but also cognitive, we leave the door ajar for scenarios of territorial rebundling marked, roughly, by calculated convergences and understandings among states and other actors. In such scenarios, epistemologically more flexible than tug-of-war scenarios, practiced identities engage each other and are, perhaps, revisited.

In a more malleable exchange environment, some regional institutions (the European Commission, the Court of Justice) may exhibit capacity for epistemic innovation. They may frame the policy deliberations of member states in such a way that their decisions may end up propelling supranational integration. These institutions may act as facilitators (rather than hegemons replacing states). In the process, sovereign states may sovereignly authenticate what are actual abdications of sovereignty, and do it out of neither legal coercion nor defensive calculations. As Caporaso and Jupille put it in their chapter, states may preserve their Westphalian ultimate right to decide, but also significant is the possible factual erosion of their equally Westphalian inclination to exclude external authority. If so, something more may occur, in a further scenario, than a self-imposed but possibly contingent and legally reversible sacrifice of sovereignty. State practices and notions of sovereignty may so recast themselves that, even when legal parchments continue to separate national from regional institutions, the latter may no longer be the only engines of supranationalism.

State institutions may slow down and abort change, but they may also initiate it (Krasner 1984). It seems testily conservative to assume that state institutions will be driven by a range of interests necessarily frozen and insensitive to developments endogenous to domestic and extranational interactions. Interests are a function of identities. Venal or not, they are experientially acquired and inseparable from identities, of which they are but a component, and from which they draw meaning and justification. Let me suggest some ways in which state actors may contribute to reshaping their identities and hence their interests. In the European case, the long road toward the present regional setup was started in concert by national actors, mainly political leaders and government officials. Some dreamt ambitiously of a differently constituted, possibly federated political Europe. But the most influential among them stuck to pragmatic, policy-driven, incremental choices. None of them had and only few envisioned an ultimate template and a set of working blueprints. But all, including the firm practitioners of national identities and interests, accepted areas of interstate cooperation, in the conviction that, incrementally, cooperation would help comity replace the corrosive enmities of the past. To achieve cooperation, national actors initiated or advocated migrations of sovereign practices to larger, supranational, territorial sites. Migration of sovereignty was not repudiation of sovereignty; an "exit" was nearly unfathomable. Nor did institutional migration signal "entry into" either, as Maurizio Ferrera uses the term in his chapter. It could not involve entering supranational institutions that did not exist until the founders of Europe slowly began to craft and practice them. At first, migration was only a more permanent spatial repositioning of practices that left member states their "ultimate right to decide." It was product and manifestation of intergovernmentalism.

At the same time, a growing contingent of supranational agents, occupying and settling the new supranational space, came to flank domestic principals. Like national counterparts, supranational agents accumulate expertise and competence. More than nationals, they accumulate a degree of autonomy and self-propelling purpose that stems from the fact that they are not institutionally nested within domestic principals. They rather operate in, and become socialized by, networks of other supranational agents, so that "[c]onsiderable experience with acting together is accumulated, and a significant amount of mutual influence between [European] and domestic institutions and actors is taking place, with no clear-cut borderline between the 'national' and the 'European'" (March and Olsen 1998: 967). Agents come to exhibit elaborative capacities, proving themselves crucial promoters and facilitators of new practices and solutions – the more so if, as in the European case, the new regional order undergoes what Stone calls a process of constitutionalization beyond intergovernmentalism (Stone 1994). Constitutionalization and the intensification of transactions across formal domestic boundaries may in turn affect domestic practices, and hence identities. To borrow from Bruce Ackerman (1992), they may open a constitutional moment within EU's member states. Wendt puts it as follows:

... decades of cooperation may have transformed a positive interdependence of outcomes into a collective "European identity" in terms of which states increasingly define their "self"-interests. Even if egoistic reasons were its starting point, the process of cooperating tends to redefine those reasons by reconstituting identities and interests in terms of new intersubjective understandings and commitments (1992: 417).

Thus domestic and intergovernmental practices trespass into multilevel governance. But to return finally to the previous cautionary tale, the malleability of today's state institutions is not infinite. One difference between the territorial rebundling leading to the modern European state and the present rebundling is that the former was a far more contingent, less monitored and conditioned phenomenon than the latter. It permitted, especially in early phases of state building, greater malleability of practices and identities. The main reason for the historical difference is that there were then no hegemons with fixed and exclusive territorial identities to quell would-be rebundlers. Tugs of war were real and aplenty. But such plenitude did not reflect the hefty resistance of a well-entrenched hegemonic territorial order. It reflected the frailty of such order as well as the number and diversity of both holdovers and would-be rebundlers. For some rebundlers, such as the early merchant cities and federations, territory was largely a medium, a brute fact of convenience, often purchased by means of chartered autonomy from remnants of the feudal/patrimonial order. There was physical territory but, beyond a physically necessary minimum, no constructed territoriality and no paramount aspiration to it. Minimal physical frontiers, while enclosing and bundling politico-administrative instrumentalities and cultural practices, did not enclose merchant and trading practices (Bartolini 1999). Church and empire, on their part, embodied an a-spatial vision, whose scope and confines were more sacred and cosmopolitan than firmly territorial. Finally, feudal holdovers upheld personal prerogatives within suitably pliable borders without exclusive sovereignty.

Hence, centralizing monarchs faced a motley crew with unclear designs, diffuse resources, shifting alliances, and contingent strategies. Furthermore, innovating monarchs seeking *fortuna* enjoyed limited exposure to demonstration effects. Their opportunities to learn from the emerging practices of first movers lagged. Compared with early state building, postwar regional integration, being subject to a narrower field of forces, has been less laggard and relatively more linear. The fact that fewer players, in number and types, are engaged in today's territorial redefinitions favors more deliberate speed. A more recent contributing factor is the information revolution, which also actually adds a contemporary touch of malleability. The information revolution is a knowledge revolution, rewarding expertise, means-ends rationality, and finally goal-oriented rationality. And the knowledge is of the type that newly influential personnel bring to domestic and supranational institutions as they "commute" between institutions, and upon which interlocking epistemic communities come to form. Giangranco Poggi writes, "most of the forms of knowledge cultivated and applied by this new personnel have in common a strong orientation to the production of effects" (1990: 124). They differ from the legal-constitutional knowledge that marks historically the practices of the modern state because that knowledge is ultimately self-referential. It validates in light of what it issues; it validates public action in light of formalized precommitments. Here then is the contemporary touch of malleability: The present knowledge revolution actually makes exclusive state sovereignty more open to reconsideration than it has ever been during the state's adult career.

Still, like other sources previously mentioned, this novel source of malleability remains more focused and less contingent and open-ended. The
modern state stays a central player in processes of territorial redefinition,
narrowing the set of paths that processes are likely to travel. Aspects of collective political action, especially territorial, help explain why the longstanding
identities of sovereign states may continue to impinge on what states practice.
These aspects also help explain why new practices, if any, are likely to track
themselves on paths that, even when new, will still be traveled by and together with states. Unlike economics, politics, official institutional politics in
particular, is based on authority more than neutral exchange (Pierson 2000).
While economic practices admit the option of exiting organizations that do
not deliver, politics, where institutions are more about prescribed practices
and precommitments than about transaction costs, admits no free exit. This
authorizes resistance to the subverting power of the information revolution,
constrains institutional refounding, and thus feeds the inefficiencies of history. So, the increasing returns of prescribed politics, of politics-as-usual,
are especially hard to falsify. The grip of prescribed practices may help explain why territorial sovereignty carries a congealed, somehow mythical and
difficult to exorcise, metaphoric significance. Rooted in the collective imagi-
nation, metaphor is reified. Implicitly and without testing, it stands in for an
explicit model that may no longer hold (Landau 1979: 10–12). In Alexander
Murphy's words, "[T]he inertia of the sovereign territorial ideal [becomes]
great enough to prevent an enduring alternative from taking root" (1996:
83). And so it is that analysts may continue to treat derogations from exclusive and exclusionary sovereignty – in international commerce and contracts
(Stone Sweet in this book), in the longstanding decoupling of citizenship
and the state, and more recently in human rights – as nothing but single
exceptions.[5]

Caporaso and Jupille alert us importantly that, even in the "most difficult
case" of the United Kingdom, a country marked by an insular notion of its
distinctive sovereignty, the state's ultimate right to decide is nonetheless recently accompanied by an increasing de facto receptivity to external authority. Still, assisted by its reified metaphorical underpinning, state sovereignty
has real consequences. The British Parliament claims its ultimate right to

---

[5] Stone Sweet's chapter on the renaissance of the law merchant takes issue with treating derogations as special exceptions. He shows that subjecting international commerce to exclusive domestic legislation was always difficult. Exceptional, in his analysis, is the period during which
domestic regulation was more successful – from the late nineteenth century through the first
part of the twentieth. Interestingly, international commerce falls precisely in that domain of
economic exchange that Paul Pierson (2000) indicates as alien to the logic of prescribed state
practices and precommitments. This suggests that of the four areas Bartolini depicts as sub-
jected by state building to boundary stabilization and exit closure, the economic was the most
reluctant. Despite the role the modern state and national bourgeoisies played in constructing
economic boundaries, these boundaries proved inherently difficult to maintain and regulate.

decide even as it mollifies it in reality and sheds insularity. Sergio Fabbrini's chapter offers an account of how, until after World War II, the American state remained, exceptionally, much less sensitive than its European counterparts to the stark exit-voice logic of domestic centralization. But the American state is no less a state for that, for there is a "vigilante" side to its exceptionalism. It resides in the proud exceptionalism of its domestic and international identity, an identity as insular and sturdy as the British, and as old in its own terms: America as a creed, as the cradle of republicanism, as a beacon for humankind. Add the emergence of America as a contemporary hegemon. And so, as the European states soften their exclusive sovereignty America remains today more than ever committed to its sovereign distinctiveness. For these reasons, and for others discussed by Fabbrini, it is unlikely that, in reconfiguring its regional place, the United States will travel much past partial, soft, unstable, horizontal, and lopsided regional regimes, such as NAFTA.[6]

To be sure, the capacity of regional regimes to make a difference for their partners, and so to have "persuasive" domestic repercussions, varies with their strength. This is the brunt of Marks and Ian Down's chapter, contrasting the respective impact of NAFTA and the EU on labor movements in the United States and Europe. The transgressive inclination of labor to extend influential voice to the regional level and reconfigure its strategies accordingly is also a function of the extent to which regional regimes build a new game in town thus making defection costly. Or, to use Bartolini's language, transgression depends on the extent to which structuring of voice occurs at the regional level. In this regard, NAFTA, as conceived by the United States, is presently a much weaker persuader, much less capable than the European Union of transferring old and new collective actors to the regional arena.

But even a strong regional regime is not a regime that thereby marginalizes states. The territorial repositioning of voices from member states to

---

[6] While the United States nowadays exhibits a weak disposition to convergence toward an inclusive regional regime, it is however responding to new regional and global migrations with *domestic* policies more open and adaptable than those of European states. But is the contrast between America's regional and domestic behavior surprising? I submit that it restates the culturally rooted distinctiveness of the American state. In his chapter, Bruce Cain shows how the difference between American and European immigration policies rests crucially on differences in their respective institutional setups. The American setup makes it harder for outlier states, with no veto power, to condition federal immigration policies. In addition, American states and their policies are open to pressures and preferences by median voters. But the setup, though crucial, is not sufficient. What finally counts is that American public opinion is presently favorable to regulated migration. And more important, Cain argues, is the role of courts, for it touches upon lasting national consensus. By variously appealing to the fourteenth Amendment and fundamental rights doctrine, the courts have curbed restrictive immigration policies. We could say, to tinker with Ruggie's quote, that American constitutional consensus is the reason that causal factors such as institutional setups produce immigration policies that are so and not otherwise.

the EU is not zero-sum. It admits concurrent or alternative levels of voice, both national and transnational. In addition, as Monti implies in the earlier quote, the performance of member states may gain in those areas upon which the treaties, the Council, or the ECJ have imposed standards and constraints. Further, even as it builds its institutions, a regional regime may continue to rely on the authenticity conferred by member states as these share jurisdictions with and within the regime. As a work in progress marked by changing practices of territoriality, the EU is not dissimilar from American federalism. While not aimed at federalism, the EU draws legitimacy, at least as much as America, from its founding states, and from later members. The long, contentious, at times turbulent, story of American federalism is itself a permanent work in progress. It has been marked by a twentieth-century accumulation of authority around federal institutions, but accumulation has not altered, indeed it has called for recurring reaffirmations of, the covenantal identity of the North American community.

Sic Europa? In a European (or world) order dominated by sovereign states, there is little evidence that other collective actors are working toward an inclusive European (let alone world) order that, on all collective matters, would discount states and interstate systems. True, in matters of politics, as the inefficiencies of history attest, broader unanticipated consequences, themselves path-channeling results of narrower short-term choices, should never be dismissed; their subjective decisiveness rests exactly on their contingent quality. But they would have to come to terms with the more lumbering dependencies long constructed by the "invention" of sovereignty and territoriality. The logic of territoriality, while significantly repositioned, is not easily discarded. And as the logic stays, so do states, at times diminished but also reinvented by sharing in regional regimes.

Thus, to unbundle territoriality means to recompose and rebundle it. It means to recognize the presence, in the political space below and beyond the state, of a variety of territorially relevant collective actors: some private, some public and legal (or indeed illegal), some constitutionalized. A number of these actors entertain trespassing relations within their larger operative space (the space of the national state and/or the space of the system of states). The relations are not sorted out neatly along the conventional territorial divide between domestic hierarchy and supranational anarchy/intergovernmentalism, as states no longer predictably operate as exclusive authoritative gatekeepers of the divide. In some ways, the multiplicity of actors subtracts from the centrality of the national state. In other ways, it involves a repositioning of the state and the emergence of new state tasks beyond that, part ideal and part factual, of gatekeeper between domestic hierarchy and international horizontalism. Nor can we ignore that states may opt for a conscious if not exclusive role in molding a multilayered territorial reality.

The gist of this section has been that new ideas challenging practiced identities may become constitutive. But existing practices are not malleable at will. Such is the case of European integration. Processes of regionalization signal a reconstitution of what Westphalian states behold and practice, individually, collectively, and vis-à-vis other territorial actors. But the idea and presence of the state are left in place. Malleability is confined. Also, the reconstitution of practiced identities is generally neither linear nor comprehensive and cumulative. Most often, ideas are not born whole but take shape in an interstitial rapport with evolving practices. This makes the outcomes of malleability uncertain. One example will serve to wrap up this section, as well as to reconnect practiced identities with the inefficiencies of history and with the theme of the next section.

I previously described an instance of inefficiency: The knowledge revolution's potential for subverting notions of territorial sovereignty may be curbed by the fact that politics, territorial politics in particular, is about authoritative practices and precommitments. The example suggests that, in the arena of sovereign institutions, practiced identities are one sufficient ingredient in the inefficiencies of history. They may *ordinarily* deflect, slow down, and arrest knowledge-inspired change. The same institutions may also, at critical junctures, take the lead: They may accelerate change by sovereignly appropriating knowledge-inspired change and subverting notions of sovereignty. I will return to this at the close of the next section. To borrow from Stephen Krasner (1984), we may speak here of an instance of revolution from above altering domestic practices and identities. Revolutions from above are not typical occurrences, but they typically occur in response to international or global challenges: military or economic challenges from other international actors; challenges from the emergence of new forms of supranational governance; or challenges from knowledge and scientific advances that do not allow free riding. Responses, perhaps after some institutional resistance, may open a period of domestic policy and institutional innovation. My point, at any rate, is that both institutional resistance and innovation throw off course the presumed linearity of history. Therefore, both are, in the language of my opening section, particular instances of history's inefficiencies, reflecting the weight, pull or push, of sovereign institutions.

DEMOCRACY BEYOND THE STATE

Is democracy conceivable only within the modern state? The contributors to this book do not address the topic directly. Some, however, touch on it indirectly, in sufficiently intriguing ways for me to pursue the matter. The issue is not of immediate relevance for the contemporary United States and its regional neighbors, but it is for Europe and the European Union. At the same time, the historical exceptionalism of U.S. democratic institutions offers a useful background against which to appraise democracy in the context of European integration. On this point, I have in mind the comparative chapters by Alberta Sbragia, Cain, and Fabbrini, to which I return at the end of this chapter.

There is a reductive way of reasoning on democracy beyond the state. It focuses on Europe and goes as follows: Only democracies qualify for membership in the European Union. At the same time, all members are called to sacrifice, whether de jure or de facto, parts of their sovereignty. Hence their democratic sovereignty is undermined. Since the Union is itself not a democracy, the trade-off amounts to a democratic deficit. In its naked form, the assertion is, for the sake of the argument, unassailable. But it is not profoundly revealing – not unless we show additionally that democracy is possible only within a state, and that Europe is not a state, so far at least.

I grant, though the point is debatable, that European integration produces sacrifices of domestic sovereignty. But I take issue with the assertion that the EU suffers from a democratic deficit. The assertion is usually justified by pointing out that the European Parliament is not sovereign, the Commission is not clearly accountable to Parliament, and the Council of Ministers is not an elected senate but an intergovernmental body. But the justification implies that the EU can be a democracy only if it takes the institutional trappings of yet another, larger, perhaps federal, state – *e pluribus* yet *unum*. As John Coultrap (1999) points out, this justification negates democracy outside the state, since a community with the institutional trappings just invoked is not simply a democracy, it is a democratic (in fact, parliamentary) state. I grant that Europe may never be a state. I later assert that it should never be one. All the same, is democracy conceivable outside the modern state, and if so, under what conditions, in what contexts?

The EU and domestic democracy do have something in common that places the EU beyond merely a-democratic intergovernmentalism. Both are, within their specific institutional setup, manifestations of liberal constitutionalism. They are, first, instances of constitutional regimes, that is, regimes regulated by "a body of metanorms, rules that specify how legal norms are to be produced, applied, and interpreted" (Stone 1994: 444). In addition, a democratic state is a later and demanding development of domestic constitutionalism; it is an instance of liberal constitutionalism. I will explicate later what I mean by *liberal*. Similarly, the EU is today a demanding gradual development of an international constitutional regime. It is in fact another instance of liberal constitutionalism resulting from a sort of spillover from domestic liberalism. Modern Western democracy developed, contentiously, within the formative institutional context of the state. Structures of authority impinging on the private denizens of the state came first, structures of public accountability and participation came later. Since the *demos* and the state came to coincide, the solution to the problem of how to practice democracy in a large territory with a large population (representation, elections, and accountability) was readily available, and at once confined, within already existing state and territorial institutions. For a long stretch, questions as to who governs, who has a voice, and how voice gets structured continued to posit themselves almost exclusively within the parameters of the state.

The international arena was construed entirely differently. It was intended as an arena of relations almost exclusively and legitimately occupied by states – fixed isomorphic and select collectivities speaking each with one voice, and mutually recognizing their indivisible domestic authority as well as their legally equal international standing. By way of treaties, states created ad hoc international rules and institutions. But veritable international *constitutional* regimes were largely unimaginable, difficult to theorize, and difficult to construe. Their metanorms enjoyed little if any enduring autonomy with respect to the sovereign states that adopted them. Metanorms and the institutions they regulated were epiphenomena.

What, then, made international constitutional regimes imaginable, indeed possible? Among the factors, one is significant, and a key to why and how we can conceive of democracy in the international arena: the changed composition of the international institutional environment. The international environment following World War II, especially after the fall of communism, presents three in part objective and in part constructed features. When it comes to states, the environment is progressively hegemonized by advanced democracies. But, second, their international hegemony is of a special sort. Despite hegemony, yet not ironically, each democracy no longer speaks with a single, monotonic, and fixed commanding voice. The more the advanced democracies operate within materially and normatively resourceful civil societies and economies, the more each speaks, domestically *and* internationally, with many voices. The international environment of liberal democracies hosts a number of non-state actors who, nurtured within openly competitive domestic venues, speak with voices that straddle and transcend those venues. To speak autonomously, they feel more comfortable if the status of their new venues is constitutionalized. In turn, if nothing else, it may not be cost-effective for states operating in an international liberal regime to resist the constitutionalization of newcomers. Third, after the fall of communism, multilateral supranational relations and cooperation are revived by the fact that Western policies and strategies are less confined within the dominant logic of block and security politics. They are more forcefully defined by iterative economic interdependence giving status, significantly constitutional status, to cooperative relations. Stone writes: "liberal regimes are more likely to produce not only constraining rules but 'enabling rules,' rules that 'set actors free to pursue their own goals'" (1994: 465). Multilateral relations and cooperation are marked by an incipiently shared understanding of what hegemons, qua hegemons, may or may not appropriately practice in the international arena.[7] Coarsely put, and as a starter, hegemons may no longer get away with their preeminent power. Hegemony may in fact prescribe moral responsibilities with a constitutive self-enforcing quality.

Still, is international constitutionalism, as practiced by liberal democracies, different from domestic constitutionalism? Are differences unbridgeable? True, the Euro-polity will always lack the symmetry, hierarchy, and order we classically attribute to the ideal-typical European nation-state. Other social forces, claiming a measure of constitutional recognition, enter the Euro-polity with referents and anchorings that, though often territorial, are at once local, national, and variously regional/supranational. Philippe Schmitter submits that this state of affairs makes the expanding Euro-polity a governing entity where the boundary of authority, "... the boundary between insiders and outsiders [,] remains uncertain and/or follows no uniform criterion" (2000: 15).

But the point I want to make is that all of this has in turn repercussions on individual states and their own internal order. If the Euro-polity lacks the symmetry, hierarchy, and order of the ideal-typical state, the European states on the ground are themselves losing some of those ideal features. They partially lose that center–periphery, hierarchical, public-private bias that was responsible, as Bartolini shows, for domestically structuring/ constitutionalizing voice and representation. These trends on the ground are substantial enough to suggest a restructuring of domestic constitutionalism, such that differentiation between domestic and supranational constitutionalism is now less tenable. Referring to a converging national and global turbulence in international affairs, Haas submits that, while by no means fading away, "[t]he nation-state, under conditions of turbulence, ceases being humankind's terminal community. People learn to play different roles in different contexts, profess different loyalties and form different attachments for different purposes" (2000: 450). Thus domestic and regional politics converge toward a civic and politico-institutional reality in flux, marked by pluralism of voices and entries, contingent jurisdictions, constitutional experimentation accented by abrading spaces and temporalities (Orren and Skowronek 1995).

What then of constitutionalism in an experimenting environment? Should the turbulence of that environment be a matter of concern for Europe? My answer is that constitutionalization typically takes shape in an experimenting, often turbulent, environment. The constitutionalism proper of the modern state was not delivered whole, Athena-like, from Zeus's forehead. In addition, the environment may well stay experimental, and constitutionalism

---

[7] Much neorealist perspective on these matters is the opposite of the one I am embracing: The cold war and bilateralism forced European cooperation in the name of international alignments, and the end of communism removes the incentives and may even unravel Europe (Mearsheimer 1990).

may prove a work in progress. I made the point for the United States. In the United States, the legal-constitutional boundaries between member states and the federal government remain in practice a matter of negotiation and jurisprudence driven by shifting interests and interpretations.

A similarly experimental environment, if still in infancy, seems to mark European states, as the increasing importance of national constitutional courts suggests. Modern constitutionalism first manifested itself as the firm specifier of the self-referential modern state. But in the greater scheme of things, the modern state, despite endurance, is a contingent phenomenon. This indicates that the rationale of constitutionalism, its foundations, go deeper than, and can survive, its previous host. Hence we benefit by conceptually unhooking constitutionalism from the contingency of the state. Nicola Matteucci, speaking of constitutionalism in its most advanced incarnation within the state, reminds us:

[Constitutionalism] is the technique of freedom... by means of which citizens are guaranteed the exercise of individual rights and, at the same time, the state is prevented from violating them. If the techniques vary..., the ideal of individual freedom is the ultimate goal in view of which those techniques are preordained or organized (1983: 271, my translation).

Simply put, Matteucci's constitutionalism is the technique of liberalism. And as his definition pithily highlights, liberalism is not only freedoms *from* (freedom from state interference). By empowering society, freedoms *from* nurture freedoms *to* (Holmes 1995). Hence the divide, empirical and conceptual, often drawn between liberalism and democracy is overstated. Democracy is active liberalism. And liberalism is driven to action by its inherent universalism as well as by a cognitive and prescriptive perspective on collective problem solving that is experimental, pragmatically open, and entrusted to recurrent testing. The perspective is universally constitutive – that is, foundational – of active liberalism, whether or not liberalism is practiced within the container "state." To recognize that the state is a contingent container is equivalent to recognizing that there is nothing contractarian, except metaphorically, let alone primary, primordial, and unshakable, about membership in the liberal state. Haas (1997: ch. 1) ties liberalism to the scientific revolution and the Enlightenment. Richard Rorty (1991: 175–202) casts it in a larger perspective akin to John Dewey's philosophical pragmatism. And Max Weber evokes liberalism's endurance when theorizing the superiority of formal (processual) over substantive rationality. The state is a central referent in their analyses of liberalism and its progress, but is not foundational: Their brands of liberalism do not necessitate the state. Foundational to their analyses is liberalism as an open problem solver.

As problem solving becomes less confined within the state, opportunities for liberal practices bearing on active freedoms as well as on access to and creation of shared renewable knowledge should not diminish but increase.

Freedom from state confinement signals the opportunity. Previously, I quoted Haas to the effect that the nation-state might not be humankind's terminal community. Haas (1997: 18–19) offers one account for his assertion. For a long time, the divide between anarchic international life and life in the rationalized sovereign state marked a divide between collective bads (international) and collective goods (national), the former a tragic side-cost of the latter. But the superiority of the state, even liberal, as problem solver ebbs under the pressure of external bads, whether global or spun by other states. Superiority ebbs, first, because external bads visibly impinge on our rational domestic life; second, because, as liberal agents, we are cognitively endowed to recognize the plight; third, because domestic responses to external bads prove inadequate; finally, because the affected *demos* who can cognitively address bads is no longer factually and normatively confined to any single country. One professional problem we now face as social scientists is that, just as we are not at ease with a postbipolar world and cannot imagine what replaces it, so also we are not comfortable with instantiating the practices of active liberalism outside the state. The habitual hierarchy, order, coordination, and predictability of the state (the European state especially) made players and rules of liberalism fairly explicit. We may broadly imagine liberalism beyond the state, but we cannot (I cannot) pin down its exact shape and practices. Should we be embarrassed or concerned?

I take comfort in a point I repeatedly made: As the story of early state formation shows, rules and institutions are accumulated practices. They take shape not in advance of but in concomitance with or response to concrete problem solving and targeted policy making. We should feel at ease, therefore, with the experimental nature of constitutionalism, within and without borders. And we may take comfort in an already-quoted statement that, at any rate, the constitutive norms of a liberal world where the state is no longer the terminal community:

> ...cannot arise merely in the mind of the philosopher who then observes how real-life actors gradually come to agree with him. New constitutive norms...may evolve piecemeal and incrementally from regulatory rules deliberately changed by the actors who are not even conscious of creating new orders (Haas 2000: 454).

Simply put, social scientists are not philosopher kings but rather roosters announcing, yet not thereby conjuring, the sun. This is not a mean nor unbecoming charge nonetheless.[8]

Besides, there is something about liberal practices beyond and across states that as social scientists we can already announce, or possibly only anticipate, but by anticipating also help advocate. First, we can anticipate something

---

[8] I concede that the matter is rather more complex. One should not rule out the role of social scientists, or particular categories thereof, and of socioscientific institutions in epistemic communities.

about the endowments and resources of liberal players. Second, since territoriality does not vanish, we may say something about the territorial distribution of interests and its propriety in such a new liberal order.

When active liberalism reaches beyond the state, one concern is the fate of those equal opportunities for participation of which the democratic state made itself the domestic guarantor. One strong ingredient of the democratic deficit thesis, applied to the Euro-polity but also to other supranational regimes, is that the added complexity of these new arenas is doubly damaging. It increases the distance and secrecy of the new deliberative centers, and also requires civic skills and resources to close the gap that are beyond the reach of most citizens. Political inequality increases and active liberalism becomes a reserve for the members of an exclusive club. I answer as follows: The democratic deficit is not a deficit of political rights; it is a deficit of extrapolitical resources, nonetheless essential for robust and informed participation. The same extrapolitical deficit marks, however, the domestic politics of contemporary advanced democracies. So, where is the difference? Is active liberalism across borders distinctively and inherently elitist? Secondly, *laudatores temporis acti* may miss the times when European mass parties, organized labor, corporate associations, nationalized services, and other structures of central coordination, frequently encouraged by the state, extended the opportunities for equal participation. But is there no substitute? I offer two answers.

First, one historical case suggests alternatives. On these matters, the United States of America always marched to its own tune. True, America was relatively short on the opportunities for organized participation typical of Europe. But arguing that this undermined American opportunities for participation and political equality would be a vast simplification (Di Palma 1969). America attended to substitutes – and the substitutes give us reason to pause before embracing the contemporary concern that active liberalism is turning elitist. Already by the 1830s, white American males, having largely achieved suffrage, were confronted with an apparently daunting task. "In Europe," writes Samuel Huntington, "the broadening of participation meant the extension of the suffrage for one institution [a national parliament] to all classes of society while in America it meant the extension of the suffrage . . . to all (or almost all) institutions of government" (1968: 128). But Huntington presents the American situation as less a daunting task than an opportunity to mobilize. This opportunity was seized upon thanks in part to the existing practices of horizontal associationism, but also thanks to its citizens learning fitting skills and practices stimulated precisely by the functionally and territorially dispersed, multiple-entry, competitive nature of America's plural political institutions.

In his chapter, Cain refers in the same vein to the American practice of shopping for political venues, whereby interested parties push policy issues to forums where they have better chances to succeed. He adds two important considerations. First, venue shopping driven by policy preferences may over time enact or consolidate institutional change of relevance for the way political participation gets effectively spread and organized. In American history, Cain points out, the opening of a plurality of institutional access and veto points progressively favored more direct egalitarian forms of representation. In sum, the experience has been anything but elitist. Second, the Euro-polity offers similar opportunities for venue shopping to overcome institutional obstacles, including the transfer of power from states to the larger polity. For instance, parties interested in a hypothetical future in liberalizing "extracommunitarian" immigration may try to circumvent immigration constraints currently exercised by single states by moving the matter to the Union.

In sum, Cain's study suggests that the American history of multilayered government, dispersed access and veto points, and accordingly diffused civic resources for influence and deliberation may somehow adumbrate ways for voice to structure itself in the Euro-polity, or other polities not fitting the tight Westphalian mold. My second answer to whether the claimed distance and complexity of the Euro-polity makes participation more difficult and less effective is to suggest that complexity may feed learning responses. American interests and associations responded to multilayered government by federally consolidating a dispersed organization of voice and access (Skocpol 1999). Will European people and interests caught in an environment of complexity respond instead with frozen and obsolete repertoires and show themselves incapable of retooling? For one thing, we should not rule out that environmental complexity may itself at least partially reflect a growth in individual skills, largely cognitive skills of the liberal-experimental type. Such skills lead in turn to the invention of more advanced problem-solving strategies and institutions.[9] This scenario may start with a selected coterie of insiders, engendering steeper inequalities and resentment. But, on the other side, I am struck that many who denounce distance, complexity, and the ensuing participatory deficit have mobilized resentment in creative ways that reveal a steep learning curve and belie their accusations (Meyer and Tarrow 1998). This raises a largely rhetorical question: What skills does complexity require that active experimental liberalism cannot by its nature provide? Ansell's conclusions lend a hand. His reading of regional development in Europe as potentially a networked polity speaks of complexity, but complexity with a learning experimental dimension. According to Ansell, the networked polity entails a cognitive shift: from bureaucratic rationality intent on marking

---

[9] James N. Rosenau and W. Michael Fagen (1997) suggest as a testable hypothesis that if, as they attempt to document, the level of autonomous skills has increased, then the new sensitivities of informed publics may become instrumental in fostering a pluralistic global order. As I see it, the broader implication of the hypothesis is that what begins as a learning and knowledge revolution may, by fostering a sense of personal autonomy and consciousness, contribute in turn to spreading values with an affinity for pragmatic liberalism.

"turf" to more inclusive problem-solving styles intent on "integrative solutions." To put a spin on Ansell, the polity entails a shift from a politics
of "turfing" to a politics of "surfing," where knowledge and initiative are
decentralized and dispersed.

CONCLUSIONS

The final issue to address regards the place, actual and ideal, of territorial voices and interests in an actively liberal Euro-polity. This book does
not speak univocally on their actual place, since much depends, as shown
in Stone Sweet's chapter, on specific policy domains. However, one thrust
of the book is that functional interests are not destined to break free of
territorial containers. Rather, other territorial containers repositioning and
clustering interests and voices flank the container "state." In their respective chapters, Cain and Fabbrini highlight this development by illustrating
contrasting trends in Europe and the United States. If at all, given its past,
it is the United States that has softened the role of locality and territory.
American history, say Cain and Fabbrini, shows a tendency to shed many
original forms of indirect and territorial representation in favor of more
direct, majoritarian, and egalitarian ones. European integration and community institutions, on the other hand, have introduced a degree of indirect
and territorially dispersed representation unprecedented in single European
states.

The question is whether these European features are likely to endure. One
aspect of the American experience, as Sbragia presents it in her chapter, suggests possible endurance. America exhibits economic specialization of many
of its regions, such that homogeneous economic interests cluster territorially, functional and territorial policies tend to overlap, and federal economic
policies have often regionally redistributive consequences. Combined with
the American system of checks and balances and constituency politics, this
confers upon much regulatory policy a subnational territorial dimension.
Sbragia observes similar or stronger nonmajoritarian attention to territory
in the way the European Union and its Council of Ministers package environmental policies. The interesting possibility, also articulated in Bartolini's
chapter, is that further economic integration of Europe may favor, as in the
United States, regional economic specialization. In turn, specialization may
favor further territorial clustering of interest representation and regulatory
politics. It may also help stabilize, depending on its timing, the quasifederal
nonmajoritarian features of the Union, those features that (as suggested in
Bartolini's chapter) already assist the restructuring of territoriality.

But Sbragia and Cain go one step further. They provide material for reflection on what the role of territorial and by extension nonmajoritarian voices
should be in the Euro-polity – or any liberal polity other than a top-down
parliamentary democracy. Sbragia shows how the nature of the European

Union as a regime in which territorial considerations remain central does not prevent but in fact assists a more effective pursuit of change in environmental policies. Cain raises issues as to whether democratic deficits – embodied, for instance, in the more equal decisional weight assigned to unequally populated EU states – are undesirable. Using as example the presently restrictive immigration policies of member states, he argues that democratic deficit is not thereby democratic deficiency. Domestically restrictive policies adopted by national agencies may happen to coincide with the majority preferences of Europeans at large, even though those agencies obviously do not represent the European *demos*. Second, and more to the point in the perspective on active liberalism *sans frontières*, Cain also points out that the rule of unmediated majority, one that would turn the Euro-polity into a superstate run as a parliamentary democracy, is not necessarily the ultimate goal. This is at least the case unless we are ready to overlook that in the Euro-polity, and so also in similarly liberal regimes of the future, intense minority interests, often territorially nested, may justly call for special attention. Majoritarian deficit, in matters that may touch on rights, is not thereby democratic deficiency, as democracy is not always counting heads. Intensity of preference raises the issue of the limits of the "one person, one vote" principle. Otherwise, prudence inspired by liberal commitment suggests recognizing that if the democratic state is not humankind's terminal community, greater attention must then be paid to the fact that individuals carry different collective attachments, some with territorial dimensions. As Jack Citrin and John Sides (2003) show, Europeans do not rank and prioritize these attachments – not across the board, not permanently, and not consistently. Individuals engage in different roles of collective relevance, embrace different identities, and properly express contextually different selves. Liberalism, in turn, is about recognizing, in the interest of pragmatic openness, this diversity (without essentializing it), so that no single identity or loyalty asserts itself as the conduit to problem solving. Liberalism is also about recognizing that specific loyalties and identities may contingently acquire salience and intensity. Thus, first, arguing that the Euro-polity needs a singular prioritizing collective identity runs afoul of empirical justification. Second, such an argument would be problematic in a profound sense. For one thing, a European identity could not and should not be forged by legislative/institutional fiat. In such constructions as the Euro-polity, such a move would impose a majoritarian strain on a reality with little if any evidence of such strain. For another, whatever the means used to build the strain – legal or cultural and socializing – the result would be a sort of liberal exclusionism, a closing of Europe that is antithetical, especially in the present rebundling context, to liberalism's pragmatic openness (Weiler 1996: 522–5).

A Euro-polity turned into a Euro-state is not a liberal answer. Nor, for that matter, is a global democracy the answer.

Reference List

Ackerman, Bruce A. 1992. *The Future of Liberal Revolution.* New Haven, CT: Yale University Press.

———. 1991. *We the People: Foundations.* Cambridge, MA: Harvard University Press.

Ackerman, Bruce A. and William T. Hassler. 1981. *Clean Coal/Dirty Air: Or How the Clean Air Act Became a Multibillion Dollar Bail-Out for High-Sulfur Coal Producers and What Should Be Done about It.* New Haven, CT: Yale University Press.

Agnew, John. 1994. "The Territorial Trap: The Geographical Assumptions of International Relations Theory." *Review of International Political Economy* 1, 1: 53–80.

Alber, J. 1982. *Von Armenhaus zum Wohlfahrtsstaat.* Frankfurt: Campus.

Alestalo, M. and S. Kuhnle. 2000. "Introduction: Growth, Adjustments and Survival of the European Welfare State," in M. Alestalo and S. Kuhnle (eds.). *Survival of the Welfare State.* London: Routledge, pp. 3–18.

Alt, James and Michael Gilligan. 1994. "Survey Article: The Political Economy of Trading States: Factor Specificity, Collective Action Problems and Domestic Political Institutions." *Journal of Political Philosophy* 2, 2: 165–92.

Alter, Karen J. 2001. *Establishing the Supremacy of European Law: The Making of an International Rule of Law in Europe.* Oxford, UK: Oxford University Press.

Anderson, James. 1996. "The Shifting Stage of Politics: New Medieval and Postmodern Territorialities." *Environment and Planning D: Society and Space* 14, 2: 133–53.

Anderson, Jeffrey (ed.). 1999. *Regional Integration and Democracy: Expanding on the European Experience.* Lanham, MD: Rowman and Littlefield.

———. 1996. "Germany and the Structural Funds: Unification Leads to Bifurcation," in Liesbet Hooghe (ed.). *Cohesion Policy and European Integration: Building Multi-Level Governance.* Oxford, UK: Oxford University Press, pp. 163–94.

Anderson, Perry. 1974. *Lineages of the Absolutist State.* London: New Left Books.

Ansell, Christopher. 2001. *Schism and Solidarity in Social Movements: The Politics of Labor in the French Third Republic.* Cambridge, UK: Cambridge University Press.

———. 2000. "The Networked Polity: Regional Development in Western Europe." *Governance* 13, 3: 303–33.

Ansell, Christopher and Giuseppe Di Palma. 1998. "Beyond Center–Periphery or the Unbundling of Territoriality: Institutions and Policies in and between Western

Democracies." Paper presented at the conference on Beyond Center–Periphery or the Unbundling of Territoriality, Berkeley, CA.

Ansell, Christopher K., Craig A. Parsons, and Keith A. Darden. 1997. "Dual Networks in European Regional Policy." *Journal of Common Market Studies* 35: 347–76.

Archdeacon, Thomas J. "Reflections on Immigration in Light of US Immigration History." *International Migration Review* 26, 2: 525.

Association Internationale de la Mutualité (AIM). 2000. *Implications of Recent Jurisprudence on the Co-ordination of Health Care Protection Systems.* Brussels: AIM.

Axelrod, Robert. 1986. "An Evolutionary Approach to Norms." *American Political Science Review* 80: 1095–1111.

Bailey, Christopher J. 1998. *Congress and Air Pollution: Environmental Politics in the US.* Manchester, UK: Manchester University Press.

Baldwin, Peter. 1990. *The Politics of Social Solidarity: Class Bases of the European Welfare States 1875–1975.* Cambridge, UK: Cambridge University Press.

Balme, Richard and Laurence Bonnet. 1995. "From Regional to Sectoral Policies: The Contractual Relations between the State and the Regions in France," in John Loughlin and Sonia Mazey (eds.). *The End of the French Unitary State? Ten Years of Regionalization in France (1982–1992).* London: Cass, pp. 51–71.

Banting, K. 1995. *The Welfare State as Statecraft: Territorial Politics and Canadian Social Policy,* in S. Leibfried and P. Pierson (eds.). *European Social Policy between Fragmentation and Integration.* Washington, DC: Brookings Institution, pp. 269–300.

Bartelson, Jens. 1993. *A Genealogy of Sovereignty.* Stockholm: University of Stockholm.

Bartolini, Stefano. 2000a. *Old and New Peripheries in the European Process of Territorial Expansion.* Madrid: Juan March Institute, Working Paper 2000/53.

———. 2000b. *The Political Mobilization of the European Left, 1860–1980.* New York and Cambridge, UK: Cambridge University Press.

———. 1999. "Political Representation in Loosely Bounded Territories: Between Europe and the Nation-State." Paper prepared for the conference Multi-Level Party Systems: Europeanisation and the Reshaping of National Political Representation. Florence, Italy.

———. 1998d. *Exit Options, Boundary Building and Political Structuring.* Florence: European University Institute Working Paper 1.

———. 1998b. "Old and New Peripheries in the Processes of Territorial Retrenchment/Expansion: Europe from State Formation to Regional Integration." Paper presented at the conference Beyond Center–Periphery or the Unbundling of Territoriality. Berkeley, CA.

Beard Charles (ed.). 1964. *The Enduring Federalist,* 2nd ed. New York: Ungar.

Beer, S. H. 1993. *To Make a Nation: The Redescovery of American Federalism.* Cambridge, MA: Harvard University Press.

Bennett, Graham. 1992. *Dilemmas: Coping with Environmental Problems.* London: Earthscan.

Bensel, R. F. 1987. *Sectionalism and American Political Development: 1880–1980,* Madison, WI: University of Wisconsin Press.

Benson, Bruce L. 1992. "Customary Law as a Social Contract: International Commercial Law." *Constitutional Political Economy* 3: 1–27.

Berezin, Mabel. "Territory Emotion and Identity: Spatial Re-Calibration in a New Europe," in Mabel Berezin and Martin Schain (eds.). *Re-Mapping Europe: Territory, Membership and Identity in a Supranational Age*. Baltimore, MD: Johns Hopkins University Press. In press.

Berger, Klaus Peter. 1999. *The Creeping Codification of the Lex Mercatoria*. The Hague: Kluwer.

Berman, Harold J. and Felix J. Dasser. 1998. "The 'New' Law Merchant and the 'Old': Sources, Content, and Legitimacy," in Thomas E. Carbonneau (ed.). *Lex Mercatoria and Arbitration: A Discussion of the New Law Merchant*. Yonkers, NY: Juris, pp. 53–70.

Beyers, Jan. 2002. "Gaining and Seeking Access: The European Adaptation of Domestic Interest Associations." *European Journal of Political Research*, 41, 5: 585–612.

Biersteker, Thomas J. and Cynthia Weber (eds.). 1996. *State Sovereignty as Social Construct*. Cambridge, UK: Cambridge University Press.

Blaurock, Uwe. 1998. "The Law of Transnational Commerce," in *The Unification of International Commerical Law*. Baden-Baden: Nomos.

Blessing, Marc. 1997. "Choice of Substantive Law in International Arbitration." *Journal of International Arbitration* 14: 39–65.

Blondel, Jean, Richard Sinnott, and Palle Svensson. 1998. *People and Parliament in the European Union: Participation, Democracy, and Legitimacy*. Oxford, UK: Clarendon Press.

Boehmer-Christiansen, Sonja and Jim Skea. 1991. *Acid Politics: Environmental and Energy Policies in Britain and Germany*. London: Belhaven.

Boehmer-Christiansen, Sonia and Helmut Weidner. 1992. *Catalyst versus Lean Burn. A Comparative Analysis of Environmental Policy in the Federal Republic of Germany and Great Britain with Reference to Exhaust Emission Policy for Passenger Cars 1970–1990*. Berlin: Wissenschaftszentrum Berlin fur Sozialforschung, FS II 92-304.

Bogaards, Matthijs. 2002. "Consociational Interpretations of the EU: A Critical Appraisal." *European Union Politics* 3, 3: 357–81.

Bonell, Michael J. 1998. "UNIDROIT Principles and the Lex Mercatoria," in Thomas E. Carbonneau (ed.). *Lex Mercatoria and Arbitration: A Discussion of the New Law Merchant*. Yonkers, NY: Juris, pp. 249–55.

Bonoli, G. 2000. *The Politics of Pension Reform*. Cambridge, UK: Cambridge University Press.

Boon-Thong, Lee and Tengku Shamsul Bahrin. 1998. *Vanishing Borders: The New International Order of the 21st Century*. Aldershot, UK: Ashgate.

Booysen, Hercules. 1995. *International Transactions and the International Law Merchant*. Pretoria: Interlegal.

Borras-Alomar, S. 1995. *Interregional Co-operation in Europe during the Eighties and Early Nineties*, in N. A. Sorensen (ed.). *European Identities. Cultural Diversity and Integration in Europe since 1700*. Odense: Odense University Press, pp. 127–46.

Borras-Alomar, S. T. Christiansen, and A. Rodriguez-Pose. 1994. "Towards a 'Europe of Regions'? Visions and Reality from a Critical Perspective." *Regional Politics and Policy* 4: 1–27.

Bosco, A. 2000. *Are National Social Protection Systems under Threat?* European Issues, No. 7. Paris: Notre Europe.

Bostock, David. 2002. "COREPER Revisited." *Journal of Common Market Studies* 40, 2: 215–34.

Brady, David W. and Craig Volden. 1998. *Revolving Gridlock.* Boulder, CO: Westview Press.

Briggs, A. 1961. "The Welfare State in Historical Perspective." *European Journal of Sociology* 2: 251–8.

Brochmann, Grete. 1996. *European Integration and Immigration from Third Countries.* Oslo: Scandinavian University Press.

Brulhart, Marius. 1998. "Trading Places: Industrial Specialization in the European Union." *Journal of Common Market Studies,* September: 319–46.

Bryner, Gary C. 1995. *Blue Skies, Green Politics: The Clean Air Act of 1990 and Its Implementation,* 2nd ed. Washington, DC: Congressional Quarterly.

Bueno de Mesquita, Bruce. 2000. "Popes, Kings, and Endogenous Institutions: The Concordat of Worms and the Origins of Sovereignty." *International Studies Review* 2, 2: 93–118.

Bussani, Mauro and Ugo Mattei. 1997/98. "The Common Core Approach to European Private Law." *Columbia Journal of European Law* 3: 339–56.

Cain, Bruce E. and Kenneth Miller. 2001. "The Populist Legacy," in Larry J. Sabato, Howard R. Ernst, and Bruce A. Larson (eds.). *Dangerous Democracy?: The Battle Over Ballot Initiatives in America.* Lanham, MD: Rowman and Littlefield, pp. 33–62.

Camilleri, Joseph and Jim Falk. 1992. *The End of Sovereignty: The Politics of a Shrinking and Fragmenting World.* Cheltenham, UK: Edward Elgar.

Campbell, A. I. L. 1990. "Adrift on a Sea of Community Law?" *Scots Law Times* 12: 89–93.

Caporaso, James. 1996. "The European Union and Forms of State: Westphalian, Regulatory, or Postmodern." *Journal of Common Market Studies* 34, 1: 29–52.

Caporaso, James, and Joseph Jupille. 2000. "Sovereignty and Territoriality in the European Union: Transforming the UK Institutional Order." Paper presented at the third workshop on Territoriality and the Nation-State. Berkeley, CA.

Carbonneau, Thomas E. (ed.). 1998a. "A Definition and Perspective upon the Lex Mercatoria Debate." in T. Carbonneau, ed. *Lex Mercatoria and Arbitration: A Discussion of the New Law Merchant.* Yonkers, NY: Juris, pp. 11–21.

————. (ed). 1998b. *Lex Mercatoria and Arbitration: A Discussion of the New Law Merchant.* Yonkers, NY: Juris.

————. 1995. "Beyond Trilogies: A New Bill of Rights and Law Practice through the Contract of Arbitration." *American Journal of International Arbitration* 6: 1–27.

————. 1992. "National Law and the Judicialization of Arbitration: Manifest Destiny, Manifest Disregard, or Manifest Error," in Richard B. Lillich and Charles N. Brower (eds.). *International Arbitration in the 21st Century: Towards "Judicialization" and Conformity?* Irvington, NY: Transnational.

Carchedi, Bruno and Guglielmo Cardechi. 1999. "Contradictions of European Integration." *Capital and Class* 67: 119.

Carpenter, Daniel. 2001. *The Forging of Bureaucratic Autonomy: Reputations, Networks, and Policy Innovation in Executive Agencies, 1862–1928*. Princeton, NJ: Princeton University Press.

Castel, R. 1995. *Les Métamorphoses de la Question Sociale*. Paris: Fayard.

Cerny, P. G. 1995. "Globalization and the Changing Logic of Collective Action." *International Organization* 49: 595–625.

Chisholm, Donald. 1989. *Coordination without Hierarchy: Informal Structures in Multiorganizational Systems*. Berkeley, CA: University of California Press.

Christiansen, Thomas. 2001. "Intra-Institutional Politics and Inter-Institutional Relations in the EU: Towards Coherent Governance?" *Journal of European Public Policy* 8, 5: 747–69.

————. 1995. "Interests, Institutions, Identities: The Territorial Politics of the 'New Europe,'" in N. A. Sorensen (ed.). *European Identities. Cultural Diversity and Integration in Europe since 1700*. Odense: Odense University Press, pp. 241–55.

Christiansen, Thomas and K. E. Jorgensen. 1995. "Toward the 'Third Category' of Space: Conceptualizing the Changing Nature of Borders in Western Europe." Paper presented at the Second Pan-European ECPR Standing Group on International Relations. Paris.

Chryssochoou, Dimitris. 2002. "Civic Competence and the Challenge to EU Polity-Building." *Journal of European Public Policy* 9, 5: 756–73.

————. 1997. "New Challenges to the Study of European Integration: Implications for Theory-Building." *Journal of Common Market Studies* 35, 4: 521–42.

————. 1994. "Democracy and Symbiosis in the European Union: Towards a Confederal Consociation?" *West European Politics* 17, 4: 1–14.

Citrin, Jack and John Sides. 2003. "Can There Be Europe without Europeans? Problems of Identity in Multinational Communities," in R. Hermann, M. Brewer, and T. Risse (eds.). *Institutions and Identities in the New Europe*. London: Cambridge University Press.

Cohen, Richard E. 1992. *Washington at Work: Back Rooms and Clean Air*. New York: Macmillan.

Coheur, A. 2001. "Integrating Care in Border Regions: An Analysis of the Euroregio Projects." *Eurohealth* 7, 4: 10–12.

Cole, Alistair. 1996. "The French Socialists," in John Gaffney (ed.). *Political Parties and the European Union*. New York: Routledge, pp. 71–85.

Coleman, James. 1990. *Foundations of Social Theory*. Cambridge, MA: Harvard University Press.

Colino, Stacey. 1995. "The Fallout from Proposition 187." *Human Rights*, 22: 16–18.

Collier, Jane Fishburne. 1973. *Law and Social Change in Zinacantan*. Stanford, CA: Stanford University Press.

Collins, Hugh. 1998. "Formalism and Efficiency." Paper presented at the workshop Private Law Adjudication in the European Multi-Level System. San Domenico di Fiesole.

Convey, Andrew and Morek Kupiszewski. 1995. "Keeping Up with Schengen: Migration and Policy in European Union." *International Migration Review* 29: 939.

Cornelissen, V. R. 1996. "The Principle of Territoriality and the Community Regulations on Social Security." *Common Market Law Review* 33: 13–41.

Cornelius, Wayne A., Phillip L. Martin, and James F. Hollifield (eds.). 1994. *Controlling Immigration: A Global Perspective*. Palo Alto, CA: Stanford University Press.

Coultrap, John. 1999. "From Parliamentarism to Pluralism: Models of Democracy and the European Union's 'Democratic Deficit.'" *Journal of Theoretical Politics* 11, 1: 107–35.

Culpepper, Pepper D. 2002. "Powering, Puzzling, and 'Pacting': The Informational Logic of Negotiated Reforms." *Journal of European Public Policy* 9, 5: 774–90.

Cusimano, Maryann. 2000. *Beyond Sovereignty: Issues for a Global Agenda*. Boston, MA: St. Martin's Press.

Cutler, A. Claire, Virginia Haufler, and Tony Porter (eds.). 1999. *Private Authority and International Affairs*. Albany, NY: SUNY Press.

Dahl, Robert A. 1999. "Can International Organizations Be Democratic?" in Ian Shapiro and Casiano Hacker-Cordon (eds.). *Democracy's Edges*. Cambridge, UK: Cambridge University Press.

———. 1994. *The New American Political (Dis)order*. Berkeley, CA: Institute of Governmental Studies Press.

———. 1976. *Democracy in the United States: Promise and Performance*. Chicago: Rand McNally.

Deakin, R. 1996. "Labour Law as Market Regulation," in P. Davies et al. (eds.). *European Community Law. Principles and Perspectives*. Oxford, UK: Oxford University Press, pp. 52–78.

Decker, Frank. 2002. "Governance beyond the Nation-State: Reflections on the Democratic Deficit of the European Union." *Journal of European Public Policy* 9, 2: 256–72.

de la Porte, Caroline. 2002. "Is the Open Method of Coordination Appropriate for Organising Activities at the European Level in Sensitive Policy Areas?" *European Law Journal* 8, 1: 38–58.

Delaume, Georges R. 1996. "Choice-of-Forum and Arbitration Clauses in the United States: A Judicial Crusade." *Journal of International Arbitration* 13: 81–92.

———. 1995. "Reflections on the Effectiveness of International Arbitral Awards." *Journal of International Arbitration* 12: 5–19.

De Matteis, A. and S. Giubboni. 1998. "Rapporti di Lavoro con Elementi di Internazionalità e Sicurezza Sociale," in F. Carinci, R. De Luca Tamajo, P. Tosi, and T. Ten (eds.). *I Contratti di Lavoro Internazionali*. Turin: Utet, pp. 97–114.

De Swaan, A. 1987. *In Care of the State*. Cambridge, UK: Cambridge University Press.

Deudney, Daniel. 1996. "Binding Sovereigns: Authorities, Structures, and Geopolitics in Philadelphian Systems," in Thomas J. Biersteker and Cynthia Weber (eds.). *Sovereignty as a Social Construct*. Cambridge, UK: Cambridge University Press, pp. 190–239.

Dezelay, Yves and Bryant G. Garth. 1996. *Dealing in Virtue: International Commerical Arbitration and the Construction of a Transnational Legal Order*. Chicago: University of Chicago.

Dicey, A.V. 1959. *Introduction to the Study of the Law of the Constitution*, 10th ed. London: Macmillan.

Di Palma, Giuseppe. 1990. *To Craft Democracies*. Berkeley, CA: University of California Press.

———. 1969. *Apathy and Participation: Mass Politics in Western Societies*. Glencoe, IL: Free Press.

Donahey, M. Scott. 1996. "From *The Bremen* to *Mitsubishi* (and Beyond): International Arbitration Adrift in U.S. Waters." *American Journal of International Arbitration* 7: 149–61.

Drobnig, Ulrich. 1998. "Assessing Arbitral Autonomy in European Statutory Law," in Thomas Carbonneau (ed.). *Lex Mercatoria and Arbitration: A Discussion of the New Law Merchant*. Yonkers, NY: Juris, pp. 195–201.

Duchêne, François. 1994. *Jean Monnet: The First Statesman of Interdependence*. New York: W.W. Norton.

The Economist. "The New Trade War." December 4, 1999, pp. 25–6.

The Economist. "Countdown to Ruckus." December 4, 1999, p. 26.

Egeberg, Morten. 2001. "How Federal? The Organizational Dimension of Integration in the EU (and Elsewhere)." *Journal of European Public Policy* 8, 5: 728–46.

Elazar D. J. 1994. *The American Mosaic: The Impact of Space, Time, and Culture on American Politics*. Boulder, CO: Westview Press.

Elkins, David J. 1995. *Beyond Sovereignty: Territory and Political Economy in the Twenty-First Century*. Toronto: University of Toronto Press.

Ellickson, Robert C. 1991. *Order without Law: How Neighbors Settle Disputes*. Cambridge, MA: Harvard University Press.

Epstein L. 1986. *Political Parties in the American Mold*. Madison, WI: University of Wisconsin Press.

Eriksen, Erik Oddvar and John Erik Fossum. 2002. "Democracy through Strong Publics in the European Union?" *Journal of Common Market Studies* 40, 3: 401–24.

Esping-Andersen, Gøsta. 1990. *The Three Worlds of Welfare Capitalism*. New York: Polity Press.

———. 1985. *Politics against Markets*. Princeton, NJ: Princeton University Press.

European Commission. 2001. *Commission Communication: The Elimination of Tax Obstacles to the Cross-Border Provision of Occupational Pensions*. COM(2001) 214.

———. 1999. *Commission Communication: Towards a Single Market for Supplementary Pensions*. COM(99) 134.

———. 1997. *Supplementary Pensions in the Single Market: A Green Paper*. COM(97) 283.

Ewald, F. 1986. *L'Etat Providence*. Paris: Grasset.

Fabbrini, Sergio. 1999a. "American Democracy from a European Perspective." *Annual Review of Political Science* 2: 465–91.

———. 1999b. "The American System of Separated Government: An Historical-Institutional Interpretation." *International Political Science Review* 20, 1: 95–116.

Fairbrass, Jenny and Andrew Jordan. 2000. "National Barriers and European Opportunities? The Implementation of EU Biodiversity Policy in Great Britain." CSERGE Working Paper GEC 2000-15.

Falkner, Gerda 2002. "How Intergovernmental Are Intergovernmental Conferences? An Example from the Maastricht Treaty Reform." *Journal of European Public Policy* 9, 1: 98–119.

Farnsworth, Allan. 1985. "Conflict of Laws: Problems That Face Transnational Business and How to Avoid Them," in Beverly A. Allen and Christian S. Ward (eds.). *The United States, Transnational Business, and the Law.* New York: Oceana.

Fassman, Heinz and Rainer Munz. 1992. "Patterns and Trends of International Immigration in Western Europe." *Population and Development Review* 18, 3: 457.

Ferrari, Franco (ed.). 1998. *The Unification of International Commercial Law.* Baden-Baden: Nomos.

Ferrera, Maurizio. 1996. "Il Modello Sud-Europeo di Welfare State." *Rivista Italiana di Scienza Politica* 1: 67–101.

———. 1993a. *EC Citizens and Social Protection.* Brussels: European Commission, DGV Report.

———. 1993b. *Modelli di Solidarietà.* Bologna: Il Mulino.

Ferrera, Maurizio, A. Hemerijck, and Martin Rhodes. 2000. *The Future of Social Europe.* Lisbon: Celta Editora.

Ferrera, Maurizio and Martin Rhodes. 2000. "Building a Sustainable Welfare State," in Maurizio Ferrera and Martin Rhodes (eds.). *Recasting the European Welfare States.* London: Frank Cass, pp. 257–82.

Financial Times, "Clinton – Off the Right Track?" November 12, 1997, p. 23.

Finer, S. E. 1997. *The History of Government from the Earliest Times.* 3 vols. Oxford, UK: Oxford University Press.

Fligstein, Neil and Alec Stone Sweet. 2002. "Constructing Polities and Markets: An Institutionalist Account of European Integration." *American Journal of Sociology* 107, 5: 1206–43.

Flora, Peter. 2000. *Externe Grenzbildung und Interne Strukturierung: Europa und seine Nationen. Eine Rokkanische Forschungsperspektive.* EUI-RSC seminar paper.

———. 1999. "Introduction and Interpretation," in Peter Flora, Stein Kuhnle, and Derek Urwin (eds.). *State Formation, Nation-Building and Mass Politics in Europe: The Theory of Stein Rokkan.* Oxford, UK: Oxford University Press, pp. 1–91.

———. 1986. "Introduction," in Peter Flora (ed.). *Growth to Limits. The Western European Welfare States since World War II.* Berlin/New York: De Gruyter, pp. 11–36.

Flora, Peter and J. Alber. 1981. "Modernization, Democratization and the Development of Welfare States in Western Europe," in Peter Flora and A. J. Heidenheimer (eds.). *The Development of Welfare State in Europe and America.* New Brunswick, NJ: Transaction Books, pp. 37–80.

Flora, Peter, Stein Kuhnle, and Derek Urwin. (eds.). 1999. *State Formation, Nation Building and Mass Politics in Europe: The Theory of Stein Rokkan.* New York: Oxford University Press.

Forsyth, Murray. 1981. *Union of States.* Leicester, UK: Leicester University Press.

Frieden, Jeffrey and Ronald Rogowski. 1996. "The Impact of the International Economy on National Policies: An Analytical Overview," in Robert Keohane and Helen Milner (eds.). *Internationalization and Domestic Politics.* Ithaca, NY: Cornell University Press.

Friedman, K.V. 1981. *Legitimation of Social Rights and the Welfare State: A Weberian Perspective.* Chapel Hill, NC: University of North Carolina Press.

Frey, Bruno and Reiner Eichenberger. 1999. *The New Democratic Federalism for Europe: Functional, Overlapping, and Competing Jurisdictions.* Cheltenham, UK: Edward Elgar.

Fudenberg, Drew and Eric Maskin. 1986. "The Folk Theorem in Repeated Games with Discounting or with Incomplete Information." *Econometrica* 54: 533–54.

Garrett, Geoffrey and Peter Lange. 1991. "Political Responses to Interdependence: What's 'Left' for the Left?" *International Organization* 45, 4: 539–64.

Geddes, Andrew. 1995. "Immigrant and Ethnic Minorities and the EU Democratic Deficit." *Journal of Common Market Studies* 33: 2.

Gerber, Elizabeth. 1996. "Legislative Responsiveness to the Threat of Popular Initiatives." *American Journal of Political Science* 40: 639–56.

Giubboni, S. 2001. "Politiche Sociali e Leggi dell'Economia. L'Iintegrazione Sociale Europea Rivisitata." *Rivista del Diritto della Sicurezza Sociale* 1: 26–102.

———. 1997. "Cittadinanza Comunitaria e Sicurezza Sociale: un Profilo Critico." *Argomenti di Diritto del Lavoro* 6: 67–126.

Gladwell, Malcolm. 2000. *The Tipping Point: How Little Things Can Make a Big Differences*. New York: Little, Brown.

Golden, Miriam, Michael Wallerstein, and Peter Lange. 1999. "Postwar Trade-Union Organization and Industrial Relations in Twelve Countries," in Herbert Kitschelt, Peter Lange, Gary Marks, and John D. Stephens (eds.). *Continuity and Change in Contemporary Capitalism*. New York: Cambridge University Press, pp. 194–230.

Goldsmith, Jack L. (ed.). 1997. *International Dispute Resolution: The Regulation of Forum Selection*. Irvington, NY: Transnational.

Goldstein, Leslie Friedman. 2001. *Constituting Federal Sovereignty: The European Union in Comparative Context*. Baltimore, MD: John Hopkins University Press.

Greenfeld L. 1992. *Nationalism: Five Roads to Modernity*. Cambridge, MA: Harvard University Press.

Greif, Avner. 1993. "Contract Enforceability and Economic Institutions in Early Trade: The Maghribi Trader's Coalition." *American Economic Review* 83: 425–48.

———. 1989. "Reputation and Coalitions in Medieval Trade: Evidence on the Maghribi Traders." *Journal of Economic History* 49: 857–82.

Greif, Avner, Paul Milgrom, and Barry R. Weingast. 1994. "Coordination, Commitment, and Enforcement: The Case of the Merchant Guild." *Journal of Political Economy* 102: 745–76.

Greven, Michael Th. and Louis W. Pauly. 2000. *Democracy beyond the State? The European Dilemma and the Emerging Global Order*. Lanham, MD: Rowman and Littlefield.

Griffiths, R. T. (ed.). 1993. *Socialist Parties and the Question of Europe in the 1950s*. Leiden: E. J. Brill.

Guillemard, A.-M. 1986. *Le Déclin du Social*. Paris: PUF.

Haas, Ernst. 2000. *Nationalism, Liberalism, and Progress*. vol. 2. Ithaca, NY: Cornell University Press.

———. 1997. *Nationalism, Liberalism, and Progress*. vol. 1. Ithaca, NY: Cornell University Press.

———. 1958. *The Uniting of Europe*. Palo Alto, CA: Stanford University Press.

Habermas, Jürgen. 1992. "Citizenship and National Identity: Some Reflections on the Future of Europe." *Praxis International* 12: 1–19.

Hagen, K. 1999. "Towards a Europeanization of Social Policies? A Scandinavian Perspective," in Denis Bouget and Bruno Palier (eds.). *Comparing Social Welfare Systems in Nordic Europe and France*. vol. 4. Paris: MIRE, pp. 661–87.

Haigh, Nigel. 1996. "Climate Change Policies and Politics in the European Community," in Tim O'Riordan and Jill Jager (eds.). *Politics of Climate Change: A European Perspective*. London: Routledge, pp. 155–85.

Hardin, Russell. 1982. *Collective Action*. Baltimore, MD: Johns Hopkins University Press.

Harlow, Carole and Erika Szyszczak. 1995. "Case Note: *R. v. Secretary of State for Employment Ex Parte Equal Opportunities Commission*." *Common Market Law Review* 32, 2: 641–54.

Hart, H. L. A. 1994. *The Concept of Law*. Oxford, UK: Clarendon.

Hatzfeld, H. 1989. *Du Paupérisme à la Sécurité Sociale. Essai sur les Origines de la Sécurité Sociale*, 2nd ed. Nancy: Presses Universitaires de Nancy.

Hayes-Renshaw, Fiona and Helen Wallace. 1997. *The Council of Ministers*. New York: St. Martin's Press.

Heclo, H. 1981. "Towards a New Welfare State," in Peter Flora and A. J. Heidenheimer (eds.). *The Development of Welfare States in Europe and America*. New Brunswick, NJ: Transaction Books, pp. 137–80.

———. 1974. *Modern Social Politics in Britain and Sweden*. New Haven, CT: Yale University Press.

Heiner, Ronald A. 1986. "Imperfect Decisions and the Law: On the Evolution of Precedent and Rules." *Journal of Legal Studies* 15: 227–61.

Héritier, Adrienne. 2001. "Overt and Covert Institutionalization in Europe," in Alec Stone Sweet, Wayne Sandholtz, and Neil Fligstein (eds.). *The Institutionalization of Europe*. Oxford, UK: Oxford University Press.

———. 1999. "Elements of Democratic Legitimation in Europe: An Alternative Perspective." *Journal of European Public Policy* 6, 2: 269–82.

———. 1997. "Policy-Making by Subterfuge: Interest Accommodation, Innovation and Substitute Democratic Legitimation in Europe–Perspectives from Distinctive Policy Areas." *Journal of European Public Policy*, June: 171–89.

Héritier, Adrienne, Christoph Knill, and Susanne Mingers. 1996. *Ringing the Changes in Europe: Regulatory Competition and the Transformation of the State. Britain, France, Germany*. Berlin: Walter de Gruyter.

Hermans, H. 2000. "Assistenza Sanitaria Transfrontaliera e Conseguenze delle Sentenze Dekker e Kohll." *Politiche Sanitarie* 2: 56–63.

Hill, Jonathan. 1997. "Some Private International Law Aspects of the Arbitration Act 1996." *International and Comparative Law Quarterly* 46: 274.

Hinsley, F. H. 1986. *Sovereignty*. New York: Cambridge University Press.

Hintze, O. 1962. *Soziologie und Geschichte Staat und Verfassung*. G. Oestreich (ed.). Goettimgen: Vandenhoeck and Ruprecht.

Hirschman, Albert O. 1981. "Exit, Voice and the State." *World Politics* 31: 90–107.

———. 1970. *Exit, Voice, and Loyalty: Responses to Decline in Firms, Organizations, and States*. Cambridge, MA: Harvard University Press.

Hiscox, Michael. 2001. "Class versus Industry Cleavages: Inter-Industry Factor Mobility and the Politics of Trade." *International Organization* 55, 1: 1–46.

Hix, Simon. 1999. *The Political System of the European Union*. New York: St. Martin's Press.

———. 1994. "The Study of the European Community: The Challenge to Comparative Politics." *West European Politics*, January: 1–30.

Hodson, Dermot and Imelda Maher. 2001. "The Open Method of Coordination as a New Mode of Governance: The Case of Soft Economic Policy Co-ordination." *Journal of Common Market Studies* 39, 4: 719–46.

Holmes, Stephen. 1995. *Passions and Constraint: On the Theory of Liberal Democracy*. Chicago, IL: University of Chicago Press.

Hooghe, Liesbet (ed.). 1996. *Cohesion Policy and European Integration: Building Multilevel Governance*. New York: Oxford University Press.

Hooghe, Liesbet and Gary Marks. 2001a. *Multi-Level Governance and European Integration*. Boulder, CO: Rowman and Littlefield.

———. 2001b. "Types of Multi-Level Governance." European Integration Online Papers, 5, 11 (http://eiop.or.at/eiop/texte/2001-011a.htm).

———. 1999. "The Making of a Polity: The Struggle over European Integration," in Herbert Kitschelt, Peter Lange, Gary Marks, and John Stephens (eds.). *Continuity and Change in Contemporary Capitalism*. Cambridge, UK: Cambridge University Press, pp. 70–97.

Hoskyns, Catherine and Michael Newman (eds.). 2000. *Democratizing the European Union: Issues for the Twenty-First Century*. Manchester, UK: University of Manchester Press.

Huntington, Samuel P. 1968. *Political Order in Changing Societies*. New Haven, CT: Yale University Press.

Hurrell, Andrew and Anand Menon. 1996. "Politics Like Any Other? Comparative Politics, International Relations and the Study of the EU." *West European Politics* 19, 2: 386–402.

Imig, Doug and Sidney Tarrow (eds.). 2001. *Contentious Europeans: Protest and Politics in an Emerging Polity*. Lanham, MD: Rowman and Littlefield.

———. 2000. "Political Contention in a Europeanising Polity." *West European Politics* 23: 73–93.

International Chamber of Commerce. 1997. *The ICC Model International Sale Contract*. Paris: ICC Pub. No. 556 (E).

Ireland, Patrick. 1991. "Facing the True (Fortress Europe): Immigrant and Politics in the EC." *Journal of Common Market Studies* 29: 457–80.

Jabko, Nicolas. 2001. "European Union through the Market: A Political Formula for Institutional Change." Ph.D. dissertation. University of California, Berkeley.

Jachtenfuchs, Markus. 2001. "The Governance Approach to European Integration." *Journal of Common Market Studies* 39, 2: 245–64.

Jacobs, F. G. 1999. "Public Law – The Impact of Europe." *Public Law*, Summer: 232–45.

Jin, Ning. 1996. "The Status of *Lex Mercatoria* in International Commerical Arbitration." *American Journal of International Arbitration* 7: 163–98.

Jobert, B. and P. Muller. 1987. *L'État en Action. Politiques Publiques et Corporatismes*. Paris: PUF.

Joerges, Christian. 2002. "'Deliberative Supranationalisms' – Two Defences." *European Law Journal* 8, 1: 133–51.

Joerges, Christian and Jurgen Neyer. 1997. "Transforming Strategic Interaction into Deliberative Problem-Solving: European Comitology in the Foodstuffs Sector." *Journal of European Public Policy* 4, 4: 609–25.

Joerges, Christian and Ellen Vos (eds.). 1999. *EU Committee: Social Regulation, Law, and Politics*. Oxford, UK: Hart Publishing.

Johnson, Kevin. 1995. "An Essay on Immigration Politics, Popular Democracy and California's Proposition 187." *Washington Law Review* 70: 629–73.

Jordan, Andrew. 2002. *The Europeanization of British Environmental Policy: A Departmental Perspective*. Houndsmills, UK: Palgrave.

Juenger, Friedrich K. 1998. "The Lex Mercatoria and the Conflict of Laws," in Thomas E. Carbonneau (ed.). *Lex Mercatoria and Arbitration: A Discussion of the New Law Merchant*. Yonkers, NY: Juris, pp. 265–77.

Kagan, Robert A. 1997. "Should Europe Worry about Adversarial Legalism?" *Oxford Journal of Legal Studies* 17: 165–83.

Kandori, Michihiro. 1992. "Social Norms and Community Enforcement." *Review of Economic Studies* 59: 63–80.

Katz, Richard. 2001. "Models of Democracy: Elite Attitudes and the Democratic Deficit in the European Union." *European Union Politics* 2, 1: 53–79.

Katz, Richard and Bernard Wessels. 1999. *The European Parliament, the National Parliaments, and European Integration*. Oxford, UK: Oxford University Press.

Keating, M. 1997a. "Les Régions Constituent-elles un Niveau de Gouvernement en Europe?" in P. LeGalès and C. Lequesne (eds). *Les Paradoxes des Régions en Europe*. Paris: La Découverte, pp. 19–35.

———. 1997b. "The Political Economy of Regionalism," in M. Keating and J. Loughlin (eds). *The Political Economy of Regionalism*. London: Frank Cass, pp. 17–40.

Keegan, John. 1976. *The Face of Battle*. New York: Viking Press.

Kersbergen, Kees van. 2000. "Political Allegiance and European Integration." *European Journal of Political Research* 37, 1: 1–17.

Kettnaker, Vera. 2001. "The European Conflict over Genetically-Engineered Crops," in Doug Imig and Sidney Tarrow (eds.). *Contentious Europeans*. Lanham, MD: Rowman and Littlefield, ch. 10.

Key, V. O., Jr., 1964. *Politics, Parties, and Pressure Groups*. New York: Thomas Y. Crowell.

Kincaid, John. 1999. "Confederal Federalism and Citizen Representation in the European Union." *West European Politics* 22, 2: 34–58.

King, Gary and Langche Zeng. 2001a. "Explaining Rare Events in International Relations." *International Organization* 55, 3: 693–715.

———. 2001b. "Logistic Regression in Rare Events Data." *Political Analysis* 9, 2: 137–63.

Knill, Christoph. 2001. "Private Governance across Multiple Arenas: European Interest Associations as Interface Actors." *Journal of European Public Policy* 8, 2: 227–46.

Kohler-Koch, Beate 1999. "The Evolution and Transformation of European Governance," in Beate Kohler-Koch and Rainer Eising (eds.). *The Transformation of Governance in the European Union*. London: Routledge, pp. 14–35.

Kohler-Koch, Beate and Rainer Eising. 1999. *The Transformation of Governance in the European Union*. London: Routledge.

Koppenol-Laforce, Marielle. 1996. "Contracts in Private International Law," in Marielle Koppenol-Laforce (ed.). *International Contracts: Aspects of Jurisdiction,*

Arbitration, and Private International Law. London: Sweet and Maxwell, pp. 141–9.

Korpi, W. 2000. *Contentious Institutions.* Stockholm: SOFI, WP 4/2000.

———. 1980. "Social Policy and Distributional Conflict in the Capitalist Democracies. A Preliminary Comparative Framework." *West European Politics* 3, 3: 296–316.

Koslowski, Rex. 1994. "Intra-EU Migration Citizenship and Political Union." *Journal of Common Market Studies* 32: 3.

Kostakopoulou, Theodora. 1997. "Why a Community of Europeans Could Be a Community of Exclusion: A Reply to Howe." *Journal of Common Market Studies* 35, 2: 302.

Kraft, Michael E. 1990. "Environmental Gridlock: Searching for Consensus in Congress," in Norman J. Vig and Michael E. Kraft (eds.). *Environmental Policy in the 1990s: Toward a New Agenda.* Washington, DC: Congressional Quarterly Press, pp. 103–24.

Krasner, Stephen D. 1999. *Sovereignty: Organized Hypocrisy.* Princeton, NJ: Princeton University Press.

———. 1995/96. "Compromising Westphalia." *International Security* 20, 3: 115–51.

———. 1993. "Westphalia and All That," in Judith Goldstein and Robert O. Keohane (eds.). *Ideas and Foreign Policy: Beliefs, Institutions, and Political Change.* Ithaca, NY: Cornell University Press.

———. 1984. "Approaches to the State: Alternative Conceptions and Historical Dynamics." *Comparative Politics* 16: 223–46.

Kratochwil, Friedrich. 1986. "Of Systems, Boundaries, and Territoriality: An Inquiry into the Formation of the State System." *World Politics* 39: 27–52.

Krehbiel, Keith. *Pivotal Politics: A Theory of U.S. Lawmaking.* Chicago, IL: University of Chicago Press, 1998.

Kreppel, Amie. 2002. *The European Parliament and Supranational Party System.* Cambridge, UK: Cambridge University Press.

Kreps, David M. and Robert Wilson. 1982. "Reputation and Imperfect Information." *Journal of Economic Theory* 27: 253–79.

Krugman, Paul. 1993. "Lessons of Massachusetts for EMU," in F. Torres and F. Giavazzi (eds). *Adjustment and Growth in the European Monetary Union.* Cambridge, UK: Cambridge University Press, pp. 241–61.

———. 1991. *Geography and Trade.* Cambridge, MA: MIT Press.

Krygier, Martin. 1999. "Institutional Optimism, Cultural Pessimism and the Rule of Law," in Martin Krygier and Adam Czarnota (eds.). *The Rule of Law after Communism.* Aldershot, UK: Ashgate Publishing.

Kulahci, Erol. 2002. "Explaining the Absence of a Genuine European Social-Democrat Consensus: The Case of 'Une Stratégie pour la Solidarité.'" European Integration Online Papers (http://eiop.or.at/eiop/texte/2002-004a.htm).

Ladrech, Robert and Philippe Marlière (eds.). 1999. *Social Democratic Parties in the European Union: History, Organization, Policies.* London: Macmillan.

Lagneau, Eric and Pierre Lefebure. 2001. "Media Construction in the Dynamics of Europrotest," in Doug Imig and Sidney Tarrow (eds.). *Contentious Europeans: Protest and Politics in an Emerging Polity.* Lanham, MD: Rowman and Littlefield, ch. 9.

Lahav, Gallya. 1997. "Ideological and Party Constraints on Immigration Attitude on Europe." *Journal of Common Market Studies* 35, 3: 377.

Landau, Martin. 1979. *Political Theory and Political Science*. New Jersey: Humanities Press.

Lando, Ole. 1998. "Optional or Mandatory Europeanisation of Contract Law." Paper presented at the workshop Private Law Adjudication in the European Multi-Level System, San Domenico di Fiesole.

Landy, Marc K., Marc J. Roberts, and Stephen R. Thomas. 1994. *The Environmental Protection Agency: Asking the Wrong Questions from Nixon to Clinton*, expanded ed. Oxford, UK: Oxford University Press.

Laponce, J. 1974. "Hirschman's Voice and Exit Model as a Spatial Archetype." *Social Science Information* 13, 3: 67–81.

Lasok, Dominik and John W. Bridge. 1991. *Law and Institutions of the European Communities*, 5ᵗʰ ed. London: Butterworths.

Lasswell, Harold and Abraham Kaplan. 1950. *Power and Society: A Framework for Political Inquiry*. New Haven, CT: Yale University Press.

Leamer, Edward. 1984. *Sources of International Comparative Advantage: Theory and Evidence*, Cambridge, MA: MIT Press.

Leibfried, Stephan and Paul Pierson. 2000. "Social Policy," in Helen Wallace and William Wallace (eds.). *Policy-Making in the European Union*, 4ᵗʰ ed. Oxford, UK: Oxford University Press, pp. 267–91.

———. (eds.). 1995. *European Social Policy: Between Fragmentation and Integration*. Washington, DC: Brookings Institution.

Levitsky, Jonathan E. 1994. "The Europeanization of the British Legal Style." *American Journal of Comparative Law* 42, 2: 347–80.

Lewis, Clive. 1989. "Statutes and the E.E.C. – Interim Relief and the Crown." *Cambridge Law Journal* 48, 3: 347–9.

Lewis, Jeffrey. 2000. "The Methods of Community in EU Decision-Making and Administrative Rivalry in the Council's Infrastructure." *Journal of European Economic Policy* 7, 2: 261–89.

———. 1998. "Is the 'Hard Bargaining' Image of the Council Misleading? The Committee of Permanent Representatives and the Local Elections Directive." *Journal of Common Market Studies* 36, 4: 479–504.

Lillich, Richard B. and Charles N. Brower (eds.). 1992. *International Arbitration in the 21ˢᵗ Century: Towards "Judicialization" and Conformity?* Irvington, NY: Transnational.

Lipset, Segmour Martin. 1996. *American Exceptionalism: A Double-Edge Sword*. New York: W. W. Norton.

———. 1979. *The First New Nation: The United States in Historical and Comparative Perspective*, 2ⁿᵈ ed. New York: W. W. Norton.

Lipset, S. M. and Stein Rokkan. 1967. *Party Systems and Voter Alignments*. New York: Free Press.

Lipsitz L. and D. M. Speak. 1989. *American Democracy*, 2ⁿᵈ ed. New York: St. Martin's Press.

Lipstein, K. 1981. *Principles of the Conflict of Laws, National and International*. The Hague: Martinus Nijhoff.

Lister, Frederick K. 1996. *The European Union, the United Nations, and the Revival of Confederal Governance*. Westport, CT: Greenwood Press.

Litfin, Karen T. 2000. "Environment, Wealth, and Authority: Global Climate Change and Emerging Modes of Legitimation." *International Studies Review* (special issue, Continuity and Change in the Westphalian Order) 2, 2: 119–48.

———. 1997. "Sovereignty in World Ecopolitics." *Mershon International Studies Review* 41, supplement 2: 167–204.

Lörchner, Gino. 1998. "The New German Arbitration Act." *Journal of International Arbitration* 15: 85–93.

Lowi, Theodore J. 1988. "American Democratic Experience(s) in Perspective," in F. Krinsky (ed.). *Crisis and Innovation: Constitutional Democracy in America*. New York: Basil Blackwell, pp. 31–46.

———. 1985. *The Personal President. Power Invested Promise Unfulfilled*. Ithaca, NY: Cornell University Press.

———. 1978. "Europeanization of America? From United States to United State," in T. Lowi and A. Stone (eds.). *Nationalizing Government: Public Policies in America*. Beverly Hills, CA: Sage Publications, pp. 15–29.

———. 1972. "Four Systems of Policy, Politics, and Choice." *Public Administration Review* 32: 298–310.

———. 1964. "American Business, Public Policy, Case Studies and Political Theory." *World Politics* 16: 677–715.

Lowi, Theodore J. and Alec Stone (eds.). *Nationalizing Government: Public Policies in America*. Beverly Hills, CA: Sage, pp. 15–29.

Mabbet, D. 2000. "Social Regulation and the Social Dimension in Europe: The Example of Insurance." *European Journal of Social Security* 2, 3: 241–57.

Mabbet, D. and H. Bolderson. 2000. "Non-Discrimination, Free Movement and Social Citizenship in Europe: Contrasting Provisions for the EU Nationals and Asylum-Seekers." In ISSA, *Social Security in the global Village*, International Social Security Association (ed.). New Brunswick, NJ: Transaction Books.

MacCormick, Neil. 1978. *Legal Reasoning and Legal Theory*. Oxford, UK: Clarendon.

MacDonald, Karin and Bruce E. Cain. 1998. "Nativism, Partisanship and Immigration: An Analysis of Prop 187," in Michael B. Preston, Bruce E. Cain, and Sandra Bass (eds.). *Racial and Ethnic Politics in California*. Berkeley, CA: IGS Press.

Mackenzie-Stuart, Lord. 1995. "The Equal Opportunities Case – A Preliminary Comment," in Ole Due, Marcus Lutter, and Jürgen Schwarze (eds.). *Festschrift für Ulrich Everling*. Baden-Baden: Nomos Verlagsgesellschaft, pp. 783–8.

Magee, Stephen P., William A. Brock, and Leslie Young. 1992. *Black Hole Tariffs and Endogenous Policy Theory*. Cambridge, UK: Cambridge University Press.

Maino, F. 1999. *La Politica Sanitaria*. Bologna: Il Mulino.

Mair, P. 1998. "I Conflitti Politici in Europa. Persistenza e Mutamento." *Rivista Italiana di Scienza Politica* 3: 425–50.

Majone, Giandomenico. 2001. "Two Logics of Delegation: Agency and Fiduciary Relations in EU Governance." *European Union Politics* 2, 1: 103–22.

———. 2000. "The Credibility Crisis of Community Regulation." *Journal of Common Market Studies* 38, 2: 273–302.

———. (ed.). 1996. *Regulating Europe*. London: Routledge.

———. 1993. "The European Community between Social Policy and Social Regulation." *Journal of Common Market Studies* 31, 2: 153–69.

———. 1992. "Regulatory Federalism in the European Community." *Government and Policy* 10, 3: 253–374.

Mamadough, Virginie. 2001. "The Territoriality of European Integration and the Territorial Features of the European Union: The First Fifty Years." *Tidjschrift voor Economische en Sociale Geographie* 92, 4: 420–36.

Mancini, G. Federico and David T. Keeling. 1994. "Democracy and the European Court of Justice." *Modern Law Review* 57, 2: 175–90.

Mann, Michael 1984. "The Autonomous Power of the State: Its Origins, Mechanisms and Results." *European Journal of Sociology*, 25: 185–213.

————. 1993. *The Sources of Social Power*, vol. 2: *The Rise of Classes and Nation-States, 1760–1914*. Cambridge, UK: Cambridge University Press.

March, James G. and Johan P. Olsen. 1998. "The Institutional Dynamics of International Political Orders." *International Organization* 52: 943–69.

————. 1989. *Rediscovering Institutions: The Organizational Basis of Politics*. New York: Free Press.

————. 1984. "The New Institutionalism: Organizational Factors in Political Life." *American Political Science Review* 78: 734–49.

Marks, Gary. 1997. "A Third Lens: Comparing European Integration and State Building," in Jitte Klausen and Louise Tilly (eds.). *European Integration in Social and Historical Perspective: 1850 to the Present*. Lanham, MD: Rowman and Littlefield.

Marks, Gary, Liesbet Hooghe, and Kermit Blank. 1996. "European Integration from the 1980s: State-Centric v. Multilevel Governance." *Journal of Common Market Studies* 34, 3: 341.

Marks, Gary and Marco Steenbergen (eds.). *European Integration and Political Conflict*. Cambridge, UK: Cambridge University Press, forthcoming.

Marks, Gary and Carole J. Wilson. 2000. "The Past in the Present: A Theory of Party Response to European Integration." *British Journal of Political Science* 30, 4: 433–59.

Marshall, Geoffrey. 1997. Parliamentary Sovereignty: The New Horizons. *Public Law* (Spring): 1–5.

Marshall, T. H. 1950. *Citizenship and Social Class*. Cambridge, UK: Cambridge University Press.

Martin, Andrew and George Ross. 2001. "Trade Union Organizing at the European Level: The Dilemma of Borrowed Resources," in Doug Imig and Sidney Tarrow (eds.). *Contentious Europeans: Protest and Politics in an Emerging Polity*. Lanham, MD: Rowman and Littlefield, ch. 3.

Martin, Phillip. 1994. "Good Intentions Gone Awry: IRCA and the US Agriculture," in Mark Miller (ed.). *The Annals* 534: 44.

Matteucci, Nicola. 1983. "Costituzionalismo," in Norberto Bobbio, Nicola Matteucci, and Gianfranco Pasquino (eds.). *Dizionario di Politica*. Torino: UTET.

Mattli, Walter. 2001. "Private Justice in a Global Economy: From Litigation to Arbitration." *International Organization* 55: 919–47.

Maxwell, Patricia. 1995. "Discrimination against Part Time Workers." *Web Journal of Current Legal Issues* 1. (http://webjcli.ncl.ac.uk/generics1/maxwell1.html).

May, Thomas. 1995. "Sovereignty and International Order." *Ratio Juris* 8, 3: 287–95.

McAdam, Doug, Sidney Tarrow, and Charles Tilly. 2001. *Dynamics of Contention*. New York and Cambridge, UK: Cambridge University Press.

McColgan, Aileen. 1996. "The Employment Protection (Part-Time Employees) Regulations 1995." *Industrial Law Journal* 25, 1: 43–4.

McCubbins, Matthew D. 1985. "The Legislative Design of Regulatory Structure." *American Journal of Political Science* 29, 721–48.

McKee, M., E. Mossialos, and P. Belcher. 1996. "The Influence of European Law on National Health Policy. *Journal of European Social Policy* 6: 263–86.

McMahon, Christopher. 1994. *Authority and Democracy: A General Theory of Government and Management*. Princeton, NJ: Princeton University Press.

Mearsheimer, J. J. 1990. "Back to the Future: Instability in Europe after the Cold War." *International Security* 15: 5–56.

Messina, Anthony M. 1995. "Immigration as a Political Dilemma in Britain: Implication for Western Europe." *Policy Studies Journal* 23, 4: 686–98.

———. 1990. "Political Impediments to the Resumption of Labour to Western Europe." *West European Politics* 13, 1: 31–46.

Meyer, David S. and Sidney G. Tarrow (eds.). 1998. *The Social Movement Society: Contentious Politics for a New Century*. Lanham, MD: Rowman and Littlefield.

Miles, Robert and Diana Kay. 1994. "The Politics of Immigration to Britain: East-West Migration in the Twentieth Century." *West European Politics* 17, 2: 17–32.

Milgrom, Paul R., Douglas C. North, and Barry R. Weingast. 1990. "The Role of Institutions in the Revival of Trade: The Law Merchant, Private Judges, and the Champagne Fairs." *Economics and Politics* 2: 1–23.

Milgrom, Paul R. and John Roberts. 1992. *Economics, Organization, and Management*. Englewood Cliffs, NJ: Prentice Hall.

Mioset, L. 2000. "Stein Rokkan's Thick Comparisons." *Acta Sociologica* 4/3: 381–97.

Mosher, James S. and David M. Trubek. 2003. "Alternative Approaches to Governance in the EU: EU Social Policy and the European Employment Strategy." *Journal of Common Market Studies* 41, 1: 63–88.

Money, Jeannette. 1994. *Fences and Neighbors: The Political Geography of Immigration Control*. Ithaca, NY: Cornell University Press.

Moore, J. Barrington, Jr. 1966. *Social Origins of Dictatorship and Democracy: Lord and Peasants in the Making of the Modern World*. Boston, MA: Beacon Press.

Moore, Sarah. 1994. "Sex Discrimination and Judicial Review." *European Law Review* 19, 4: 425–33.

Moravcsik, Andrew. 1998. *The Choice for Europe: Social Purpose and State Power from Messina to Maastricht*. Ithaca, NY: Cornell University Press.

———. 1997. "Taking Preferences Seriously: A Liberal Theory of International Politics." *International Organization* 51: 514–48.

Munz, R. 1996. "A Continent of Migration: European Mass Migration in the 20th Century." *New Community* 22: 201–26.

Murphy, Alexander B. 1996. "The Sovereign State as Political-Territorial Ideal," in Thomas J. Biersteker and Cynthia Weber (eds.). *State Sovereignty as Social Construct*. Cambridge, UK: Cambridge University Press.

Musalo, Karen. 1999. "Fortress American – The United States' Response to Refugees." Paper presented at the Conference on Cosmopolitanism and Nationalism. Stanford, CA: Stanford University.

Myles, J. and P. Pierson. 2001. "The Comparative Political Economy of Pension Reform," in P. Pierson (ed.). *The New Politics of the Welfare State*. Oxford, UK: Oxford University Press, pp. 305–33.

Napier, Brian. 1994. "Victory for Part-Time Workers." *New Law Journal* 18: 396–7.

Newman, Lawrence W. 1998. "A Practical Assessment of Arbitral Dispute Resolution," in Thomas E. Carbonneau (ed.). *Lex Mercatoria and Arbitration: A Discussion of the New Law Merchant*. Yonkers, NY: Juris, pp. 1–10.

Neyer, Jürgen. 2003. "Discourse and Order in the EU: A Deliberative Approach to Multi-Level Governance." *Journal of Common Market Studies* 41: 3.

Nicol, Danny. 1996. "Disapplying with Relish? The Industrial Tribunals and Acts of Parliament." *Public Law*, Winter: 579–89.

North, Douglas C. 1991. "Institutions, Transaction Costs, and the Rise of Merchant Empires," in James D. Tracy (ed.). *The Political Economy of Merchant Empires*. Cambridge, UK: Cambridge University Press.

———. 1990. *Institutions, Institutional Change, and Economic Performance*. Cambridge, UK: Cambridge University Press.

Ohmae, Kenichi. 1991. *The Borderless World: Power and Strategy in the Interlinked Economy*. New York: Harper.

Okekeifere, Andrew I. 1998. "Commercial Arbitration as the Most Effective Dispute Resolution Method: Still a Fact or Now a Myth?" *Journal of International Arbitration* 15: 81–105.

Olsen, J. P. 2000. *Organizing European Institutions of Governance*. ARENA Working Papers 00/2.

Orren, Karen and Stephen Skowronek. 1995. "Order and Time in Institutional Study: A Brief for the Historical Approach," in John S. Drgzek, James Farr, and Stephen T. Leonard (eds.). *Political Science in History: Research Programs and Political Traditions*. Cambridge, UK: Cambridge University Press.

Ostrom Victor. 1987. *The Political Theory of a Compound Republic: Designing the American Experiment*, 2nd revised ed. Lincoln, NE: University of Nebraska Press.

Page E. C. 1995. "Patterns and Diversity in European State Development," in J. Hayward and E. C. Page (eds.). *Governing the New Europe*. Durham, NC: Duke University Press, pp. 9–43.

Palier, Bruno. 1999. "Reformer La Securité Sociale." Ph.D. dissertation. Institut d'Études Politiques de Paris.

Papademetriou, Demetrios G. 1996. *Coming Together or Pulling Apart? The European Union's Struggle with Immigration and Asylum*. Washington, DC: Carnegie Endowment for International Peace.

Papademetriou, Demetrios G. and Kimberly A. Hamilton. 1996. *Converging Paths to Restriction: French, Italian and British Responses to Immigration*. Washington, DC: Carnegie Endowment for International Peace.

Pappi, Franz and Christian Henning. 1999. "The Organization of Influence on the EC's Common Agricultural Policy: A Network Approach." *European Journal of Political Research* 36, 6: 257–81.

Party of European Socialists, PES. (1999). *Manifesto for the 1999 European Elections* (http://www.eurosocialists.org/upload/publications/39EN14-en.pdf, accessed August 4, 2002).

Pechota, Vratislav. 1998. "The Future of the Law Governing the International Arbitral Process," in Thomas E. Carbonneau (ed.). *Lex Mercatoria and Arbitration: A Discussion of the New Law Merchant*. Yonkers, NY: Juris, pp. 257–64.

Pennings, F. 2001. *Introduction to European Social Security Law*. The Hague: Kluwer Law International.

Perrin, G. 1969. "Reflections on Fifty Years of Social Security." *International Labour Review* 99: 242–92.

Persily, Nathaniel. 1997. "The Peculiar Geography of Direct Democracy: Why the Initiative, Referendum and Recall Developed in the American West." *Michigan Law and Policy Review* 2: 11–41.

Pettigrew, Thomas F. 1998. "Reactions toward the New Minorities of Western Europe." *Annual Review of Sociology* 24(1): 77–104.

Philip, Alan Butt. 1994. "European Union Immigration Policy: Phantom, Fantasy, or Fact?" *West European Politics* 17(2): 168–80.

Pierson, Paul (ed.). 2001. *The New Politics of the Welfare State*. Oxford, UK: Oxford University Press.

———. 2000. "Increasing Returns, Path Dependence, and the Study of Politics." *American Political Science Review* 92, 4: 251–67.

———. 1996. "The Path to European Integration." *Comparative Political Studies* 29, 2: 123–63.

Poggi, Gianfranco. 1990. *The State: Its Nature, Development and Prospects*. Stanford, CA: Stanford University Press.

Polanyi, Karl. 1957. *The Great Transformation: The Political and Economic Origins of Our Time*. Boston, MA: Beacon Press.

Pollack, Mark A. 2000. "Blairism in Brussels: The 'Third Way' in Europe since Amsterdam," in Maria Green Cowles and Michael Smith (eds.). *The State of the European Union: Risks, Reform, Resistance, and Revival*, vol. 5. Oxford, UK: Oxford University Press, pp. 266–91.

Preuss, U. K. 1996. "The Political Meaning of Constitutionalism," in R. Bellamy (ed.). *Constitutionalism, Democracy and Sovereignty: American and European Perspective*. Aldershot, UK: Avebury, pp. 11–27.

Puetter, Uwe. 2003. "Informal Circles of Ministers: A Way Out of the EU's Institutional Dilemmas?" *European Law Journal*, 9, 1: 109–24.

Ray, Leonard. 1999. "Measuring Party Orientations towards European Integration: Results from an Expert Survey," *European Journal of Political Research* 36, 2:283–306.

Rensmann, Thilo. 1998. "Anational Arbitral Awards: Legal Phenomenon or Academic Fiction." *Journal of International Arbitration* 15: 37–65.

Rhinard, Mark. 2002. "The Democratic Legitimacy of the European Union Committee System." *Governance*, 15, 2: 185–210.

Riker, William H. 1987. *The Development of American Federalism*. Boston, MA: Kluwer.

———. 1964. *Federalism: Origin, Operation, Significance*. Boston, MA: Little, Brown.

Rimlinger, G. 1971. *Welfare Policy and Industrialisation in Europe, North America and Russia*. New York: John Wiley and Sons.

Rodrik, Dani. 1997. *Has Globalization Gone Too Far?* Washington, DC: Institute for International Economics.

Roederer, Christilla. 2000. "Popular Struggle and the Making of Europe's Common Agricultural Policy: Farm Protest in France, 1983–1993." Unpublished Ph.D. thesis. University of South Carolina Department of Government and International Studies.

Rogowski, Ronald. 1989. *Commerce and Coalitions*. Ithaca, NY: Cornell University Press.

Rokkan, Stein. 1999. *State Formation, Nation Building, and Mass Politics in Europe: The Theory of Stein Rokkan*. Peter Flora with Stein Kuhnle and Derek Urwin (eds.). Oxford, UK: Oxford University Press.

———. 1974. *Dimension of State Formation and Nation Building*, in C. Tilly (ed.). *The Formation of National States in Western Europe*. Princeton, NJ: Princeton University Press.

———. 1973a. *Centre-Formation, Nation-Building and Cultural Diversity: Report on a Unesco Programme*, in S. N. Eisenstadt and Stein Rokkan (eds.). *Building States and Nations: Models and Data Resources*, vol. 1. Beverly Hills, CA: Sage, pp. 13–38.

———. 1973b. *Cities, States, and Nations: A Dimensional Model for the Study of Contrasts in the Development*, in S. N. Eisenstadt and Stein Rokkan (eds.). *Building States and Nations: Models and Data Resources*, vol. 1, Beverly Hills, CA: Sage, pp. 73–97.

———. 1973c. "Entries, Voices, Exits: Towards a Possible Generalization of the Hirschman Model." *Social Sciences Information*, 13, 1: 39–53.

———. 1970. *Citizens, Elections, Parties: Approaches to the Comparative Study of the Processes of Development*. Oslo: Universitetsforlaget.

———. (ed.). 1968. *Comparative Research across Cultures and Nations*. Paris: Mouton.

Rokkan, Stein and Segmour Martin Lipset. 1967. "Cleavage Structures, Party Systems, and Voter Alignments: An Introduction," in Stein Rokkan and S. Lipset (eds.). *Party Systems and Voter Alignments: Cross-National Perspective*. New York: Free Press, pp. 1–64.

Rokkan, Stein and R. Meritt (eds.). 1968. *Comparing Nations. The Use of Quantitative Data in Cross-National Research*. New Haven, CT: Yale University Press.

Rokkan, Stein, Derek Urwin, F. H. Aerebrot, P. Malaba, and T. Sande. 1987. *Centre–Periphery Structures in Europe*. Frankfurt: Campus Verlag.

Rorty, Richard. 1991. *Objectivity, Relativism, and Truth*, vol. I. Cambridge, UK: Cambridge University Press.

Rose Richard. 1996, *What Is Europe? A Dynamic Perspective*. New York: Harper-Collins.

Rose, Richard. 1990. "Inheritance before Choice in Public Policy." *Journal of Theoretical Politics* 2: 263–91.

Rosenau, James N. 1966. "Transforming the International System: Small Increments along a Vast Periphery." *World Politics* 18, 3: 525–45.

Rosenau, James N. and W. Michael Fagen. 1997. "A New Dynamism in World Politics: Increasingly Skillful Individuals?" *International Studies Quarterly* 41: 655–86.

Rosenbaum, Walter A. 1991. *Environmental Politics and Policy*, 2nd ed. Washington, DC: CQ Press.

Rubino-Sammartano, Mauro. 1995. "New International Arbitration Legislation in Italy." *Journal of International Arbitration* 12: 77.

Ruggie, John Gerard. 1998. "What Makes the World Hang Together? Neo-Utilitarianism and the Social Constructivist Challenge." *International Organization* 52: 855–85.

———. 1993. "Territoriality and Beyond: Problematizing Modernity in International Relations." *International Organization* 47, 1: 139–74.

Rustow, Dankwart. 1970. "Transitions to Democracy." *Comparative Politics* 2: 337–63.

Saint Jours, Y. 1982. "France," in P. A. Koehler and H. F. Zacher (eds.). *The Evolution of Social Insurance 1881–1981*. London: Pinter, pp. 93–148.

Sandholtz, Wayne and Alec Stone Sweet (eds.). 1998. *European Integration and Supranational Governance*. Oxford, UK: Oxford University Press.

Sbragia, Alberta. 2002. "The European Union, Federation and Sovereignty: The EU as a 'Mirror Image' of Traditional Federations?" Paper presented at the American Political Science Association (APSA) annual meeting, Boston, MA.

———. 1996a. *Debt Wish: Entrepreneurial Cities, U.S. Federalism, and Economic Development.* Pittsburgh, PA: University of Pittsburgh Press.

———. 2000b. "Environmental Policy: Economic Constraints and External Pressures," in Helen Wallace and William Wallace (eds.). *Policy-Making in the European Union,* 4th ed. Oxford, UK: Oxford University Press, pp. 293–316.

———. 1996c. "Environmental Policy: The Push-Pull of Policy-Making," in Helen Wallace and William Wallance (eds.). *Policy-Making in the European Union,* 3rd ed. Oxford, UK: Oxford University Press, pp. 235–55.

———. 1993. "The European Community: A Balancing Act," *Publius* 23: 23–38.

———. 1992. *Euro-Politics: Institutions and Policymaking in the "New" European Community.* Washington, DC: Brookings Institution.

Sbragia, Alberta with Chad Damro. 1999. "The Changing Role of the European Union in International Environmental Politics: Institution Building and the Politics of Climate Change. *Environment and Planning C: Government and Policy* 17, 1: 53–68.

Scarbrough, E. 2000. "West European Welfare States: the Old Politics of Retrenchment." *European Journal of Political Research* 38, 2: 225–59.

Scharpf, Fritz. 2001. *European Governance: Common Concerns vs. the Challenge of Diversity.* Jean Monnet working paper (http://www.iue.it/RSC/Governance/).

———. 2000a. *Governing Europe: Effective and Democratic?* Oxford, UK: Oxford University Press.

———. 2000b. "The Viability of Advanced Welfare States in the International Economy: Vulnerabilities and Options." *Journal of European Public Policy* 7, 2: 190–228.

———. 1996. "Negative and Positive Integration in the Political Economy of European Welfare States," in Gary Marks, Fritz Scharpf, Philippe Schmitter, and Wolfgang Streeck (eds.). *Governance in the European Union.* London: Sage, pp. 15–39.

———. 1988. "The Joint-Decision Trap: Lessons from German Federalism and European Integration." *Public Administration* 61: 239–42.

Scharpf, Fritz and Vivien Schmidt (eds.). 2000. *Welfare and Work in Open Economies.* 2 vols. Oxford, UK: Oxford University Press.

Schild, Joachim. 2001. "National v. European Identities? French and Germans in the European Multi-Level System." *Journal of Common Market Studies* 39, 2: 331–51.

Schmitt, Hermann and Jacques Thomassen. 1999. *Political Representation and Legitimacy in the European Union.* Oxford, UK: Oxford University Press.

Schmitter, Philippe C. 2000. *How to Democratize the European Union...and Why Bother?* Lanham, MD: Rowman and Littlefield.

Schmitter, Philippe C. and M. W. Bauer. 2001. "A (Modest) Proposal for Expanding Social Citizenship in the European Union." *Journal of European Social Policy* 11, 1: 55–66.

Schockman, H. Eric. 1998. "California's Ethnic Experiment and the Unsolvable Immigration Issue: Proposition 187 and Beyond," in Michael B. Preston, Bruce E. Cain, and Sandra Bass (eds.). *Racial and Ethnic Politics in California,* vol. 2. Berkeley, CA: IGS Press.

Schofeld, N. 1985. "Anarchy, Altruism, and Cooperation." *Social Choice and Welfare* 2: 207–19.

Schwartz, M. A. 1974. *Politics and Territory*. Montreal: McGill-Queen's University Press.

Scott, Joanne and David M. Trubek. 2002. "Mind the Gap: Law and New Approaches to Governance in the European Union." *European Law Journal* 8, 1: 1–18.

Searle, John R. 1995. *The Construction of Social Reality*. New York: Free Press.

Selznick, Philip. 1992. *The Moral Commonwealth*. Berkeley, CA: University of California Press.

Seventh Geneva Global Arbitration Forum. 1999. "Reconsidering a Key Tenet of International Commercial Arbitration: Is Finality of Awards What Parties Really Need? Has the Time of an International Appellate Arbitral Body Arrived?" *Journal of International Arbitration* 16: 57.

Shapiro, Martin J. 2000. "Subsidiarity as a Legal Standard for the European Union." Paper presented at the conference Beyond Center–Periphery or the Unbundling of Territoriality. San Domenico di Fiesole.

———. 1996. "Globalization and Freedom of Contract." Jean Monnet chair lecture. San Domenico di Fiesole.

———. 1980. *Courts: A Comparative and Political Analysis*. Chicago, IL: University of Chicago Press.

Shapiro, Martin J. and Alec Stone Sweet. 2002. *On Law, Politics, and Judicialization*. Oxford, UK: Oxford University Press.

Shinoda, Hideaki. 2000. *Re-examining Sovereignty*. New York: St. Martin's Press.

Schoukens, P. (ed.). 1997. *Prospects of Social Security Co-ordination*. Leuven, Belgium: Acco.

Sigueiros, Jose Luis. 1998. "Arbitral Autonomy and National Sovereign Authority in Latin America," in Thomas Carbonneau (ed.). *Lex Mercatoria and Arbitration: A Discussion of the New Law Merchant*. Yonkers, NY: Juris, pp. 219–31.

Sinclair, Barbara. 1997. *Unorthodox Lawmaking: New Legislative Processes in the U.S. Congress*. Washington, DC: Congressional Quarterly Press.

Skocpol, Theda. 1999. "How Americans Became Civic," in Theda Skocpol and Morris Fiorina (eds.). *Civic Engagement in American Democracy*. Washington, DC: Brookings Institution and Russell Sage Foundation.

———. 1992. *Protecting Soldiers and Mothers: The Political Origins of Social Policy in the United States*. Cambridge, MA: Harvard University Press.

Skowronek, Stephen. 1987. *Building a New American State. The Expansion of National Administrative Capacities 1877–1920*, 3rd ed. Cambridge, UK: Cambridge University Press.

Slaughter, Anne-Marie and Alec Stone Sweet. 1995. "Assessing the Effectiveness of International Adjudication." *Structures of World Order: Proceedings of the 89th Annual Meeting*. Washington, DC: American Society of International Law.

Smith, A. D. 1995. "The Nations of Europe after the Cold War," in J. Hayward and E. C. Page (eds.). *Governing the New Europe*. Durham, NC: Duke University Press, pp. 44–66.

Smith, Anthony D. 1991. *National Identity*. London: Penguin Books.

Sorensen, Jens Magleby. 1996. *The Exclusive European Citizenship*. Aldershot, UK: Avebury Press.

Spruyt, Hendrik. 1994. *The Sovereign State and Its Competitors*. Princeton, NJ: Princeton University Press.

Stephens, John D., Evelyne Huber, and Leonard Ray. 1999. "The Welfare State in Hard Times," in Herbert Kitschelt, Peter Lange, Gary Marks, and John D. Stephens (eds.). *Continuity and Change in Contemporary Capitalism*. New York: Cambridge University Press.

Stewart, David P. 1992. "National Enforcement of Arbitral Awards under Treaties and Conventions," in Richard B. Lillich and Charles N. Brower (eds.). *International Arbitration in the 21ˢᵗ Century: Towards "Judicialization" and Conformity?* Irvington, NY: Transnational.

Stolper, Wolfgang and Paul Samuelson. 1941. "Protection and Real Wages." *Review of Economic Studies* 9: 58–73.

Stone, Alec. 1994. "What Is a Supranational Constitution? An Essay in International Relations Theory." *Review of Politics* 55, 3: 441–74.

Stone Sweet, Alec. 2000. *Governing with Judges: Constitutional Politics in Europe*. Oxford, UK: Oxford University Press.

———. 1999. "Judicialization and the Construction of Governance." *Comparative Political Studies* 31: 147–84.

———. 1998. "Rules, Dispute Resolution, and Strategic Behavior." *Journal of Theoretical Politics* 10: 327–38.

Stone Sweet, Alec and Thomas L. Brunell. 1998. "Constructing a Supranational Constitution: Dispute Resolution and Governance in the European Community." *American Political Science Review* 92: 63–81.

Stone Sweet, Alec and James A. Caporaso. 1998a. "La Cour Européenne et L'intégration." *Revue Française de Science Politique* 48: 195–244.

Stone Sweet, Alec, and James A. Caporaso. 1998b. "From Free Trade to Supranational Polity: The European Court and Integration," in Wayne Sandholtz and Alec Stone Sweet (eds.). *Supranational Governance: The Institutionalization of the European Union*. New York: Oxford University Press, pp. 92–133.

Stone Sweet, Alec and Wayne Sandholtz. 1997. "European Integration and Supranational Governance." *Journal of European Public Policy* 4, 3: 297–317.

Stone Sweet, Alec, Wayne Sandholtz, and Neil Fligstein (eds.). 2001. *The Institutionalization of Europe*. Oxford, UK: Oxford University Press.

Streeck, Wolfgang and Philippe Schmitter. 1991. "From National Corporatism to Transnational Pluralism: Organized Interests in the Single European Market." *Polity and Society* 19: 133–164.

Swidler, Ann. 1986. "Culture in Action: Symbols and Strategies." *American Sociological Review* 51: 273–86.

Swiss Re-insurance Company. 1998. *Financial Difficulties of Public Pension Schemes: Market Potential for Life Insurers*. Zurich: prospect no. 8 of Sigma.

Tarello, G. 1998. *Storia della Cultura Giuridica Moderna: Assolutismo e Codificazione del Diritto*. Bologna: Il Mulino.

Tarrow, Sidney. 1998. "Building a Composite Polity: Popular Contention in the European Union." Discussion paper. Stanford, CA: Stanford University.

Tarrow, Sidney. 1998. "Fishnets, Catnets, Internets: Globalization and Transnational Collective Action," in Michael Hanagan, Leslie Page Moch, and Wayne te Brake (eds.). *Challenging Authority: The Historical Study of Contentious Politics*. Minneapolis and St. Paul, MN: University of Minnesota Press, pp. 228–44.

Tarrow, Sidney, Peter J. Katzenstein, and Luigi Graziano (eds.). 1978. *Territorial Politics in Industrial Nations*. New York: Praeger.

Taylor, Michael. 1982. *Community, Anarchy, and Liberty*. Cambridge, UK: Cambridge University Press.

———. 1976. *Anarchy and Cooperation*. Cambridge, UK: Cambridge University Press.

te Brake, Wayne. 1997. *Making History: Ordinary People in European Politics, 1500–1700*. Berkeley, CA: University of California Press.

Therborn, G. 1989. "Pillarization and Popular Movements. Two Variants of Welfare State Capitalism: The Netherlands and Sweden," in F. G. Castles (ed.). *The Comparative History of Public Policy*. New York: Oxford University Press, pp. 192–241.

Thomson, Janice E. 1995. "State Sovereignty in International Relations: Bridging the Gap between Theory and Empirical Research." *International Studies Quarterly* 39: 213–33.

Thraenhardt, D. 1996. "European Migration from East to West: Present Patterns and Future Directions." *New Community* 22: 227–42.

Tilly, Charles. 1995. *Popular Contention in Great Britain, 1758–1834*. Cambridge, MA: Harvard University Press.

———. 1990. *Coercion, Capital, and the European States, AD 990–1990*. Cambridge, UK: Basil Blackwell.

———. 1985. "War Making and State Making as Organized Crime," in Peter B. Evans, Dietrich Rueschemeyer, and Theda Skocpol (eds.). *Bringing the State Back In*. Cambridge, UK: Cambridge University Press.

The Times. 1994. "Profound Judgment: How the Law Lords Tipped Britain's Constitutional Balance." March 5.

Tinbergen, J. 1965. *International Economic Integration*. Amsterdam: Elsevier

Tsebelis, George. 1999. "Veto Players and Law Production in Parliamentary Democracies: An Empirical Analysis." *American Political Science Review* 93: 591–608.

———. 1994. "The Power of the European Parliament as a Conditional Agenda-Setter." *American Political Science Review* 88: 128–42.

———. 1990. *Nested Games: Rational Choice in Comparative Politics*. Berkeley, CA: University of California Press.

Turner, Ian. 1988. *Environmental Policy in Europe: Uniformity or Diversity? A Case Study of the EEC Car Emissions Decisions*. CEED Discussion Paper No. 7. London: UK Centre for Economic and Environmental Development.

Turner, Lowell. 1996. "The Europeanization of Labor: Structure before Action." *European Journal of Industrial Relations* 2:3, 325–44.

Ucarer, Emek M. and Donald J. Puchala (ed.). 1997. *Immigrations into Western Societies: Problems and Policies*. London: Pinter.

Van Waarden, Frans and Michaela Drahos. 2002. "Courts and (Epistemic) Communities in the Convergence of Competition Policies. *Journal of European Public Policy* 9, 6: 913–34.

Veitch, John M. 1986. "Repudiations and Confiscations by the Medieval State." *Journal of Economic History* 46: 31–6.

Verdier, Daniel. 1994. *Democracy and International Trade: Britain, France, and the United States, 1860–1990*. Princeton, NJ: Princeton University Press.

Villiers, Charlotte and Fidelma White. 1995. "Agitating for Part-Time Workers' Rights." *Modern Law Review* 58, 560–74.

Wade, H. W. R. 1996. "Sovereignty – Revolution or Evolution?" *Law Quarterly Review* 112: 568–75.

———. 1991. "What Has Happened to the Sovereignty of Parliament?" *Law Quarterly Review* 107: 1–4.

———. 1980. *Constitutional Fundamentals*. London: Stevens and Sons.

Walker, R. B. J. 1993. *Inside/Outside*. New York: Cambridge University Press.

Wallerstein, Immanuel. 1974/1980. *The Modern World System*, vols. I, II. New York: Academic Press.

Walzer Michael. 1996. *What It Means to Be an American. Essays on the American Experience*. New York: Marsilio.

Warleigh, Alex. 2000. "The Hustle: Citizenship Practice, NGOs, and 'Policy Coalitions' in the European Union – the Cases of Auto Oil, Drinking Water, and Unit Pricing." *Journal of European Public Policy* 7, 2: 229–43.

Watts, Ronald. 1998. "Federalism, Federal Political Systems, and Federations." *Annual Review of Political Science* 1: 117–37.

Weale, Albert and Michael Nentwich. 1998. *Political Theory and the European Union: Legitimacy, Constitutional Choice, and Citizenship*. London: Routledge.

Weiner, Merle. 1990. "Fundamental Misconceptions about Fundamental Rights: The Changing Nature of Women's Rights in the EEC and Their Application to the United Kingdom." *Harvard International Law Journal* 31, 2: 565–610.

Weber, Cynthia. 1995. *Simulating Sovereignty*. Cambridge, UK: Cambridge University Press.

Wedgewood, C. V. 1981. *The Thirty Years' War*. London: Methuen.

Weiler, J. H. H. 1996. "European Neo-Constitutionalism: In Search of Foundations for the European Constitutional Order." *Political Studies* 44 (special issue): 517–33.

Weiler J. H. H. 1999. *The Constitution of Europe: "Do the New Clothes Have an Emperor?" and Other Essays on European Integration*. Cambridge, UK: Cambridge University Press.

Weintraub, Sidney. "North American Free Trade and the European Situation Compared." *International Migration Review* 26, 2: 506–24.

Wendt, Alexander. 1992. "Anarchy Is What States Make of It: The Social Construction of Power Politics." *International Organization* 46, 2: 391–425.

Werner, Heinz. 1994. "Regional Economic Integration and Migration: The European Case." *Annals of the American Academy of Political and Social Science* 534: 147–64.

Werner, Jacques. 1999. "Reconsidering a Key Tenet of International Commercial Arbitration: Is Finality of Awards What Parties Really Need? Has the Time for an International Appellate Arbitral Body Arrived?" *Journal of International Arbitration* 16: 57–61.

———. 1997. "The Trade Explosion and Some Likely Effects on International Arbitration." *Journal of International Arbitration* 14: 2–15.

Wessels, Bernhard. Forthcoming. "Interest Groups in the EU: The Emergence of Contestation Potential," in Gary Marks and Marco Steenbergen (eds.). *Dimensions of Contestation in the European Union*. Boulder, CO: Rowman and Littlefield.

Wessels, Wolfgang. 2001. "Nice Results: The Millennium IGC in the EU's Evolution." *Journal of Common Market Studies* 39, 2: 197–219.

———. 1997. "An Ever Closer Fusion? A Dynamic Macropolitical View on Integration Processes." *Journal of Common Market Studies* 35, 2: 267–99.

Wiebe R. H., 1995. *Self Rule: A Cultural History of American Democracy.* Chicago, IL: Chicago University Press.

Woldendorp, Jaap, Hans Keman, and Ian Budge. 2000. *Party Government in 48 Democracies (1945–1998): Composition, Duration, Personnel.* Dordrecht: Kluwer.

Wright, Vincent. 1997. "Relations Intergouvernementales et Gouvernement Régional en Europe: Réflexions d'un Sceptique," in P. LeGalès and C. Lequesne (eds). *Les Paradoxes des Régions en Europe.* Paris: La Découverte, pp. 47–55.

Yu, Hong-lin. 1998. "Total Separation of International Commerical Arbitration and National Court Regime." *Journal of International Arbitration* 15: 145–66.

Zincone, G. 1992. *Da Sudditi a Cittadini.* Bologna: Il Mulino.

Zito, Anthony R. 2001. "Epistemic Communities, Collective Entrepreneurship and European Integration." *Journal of European Public Policy* 8, 4: 585–603.

———. 2000. *Creating Environmental Policy in the European Union.* New York: St. Martin's Press.

Index

air pollution policy 14, 207, 211
Ansell, Christopher 14–16, 57, 61,
    122, 163, 229, 243, 246, 252,
    267
Austria 118, 148, 157, 184
authority 3, 4, 8, 11–18, 70–3, 123,
    136–42, 145, 151, 158, 165, 169,
    184, 186, 226, 229, 232
    Kompetenz-Kompetenz, 137
    medieval 67–8, 128–30, 225
    private 7, 16, 71, 122, 133–6
    sovereignty 5–8, 69–89, 105,
        163
    territoriality 5–8, 67, 69, 246,
        252

Bartolini, Stefano 8, 9–11, 12, 14, 16,
    18, 24–5, 35, 49, 53, 59, 62–3,
    91, 119, 158, 172, 180, 228, 238,
    246, 252, 258, 263, 268
Belgium 45–7, 54–5, 97, 115, 118, 148,
    169, 184, 194
borders and boundaries 4, 9–10, 19–25,
    27–44, 91–102, 107, 109, 111–13,
    121–2, 175, 190, 200, 244
    exit and voice 22–44, 61, 99, 105–6,
        118, 120, 158, 180–1
    membership 92, 110–12, 121
    structuring, destructuring, and
        restructuring 92–103, 116,
        117–21
Borras Alomar, Susana 33

Cain, Bruce 14, 18, 240, 250, 261, 266,
    268
Caporaso, James 6, 229, 241, 249, 254,
    257
center–periphery relations 9–11,
    19–45, 51, 60, 91, 118, 206–7,
    263
citizenship 11, 90, 92–3, 95–6, 181,
    188, 202, 236, 244
    social 101–2, 111–12, 116, 121, 244
Citrin, Jack 12, 269
constitutionalism 172, 186–7, 202, 233,
    241, 255, 261

decentralization 32, 115, 182
Delors, Jacques 159
democracy 4, 64, 138, 246
    consociationalism 239, 241
    corporatism 239, 241
    democratic deficit 50, 62–4,
        189–204, 206, 236, 240
    direct 203
    pluralism 184–5, 240–1, 243
    veto points 189, 197, 199, 208, 210,
        212, 214–15, 240–1
    Westminster model 239, 241
democratization 22, 175–9
    voice options 23
Denmark 97, 148
Di Palma, Giuseppe 17, 158, 164, 176,
    186, 240, 245
Downs, Ian 17, 238, 258

elite consolidation 37, 45, 51, 53, 242
European integration 3, 18–19, 23, 29,
    32, 47, 90–1, 95, 104, 111–12,
    118, 120–1, 146, 150, 159, 191,
    205, 229, 249, 253, 260–1, 269
European law 75–7, 89, 105, 110, 121,
    141
European Monetary System 227, 232
European Union 15, 17–18, 25, 29, 32,
    45–7, 50, 55, 62, 68–9, 73–89, 95,
    105, 113–14, 145, 148, 151,
    154–5, 158, 163, 186, 205, 225,
    251, 260
  citizenship 115–16, 121, 232, 238–9,
    243–4
  Commission 45–7, 56, 58, 63, 80–1,
    105, 184, 239, 253–4, 261
  Council of Ministers 105, 153–4,
    184, 205–11, 232–3, 239, 242,
    259, 261
  democracy 185, 189–204, 206, 236,
    238–45, 261–9
  enlargement 117
  environmental policy 153, 207,
    217–22
  European Court of Justice 13, 69,
    73, 76–89, 105, 108–12, 114,
    184, 191, 203–4, 229, 233, 242,
    249, 253–4, 259
  European Parliament 46–7, 63, 134,
    154, 158, 184–5, 191, 194–5,
    201, 217, 229, 232–3, 239, 243,
    261
  federalism 206–22, 230–4, 242
  hybrid nature 226, 230, 234–6, 242
  immigration policy 188–204
  intergovernmentalism 48, 191, 197,
    199, 208, 226, 230, 236, 242,
    244, 253, 255, 261
  Maastricht Treaty 13, 54, 151–4,
    217, 229, 239, 251
  market integration 157
  regional policy 119, 153
  "semipolity" 205
  Single European Act 154, 229, 234
  social policy 115, 153–4
  territoriality 227–8
  Treaty of Amsterdam 151–3, 239

exit-voice framework 9, 15–16, 53, 59,
    92, 244, 246, 252, 255
  hiding 99

Fabbrini, Sergio 11–12, 18, 240, 257–8,
    261, 268
federalism 151, 164, 170–5, 181, 183–4,
    205–22, 226–7, 230, 234, 238
  confederalism 171–3, 226, 231–4,
    242
Ferrera, Maurizio 11, 13, 16, 30,
    228–45, 255
Finland 97, 148
France 45–7, 55–6, 69, 97, 100, 103–4,
    110, 118, 131, 140–1, 148, 157,
    167, 171, 174, 178, 194, 196,
    218

Germany 57, 97, 99, 103, 111, 118,
    140–1, 148, 167, 169, 174, 184,
    194, 196–7, 218
globalization 3–4, 15, 23, 27, 32, 69,
    90, 118, 122, 144, 146, 188, 226
governance 122, 127–8, 144, 190, 193,
    234
  transnational 128
Greece 197, 218

Haas, Ernst 48, 76–7, 89, 145, 230,
    253, 263, 264
Hirschman, Albert 9, 11, 16, 24, 49,
    92, 121, 244, 252
Hooghe, Liesbet 49, 53, 202

Imig, Doug 45–7, 55
immigration 14
interests and identities 8, 16–17, 37,
    185, 207, 236–44
  crosslocal and functional 19, 35, 52,
    209, 211, 217, 237
  European 12, 62, 153, 238, 241
  national 12, 174, 220, 238, 243
  practiced identities 253–60
  territorial 207, 209, 211, 217, 256
  transnational 10, 36, 46, 58, 131–3,
    194, 237, 243
international organizations 205, 207,
    222, 228, 230, 237

Ireland 118, 148, 218
Italy 45–7, 54–5, 97–100, 111, 115,
    117, 119, 131, 140–1, 148, 167,
    169, 174, 194, 196, 218

Jupille, Joseph 6, 229, 249, 254, 257

Kettnaker, Vera 58
Krasner, Stephen 4, 5, 71, 73, 93,
    260
Krugman, Paul 209, 220

labor unions 46, 145, 150, 159, 209
legitimacy 25, 175, 177–9, 185, 232–3
Lex Mercatoria 15–16, 123, 132–44
liberalism 261–9
Lowi, Theodore 210, 250
Luxembourg 118, 148

Marks, Gary 17, 49, 53, 202, 238, 249,
    258
Marshall, T. H. 98
McMahon, Christopher 6–8
Monnet, Jean 145
Moore, Barrington 34
multilevel governance 36, 49, 151

national/supranational/local alignment
    55
neofunctionalism 5, 10, 48, 237
neomedievalism 3, 10–18, 67, 128–33,
    225
Netherlands 99, 118, 131, 148, 167,
    169, 218
North American Free Trade Agreement
    (NAFTA) 17, 145–6, 148, 151,
    155, 158–9, 258
Norway 97, 197

Orren, Karen 248

Pizzorno, Alessandro 10
Poggi, Gianfranco 227, 255–6
political opportunity structures 53,
    246
political parties, 145–59, 179–82, 203,
    211, 266
    European 185, 238, 241

regional integration 145–59
regulation 210–11
relational explanation 10–15, 47–8,
    243, 246
    brokerage 48, 60
    object shift 48, 60–1
    scale shift 48
representation 62, 188, 230, 232
    functional 3, 14, 16–17, 34–44, 201,
        209
    countermajoritarian 199, 204, 240,
        268
    majoritarian 14, 194, 197, 201–2,
        268–9
    supermajoritarian 197–8, 208, 242
    territorial 8, 12, 14, 17, 19, 34–44,
        201, 203, 206, 209, 221, 227,
        268
Riker, William 171–2
Rokkan, Stein 9, 11, 16, 18, 22, 34, 49,
    91–104, 107, 116–18, 121,
    165–9, 175, 185, 244, 252
Ruggie, John Gerald 3, 7–8, 23, 225–9,
    232, 234, 243–4, 253

Sbragia, Alberta 14, 16–18, 164, 241,
    261, 268
Scharpf, Fritz 150–1
Schmitter, Philippe 227, 263
Shapiro, Martin 13, 15
Sides, John 12, 269
Skowronek, Stephen 185, 248
social cleavages 92, 95, 118, 175,
    179–82, 240
sovereignty 4–8, 68, 71–2, 74, 90–1,
    107, 111–12, 122, 141–2, 163–4,
    172, 188, 225–6, 231, 254–5,
    257–8
    authority 5–8, 70–3, 137, 163
    constructivist views of 5–6
    Krasner, Stephen 4–5
    Rokkanian view 93
    semisovereign state 106–12, 120
    social 91, 104–5
    territoriality 5–8, 18, 72–3, 169,
        246, 251
Spain 45–7, 55–6, 77, 115, 148, 167,
    171, 218

state, the 3–4, 6, 122, 227–30
    composite or compound 50–3, 62,
        164, 174, 182, 184, 186, 227,
        230, 234, 243, 265
    consociational 169–70
    corporateness 6, 170–1, 227, 231
    federal 227, 230–4
    general competences 228–9
    infrastructural power 25–7
    semisovereignty 106–12
    separation of powers 164, 173
    state building 9, 11, 20–3, 36, 51–3,
        90, 107, 165, 249, 256
    welfare, *see* welfare state
    Westphalian 6, 17–18, 67–8, 73,
        76–7, 88, 93, 97, 122–3, 128,
        130, 163–4, 249, 254, 260, 267
Stone Sweet, Alec 15–16, 229, 255, 257,
        262, 268
subnational regions 5, 10, 16, 24–44,
        54, 57, 118–21, 201, 243
subsidiarity 13, 234
Sweden 69, 98, 103, 148
Switzerland 169, 184, 230

Tarrow, Sidney 10–14, 16, 36, 119, 145,
        237–8, 241, 243, 246, 252
Te Brake, Wayne 34, 37, 50–3
territoriality 3–9, 15, 68, 72–3, 101,
        107, 111–13, 225–7, 231, 259,
        268
    democracy 4
    differentiation 25–44, 91
    interests and identities 8, 93
    monocephalic and policephalic 21
    rebundling 5, 7, 10–13, 15, 145, 255
    sovereignty 4–8, 48, 169, 246
    stratarchy, 10–18, 35, 37
    territorial incorporation 175
    unbundling 3, 5, 7, 10–13, 15, 46,
        144, 225, 259
Tilly, Charles 10, 64, 165

United Kingdom 56, 69–70, 74–89, 98,
        103, 118, 140, 167, 171, 196,
        197, 208, 217–18, 257–8
    courts 69, 74, 78–89
    Equal Opportunities Commission
        case 82–6
    Factortame case 76–7, 82–4
    judicial review 74, 76–7, 83, 87, 89,
        229
    parliament 12, 68, 69, 74–7, 89, 249
    rights 75
United States 17–18, 29, 120, 138–41,
        146–8, 155, 240, 260, 264, 266
    air pollution policy 207, 211–16,
        219–22
    Congress 173, 183, 197–200, 206,
        207–17, 219
    courts 182, 184–5, 196–7
    democracy 177–9, 197, 199
    federalism 164, 170–5, 181, 183,
        196–9, 205–22, 259
    immigration 188–204, 250, 258
    social cleavages 179–82
    sovereignty 169
    state building 165, 169–75, 176–9,
        182, 228, 258

venue shopping 14–15, 202, 240, 250,
        266

Wallerstein, Immanuel 21
Weber, Cynthia 5–8
Weber, Max 70, 227, 264
welfare state 11, 13, 25, 27, 90–102,
        106–21
    health care 107, 109, 114, 118–19
    historical development 91–102
    pensions 114, 116–17
    social assistance 109–10, 114–15,
        119
    social insurance 96–107, 113–14,
        116